Tripping Down the Ganga

TRIPPING DOWN THE GANGA

A Son's Exploration of Faith

Siddharth Kapila

SPEAKING TIGER

SPEAKING TIGER BOOKS LLP
125A, Ground Floor, Shahpur Jat, near Asiad Village,
New Delhi 110049

First published by Speaking Tiger in 2024

ISBN: 978-93-5447-890-1
eISBN: 978-93-5447-813-0

All photographs courtesy the author unless specified otherwise

10 9 8 7 6 5 4 3 2 1

Typeset in Adobe Garamond Pro by SÜRYA, New Delhi
Printed at Chaman Enterprises, New Delhi

For mummy

Contents

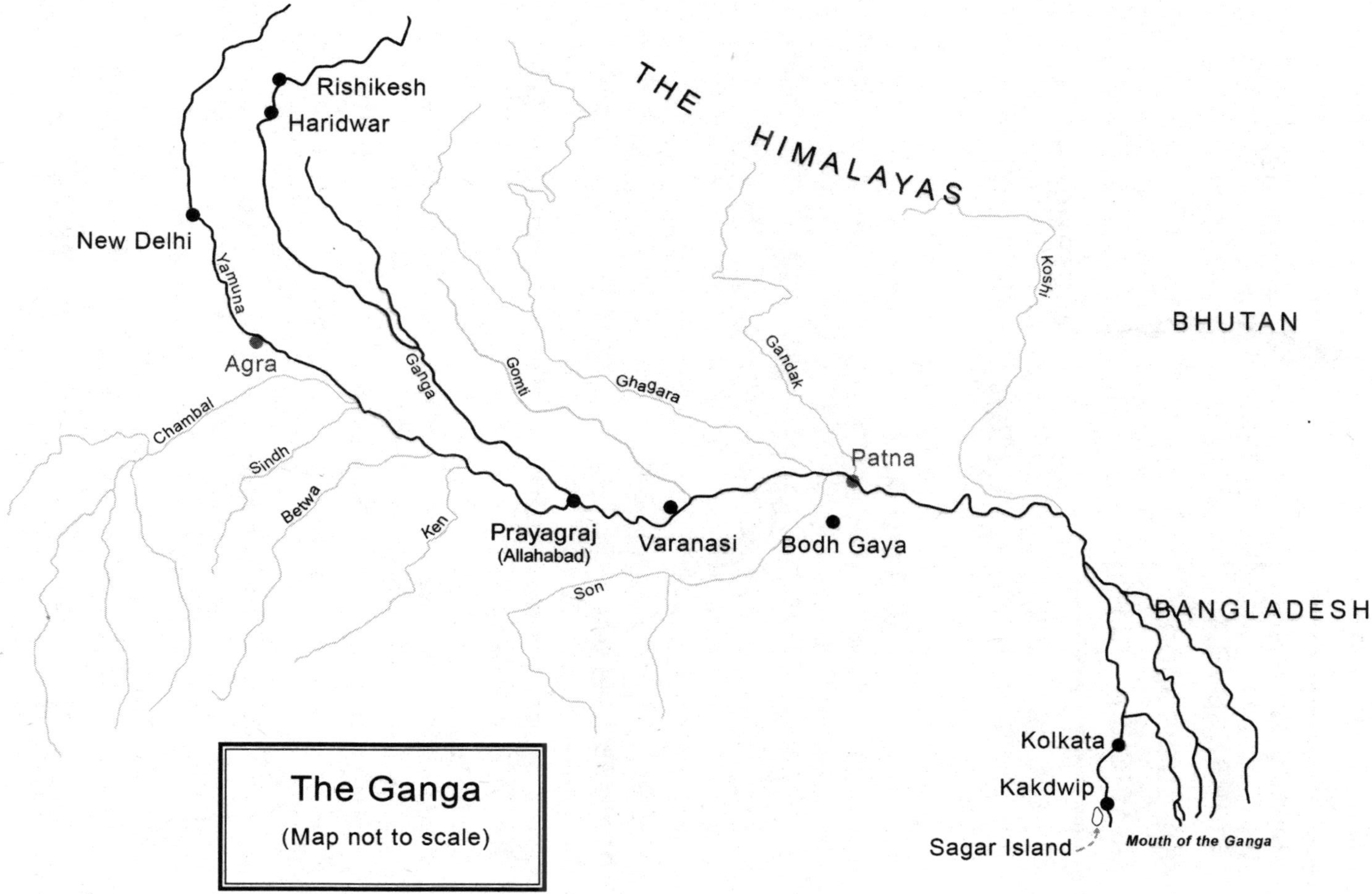
THE HIMALAYAS
Rishikesh
Haridwar
New Delhi
Yamuna
Agra
Ganga
Gomti
Ghagara
Gandak
Koshi
BHUTAN
Chambal
Sindh
Betwa
Ken
Prayagraj
(Allahabad)
Varanasi
Patna
Bodh Gaya
Son
BANGLADESH
Kolkata
Kakdwip
Sagar Island
Mouth of the Ganga
The Ganga
(Map not to scale)

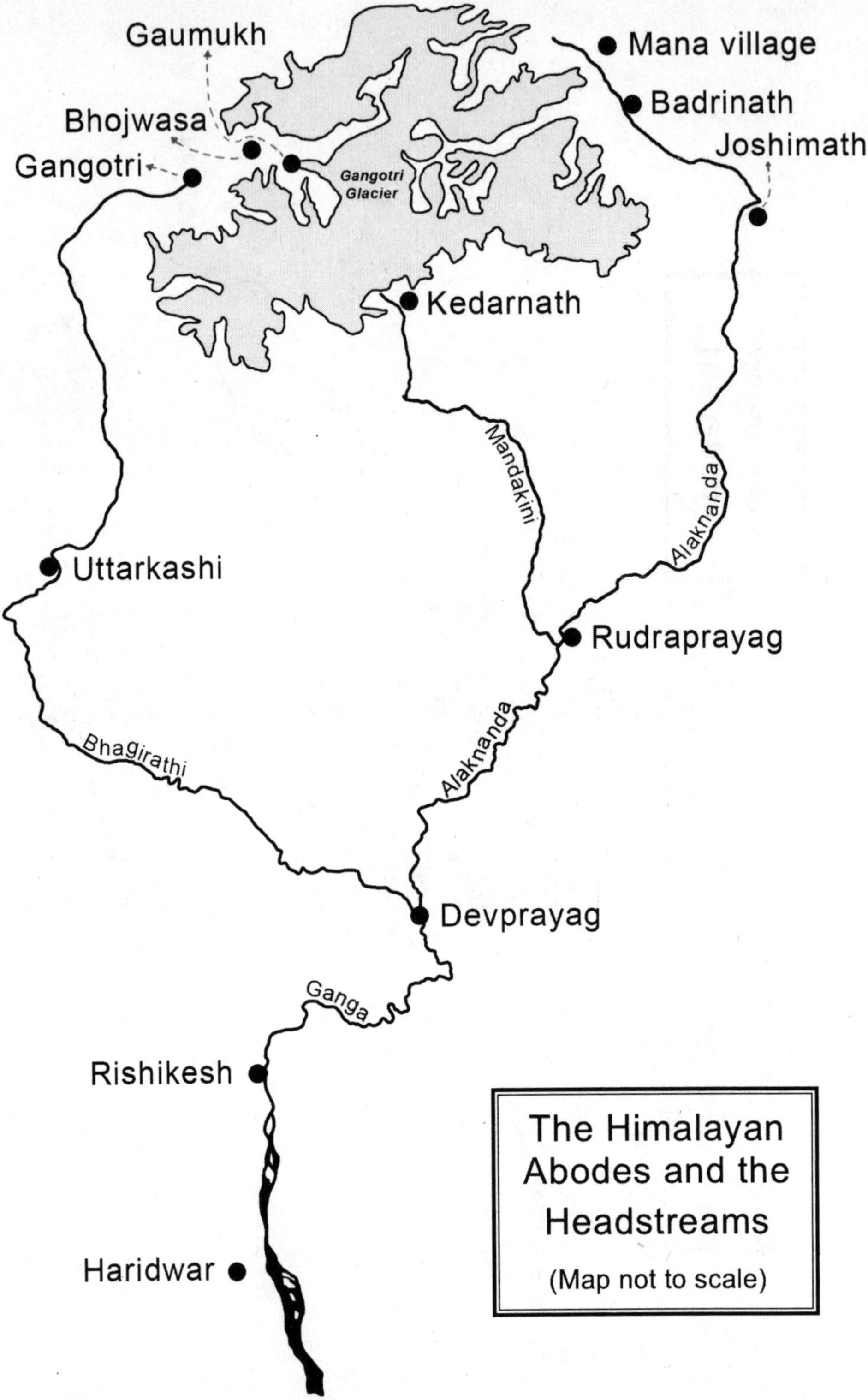

The Himalayan Abodes and the Headstreams

(Map not to scale)

Author's Note

Dear Reader, everything I relate in this memoir is true. By which I mean it is an accurate representation of my memory, interviews, notes and pictures. However, save for my mother, sister and myself, I've changed the names and identifying details of some, but not all, individuals who appear in my accounts for their privacy as well as that of the Rishikesh ashram with which my family has been associated for a long time. I have also merged a handful of people into composite characters and slightly reordered the sequencing of events. But really, I have not run with my imagination. Whenever I changed a detail, I did so always mindful that this should have no impact on the authenticity or substance of *what actually happened.*

A Trickle

This book is an account of my journeys, or *yaatras*, to seven major pilgrimage sites along the Ganga. Some trips I made in my thirties, between 2015 and 2022, while others I made through my adolescence and twenties. This is also my journey to find God, or 'meaning', if you will. Which, thanks to my devout mother, I could argue has been in the making since I was born.

In October 2015, when the seed for writing this book came to me, I had decided to quit my career in law—something I had invested a lot of time in and my parents had spent a lot of money on my education abroad for. I announced to everybody that I wanted to give everything up and write. When people asked, 'What about?' I couldn't quite say.

I had to figure it out. I had to pave my own way. I never did settle into the well-trod ways of our elders. So while people my age were probably deciding which play school to put their kids in, I was thinking about where to travel next. While my peers were putting down roots, I was seized by some opposite human instinct.

I wanted to break away! I wanted to travel! I wanted to seek!

Of course, all of me knew just how fortunate and privileged I was—*I am*—to put concerns of money and career on hold and simply go pursue my passions. To go figuring. For this, I am eternally grateful to my parents. And to God. (*Does the term 'Universe' fit here better than the Big G?* a side of my brain wonders.)

And so I went. In Japan, I had sushi and sake. In Greece, I filled myself with souvlaki and ouzo, and in Italy I had pasta with wine. At home, I spent long days cycling in rice fields around Hampi and many hours watching the sun slip into the Arabian Sea at Palolem. My point is—I was no spiritual hippie who had suddenly decided to grow his hair and become a yogi. I liked good food. I liked meat. I enjoyed what sadhus called *moh-maya*, the illusion of worldly pleasures.

But the farther afield I went, the more I had the urge to return to the old and familiar. The more foreign cultures I tasted, the more I yearned to dive deeper into my own.

My sister Mala and I had accompanied my mother on *tirath* yaatras, as Hindu pilgrimages are called, since we were children. But in my thirties, my mother and I dialled up our temple-going. Together we went to Dwarka in Gujarat, Jagannath Puri in Odisha, and Rameswaram in Tamil Nadu. We attended the Mahakumbh Mela in Allahabad in 2013, and the next year, we watched the spirit of God enter a dancer's body in a village near Mangalore, Karnataka. We went again and again to the old ashram in Rishikesh to which our family has been associated for many decades and many times to Varanasi. And finally, in 2015, we went to Ganga Sagar, where the Ganga merges with the Bay of Bengal.

And it was during this time that I also started going on yaatras all on my own.

As my mother said to me one day, 'After travelling the whole world, you are coming back to what I taught you.' I rolled my eyes. But I couldn't disagree.

The thing is, mummy and I were always fighting about her obsession with faith and ritual. If there was a *pooja* our Swamiji told her to do, a fast a pandit told her to keep, or a temple somebody said she should visit, she would do it. And a gazillion times more. On our yaatras, she would show such deep faith, and perform such fevered rituals that the whole exercise would leave me exhausted. Every time I told myself I'd never go with her again. And every time I went. Again and again.

(To give you a peek into my mother's religiosity, allow me to share a text she sent me a few days back:

Sid, for invoking Higher Beings, please wait to give or take meat until November 30th. Yesterday was Ekaadashi. I did a BIG pooja for the marriage of Lord Vishnu and Tulsi. So at least till the 30th, which is Poornima, you should be vegetarian.

OK, I replied, knowing I would do just as I pleased. Which, by the way, was often just as she said.)

It was while I was travelling and figuring and arguing with my mother that I got this idea: *Why don't I write about my yaatras? Why don't I write a travelogue on the Hindu faith?*

I habitually believed in God, but also disbelieved in Him. Yes, I prayed, but I didn't pray like mummy did. I didn't understand what faith meant to me precisely, but I knew it meant something, because I saw myself becoming curious about how our beliefs moulded truth. How oral histories informed our worldview.

But where would I begin? The subject of religion is fraught with difficulties. And while all faiths are vast and complex, because Hinduism is among the oldest and not bound to a single holy book—or arguably, not tied to *any* book at all—it is, I think, exceedingly so.

I had to be clear about my project's scope. I had to fix my milestones.

I decided to focus on specific key sites, all of which I'd previously visited. Doing so would provide a nice contrast between the past and present—about how these places had changed and how my own perspective had as well. I would speak with other *yaatris* about their beliefs. I would talk to my family, friends, Swamiji and other holy men about what they remembered from our yaatras together. I would dig into my memory. I would open my subliminal mind.

This was exciting—and intimidating.

The locations I finally ended up choosing are all along the Ganga, and the reason for this is two-fold. One, as Delhi-ite and Hindi speaker, I was most comfortable writing about sites in northern India. I wanted to avoid misinterpreting things people said to me in places where I needed help understanding the primary language. Second, for an exploration of the relationship of Hindus with their faith, and mine with my mother, the waters of Ma Ganga seemed apposite.

From the start, I was clear I wanted to spend much time in the Himalayas. This is because three of the *Chhota Char Dham*—or the four sacred Himalayan abodes—each sit by one significant source stream of the Ganga. (The fourth, Yamunotri, is the place of origin of the river Yamuna that passes through Delhi.) The Mandakini flows alongside Kedarnath, the Alaknanda cuts through Badrinath, and the Bhagirathi originates from the Gaumukh glacier eighteen kilometres ahead of Gangotri town. The Mandakini flows into the Alaknanda at Rudraprayag, and the Alaknanda joins the Bhagirathi at Devprayag. While both the Alaknanda and the Bhagirathi are regarded as the two headstreams of the Ganga, the Bhagirathi is considered by devout Hindus as the river's *true* source stream.

I decided to begin my journey by paying my respects at Kedarnath to Lord Shiva, for whom I have long felt a special affinity, after which I'd offer my prayers to Lord Vishnu at Badrinath. Then I'd go to Gangotri, Mother Ganga's main temple. In the Himalayan foothills, I'd revisit Rishikesh, of course. And in the plains, I'd once again attend the Kumbh Mela at Allahabad and partake in the Mahashivratri (Shiva's grand night) celebrations at Varanasi. I'd end my journey by revisiting the beach at Ganga Sagar in Bengal.

And this is broadly how my journey panned out, too. In 2016, I revisited Kedarnath with a pandit from Rishikesh. It was my first time there after the devastating flash floods of 2013. Then we both went to Badrinath with a German backpacker who'd joined us on the way. I made my way to Gangotri along with an Afghan spiritual seeker in 2018, and the same year, I walked with the *kanwariyas* in Rishikesh. In 2019, I interacted with the Naga sadhus at the Prayagraj Kumbh Mela. I sought out the Aghori babas of Varanasi in February 2020 and returned to speak with them in the summer of 2022. I was all set to revisit Ganga Sagar in March 2020, too, but when both time and travel stopped due to the Covid-19 pandemic, I felt that perhaps this was *kismet*. Perhaps, in keeping with the cyclical nature of time core to Hindu beliefs, it was best to end my book at my journey's beginning, by recounting my trip to Ganga Sagar in 2015.

Initially, I had intended to write a straightforward travelogue. I wanted to record the legends and faiths of devotees at major Hindu pilgrimage sites. But the deeper I got into this project, the more I saw that my place in society as an English-speaking, upper-caste Hindu man could not be so neatly divorced from what I observed in others.

The more extensive my travels grew, the more my project morphed from a plain journalistic account into a memoir about what Hinduism means not simply to believers in general, but to me—somebody who, because of his upbringing, is undoubtedly an insider, but is also something of an outsider in that he often finds himself outside the bounds of established convention. Thus, this book is about my co-travellers' attitudes on faith, from utterly devout sadhus and pandits to unqualified atheists, as much as it is about what it means to be a young, educated man in India today, juggling tradition and modernity, science and superstition, Reason and Faith.

While I dip in and out of the galaxy of divinities, stories and philosophies encompassing the Hindu faith, I never intended to produce an exhaustive account of even the religious stories I (re) tell, let alone some kind of treatise on Hinduism. Moreover, as I was concerned only with the *nature* of faith, other than to a small extent in the Varanasi sections, I've made no attempt, other than in passing, to delve into what academics might consider the *actual history* of the places I visited or the historicity of the stories I heard along the way. That is a subject better left to the historian. Which I'm not. The folklores and traditions I narrate should be seen, then, more as a reflection of the Hindu faith I was exposed and drawn to rather than the product of a rigorous ethnographic or theological study. Put another way, my mythological asides, book references and philosophical musings are but my relishes in my own *thaali* of religious experiences.

Nevertheless, I can't get away from the fact that this is still very much a book about Hindu beliefs. So, for the uninitiated, here is a very, *very*, bare primer to help put my account into some context:

We Hindus have no one holy book and no prophet. Instead, we have many sacred texts and an even more significant number of sages, or *rishis*. In the hierarchy of these texts, it is generally accepted that the Four Vedas (the Upanishads contained in them) sit at the very top. With the Puranas (ancient lore) and Itihasas (epics such as the Mahabharata and Ramayana) just below.

In extremely brief, the initial part of the Vedas deifies the Forces of Nature, making allusions to the larger ideas of Truth and Reality and the Universe. The second part speaks of Hindu rituals. How you should do a *yagnya* (invoking the Gods around a fire), for example. At the end of the Vedas, we arrive at the philosophical heart of Hinduism: the Upanishads.

The image of God in Hinduism takes on different shapes depending on how—or rather, where—you want to see Him or Her. The Upanishads imagine the mega entity, *Brahman*—described variously as the Transcendent Reality; That which is formless, timeless and eternal; That which is without beginning and end; That which has no parent, no origin; That which is boundless joy.

A core principle of Hindu philosophy is that the Brahman and the *aatman* (soul, self) are One. However, as these concepts were probably considered too remote for the human mind to grasp, the Vedas distil the Brahman into human-like deities. The stories in the Puranas about Hindu gods are rich with symbolism echoing higher level concepts of *dharma* ('Duty' or 'Righteous Behaviour'), *karma* ('Action, and its consequences') and *moksha* ('Freedom from the cycle of rebirths'), among others.

In the Hindu scheme, things tend to move in cycles. The central tenet of reincarnation, the cycle of rebirths, is based on the idea that your present life is determined by an accumulation of your past karma, and likewise, your future lives depend on your current actions. The process of birth and rebirth—i.e. transmigration of souls—continues until one achieves moksha and the Oneness of one's soul with the Brahman, the Eternal Universal Soul. While Buddhists also believe in rebirth and reincarnation, they do not believe in a soul or the Brahman.

Another Hindu cycle concerns the nature of Time. According to ancient lore, there are four ages, or *yugas*, that become progressively shorter and less virtuous. The first is the *Satyug*, or *Satya Yuga*, followed by the *Treta Yuga*, the *Dwaapar Yuga*, and finally, our present age, which is the shortest and most corrupt of all, the *Kalyug*, or *Kali Yuga*. At the end of each yuga, declining human morality leads to the total destruction of Reality. After which Everything begins anew.

It is Lord Shiva who destroys.

It is Lord Vishnu who preserves, coming down to the world as an avatar for this purpose. (Vishnu's first avatar in the Satyug was the fish Matsya who rescued the first man, Manu, from a great deluge. Ram and Krishna were His avatars in the Treta Yuga and Dwaapar Yuga, respectively.)

And it is Lord Brahma who creates.

Together, the three Gods make up the Hindu Triad.

While traditionally, only the Brahmins read the Vedas, their knowledge was disseminated to ordinary Hindus through numerous channels. For example, the Puranas, the Ramayana and Mahabharata still reach the common man via sermons made by sadhus and pandits at poojas, and stories told at temples. Of course, nowadays, there is also television and the internet, not to mention greater personal agency.

Other than those who have an interest in theology, I know only a few Hindus who've read the Upanishads. Still, many educated believers have a copy of the Bhagavad Gita, which contains many Upanishadic teachings, in their homes. A part of the Mahabharata, the Gita is a dialogue about the nature of dharma (and other Hindu ideas) between the Pandava Prince Arjuna and Lord Krishna. Krishna counsels Arjuna to 'fulfil his Kshatriya [warrior] duty to uphold dharma' through 'selfless action'.

It is true, as many say, that Hinduism is more a way of life than a religion. But I would argue that there are enough points of unity between its disparate practices to make it a composite faith, too. One such practice is the act of undertaking yaatras to temples.

The devout across the subcontinent make yaatras in their neighbouring regions. So, while Bengalis tour the various *Shaktipeethas* (energy centres) strewn across eastern India, South Indians go in large numbers to Venkateswara Temple in Tirumala. Likewise, North Indians flock to the Himalayas and the holy cities of Haridwar and Varanasi.

For a very long time, however, the Hindus who had the means or grit have also travelled across the length and breadth of the country for tirath yaatras. One ancient nationwide route, the *Char Dham*, covering the four corners of the country (Rameswaram in the South, Dwarka in the West, Puri in the East and Badrinath in the North) is said to be established by the philosopher Adi Shankaracharya in the eighth century. The Chhota Char Dham in the Indian Himalayas is possibly just as old.

But travelling down the Ganga, one might say, is the most ancient yaatra of all—considering that it must be at least as old as the Ganga has been regarded as sacred.

PART I

Churnings

October 2016, May 1998 & May 2000

A Metamorphosis of God in Kedarnath

At a height of 3,583 metres, Kedarnath lies in the Garhwal Himalayas on the banks of the Mandakini River. As a *jyotirlingam*, or *jyotirlinga*, a spot where Lord Shiva's light, *jyoti*, illuminates the Earth, Kedarnath is among India's most revered Shiva temples.

The Kedarnath Valley was hit by unprecedented flash floods in June 2013. Over 5,000 people in the state of Uttarakhand were 'presumed dead'. Even though the Kedarnath temple stayed intact, its surroundings—hotels, resthouses, shops—all flowed away with the waters. The search for bodies continued for several months afterwards. Approximately four hundred bodies were found in the valley 'in highly decomposed states', the newspapers said.

October 2016

Hanging by a string from the rear-view mirror, Lord Hanuman was dancing to his *chalisa* playing on the stereo. The Innova shook and the words '*Jai Bhole Baba*' stickered on the rear screen came into my focus, and I thought, *Yes, God's signal is spot on today.* Shiva's blessings fit my journey perfectly indeed.

Panditji, seated behind me, had his hands joined in supplication. He began chanting and handed me a little prayer book. I knew most of the words to the *Hanuman Chalisa,* but not by heart.

'*Jai Hanuman gyaan gun sagar, Jai Kapees tihun lok ujagar.*' He pulled up his legs and crossed them under his dhoti. '*Ramdoot atulit bal dhama...*'

At about five-foot-ten, Panditji, or Pandit Hemant, was taller than me by a couple of inches. And even though he was thirty-four, my equal in age, I had to treat him with that special reverence reserved for people much older than myself. This was not just because Panditji was, well, a Hindu priest, and we were going to one of the most sacred Shiva temples in the country. It was also because he was one of my mother's legion of Rishikesh contacts. A pandit at Shivsagar Ashram.

Panditji clapped his hands and met my eyes, encouraging me to continue. His eyes were a kind brown, and his scant stubble was the main masculine aspect to his soft-featured Himachali face. He had a red *tika*, now dried, on his forehead. It split as he furrowed his brow in concentration.

I attempted to add to what was now a chorus (for the driver, Sanjay, too, I spied lip-syncing), but I sensed immediately that my words came more as strained echoes. So I motioned Panditji to carry on. I would listen to him quietly. How could I be expected to strike a beat of devotion in this state of undulating turbulence?

To my right, the road disappeared into a sheer drop. In the valley far below, the Ganga gleamed under the sun and across it a thick carpet of greens unfurled on the hills as if without end.

The trees were getting darker. They were taller, slenderer. I rolled down my window and a bracing piny scent took me over. Rishikesh was now some hundred kilometres behind me. Why, Rishikesh was where my religious journey began, I thought smiling to myself, long before I was even conceived in my mother's womb!

The car banked a hard left and I roused up. 'Sanjay, please take it easy!'

'Don't worry, bhaiyya. I've been driving in these mountains for ten years, and on this route, I can go eyes closed.' Sanjay, a Rishikesh resident, looked no older than twenty-five, but the ease with which he steered over the bends belied his years. 'You must know the story of Kedarnath?' he turned back and asked with a twinkle in his eyes. I did, but I was curious to hear this young man's narration. Like many millennials, Sanjay's hair was up in spikes, and his ears were blocked with earphones. The rest of him though was all Hindu Indian. The back of his steering hand was tattooed with a fading 'Om' and his left bicep bore the stamp of Lord Shiva's Trident.

'After the Pandavas won the battle of Mahabharata, they prayed to Lord Krishna asking for forgiveness,' Sanjay said. 'They begged him to open the gates to heaven. But he told them clearly, the decision was not his. The Pandavas had spilt the blood of their grandfather, their gurus, their brothers, and the only way they could get to heaven was by asking Shivji for forgiveness.'

Panditji's prayers came to an abrupt stop.

'Sanjay, stop the car!' I said. 'Why didn't you tell me you were feeling sick, Panditji?'

The priest clogged his mouth with his orange scarf. 'I just…I didn't realize it. It happened so suddenly, Siddharthji.'

We got off the car and I took in a deep breath. The last time I came up this way was almost twenty years ago. Back then, the in-vogue men's hairstyle was long and wavy, the front falling over the forehead in leisurely droops, inspired by Ajay Devgn rather than Instagram. Kedarnath was, I believed, a place refined by the Himalayas and unspoiled by man. And I was an energetic teenager in whose recall lay stored a volume of prayers, the uppermost of which was the *Hanuman Chalisa*.

I helped Panditji get cleaned up, and we got back on our way. A milestone peeking out from a clutch of rhododendrons said: 'You are in The Himalayas. This is Devbhoomi: The Abode of the Gods.'

May 1998

In the summer of '98, India had just conducted its nuclear tests, and I, at sixteen, had just taken my Class X exams. Delhi was raging with hot loo winds. And with rumours of an imminent war with Pakistan, drawing rooms across the country were growing restless. I was a bit edgy too. But for a different reason.

My best friend Arjun and I had been denied permission to go on a trek to Dodital, and my barrage of pleases to my mother had resulted only in bickering. But then, one day, I heard mummy making excited noises over the phone and just like that a possibility opened up.

'What happened?'

Mummy smiled. 'It seems you can go on your trek.'

'Seriously?'

'Yes.' She had that look in her eyes. 'But I will be going with you.'

As it happened, my mother and her sisters, Minna Masi and Rashmi Masi, had been quietly planning a yaatra to Kedarnath and Badrinath that summer. It had been ages since the sisters had vacationed together, and with them there was never a doubt about where to go.

I should tell you, Dear Reader, that my mother's side of the family, the Malhotras, like to make yaatras as frequently as millennials download smartphone apps. In contrast, my father and his siblings, the Kapilas, had stayed on the path of consummate atheism for as long as I can remember. Only my Dadaji, my paternal grandfather, was somewhat religious, and even of this, I have little recollection. My parents' differing approaches probably came down to the fact that my mother's family adhered to the *Sanatan Dharma*, the Eternal Hindu Order with all its gods, goddesses and their myriad avatars, while my father's side followed the Arya Samaj sect of Hinduism. The Arya Samajis are the product of a reform movement dating back to the early 1870s. Their practices, essentially a mix of mantras and *havans*, prayers around a sacred fire, are predicated on the soundness of the Vedas. The Arya Samajis rejected idol worship, and my mother rejected *them*.

Mummy said Sehdev Uncle was going with us too. Sehdev Uncle, a short but sturdy man with a humpback, was then a bachelor in his fifties.

While my mother was a tax lawyer, Sehdev Uncle was a salesman at MDH, the masala manufacturer. While we spoke mainly in English at home and lived in a three-bedroom flat in Delhi's tony Greater Kailash, Sehdev Uncle spoke only Punjabi and Hindi. He lived with his three brothers and their wives in a tenement in the gullies of Paharganj. It's not that I believed my parents were big people and that Sehdev Uncle was small. (Although class differences matter. So yes, I thought that way, too.) What bothered me was how uneducated he was. How steeped in faith he was.

But mostly, I didn't care. I didn't give the man much thought except when he happened to accompany mummy on her various yaatras—which was fairly often—to Varanasi or Pashupati Nath, or her endless sojourns near Delhi. Indeed, if there was somebody who could rival mummy in temple-going, it was Sehdev Uncle. The two had been committed patrons at Shivsagar Ashram in Rishikesh for well over thirty-five years, where under the auspices of Swami Vairagya Teerath, Sehdev Uncle's mother and my grandmother had first met.

Swami Vairagya Teerathji, or Maharajji, as I knew him, was not just mummy's guru. He was a saint so peerless and supreme that he informed every aspect of her life. Whether it was her career (she'd not passed her pre-medical exam because 'law is your calling' Maharajji had said); or her marriage ('Your husband will not be religious, but he will have a sharp mind'); or even her diet ('No rice for me today, it's *Ekaadashi*,' and 'It's *Pradosh*, so I'll eat after praying to Shivji in the evening,' are the kind of utterances mummy makes even today). More than thirty years after his passing, I realize that Maharajji's teachings dwell not only in mummy's actions but echo in mine too.

Mala, my younger sister, once said that mummy considered Maharajji no less than Lord Vishnu. But I disagreed. He was more like Shivji, I said. Mummy used to say Maharajji was her father and mother in ways her own parents couldn't be. He could see both into your past and future. And not just that. He could even change it at will, if he desired. 'Did he ever?' I once asked, and mummy looked at me reprovingly and said, 'You had to see Maharajji in his glory.'

But I never did see him in his glory, you see, for I was only eight years old when he passed on. All I could go on was hearsay and images of a grey-bearded man. Still, I knew from the very beginning of Maharajji's realness, and also his omnipotence, his beneficence. Maharajji's sepia-tinted photograph with his long beard flowing in the Rishikesh wind, his brown eyes searching into yours, stood alongside the idols of Shiva and Lakshmi in our home's temple where mummy did her pooja every morning and evening.

It made perfect sense that one of Maharajji's disciples, another Rishikesh sadhu, a Swami Shraddhanandji, would be the one to lead us to Kedarnath. I had met Swami Shraddhanandji only a few times before and didn't know him well. I just knew he was the Swamiji to whom mummy deferred for life advice at the time.

'We are so fortunate that Swamiji will be protecting us throughout the yaatra,' mummy said. 'So many devotees have asked him before, but he always refuses.'

'He'd never say no to you,' I said.

Mummy was skilled at showering high fealty on sadhus and seldom missed an opportunity to dive at their feet in a *sashtang pranaam*, or prostrate genuflection. Her penchant for dishing out large donations had made her very popular with saints and imposters alike. Only the previous year, Arjun had prank-called her posing as a Varanasi pandit, in a voice all hoarse and crackly, speaking in terrible Hindi. Mummy went along with the ruse for several minutes until he finally asked for a donation. 'Five Lakhs? What do you need five lakhs for?' she yelled into the phone. Years later, even she would admit the joke was funny. Not that it did much to change her ways.

'Anyway, Neha is also coming,' she said.

'Who?'

'You remember Mrs Khanna from Bombay? Her daughter. She's a big Shiva devotee. Her mother says she's desperate to get married. Her father died last year, and Mrs Khanna doesn't keep well. Neha really...'

I cut in. 'Can Arjun come with us?'

Mummy stared at me. 'Only if he's interested. He's used to all these fancy-mancy holidays, so please tell him that up in the Himalayas there are no comforts.' She let her words sink in. 'None. At. All. This is a yaatra and not one of his trips to the Alps.'

She did have a point. At a time in life when most of my classmates had to content themselves with a week in Mussoorie or Shimla, and the term 'abroad' only meant places like Paris and London, Arjun's family was used to regular foreign holidays. Mala and I, on the other hand, seemed perennially to end up in Rishikesh. The evening *aarti* ceremony in Shivsagar Ashram, surrounded by devotees chanting *shlokas*, being our most exciting time of day. 'Go do sashtang pranaam,' mummy would tell us, and we'd drop to the floor all reverent and flat saying, '*Om Namo Narayana, Swamiji*,' before the feet of sadhu after orange-robed sadhu.

After the aarti, we would prostrate ourselves before the *Shivalingam* in the ashram's temple. Mummy said this rock, an embodiment of Lord Shiva, had been lifted from the Ganga by Maharajji himself. Maharajji had once had a dream. In it, Shivji had asked him to go down to the banks of the Ganga, where He, Lord Shiva, would present himself in the water. Maharajji had such divine powers.

It was an auspicious pre-dawn 5:30 am in the May of '98 when the lot of us yaatris—mummy, my aunts, Minna Masi and Rashmi Masi, Sehdev Uncle, Neha, Arjun and I—all bundled into a tempo-traveller and set off from Delhi for Rishikesh. (Mala couldn't make it. She had been allowed to go on a school trip to Jaipur.)

Our first stop was at an old Satya Narayan temple outside Haridwar, a place I remembered well. Inside, there stood an ancient banyan tree under which Mala and I used to play hopscotch when we were little. I always paid 'strict attention' as my Nani stopped here en route to Rishikesh to offer her prayers. As my grandmother joined her palms, her lips fish-puckering shlokas, I'd spring up to gong the bell, then ride on the rise-and-fall of her unpronounceable Sanskrit intonations and then pop into my mouth the sweet *prasad* the pandit dropped into my hands after he marked my forehead with cooling red tika.

What really caught my eye, though, were the black commas zigzagging in the pond behind her. They seemed so small, so insignificant. And yet they were always struggling and vibrating as if searching for a way to escape their trap.

'For these fish, their whole world is this pond, na?' I once asked my Nani.

'They are not fish, beta. They are tadpoles,' she said. 'And one day, they will grow into frogs and discover how big this world is. Now close your eyes and pray.'

I cast a glance around the temple courtyard. The place looked much the same, but it also felt different somehow.

I surveyed the temple's grounds. The sagely-bearded banyan tree was the same. The idols of Vishnu and Lakshmi, they too emitted that late-afternoon sleepiness. So what had changed? Something had, but I couldn't tell what.

The answer came a few hours later, as our tempo-traveller drove uphill into wafts of cool misty clouds. Yes, the old pond had gone. And so had the tadpoles.

October 2016

Panditji and I went down a path, passing first a group of college students frozen in selfie-poses, the dam-stilled blue water acting as their backdrop, followed by a cluster of *bhajan*-singing orange-robed mendicants.

'This is a very *siddh devi*, Siddharthji,' Panditji said, describing the goddess by an adjective I thought fell somewhere between 'realized' and 'proven' but elicited yet weightier emotions.

Twenty kilometres shy of Rudraprayag, where the Alaknanda and Mandakini merge, we stopped at the temple of goddess Dhari Devi. Its pillars went deep into the Alaknanda.

'Dhari Devi is the protector of the Char Dham. Do you know her significance?'

I shook my head.

'The original Dhari Devi temple was found deep inside the Ganga.'

'They discovered a temple under the riverbed?' I felt a familiar creeping scepticism.

'No, no, Siddharthji. Hundreds of years ago, a raja threw a golden statue of Ma Kaali into the river, and that idol became a massive rock. It is her statue that is in the water. This rock arose from it. It is a form of *Bhadrakaali*,' he said, referring to Goddess Kaali in fierce form.

I looked over the railing at a huge rock jutting from the water.

'I'm telling you, they've done science tests too. The Devi should never have been lifted from her resting place. But in 2013, they decided to move her over here because of this that they built.' Panditji pointed at a dam in the distance. 'And a few hours later, the cloudburst happened.'

I knelt before the temple pandit and he spooned a trickle of *Gangajal*, or water from the Ganga, into my cupped palm. 'What happened in 2013, panditji?' I asked. 'Is it true that the floods came after they removed Dhari Devi from her resting place?'

'*Na*. Many people think that,' he said. 'That when they brought the Devi to this platform, the floods got triggered. But the truth is the Devi knew the floods were coming. She knew. And this is why she chose to rise to higher ground. Had we not moved her, she would have also been swept away.'

But Panditji was doubtful. 'Some hundred years back, they had tried to lift her. And soon after that, a landslide flattened Kedarnath.'

The temple pandit regarded Pandijti with intense eyes. 'It is wrong to blame Devi,' he said. 'It is we who are to blame.'

'Yes. When man plays with nature, nature plays its hand back,' one of the gathered worshippers offered.

Panditji blinked. 'The unique thing about this devi is that her appearance changes as the day progresses. From morning to afternoon to night, she changes from a girl to a woman to an old lady,' he said.

And the temple pandit let loose a smile. '*Haan*. That is correct.'

May 1998

Bhajans dedicated to Lord Shiva blared out from the tempo-traveller as we burrowed deeper and deeper into the mountains. Having just passed through a pine forest, the road opened to a view of terrace farms that cut into the mountainside in neat wide steps, which looked altogether like the ridges on the back of a crocodile reaching far, far down to eat the long golden snake, the Ganga…

Swamiji and Neha occupied the two front seats while mummy and Sehdev Uncle sat in the middle, with Minna Masi and Rashmi Masi just behind them. Arjun and I were sprawled out on the long seat at the far back.

'I hope I do well in maths,' I said. 'I think it went well, but you can't say.' I secretly felt my exam had gone very well, but since maths had been my biggest weakness throughout school I didn't believe this. Not fully.

'I just need to do well enough to get out of here,' Arjun said. 'The other day my dad drove me to Delhi University and it looked just horrible. I've told him to get me out.' He gave a smug smile. 'He's agreed.'

Arjun often spoke in this way, and it was precisely his talk, at once utterly frank and improper, that I found amusing. Arjun was the son of a Mr Goel, who owned a chain of restaurants in North Delhi, and everybody in school knew he was filthy rich. I wasn't rich. My parents had been government servants in the Indian Revenue Service for over twenty-five years. The government was where they had met and government flats were where I grew up. My mother joined ANZ Grindlays Bank in 1995 as their tax adviser because the pay in the private sector was so much better.

Arjun's rich talk matched his countenance, too. He was six feet tall and lanky, while I was five-foot-seven and on the chubby side. He always ensured his hair was neatly gelled back and his shoes were polished and pointy whereas I wore my hair as a lazy flop, and my boots, well, I can't even remember them. Other boys would mock him for his manners, but Arjun didn't care. He prided himself on his clothes and shoes and holidays. And that was that. 'It's imported, man, you wouldn't know,' was the kind of thing he'd say to shut up a class bully. I often laughed alongside him because despite our many differences, we had much in common, too. For one, we both loved good food and hated cricket.

My gaze fell on Neha. She was looking out of the window, lost in thought. When her mother, Mrs Khanna, had come to our house to drop her off a few nights before, I heard her anxiously tell my mother about how Neha's biological clock was ticking, about how it was high time she did something about it. But what surprised me was Neha's total lack of reaction. She gave a shy smile and said nothing.

Neha was thirty-two years old, and as far as Arjun and I were concerned, she was practically antique. Assuming we were immature young boys—which, to be fair, we were—she had been somewhat standoffish towards us these past couple of days, so we'd kept our distance from each other. Neha had shoulder-length hair, black liquid eyes and a nose with a nose ring. She had a scar on her forehead which you noticed only when she pushed her hair back. As she did now to save it from scattering in the wind.

Across the aisle from her, orange-robed and bald but with a thick black beard, sat Swami Shraddhanandji. We had picked him up from Rishikesh. I guessed he was in his early forties then. Which made him about a decade younger than my mother. But the gravitas with which he spoke made him sound no less than eighty.

He was saying in Hindi: '...so yes, within a few years, north India will be hit by a big earthquake. In this Kalyug, there will be an apocalypse, and around twenty per cent of the world's coastline will go. Bombay-vombay all will go into the water. That's what my calculations say.'

Kalyug, I knew, was our present Age of Vice. But... 'Does Swamiji know that Bombay isn't in north India?' I turned to Arjun. He grinned.

'When will this happen, Swamiji?' Neha said. Her voice was a mixture of incredulity and concern.

Swamiji licked his lips. 'We cannot say,' he said. 'But it could be within your lifetime.'

The man sounded confident. I wasn't persuaded by his talk, but I felt in myself the beginnings of a curious something, a slow-wheeling interest to listen to more of the story. My teenage mind jumped from what I knew about global warming to plate tectonics. The Himalayas were young. They were still forming, in fact. (*Over 200 million years ago India was a large island separated from Eurasia by the Tethys ocean...*) And so I considered: if these unimaginable things had once happened—continents colliding to grow mountains and glaciers and rivers—then wasn't it plausible that Swamiji's story also contained some truth?

(This is how the faithful get you. Early.)

Swamiji pulled his legs up and gracefully crossed them under his robes. He was going on about the Satyug now. The Age of Truth, when humanity was governed by virtues and the sages were powerful enough to invoke the gods at will.

'You must know of the country Denmark?' he said with an appraising glance and Arjun and I nodded. Denmark was beside Sweden. Sweden was where my favourite band Roxette was from. 'That's what you call it today,' he said. 'The country's ancient name is actually *Dhenumarg*.'

Arjun and I stared at each other. Swamiji had claimed a Scandinavian word as Indian by merging the Hindi words for 'cow' and 'way'. Then we threw our heads back and burst out laughing and high-fiving.

'This is too much,' Minna Masi whispered to Rashmi Masi, and mummy shot me a glare.

Swamiji tried to hold my gaze, but I was quaking with laughter. 'Just wait and see, Siddharth. You will see Kedarnath's miracle for yourself,' he said, but I kept giggling.

'Behave properly,' mummy snapped and Sehdev Uncle backed her up. 'Do you boys study in your school or play behind it?' he said.

'Uncleji, have you tasted chicken?' I said. Sehdev Uncle didn't even touch eggs, let alone meat. Mummy and her sisters never touched meat either. Papa, Mala and I did.

'*Hai, hai! Moorkh ladke, Ram ka naam le...*you stupid boy, take Lord Ram's name.' Sehdev Uncle stuck his tongue out in horror, and Arjun and I rose to a higher pitch.

On our way to Guptkashi, a small town in the Kedarkhanda region of the Garhwal Himalayas, Swamiji returned to Kedarnath's story.

'Shiva was not willing to meet them,' he said of the Pandavas. 'It was not just that He was angry that they had sinned. Rather it was because the Lord has a good measure of his nature. You see, if anybody prays sincerely to Shivji, He can't say no. And it was well known that even *rakshasas*, demons, had got what they wanted out of him.

'So Shiva avoided the Pandavas in Kashi and in other places. Then taking the form of a bull, he eventually came here, to Uttarakhand. And when the Pandavas learnt he was hiding in the Himalayas, they came looking for him. They went to Himachal and to Kashmir, and finally landed up in this town, where despite Shiva's brilliant disguise, they recognized him. But then, when Bhima leaped to grab the bull'—Swamiji's eyes flashed as if divulging the secret to a magic trick—'Shiva slipped underground and vanished.'

'That's why this town is called Guptkashi,' Arjun said, sounding pleased with himself, and Neha gave a wry smile.

'Yes. You've understood why this town is hidden. But can you tell me why the name also has "Kashi" in it? … It is because it is as pure as Varanasi,' Swamiji said, answering his own question.

At Guptkashi, we paid our respects at the local Shiva temple, after which we took a dip in a pond, the Manikarnika Kund, which was fed by two springs. One stream, locals said, brought water from the Ganga while the other released the Yamuna. I very much doubted this was true, but mummy and Sehdev Uncle obviously didn't, as they flapped about in the water like children.

On our way to Gaurikund, the base town for the trek up to Kedarnath, the following day, we'd been on the road for a half hour when we were forced to stop. There had been a massive rockslide and we would have to wait for it to be cleared.

'Oh, shit!' Arjun threw his head back and hit play on his Walkman.

I could hear Neha's soft, self-assured voice from up in the front. She was telling Minna Masi about how she had got that scar on her forehead. '…Somewhere near Pune, aunty,' she said. 'We were driving back from Shirdi, and I saw a snake crossing the road. I'm sure it was a cobra, actually. So I swerved the car, and before I knew it, I hit a tree. It happened very fast.'

'You swerved the car off the road?' Arjun said, taking out an earphone. 'For a snake?'

'I've been a Shiva devotee since childhood, baba.' Neha looked annoyed. 'You won't get it.' She turned to Swamiji whose face was the picture of sympathetic comprehension.

Lord Shiva's neck is wrapped by a snake, a representation of all time—past, present, future—symbolizing that He simultaneously controls it and is independent of it. This much I understood. Even though I couldn't grasp how faith could make anybody drive off the road so comprehensively.

'My head hit the steering wheel and there was a little blood, but it wasn't bad. My father was next to me. He hurt his knees.' For a moment, Neha's eyes grew distant, but she brought herself back. 'He was so angry. Papa was the real Shiva devotee. It was he who took me to Kedarnath some years back.'

Sehdev Uncle, who was shelling peanuts, appeared entranced.

'Look at it, aunty.' Neha showed her scar to Rashmi Masi as Arjun and I also came closer for a look. 'It's just the shape of the moon on top of Shivji's head.'

I turned to my mother. Mummy was captivated. *Now Neha was a girl after her own heart*, as she would have put it.

It was time to make the crossing.

'Take Bhole Baba's name,' the driver said revving up the engine.

I looked out the window. The hastily cleared road, still rutted with rocks, was only truck-wide, and the chasm to my right extended downward to dizzying depths. There is no chance in hell we're surviving this fall, I thought, and tapped Arjun on the shoulder. 'Should we say the *Hanuman Chalisa*?' He put a finger to his lips.

We started to wobble down the road, jerking wildly from side to side and everybody fell silent. It was the kind of silence which emits a soundless sound and a second becomes a minute long. Then Neha began the *Shiva Kavach*, or 'Shiva's armour'. And on her cue, Sehdev Uncle broke into the *Sankat Mochan*, a prayer to ward off distressing situations, while Minna Masi and Rashmi Masi both surged with unmelodious *Om Namah Shivaays*.

I began with the *Hanuman Chalisa*. But then I was overtaken: '*Oh Shivji! Oh Bhootnath! Oh Bholenath!* Please protect us. Please take us safe, whole, complete to your haloed gates.' Mummy was standing up with her palms open towards the rattling ceiling. 'Swamiji, Sid, Rashmi, Minna, Sehdevji, Neha—please protect us. Please.' Her eyes darted to the man at the wheel. 'And, of course, Sushil. Please protect Sushil.'

The tyres skidded over loose mud and everybody gasped. There was a see-sawing and a shuddering. There was a lurch, there was a stall. Then, again a wobble.

Then, nothing. It was over. We'd made the crossing unhurt.

Arjun and I laughed a nervous laugh.

'You okay?' I asked him.

With the acute look of a spurned lover, Arjun walked up to mummy.

'You're okay, na, beta?' Mummy's eyebrows were raised in deep concern.

He looked like he was about to throw up. 'I'm fine, aunty,' he said. 'But really, how could you forget me in your prayers? I mean, you remembered even to protect the driver!'

Gaurikund. October 2016

It was 6 pm, and darkness was falling as Pandit Hemant and I paced up a solitary path lined to either side with shops that had mostly shuttered down. The peak season had gone, and the yaatris with it. This was late October, and with Diwali, the penultimate day of the Kedarnath yaatra, now barely a week away, Gaurikund was winding down to a sleep that would last until the end of April.

I was taking in the gush of the Mandakini foaming down the rocks when a Gujarati man with a towel around his neck approached us. 'Can we bathe here?' he said. A signboard behind me pointed to the *tapt kund*, the hot springs, but I could see no yaatris anywhere around.

'I don't know,' I said. 'Maybe the baths were destroyed in the floods?'

'No, no, it is absolutely functional,' a porter said. 'You must have a bath here before going up for *darshan*'—that is, the 'sacred viewing' of God or a holy person.

Swamiji had said the same thing to me once. And Sehdev Uncle had said, 'The water from this kund can cure diseases. Did you boys know that Parvati Devi bathed in this same spot?'

'Not only that,' Swamiji added, 'one day, Parvatiji moulded a boy out of the *ubtan* she applied on her body, and once he came to life, she asked him to stand guard at the entrance. When Lord Shiva arrived, the boy stopped him from entering the pond, and Shiva became so incensed—"Who is this boy to stop me from seeing my wife?"—that he cut off his head. A devastated Parvati then said to her husband, "You must bring my son back. Do whatever it takes but bring him back. Now!" At this same moment, Shiva saw a wandering elephant and he took off his head and placed it on the boy's body. And who is…?'

'Ganesha!' Arjun cried, and Neha smiled as if to say anybody could have guessed that.

A sulphurous smell floated out of the pools of hot water as a gaggle of petticoat-clad aunties and dhoti-wrapped uncles submerged themselves in the separate female and male bathing compartments. Sehdev Uncle invited us in.

Earlier, in Rishikesh, when Arjun and I stood diffidently at the top of a *ghat* leading to the Ganga, a sadhu had approached us. 'This is the purest water,' he said. 'It can never rot. Don't hesitate to come in.'

'Is it purer even than a bottle of Bisleri?' I countered.

'Bisleri may be clean. But Gangajal is pure. *Pavitra*. There is a difference,' he said.

No sooner had we gone waist-deep into the water than a little upstream from us a pig ambled in and urinated. At least the Ganga was a running river, I thought. This pond here, it's stagnant. 'No, thanks,' I said to Sehdev Uncle.

But today, all these years later, this same pool was warm and inviting. Panditji and I took a dip.

The caretaker at the state-run guesthouse, the Garhwal Mandal Nigam, a middle-aged Garhwali man with a deep-set frown, scribbled our names into the guest logbook. 'Why didn't you take the helicopter from Guptkashi or Phata, panditji?' he asked.

'What is the point of coming on yaatra if you do it through shortcuts,' Panditji said. 'There is no shortcut to God. It takes very hard *tapasya*, penance, to get anywhere near him.'

The caretaker's pursed lips broke into a smile. 'But panditji, nowadays there are many more Heli-yaatris than walking ones, na?' he said. 'Times have changed.'

A VIP, a minister to be more precise, who'd gone up by helicopter once had returned only to find that nothing had changed, I remembered somebody telling me when I was last here; his wishes from God remained unfulfilled. The *aam aadmi*, the common man, who never had a choice other than to go up by foot in the first place, though, always had his prayers answered.

'Don't you worry, Panditji,' I said. 'We'll walk up for sure.'

Gaurikund. May 1998

'Don't be foolish. You can't go up barefoot. You're asthmatic.'

'As if you can. You're old.'

'I do yoga every day and my body is hardened. Just look at Sehdev Uncle. He is older than me and he's the strongest person here.'

'So strong, like a penguin,' Arjun said, interrupting this exchange between mummy and me.

'Shut up.' I winced. 'He can understand English. And his back is like that because he fell sick as a kid.'

Sehdev Uncle had had a desperately poor childhood. When he was less than two years old the country was partitioned and his family was forced to flee their home in Western Punjab. They had come east in an open-air train carriage, packed with hundreds of refugees. After first baking under the August sun, he had nearly drowned in a rising pool of monsoon waters.

'His father died in that train,' mummy had told me. 'And what did his poor mother not do to feed her children! She stitched people's clothes and would steal bits of cloth from here and there.' She shook her head. 'You can't imagine life in those days.

'When they reached Delhi, Sehdev had a high fever. His muscles went into spasm and his spine became stiff. His mother, she stood in long lines at the refugee camp to get him medicine, and in time his fever went away but his back remained bent… Some people said it was jaundice, some said polio, but his mother was a poor, uneducated woman and she was just happy her son was talking and walking again. Then, some years later, Sehdev got typhoid. And this time he became so sickly, a total skeleton, that his mother really thought he'd die. She visited *vaids* and *hakims*. But nothing worked. Then, when Sehdev was around five or six, she came to know about a great saint in Rishikesh. She had heard that this man had healing powers. People said that whatever he touched was injected by the spirit of Shiva. People said he had vowed not to touch even a single paisa. She took Sehdev to him.'

That saint was Maharajji and the first thing he said to Sehdev's mother was that she should stop thieving. That she should learn to stand on her own two feet. Then he took little Sehdev under his wing at Shivsagar Ashram and raised him like his own boy. It was Maharajji who gave Sehdev natural treatments. Maharajji put Sehdev on a diet of fruits, nuts, vegetables and fresh cow's milk from the *gaushala* at the ashram.

And 'little by little, the boy grew strong. His back grew straighter.' Mummy grew reflective. '... Many years later, I remember Maharajji had filled up a sack with *bel* fruits. He told Sehdev, with so much love, "I picked these from the forest just for you."'

'Then?'

'Then, nothing... So, I mean, Sehdev Uncle was shaped by his Rishikesh upbringing.'

And it was true. Not only did Sehdev Uncle follow a *saatvic* pure vegetarian diet, he also followed the unwavering path of a *brahmachari*. He never married. He never touched a woman. No wonder mummy constantly said to me, as she did now: 'Sehdev Uncle is a *sanyaasi* [a renunciate]. He has such strong self-control that he can go without food for five-five days. This is the result of being raised by mahatmas rather than on a diet of Coke and pizzas like you boys.'

Sehdev Uncle meanwhile was giving Neha another précis to his life. '...I know the Shaastras at the back of my hand. But my brother has reduced me to a lackey... Behenji, I tell you, in another life I would have been a Sanskrit professor.'

'Don't call me sister, uncleji,' Neha shot back. She turned to me, switched from Hindi to English. 'He's old enough to be my father.'

'Yes, yes, uncleji's story is fascinating,' Arjun said, preoccupied with other matters. 'But can he help me get a horse porter? These Nepalis are thugs.'

'Arjun!' Neha's eyes grew big. 'They aren't Nepalis. They are Garhwalis. What's wrong with you?'

'Wait. Aren't you going to trek up?' I asked my friend. 'You were the one who wanted to trek in the Himalayas.'

'Yeah, but this place is so yucky. Just look at all this horse shit everywhere. And my Nikes are brand new. My dad just got these from the US.'

'So? Do you plan to worship your shoes?' Neha said as she took hers off.

Arjun ignored her. 'Plus, have you seen the crowd here? It's totally villagy.' At which Minna Masi shot him a glare and he shut up.

My mother and Neha began their ascent barefoot along with hundreds and hundreds of yaatris—a testament to their faith as much as a measure of some unspoken competition between them. Over the years, I've learned that, like any serious business, the belief in God comes with very high—possibly the highest—stakes.

And like them, Swamiji and Sehdev Uncle started out barefoot, too, although they slipped into footwear after only a few kilometres. Minna Masi and Rashmi Masi also started out walking, wearing sandals, however, as they had brought no shoes. But after mere metres, gasping for air and apologising profusely to Shivji, they gave up and got into hand-pulled palanquins.

On my part, I wore shoes from the start even though, perhaps driven by bravado rather than faith, I did briefly contemplate going up without them.

October 2016

By 8:30 am, Panditji and I had covered well over five kilometres.

'If we had delayed leaving any longer, *Rahu Kaal* would have begun, Siddharthji, so it's good we left in time,' he said.

The mere mention of Rahu Kaal, an inauspicious time of day for beginning any venture, hinted that the man had discussed my yaatra's particulars with my mother. But then I wondered if his talk was simply a demonstration of his piety.

With every interaction I was realizing just how immeasurably removed Panditji's world was from mine. As the overseer of poojas and havans, Panditji was, as my father might've put it, 'a star shining his light on an earth that was still flat'. To my mind, though, he was more like the nucleus of an atom. One among thousands and thousands, all circling with devotees. All filling up some alternate conception of reality.

'Actually, my family were service people,' Panditji had said earlier. 'I come from a small village near Shimla where my father is a clerk and my mother is a homemaker. From the age of five itself, I had a tremendous attachment to God. Siddharthji, I'm telling you, I was so much into prayers to Devi and Shiva, that my parents would say, "Why can't you go out and play like the other boys? Why are you always lost in your thoughts?"

'So when I was eleven, I ran away from home. I decided to become a sanyaasi, and I took the bus to Rishikesh... When I got off, I had nothing on me. No money. Only my clothes and my will. That's all. Over there, I found an ashram that kept boys like me. In the beginning, I really liked it, you know, being away from home. Following my own way. But then within a month, I became ill and there was nobody to look after me and the food was terrible, and I missed my mother a lot. So, I wrote to my father and he came right away and took me home.'

Panditji drew in a breath. 'It was good to be with my parents again. But after a month, I knew I couldn't be there. I did not belong there any more. I knew it was not the life I was meant to lead. So I returned to Rishikesh. And I've never gone back.'

'How did your family take your decision?'

'They were sad, of course. Oh, my mother wept for months. She wouldn't stop crying... When I turned eighteen, I wrote to her. I said, "Even though this is the path I have chosen, I promise you one thing: I will not take sanyaas without first telling you."'

Snowclad mountains peeked out at the head of the valley riven through by the Mandakini River that gave it its name. Groups of yaatris on horseback passed by, and I spotted the odd bobbing *tokri-waala*, carrying on his back bales of hay or a stack of suitcases. Those hand-pulled palanquins of yore were utterly absent now, though. They seemed to have all but disappeared, replaced by choppers piercing the chilly air as Heli-yaatri after Heli-yaatri flew up for darshan at a mere Rs 2,500 for a one-way trip.

'She must be quite relieved,' Panditji laughed, 'that at least I am married now and have a son.'

Rambara, a village at the halfway point. May 1998

Arjun and I stood sweating inside our track pants at a chai stall. But then there came a light drizzle, and as we started to freeze, we sought comfort in steaming bowlfuls of Maggi noodles. Later, motivated by the spirited public nose-clearings of Garhwali porters, we competed to see who could retch up the fattest blob of spit.

Neha let us know how disgusting she thought this was. But as she sat there examining her feet, her soles gone soot-black, I wanted to say how *that* was so much worse. But I kept quiet. I was getting worried now. What had been a light patter was turning to fast-gliding sleet and mummy was still not in sight. Arjun and I continued with our little game, but after half an hour passed, it was no longer fun, and my anxiety was showing.

'Isn't that her?' Neha said, peeking through the haze.

'Where?'

I caught sight of an old woman inching up the hill. To her one side was a male figure, drenched so his clothes had gone from orange to red: Swamiji. And to her other side was mummy. Her salwar-kameez was soaked, but she was bubbling with energy, chatting away.

As the trio came closer, the figure at the centre became clear. The old woman was not just frail; she was also poor. So poor in fact that she was trekking up to Kedarnath wearing just a cotton saree, which, gossamer-thin and transparent, clung wetly to her wrinkled skin. Her midriff was bare, and her chest was blouseless.

I rushed up to my mother. 'What took you so long? We've been waiting ages!'

Mummy's brow was a fount of sweat and rain. 'This *mataji* asked for my help when it started to rain, and I couldn't say no to her, na? Swamiji was keeping me company so you needn't have worried.'

'We went down looking for you twice!'

The old woman must have noticed my consternation because she embraced mummy and placed her hand on my shoulder. 'Beta,' she said, 'your mother came to me in my time of need. Like a devi [goddess]. Only because of her will I get to see God today. She is my saviour. You are so lucky to have a mother like her.' She planted a sloppy kiss on mummy's cheek. 'Please don't be angry with her.'

October 2016

After we crossed a bridge over the Mandakini at the halfway point, Panditji and I, he pointed at the other side of the valley. Like nail scratches on sapped skin, the old trekking route could be seen on a denuded mountainside. There was not a trace of what was once Rambara.

I remembered that mummy had given the old woman whatever her hands could find: Rs 200. But when the rain abated, both Swamiji and I talked her into continuing with us unencumbered. We had to complete our climb before dusk and could not afford to be slowed down.

'It is your duty to help others when you can,' Swamiji said. 'But if you keep doing this, how will you be able to complete the yaatra yourself? Your own yaatra is the most important. Never forget that... Why is Shiva so difficult to access? Why does he live so deep inside the Himalayas in such *far-far* heights? It is because if he didn't hide, anybody could come and ask him for anything.'

The Kedarnath peaks were taking on the relief of a white wall reaching the heavens.

'You see, the Char Dham and especially Kedarnath was always meant to be difficult to access,' Panditji now said to me. 'It was never meant to be a place to be conquered by people in their big cars so they could jump from one dham to the next. And in the early days, it actually was like this. People would come here after much effort at the end of their lives. In the old days, people didn't even know if they could go back down, so some would do their funeral rites at the sacred confluences of Devprayag or Rudraprayag before coming up... Now, of course...' And he let his words fade in the cold air with a wave of the hand.

It was true, I thought. Many yaatris to Kedarnath are poor. They trek up on foot wearing just rubber *chappals*. Or no footwear at all. Yet somehow, they manage. They find their way from all parts of the country, pulled by devotion. By emotion. By faith.

'Why do you mostly see these villager yaatris here?' Arjun had once asked aloud.

'Because you English-types with your Reebok shoes are too smart for such yaatras,' Sehdev Uncle had said. 'One requires *sachchi bhakti*.' Real devotion.

'I wear Nike, not Reebok,' Arjun muttered under his breath.

'This is why the floods came here,' Panditji said. 'This is why the apocalypse came to Kedarnath.'

I stared at him, startled. 'What are you saying, Panditji?'

'*Arre*, people had also started coming here for their honeymoon.' He lowered his voice, clenched his teeth. 'Prostitution was also happening here.'

Whether or not Panditji's claims held water, I can't say. But several yaatris would supply me with similar accounts, each varying slightly in the extent of the egregiousness they described but all shocking to the Shiva devotee: 'Liquor was being sold in Kedarnath,' said a man from Maharashtra; 'You won't believe it. Goats were being slaughtered near here,' said a baba from UP; 'Girls were available for booking also. From Himachal, Nepal,' said a man from Gujarat.

And while these were all contentions lacking in evidence, they demonstrated one thing to me: the widespread belief that Lord Shiva unleashed destruction due to the unchecked abuse of his abode.

'But what about the people who came here to pray with sachchi bhakti. What was their fault? They were killed by the thousands; and most who died were poor. Whole villages were wiped clean. And there are criminals. Criminals enjoying...'

But then I heard myself and stopped talking. For I've learnt that just as acts of God don't discriminate between believers and non-believers, people's faith too remains quite unmoved by the Universe's random ways.

The afternoon was a fierce blue. I passed a train of men hauling up a colossal metal beam and a lot of yaatris on horseback. 'Side...side...' the porter yelled, making clucking noises as he pushed us against the mountainside. There came a shawl-wrapped village woman. She was from Karnataka. Then rustic men with sparkling earrings. They were Rajasthani. Now, Bengalis, head-wrapped in monkey caps. And now, students from Madhya Pradesh.

We were all getting closer and closer to Shiva. The Yogi of yogis. The Deva of devas. The Sage of all sages and all ages. All of us intoning: *Jai Bhole Baba Ki! Jai Kedar Baba Ki! Har Har Mahadev!* and *Om Namah Shivaaya!*

The town ahead became visible, snowy peaks sheltering it like a halo, and it hit me. It really was difficult, wasn't it, to *not* imagine it? The presence of something awe-inspiring. Something subliminal. Something godlike, if not God Himself. How could I not see what was patently there for me to see? What was so palpable and overpowering. The river Mandakini coursing through these mountains like blood through the body was the giver of life. And the white massif ahead gave her her life in turn.

There was a convergence here—of geography and biology, of world and spirit. And like some undisclosed intuition finding legitimacy in new-found evidence, the outer physics met my imagination in a rush of sense.

Kedarnath town. May 1998

At 2 pm, I was the first of the trekkers to join my palanquin-worn aunts at a *dhaba* at the edge of town, where they were warming themselves with *pakoras* as exhausted, jubilant yaatris staggered past. Kedarnath town was a colony of mushrooms—single-storey buildings, double-storey and higher spilling every which way and on either side of the Mandakini—fringed by snow-covered mountains that glistened in the sun like the white spokes of a majestic crown.

Ten minutes later, Neha came into view. 'Ha. I beat you,' I called out to her.

'Yes. It is no small achievement, Sid. You should be proud,' she said, trudging over.

Neha's face was drained, and her forehead had creased into rigid folds. The scar on her forehead looked like it would burst open. Had she even eaten anything? She'd said she was on a fast and refused even a sip of water down at Rambara.

'Sid. Please get Neha some tea,' Minna Masi said. But Neha shook her head vigorously. Rashmi Masi turned to her. 'You sit right here and show me your feet.' She reached for her purse and fished out a roll of bandage and a bottle of Dettol. 'Lift up.' And Neha did so, reluctantly. Her feet were caked in dung and her left sole had a deep gash. 'Uff. What kind of devotion is this, beta?'

Arjun came sauntering into view.

'Oh, it's nothing, aunty. It's part of the experience,' Neha said, pulling herself away.

He dawdled over and sat down with a sigh. 'This entire way up, I saw just one decent family. Just one. Everybody else looks like a pauper of Mother India.' He gave Neha an impish glance. 'Well done. You beat me,' he said. '… So, has the holy trinity reached?'

'Don't mock them, Arjun!' Neha said. 'This Sehdev Uncle, I don't know. But Sid's mother is the biggest devotee of us. She's no less than Swamiji, actually.'

Arjun opened his mouth to make some clever remark. But seeing Neha's undrunk cup of tea and her slackly bandaged feet, he went momentarily quiet and I thought I saw a wisp of tenderness pass his face.

Kedarnath town. October 2016

At the helipad at 11,800 feet, I thrilled like a schoolboy watching choppers flying up through the lush valley—*First it was a dragonfly in the forest! Now a metallic bird in search of a ledge on a cliff!*—before moving on. The brand new trekking path cut through a green meadow, on either side of which rectangular tent blocks had been erected by the Uttarakhand State Government with surgical precision. Moreover, with the conspicuous army personnel about to oversee the town's reconstruction and the old jumble of concrete all gone, Kedarnath did look somewhat foreign, if not Swiss, I thought. The town was undoubtedly orderly, but it was also empty and therefore looked somewhat bleak. Like a house scrubbed clean, but also wiped of its homeliness.

We got to one concrete guesthouse and Panditji and I got a dorm bed each for the night. (Only five hundred rupees per person.) Then, with our bags unloaded and hands washed, we tottered over to an open courtyard where lunch was served out of steel vats.

'*Aapko sirf daal, chawal, aloo milega*…you will only get daal, rice and potato,' the manager said. Same as before, I thought. Panditji wanted to head to the temple right away, but I insisted we eat first. All we had had since dawn was a cup of chai and a bowl of Maggi.

The Kedarnath peak (at 22,769 feet) and the Kedar Dome (at 22,411 feet) sparkled under the clear blue sky like gilded steeples, and so I did the thing to do in our times. I took a bunch of pictures and posted them on Instagram. Yes, there was even wi-fi, if you please. The signal was spotty, but it was there.

I sighed. The Kedarnath town of my memory was gone. All obliterated by the floods of 2013.

... Save for the temple. Which, even from this distance of some seven hundred metres was just as I remembered it.

Kedarnath, the Garhwal Mandal Nigam Dormitory. May 1998

It was past ten, and utterly exhausted, I was drifting into sleep when I heard a scream: 'Oh my God!'

Mummy sprang up. 'Beta?'

'Shit,' Arjun said. 'Listen. They only have an Indian-style toilet here. And it's a total stink bomb.'

Neha's face emerged from under the covers like a peering rabbit. It was her turn to laugh and I couldn't resist joining in.

'Whatever, guys. This sucks.' Arjun was standing at the bathroom door with his hand on his stomach.

Sehdev Uncle, sleeping in the far corner of the dorm, made a mumbling noise. 'We have to wake up early, so you please go to sleep,' he said.

'Yes, tomorrow is a long day,' mummy said. 'Sehdev Uncle is arranging a VIP darshan for us.'

Neha rolled her eyes. 'I don't know why your mother keeps praising that man,' she whispered. 'I find him good for nothing.'

'Hmm,' Arjun said, turning off the solitary low-voltage light and got into his (German) sleeping bag.

Kedarnath. October 2016

The fragrance of incense.

The evening aarti shot through with the clapping of cymbals.

We walked on. And here, a hundred metres short of the temple, I saw it. Crumbling brick houses still standing with jagged wires sticking out from underneath, their roofs ripped bare to the sun: the residue of Lord Shiva's dance of destruction.

With a fresh spring in his step, Panditji rushed down to a stream below to wash his hands and I followed. A vendor among the scores lining the pathway shouted out, 'Only Rs 100. I have all the items for pooja. Come here, bhaiyya.' Bel leaves, Gangajal, marigold flowers, incense, ghee, milk, sugar, honey. I would need this all, and I bought a basket.

A middle-aged pandit with a round belly emerged from a tent. 'Will you do *abhishek* pooja?' he said, referring to a pooja with the ritual bathing of the deity. 'You'll need me.'

'Don't speak to anybody, Siddharthji,' Panditji whispered. 'Just follow me.' He marched on.

'Where are you from? Punjabi? What's your surname? *Gotra*?' The fat pandit was asking me about my lineage. My caste. He was blocking my way.

'I don't need your help, panditji. I'll manage,' I said.

'I'm telling you. You can't do the pooja without me.'

I pushed on. But before I could go ahead the man rushed up and pressed a piece of paper into my hand. 'My business card,' he said. 'I'm always available on WhatsApp.'

Kedarnath. May 1998

It was a cloudless night, and the ancient stone Shiva temple stood out in the darkness as a block of grey with moonbeams bouncing off its walls. It was a neat rectangle crowned by two proportional slopes. It was rock-slab over rock-slab with a towering dome at the rear. It looks so solid, I thought. Like an age-weathered fossil. No, it was not a fossil. It was a dinosaur. It did have the quality of being conceived in a world far different from mine. *Really, how did they build this back then?*

I looked at my watch: 4 am.

'Why do we have to go so early?' I had croaked a half hour earlier standing in the bathroom as I poured water over myself from a rusty steel bucket.

'It is *Brahma-muhurat*. This is the time God is most receptive to prayer,' mummy yelled. 'And Kedarnath is a jyotirlingam. I've explained all this. Now hurry up.'

A jyotirlingam was the physical embodiment of Shiva at a place where the Lord emerged from the earth. Or, in this case, where he'd once appeared briefly and gone right back into it:

Shiva was grazing among the cattle, taking on the avatar of a bull when Bhima, the second Pandava, possessed of gigantic stature and unmatched strength, stretched himself, a leg to either side of the Kedarnath peaks. Dusk was nearing, and as the cattle slowly made their way to their shelter, they all had to pass from under him. And all did. *All but one.* The bull-guised Lord, ever the hider, was sinking fast into the ground. He was again getting away. But this time, Bhima was not going to let God escape. This time he would be fast. And so he plunged his hands downward and grabbed the animal by its hump. But as soon as he did, it turned to stone. While the rest of it disappeared deep, deep, into the ground.

Then, Lord Shiva revealed himself to the Pandavas as a column of Infinite Light.

'Shiva was so impressed at the determination of the Pandavas that he forgave them for their bloodshed completely,' Swamiji said, leading us through the town's dark lanes. 'And the Pandavas were so grateful to him that they built a temple here in his honour.'

With five families ahead of us, we had been waiting in line for about fifteen minutes now, and I was more concerned about getting frostbite than the temple's genesis. Sehdev Uncle was somewhere in the front amid a flurry of pandits, their stoles flapping, their *tilaks* furrowing. *Were they trying to gain our favour or assert their power?*

He waved his hands. 'Aam aadmi is not allowed to stay inside for long! But I'm arranging for a full abhishek.'

Arjun nudged me. 'Man. I tried to balance on my haunches, but it was so difficult. I thought I'd fall into the toilet.'

'Arjun, please don't talk your nonsense in front of God,' Minna Masi said. 'We are going to a very powerful place. Just go and sleep if you're going to be like this.'

So, he finished his thought in my ear: 'I think I'll just hold it in till we go down.'

Where was the one to give him a good comeback? 'I don't see Neha…?' I asked.

'You just pray properly now,' mummy said. 'Don't be distracted.'

A couple of minutes passed and we received the green signal. 'Come fast…fast,' Swamiji said, and we hobbled forward. We bypassed the growing line of poor devotees squatting outside the temple in the cold. We passed the statue of Nandi, a bull, Shiva's most ardent admirer, standing guard at the entrance. And in one sweep, we passed from one string of Reality and into the arms of another.

The Pandavas, carved into the walls of the temple's antechamber, watch over a handful of devotees sitting at the corners.

'Are you okay, Siddharthji?'

The stones undersole are cold, and I get a whiff of a long-forgotten scent. 'Yes, Pandijti. Carry on. I'm behind you.' I'm falling into a memory I forgot was even there.

'Stay together,' mummy is saying. '*Har Har Har...* Stay together.'

'*Om Namah Shivaaya. Om Namah Shivaaya. Om Namah Shivaaya.*'

I wrestle past imploring souls chanting, '*Jai Bhole Baba Ki! Jai Kedar Baba Ki!*' I feel a shove and a push, but I float along the current. It is what I hear first *('Jai Shambho! Jai Shambho!')*, then it is what I see (an enormous jagged, misshapen rock) that tells me I've arrived in the sanctum sanctorum.

Sandwiched between Arjun and mummy, I jostle up to a corner where I can see Him, Lord Shiva. At the centre of this dark chamber and taking up by far the most space, there He is. The Kedarnath Jyotirlinga. Lacking a phallus' signature smooth cylindrical shape, this doesn't look like any Shivalingam I've seen. It looks odd. Indeed, it looks like the hump of an enormous bull.

Three other families encircle God. Each is engrossed in abhishek rituals overseen by a pandit.

'Do as I say,' Swamiji says. 'We have little time.' And mummy leans forward to make contact with the Shivalingam. '*Om. Om. Om.*'

'Where is Neha? Wasn't she with you?'

'Sid.' Mummy opens her eyes. 'Please concentrate. She's not well.' She locks her gaze on the divinity before her. 'You've come here to pray.'

Not well enough to come *here*? That's impossible. But now is not the time to muse on peripheral matters. And as a grown man with Panditji instructing me, I do as told: I sprinkle rice in all four directions. I drink a spoonful of Gangajal. I apply red tilak on the Shivalingam.

I'm about to begin my pooja when I'm interrupted by a man belching. He metamorphoses his burp into an '*Ommm...*' It's the fat pandit who waylaid me outside standing at the door to the alcove. He shoots Panditji a proprietorial glance and starts shuffling towards us. People make room for him to pass, and Panditji retreats to a space at my back. Only the designated pandits may conduct poojas inside the temple, he says to Panditji before he pleasantly asks me, 'What is your gotra?' I tell him this time.

But as I do, I think: why must another intrude on my relationship with what I choose to call, or not call, God? Why must I go through the rigours of a ritual I didn't ask for? Yet here I am of my own volition, in a chamber built upon pandit-sophistry, with a pandit of my own by my side. So doesn't a part of me also want this ritual? Don't I crave this sermonizing which at one level I find grating but is also rather comforting?

I'm sixteen again, and mummy begins the abhishek: First, she pours Gangajal over the Shivalingam—an act of cleansing for both the physical and the metaphysical realities. After which she presses into it the three-fingered bel leaves, signifying Shiva's three eyes: his vistas of past, present and future. Then she pours over the Lord milk (for the benefit of the family), followed by applications of fresh curd (for coolness of mind), ghee (for good health), honey (for healing ailments) and sugar (for prosperity).

And now as an adult I proceed to do the same, with two pandits at my side jousting each other with their invocations.

As their shlokas climb to the ceiling in warm whirls, I again find myself drawn to worlds tangential: This ceiling. It is so black. All these layers of soot. All these centuries of belief. What does it mean? What is faith? Isn't it just people blindly doing things their ancestors did blindly?

There is a spider web in a corner. *Can an insect ever learn to get unstuck?*

I feel a tremor and look to my side. It is Arjun, and I'm sixteen again. He's trembling and tears are coursing down his cheeks. He's sobbing. Can he breathe? There's not much air in here. Mummy's arm goes over my friend's shoulders even as her other one is busy in prayer. Sweat, tinged red by the tilak on her brow, is streaked across her nose like a paint stroke from God. My mother looks ecstatic—an ecstatic mess. I knew this would happen to *her*. But what's got into him?

'Arjun, can you breathe? Sehdevji, Gangajal, Gangajal,' mummy calls out, and Arjun obediently hands her the blessed receptacle of Ganga water.

Mummy's palms and forehead go flat on the Shivalingam, and a weeping Arjun begins shadowing her moves. Like everybody else, he's in the grip of some primeval force even as I'm still collected and calm. I'm still pondering.

'Sid! Pray hard for your exams. For your health. For everything. Come, come, repeat the *Shiva Mahiman* after me.'

The *Shiva Mahiman Stotra* is considered the ultimate prayer to Shiva. Composed by a king of the *Gandharvas*, or celestial beings, who'd dared to cross the outlet of a Shivalingam from which the holy bath water egresses, it is so powerful a paean to the Lord that no matter how angry He is, no matter how grave the nature of your offence, Shiva immediately melts by your recitation of it.

With my nostrils full with the scent of damp leaves and ghee, I turn my gaze to Minna Masi and Rashmi Masi. Their lips are fish-puckering prayers, like my Nani's used to. As for Sehdev Uncle, he's having a meditative seizure.

Swamiji whispers something in mummy's ear and she squeezes my shoulder. 'Here, here.' She tears open a packet of ghee.

As if at a precipice, I'm torn. Should I back off or jump in? Where's Arjun? He was just here. Where's he gone? I feel something slither over my foot and look down. Arjun is on the floor, prostrate before God, and seeing him mummy is prostrating herself too.

Mummy's following Arjun's lead now? What's going on? What should I be doing? Why am I not feeling? I know, but I don't know. All I know is that I should stop wavering…and do something. *Anything.*

So, I grab the ghee packet and rip it open and the sticky-sweet yellowness comes squirting out onto my palm. I spread it liberally on the Shivalingam.

'Sid, here is the sugar…' Then I take the packet of sugar.

'Here is the honey.' And then the honey.

'Panditji, pass me the Gangajal.'

Isn't this why I came here in the first place?

'Bel leaves. Arjun, give me the bel leaves.' To go along with everybody else. Like a tadpole caught in a loop. Like a tadpole in a pond.

I close my eyes. I pray. *Please, Shivji. Please make me do well in*

Maths. My exam went well, but given how pathetically I've performed all along, who knows? Please, Shivji, if you grant me this, I swear I will return to you. One day.

And as a grown man, I implore God again. I submerge myself deeper and deeper into that mental recess where the mystifying mathematics of faith meets the algebra of logic. To a place where, in the deific union of male and female energies, Shiva meets Shakti. At that point where one strives to be one with the Self, one with the Universe.

Is this the edge of infinity or the limit of the imagination? Or is it the weight of a meme nurtured over the ages by the sages? Is this the precious seedling of faith?

Kedarnath. October 2016

The next morning, Panditji led me to a spot behind the shrine.

Where once lay the resting place of Adi Guru Shankaracharya, philosopher and founder of the Vedanta school of Indian philosophy and the definer of the pan-India Char Dham, there was now nothing. Nothing but a moraine of rocks scattered up a steep slope until they disappeared and the snowy spires took off into the sky.

'Where are you taking me, Panditji?' I had had my fill of prayers.

'This,' he said, pointing to an enormous boulder at the temple's perimeter. Beneath it lay a picture of Kaali—Shiva's wife in her warrior avatar.

'This rock is none other than Devi,' he said. 'She is Parvatiji herself.'

'Because it stopped here when the floods came?' I said.

From the corner of my eye, I saw a baba eyeing us. His leopard-skin skirt was fake, but his magnificent dreadlocks were real. I recognized him. He was one of the *damroo*-beating, hashish-smoking, half-naked men seeking alms outside the temple yesterday.

'Siddharthji, on the day of the floods, this rock didn't just stop here. It stopped the debris and water from erasing the temple.' Panditji eyeballed the scant embryonic constructions about us. 'Can't you see? Everything got washed away. But this temple stood firm. How do you explain that?'

The baba took a step closer. 'I was here when it happened,' he said. 'When Shiva did his *tandava* of destruction, I was here.'

'You saw the floods in 2013?'

'Yes. The water came this way, and the stones came rushing down from here and here.' The baba flailed his hands. 'I was in front of the temple. I held onto Nandi as the others got swept away. It was terrible. Very terrible.' The baba appeared distressed, but I felt his voice was less fragile, more vain. 'Near me, there was a man who kept saying *Hai Bhagwaan! Hai Bhagwaan!* and then he also fell silent. That silence will remain with me always.'

Yet what the baba said did happen. Much worse things happened in June of 2013. There were stories of immense kindness. About army jawans who gave up their own food for stranded pilgrims. About villagers who trekked for days through slippery slopes in search of survivors. But there were also accounts of horrible selfishness: of the baba who wouldn't let go of his mattress while boarding a rescue helicopter, which when the police got suspicious and ripped open revealed a stash of disintegrating notes; of the goat-herder who raped a girl for weeks after she sought refuge in his shed; of the survivors who scavenged the rotting dead for gold. So, everything this baba said was true. But was it *his* truth or his stratagem?

'… And I have returned every year since that day. This is my third trip,' he said. 'I will only leave when the temple *kipat* [gate] closes on Diwali. This is my vow to Shivji.' He mimed an expression of servility. 'Panditji, you tell me, who else will look after Bhole Baba if not us? Who else will light his fire?' He stretched out his empty hands.

But Panditji was adamant. 'Isn't it true that the water came rushing down from this mountain and split into two streams right here? Isn't it true that this rock saved the temple?'

'Yes, Panditji, that is right. I saw it with my own eyes,' the baba said, and with that reply, Panditji gave the man Rs 50.

'Siddharthji, what else do you call this if not a miracle?' he said.

Kedarnath. May 1998

Back in the dormitory, bags were being packed, and porters called.

'Oh shit. I forgot to take out my Nikon,' Arjun said. 'These fools will ruin it. Bhaiyya, be careful. Put my bag down here. I need to take out something.'

'It was such a beautiful darshan, Sehdevji,' Rashmi Masi said. 'Just wonderful. The vibrations you felt were…'

'Just amazing,' Minna Masi filled in.

For once, Swamiji was silent. He had the serene look of a priest basking in the afterglow of a perfectly delivered sermon.

Blundering about the room pretending to look for lost belongings, Neha was quiet too. Her face was taut. I stopped her. 'What happened? Why didn't you come for the darshan, Neha?'

'I wasn't feeling well,' she said.

Arjun backed me up. 'Well, you look quite fine.'

'Leave it. We'll talk later,' she finished.

When we'd descended to Gaurikund, I was still at a loss as to what had happened. My mother and aunts were being evasive, while Arjun unhelpfully suggested that Neha must have experienced a 'mental issue' due to the high altitude. It took a couple of days of piecing together eavesdropped snippets of conversation to figure it out. On the morning of the darshan, Neha had gotten her period and had decided that there was no way she'd enter a place so sacred in an *impure* state. 'Don't be silly,' mummy tried to reason with her, 'You have done such hard tapasya. Please don't torture yourself now,' with little effect. Swamiji had been asked to weigh in too. But his answer was ambiguous. Certainly, Neha could enter the temple, but not the sanctum sanctorum. Plus, she'd have to do a round of pre-as-well-as-post-darshan cleansing rituals. That was the only way.

By the time we reached Rishikesh, Arjun couldn't contain himself any longer. 'That's just stupid, Neha. You worked so hard for it. How could you act so...*illiterate*?' he said, his veins inflamed at the temples. I seconded him.

'You boys won't understand. You can't.' Neha's eyes conveyed her faraway expression. 'Some things are personal,' she said.

A week after we returned to Delhi, I heard mummy making agitated noises over the phone once again. But this time, she didn't sound excited, she was shocked: 'Don't tell me... I don't believe it... Oh my god... I would never have...' She hung up.

'What happened?'

October 2016

Gaurikund was now only five kilometres away and Panditji and I stopped to rest. His knees had jammed and a blister on his foot had burst. 'I have a sitting job, na,' he said apologetically as he massaged his foot. 'All the time, I'm sitting only. I'm not used to this exercise.'

'Do you think there is a masseur around here?' I asked a *chaiwaala*. If mummy were here she'd have ordered me to give Panditji a massage. *Fat chance I'm doing that.*

Once Panditji's foot-rub got underway, I put to him the same question I had once to Swamiji: 'How did the ancients build this temple?' My tone, I remember, was genuine, and Swamiji's voice, too, was sincere.

'See, in the days of the Pandavas, the entire world was different,' Swamiji said. He went quiet, carefully weighing his next words. 'It is possible that they had an ancient flying machine. A *Pushpak Vimaan*? Or some superior technology? Who knows? But they did it somehow.'

That the Pandavas had built the original Kedarnath shrine far back in the mystical Hindu Dwaapar Yuga was a belief held by the most devout. But it was superseded by a more predominant theory that maintained that the temple was built by Adi Shankaracharya in the eighth century. Yet a third theory said that the builder was a Raja Bhoj of Malwa who had ruled this area between 1076 and 1099 CE.

Winds appeared to blow freely between fact and myth, obscuring the vision for some even as they refined it for others. Whatever Kedarnath's provenance, though, one thing to me was evident. The temple's builders, whoever they were, had a deep sensitivity to their surroundings. They appreciated the majesty and fickleness of these peaks in ways we modern inhabitants could not. Because although the temple was only slabs of stone joined without mortar onto a plinth, the nifty manner in which it had been constructed saw the structure through not just floods but also—I would later read in a news article—an ice age spanning four hundred years (from 1300 to 1900) during which time, covered under sheets of snow, the jyotirlingam was hidden away from all humanity.

Was the temple's unique architecture the reason it withstood the awful onslaught of 2013? Was its resilience a proof of its power or its fictions?

Panditji took a sip of chai. He said dreamily, 'See, in those days, they had faith, they had energy. They had everything.'

We were about to get up when a young white backpacker strode up to us. He was a lean chap with an open smile and curious bespectacled eyes. He wore a grey T-shirt and track pants and had a knapsack on his back. He looked no more than eighteen.

'Ha Ha Mahadev,' he ventured.

'Har Har Mahadev. No Ha Ha,' a bemused Panditji replied. 'Where *ju* from?'

'Germany. I am travelling around India for six months.'

'Oh, so you come holiday. *Gut. Gut.*'

The backpacker's name was Theo, and he was on a gap year before going to university. He said he had learnt basic Hindi through YouTube and was very interested in learning about Indian spirituality. After completing a trek to Gaumukh glacier, he'd hopped on a bus to Kedarnath because somebody had told him it was also worth exploring. He loved the mountains.

He pulled out a Band-Aid from his first aid kit. 'For you,' he said, and Panditji nodded a thank you.

Theo joined us on the walk downhill and in no time he and I fell into a deep conversation on some of life's tangentialities. *Will all religion evolve to become godless someday? Does a diet of excessively spicy food corrupt the tastes or sharpen them? And what of excessive rituals—what does that say about a culture?*

It was only by the time we reached Gaurikund a glacial hour later that I realized Panditji had been unusually quiet. Was he self-conscious about his spoken English? He did sound a little odd. But no more than Theo did speaking Hindi.

'Do you want to ask him something, Panditji?' I said. And as I opened my mouth, it struck me that rather than find Panditji's spoken English hilarious as I once had Swamiji's, I'd been straining to speak in Sanskrit-inflected Hindi all along. Over here, it was I who was self-conscious of my speech.

Panditji was hesitating, but I encouraged him to go on. 'I was just wondering, Siddharth,' he said, 'how does this boy fit clothes and things for six whole months into his tiny bag?'

I smiled. Panditji had finally dropped the 'ji' from my name.

Beyond 1998

Whatever her motivations were to make the yaatra to Kedarnath that year, or her reasons for staying away from the shrine, Neha remains unmarried and just as devout a Shiva devotee today. I spoke to her only last year after a gap of a decade. Having just returned from a yaatra to Kailash Mansarovar in Tibet, the abode of Shiva, she was on a high. 'The experience was even more amazing than Kedarnath,' she said, and I understood of course that she was referring not to our yaatra together but to the trip she'd made by herself a couple of years afterwards.

'I hope your mother is well,' she said. 'That trip with you was really memorable.' She let out a wistful laugh.

It was Neha who had called my mother that day, a week after we had got back home. She told mummy that on the morning of the darshan, after having somehow learned about the nature of her quandary, Sehdev Uncle came up to her.

'These things happen,' he said. 'It's only God's way of testing you.'

Neha didn't reply. She was in deep thought, wondering if ever and when she'd be able to return. And in that short hopeless moment, he leaned forward and took her in his arms. Neha was taken aback. Maybe this was just a fatherly hug? Should she tell him to back off? But then Sehdev Uncle's hands began to creep and slide over her back and she had to push him away, ask him to respect her space. Tell him that she was like his daughter.

Mummy couldn't believe her ears. Sehdev? *Sehdev*? The very suggestion was absurd. This was the same man who had once cleaned Maharajji's faeces when he had become too old and sick to move. This was the man who nursed his mother day and night after her other sons had deserted her. This was the man who had dedicated his life to God.

What Neha said made no sense. Except that, at some level, it probably did. Because as the months rolled on, and trickle by trickle disconnected episodes of the man's errant behaviour emerged, so too did mummy's behaviour towards him start to change. First ceased the invites to family poojas. Then came a stop to his inclusion in the yaatras. And soon, Sehdev Uncle became something immaterial, lingering on only as a memento of an old friendship.

But after a half-decade passed, he returned, contrite. 'It was a big misunderstanding... No, it wasn't a misunderstanding. It was mistake. Something like that would never happen again. Not in a million lifetimes, behenji,' he said. And my mother begrudgingly accepted the man's apology, although things were never the same again.

The septuagenarian Sehdev still eats no cereals after sundown and is—as Arjun might still say—almost as fit as a penguin. Speaking of whom, Arjun did end up going abroad for his studies like he wanted (Hotel Management in Switzerland), only to return and join his family's restaurant business. The man still enjoys his foreign vacations ('Machu Picchu was fab. Europe is passé, man'), and despite the demands of modern living always makes time for an annual yaatra. Shirdi is his preferred destination these days as he has contacts there and doesn't have to 'deal with the crowds'. Even today, he fondly refers to mummy as his Himalayan mother and rings her now and again to seek counsel on pooja dos and don'ts.

Meanwhile, mummy's relationship with Swamiji has only grown from strength to strength, especially after 2009 when he moved from Rishikesh, closer home to Gurgaon, where he now has an over hundred-strong following of devotees.

As for me, I returned to Kedarnath, didn't I, the conundrums about faith notwithstanding? And it was not only because I got 97% in my Class X maths exam, my highest ever, after my last darshan here.

Somewhere en route Badrinath. October 2016

'*Give me everything tonight, give me everything tonight...*' Sanjay, the driver, hummed to the song on the stereo. 'I just love this singer, Pitbull, bhaiyya,' he said with pride. As we crossed a Hanuman shrine, he took his hands off the wheel to make a namaste to the deity, and Panditji, Theo and I followed suit. We were on our way to the most powerful Vishnu temple in north India: Badrinath.

'Why are you writing about God?' Theo casually asks me.

I know how to answer him. I've given this question so much thought. And as I formulate my answer, a memory from long ago again comes to mind:

It is September 21, 1995, and I've just got home from school. The phone rings and I pick up. Mummy's breathless voice on the other end: 'Beta, the gods are drinking milk! Go to the pooja room now. I went to the temple this morning...'

'What? Hold on.' I switch on the TV. There are excited reporters, euphoric worshippers. The news is everywhere. There are long lines at temples all over Delhi. All over India. I take a spoonful of milk and hurry to the Ganesha statue in our living room. It is stony and unresponsive, and I feel ridiculous. I return to the phone and tell mummy to stop bothering me.

'No, no! Go to the gods in the pooja room!' She is insistent.

So I do. And this time, as I place a spoon of milk before Lord Ganesha, I can feel my eyes widening in my head. The sphere of white quivers then shrinks and shrinks further until it is a pin-prick. All gone into the receding depths of the elephant god's trunk. *Seeing is believing!*

I call Mala. We feed the gods again.

The story began that day with a Delhi pandit offering milk to Lord Ganesha. He had had a dream, people said. The word spread quickly so that by noon gods all over India were doing the same thing, and by late afternoon, the phenomenon had spread to Hindu temples in the UAE, the UK and Canada, too.

It was only by the evening that the scientists and rationalists weighed in. They said the miracle was nothing. It was the result of 'capillary action'. The surface tension of the milk pulled the liquid up and out of the spoon. Commentators put forward cogent arguments about group mentality and mass hysteria and called the day a communication miracle. One news channel even showed a man performing the same trick with a doll. When I saw this, I felt a little deflated, but also lighter.

What did mummy think? You can guess. She had seen the extraordinary. Millions with her had seen the unforgettable that day. So much so that even when I bring this day up now as evidence of the delusions of faith, her answer is the same: 'If science can explain everything, then tell me, why has such a thing not happened on the same scale again?'

For a long time now, the twin ideas of God and Faith have bedevilled me. It is an angst concerning which I can apportion some blame on my parents. For as far back as memory serves, my father refused to set foot in a house of worship, whereas my mother never did leave one *underworshipped*. And although I'd been with her to over a hundred temples across the country, I could never get myself to invest wholesale in the belief in a higher power. Certainly not in the way that she and so many around me were so effortlessly able to. I would be dishonest if I didn't also admit that there were times I was convinced that God is a comforting lie we tell ourselves to cope with life's random, unfair ways.

But my scepticism could go no further. Because if I often rejected ritual and its dogmatic trappings, I was just as often stirred by a belief in the existence of an extrasensory force. Even as I saw religion misused by those in power, I felt hard-pressed to dismiss the notion that there exists something profound and unquantifiable, blazing beyond the sum of all intellect and imagination. And if such transcendence was indeed real then maybe, just maybe, if I could get even a glimpse of it, my pursuit of God would be worth it, I thought.

Besides, what is Truth anyway if not fidelity to your feelings?

You could say, then, that if *with* faith I struggled, *without* it I felt unmoored. I could never grow comfortable in the utter lack of it in the way so many atheists managed to. I could not automatically presume that the belief in God was a symptom of the superstitious mind. Or that the lack of faith was the hallmark of a rational one. Still, if I could not even fathom what these concepts meant to me how could I articulate my feelings to somebody else?

I knew only one thing for sure. I wanted to better understand how God gives meaning to people's lives.

But let me not get ahead of myself. To move forward along my journey down the Ganga, I must look back again into my past. (It's true what they say about Indian boys and their mothers. We really never do break away.)

So where was I? Yes, Badrinath. I first went to Badrinath at the age of eighteen, and it was during this yaatra that I had my first acquaintance with the whys and wherefores of Hindu ritual. And what they mean to the devout.

A Synthesis of Rituals in Badrinath

Delhi. April 2000

One hot afternoon, I got home from school to find an extravagant female voice coming out of our living room. She sounded familiar.

'So, how did it go?' My father was waiting for me in the hallway with a keen look on his face. I had just taken my Economics exam, the second of my school finals, and the scary business of facing the impossible cut-off percentages at Delhi University lay ahead.

'Fine.' I lied. My exam was terrible.

'Your mother is in there.' He pointed to the door. 'Talking to her real husband.'

I smirked. This was Ritu Aunty, for sure. Ritu Mehta was my mother's old school friend. She had moved to Kolkata after getting married 'to a real estate man' sometime in the 1970s, but even so, Mala and I had got to know her quite well from her visits to Delhi—which my father said happened too often.

'But papa, she actually listens to mummy, unlike you,' Mala said.

My father made a face of mock-irritation. 'And what about her own husband, *haan*?' he said. 'She touches his feet in the morning, calls him her Lord, and then, throughout the day she bullies him. I've seen it all.'

'I think you're a male chauvinist,' I heard Mala say as I walked on.

'This is the world's way,' Ritu Aunty said to my mother. 'The problem is you're too simple. Immersed in God all the time. You need to be more'—her eyes searched for the right word—'worldly'. She tapped her diamond-ringed finger on the table. Ritu Aunty's hair was made into a prim bun, and her eyes, large and fire-sharp, flitted about when she spoke. She was a fair-skinned, slender woman who took great care to dress well. Too well, actually.

'Hello, beta,' She said to me and turned back to my mother. 'Look, last summer when Satish and I were in Paris, he injured his foot. When the doctor came, I also faked an asthmatic attack.' She arched her eyebrow. 'To be honest, that bland food was making me a little breathless anyway. But I got a full body check-up, fully covered by insurance. How could I not?' She laughed.

Mummy made a face of amused disapproval. 'You're too much.'

Still, I knew my mother well. I knew that, at some level, mummy admired her friend, too. She respected her for her gumption even if she understood that she didn't quite have it in her to live up to her ideals. For if mummy was Ritu's antithesis in everything material, then Ritu was her protege in all things religious. If Ritu was mummy's consultant in matters of jewellery and saree, then mummy was her guru on the ever-expanding rigours of pooja.

Tired, I gave aunty a wan smile and sat down. And as I sat there that afternoon, my mind still spinning with the law of diminishing marginal utility, I picked up that, like me, Ritu Aunty, had also been suffering from lack of sleep. The problem dogging her was the unmarried status of her only daughter, Shruti.

Mala and I had met Shruti, my senior by five years, only once a couple of years before and had decided that she was a *behenji*. Fairly, as you might know, behenji is the respectful Hindi term for sister, but it is not this meaning we were referring to. Shruti was one of those old-fashioned girls who clung to traditions without questioning them. Our judgement, which is to say *my* judgement, rested on the fact that Shruti had said she was keeping a Monday fast for Lord Shiva and had appeared very proud of it. She said she had eaten no cereals throughout the day and that there'd even been Mondays when she'd had nothing but fruits all day.

This show of self-restraint had prompted mummy to say that I should marry a girl *just like her*, making Ritu Aunty chuckle, and I grit my teeth in anger. Now, Shruti had returned to India after completing her studies in London. But whether this was for good or a brief while, Ritu Aunty couldn't say.

'Shruti is a *Manglik*, Shash. I didn't want to tell you earlier. And everything going on with her is only confirming my worst fears.' Ritu Aunty's bun swayed from side to side. 'My pandit has told me to get her married to a peepal tree. Then there is also a Daksh Mandir in Haridwar. Maybe I should take her there and make her fast for sixteen Mondays.' She stalled. 'Before, it was another matter, but now I think I'll have to do all this myself only.'

'Why? Shruti is such a dharmic girl.'

'Oh, she'll refuse. But'—Ritu Aunty looked uncertain—'maybe she'll listen this time.'

Mummy picked up the phone and punched in the numbers. '*Om. Swamiji*,' she said. '*Ji*, Ritu, my old girlfriend from school is here… Yes, the one you saw at the havan… Yes, exactly, the fair one…' She giggled, her voice slipping into the manner of a schoolgirl trying to impress her teacher. 'I wanted to know what could be done for her daughter. You see, she's a Manglik.'

There was a touch of concern in the way my mother enunciated this word—Manglik. As if it were a problem, but not such an insurmountable one as to not find a remedy. I now know that a Manglik is somebody who, because of the planet Mars in their astrological chart, is likely to encounter hurdles in getting married. And possibly some problems later on, too.

'I need to talk to you,' I said, but mummy shushed me.

She hung up. 'See, Ritu. You've to do your best to settle your daughter, and Swamiji is saying the same thing. You can have Shruti marry a peepal tree. But what's far better is that she marry Lord Vishnu himself. And Swamiji favours this because God is the perfect match for any girl. The wedding can take place at any temple of your choice, but it *must* be done properly.'

I was growing impatient. Surely, my academic woes were more critical than this foolishness?

'Aunty, why don't you go to Badrinath?' I said. My words were flippant. From Swamiji's talks, I knew that Badrinath was where Lord Vishnu resided in the Satyug. We had been forced to abandon our yaatra there two years back because of a landslide en route from Gaurikund and everybody was disappointed about it. The two women fell silent. *What did I say?*

'Actually, Sid,' Ritu Aunty said, 'that is a brilliant idea.'

Swamiji Shraddhanandji said *Akshaya Tritiya*—a day in the Indian almanac considered so auspicious that if any act propitiating God is done on it, it necessarily gets fulfilled—was the best date for the wedding. But as Ritu Aunty feared that Badrinath would be thronged then—since Akshaya Tritiya is also the day the Badrinath temple opens for the summer season—she decided it would be their date of departure from Delhi.

She said she'd see to it that Shruti came along. 'But would you like to guide us through the ceremony?' she asked my mother.

Mummy blushed.

Later that day, Mala announced that she was going too. Of course she was. My sister was terribly concerned about how she did in her Class X exams and relied on the good favours of God just as I did. There was no way she'd let this opportunity slip by. Certainly not after having missed the yaatra to Kedarnath.

Did I want to go? 'Hmm,' I said. And then, 'Okay, maybe.' But I wanted to clarify that I was only going because I wanted another Himalayan adventure. And because I wanted to witness this heathen ceremony. Which was true. What I didn't say was that I didn't want to be left out. I'd seen first-hand the beneficial effects of a visit to Kedarnath, and I wasn't going to deprive myself of another godly experience.

Whatever my draw, for the time being mummy was happy. Her son was following the righteous path, the *dharmic* path. It was one from which she could see I was beginning to veer away.

Haridwar. May 2000

The stop at Haridwar was only for a couple of minutes. So when the Shatabdi slowed to a crawl, and porters came trickling into our carriage, I made for the door. Mala was behind me. Ritu Aunty ordered the porters to gather her bags from below her seat and stalked off to the toilet. Shruti sighed and turned to her father. 'Why does she have to go now?'

While mummy's bags were filled with all manner of pooja items—the *Bhagavata Purana* among other prayer books, Maharajji's framed photo, and her travel-lucky idol of Ganeshji—in addition to a pile of thermal vests, homeopathic pills and Ayurvedic powders for Mala and me, Ritu Aunty's suitcases, a total of three, were packed tight with not just Shruti's bridal saree and jewellery, but with 'clothes for the poor, too'.

The suitcases landed with a thud at my feet, and Satish Uncle and mummy joined Mala and me on the platform. A minute later, Shruti appeared at the door, flustered. 'Really, papa, why does she have to disappear at the last minute?' In blue jeans and a red T-shirt with shoulder-length hair tied up in a ponytail, Shruti looked a younger version of her mother, and if it weren't for her glasses that lent her a kind of abstract demeanour, she was rather cute.

The train gave a forward lurch. 'Oh God. Papa?'

'Come. Jump.' Satish Uncle held out his hand, and Shruti hopped off the carriage and he jumped back onto it. Then, just when the train's chug seemed about to break into a race, he jumped out onto the platform. We caught up with him. 'I think let's take a taxi to the next stop,' he said, catching his breath. The train had nearly left the station, and Shruti was on the verge of tears.

'Yes, yes. Let's go,' mummy said.

We were pushing through the crowds with two porters trailing us, our suitcases on their heads, when my ears went numb with an insane screeching noise that dragged for several seconds. Far away, the Shatabdi had stopped and suddenly the hushed station was thrilling with commotion. Black-coated officials were rushing out of their rooms and porters were running across the platform.

Satish Uncle began sprinting, and Shruti gave him chase. My mother ran after Shruti, and Mala and I ran after mummy. The porters stood where they were, like stunned sheep.

Far ahead, beyond the platform's awning, I spotted Ritu Aunty. She was walking along the train tracks, muttering to herself. 'These bloody rascals. Bloody rascals.'

'Make way for memsahib,' a man said. 'Has she come from foreign?' said another.

'No, I haven't come from outside,' Ritu Aunty shrieked at the poor guy and he backed away.

Shruti attempted to suppress the panic in her voice as she embraced her mother. 'Are you fine?'

'I'm fine.' Ritu Aunty wiped her brow. 'As soon as I got out of the bathroom, I pulled the chain as hard as I could.' To the station manager, Ritu Aunty said that she had no choice. She had no money with her.

When we got into a taxi, Satish Uncle admired his wife as she smoothened her bun and patted her clothes to neatness. He turned to mummy. 'You know, Shashiji,' he said, 'Ritu will find a way out of any situation.' Shruti rolled her eyes.

Rishikesh

The first sight that met my eyes as we drove into the gates of Shivsagar Ashram was both new and discomfiting. In the ashram's front lawns, where once lay grass and thorny flower pots with buzzing bees, there now towered a massive statue of Lord Shiva. His arms were outstretched and his hair was aptly matted with the Ganga flowing out of it in solid whirls. But due to poor artistic conception or taste, the overall look was bizarre, prompting Ritu Aunty to remark: 'They've really turned our Shivji into He-Man, haven't they?' Mala and I laughed. But Shruti glanced out the window and threw her head back, her lips closed tight.

The room we stayed in at Shivsagar Ashram, the one we always stayed in, was the Lotus Room. It was beautiful only in name. Three charpoys, their frames strung up with jute and with thin stained mattresses spread over them, stood alongside paint-flaking walls linked at the corners by cobwebs. These now trembled under the whir of the heat-churning fan that could stop at any time. There was a little wire-mesh window in one corner that let in more dust than light, and I knew this because, as a kid running around the ashram, my bare feet would go black in no time.

When I was about ten, I scampered in from the lawns outside shouting, 'Snake! There's a snake outside!' and my Nani told me a story.

'Did you know there was a Raja Parikshit, who died from snake bite?' she said.

No, I didn't. Who was he?

A sage had cursed him to die in this way. So, when his son became raja, he decided to avenge his father's death and began a *sarp satra* yagnya—a snake sacrifice ceremony around a fire pit that would once and for all wipe out all the snakes in the universe. Snakes from everywhere, from the sea and the ground and even the invisible ones in the sky came flying into his fire, and as the fire crackled and grew, the snakes' panic did too.

Then the snakes learned about a sage Jaratkaru's son, Astika. They discovered that only he could save them from annihilation. So, they beseeched him: Please save us, Astika! Please protect us. Our very existence depends on you! And Astika agreed to help them. Astika wrecked the yagnya, and the carnage of snakes forthwith stopped, and since that day, snakes everywhere are indebted to him. And so I was to remember: 'If you see a snake, say aloud three times, "*Astika! Astika! Astika!*" and it will go away.'

Not that there was a chance of finding one in Shivsagar Ashram's lawns today. They had probably all been wiped out with the new constructions cropping up, even if our Lotus Room itself had stayed grimy, and the toilets filth-encrusted.

The dining hall, too, inside which devotees ate sitting down on the sticky floor smelled as much of food as of sweat. With my right foot pressing down uncomfortably on the left one, I constantly strained to sit cross-legged. Within minutes I'd have to shift positions or go numb.

The food was saatvic: vegetarian and free of onion and garlic. But even so, it was not bland, and truth be told, I'd come to like it. I looked forward to filling myself with finger-mashed lots of it, relishing every morsel with a smidgen of salt and a crunch of green chilli. Brahmin cooks came through the kitchen doors holding steel buckets—one swinging squeakily from the left arm of each, for only the right hand was meant for serving—as they announced the names of dishes by attaching at the end the name of Lord Ram. So the daal became '*daal-Ram*', rice '*chawal-Ram*', and sabzi '*sabzi-Ram*'.

My eyes would shadow these servers as they moved down the hall, dropping food from a double arm's length away into dried-leaf thaalis. Would they make the mistake of resting the bucket on the ground? They could not, for such an act would render the contents defiled. Liable to being thrown away. Would the gangly guy spill the daal? He looked perpetually unsteady. But he never did. And in all my years going to Shivsagar Ashram, no server placed his bucket on the floor either. Somehow their aim remained precise and the food always landed on my thaali. Of course the liquids ran their own course once my food was in it, sometimes seeping out from the cracks underneath, or flowing over the sides and onto the floor.

Once, Rashmi Masi took our visiting American cousin, Nina, a little younger than Mala, with us to Rishikesh. Growing up abroad had cut off her brother's daughter from her roots, so she took it upon herself to remedy the situation. We were all sitting in the dining hall, I recall, and the lanky daal server was doing the rounds. When he got to Nina, she flinched. Hot daal had splashed onto her top, and by the time she could recover her senses she was staggered by the thin yellow stream seeping from under her thaali, snaking down the uneven floor and merging with another daal tributary a metre away.

'*Arre*,' I said, laughing, 'you're supposed to bring it back into the centre like this,' deftly corralling the food in my plate with my fingers.

Nina didn't reply. Her eyes were impassive. 'I don't know how you can eat this shit,' she said. 'They feed you like dogs here.'

My first instinct was to laugh. My cousin wasn't wrong in her observation. Nina's childhood wasn't Indian, much less an ashram-hopping one. But her words stung. Even though I whined about Shivsagar Ashram non-stop, it was home, the most appealing feature of which was that it had remained unaffected by the passing of time… 'Shivsagar Ashram has been in a run-down state from the very beginning!' I used to say with childish pride.

Swami Shraddhanandji was waiting to see us that morning.

We removed our shoes and stepped into his chamber. The floor was orange carpeted, and the fragrance of incense hung in the air. A sea of yellowing Sanskrit books stared at me from the shelf in front of which he sat cross-legged on a raised square platform. He had his copy of the *Bhagavata Purana*, its pages open, lying on a low desk.

I knew that the *Bhagavata Purana*, devoted to Lord Krishna, was one of the eighteen great Puranas as mummy had been studying it at the time. Or rather, Swamiji had been teaching her shlokas from it every evening over the phone, which was therefore blocked off to me.

'*Om*, Swamiji.'

Mummy prostrated herself on the floor and Mala and I followed her. Ritu Aunty, who had covered her head flimsily with a dupatta, bowed her head slightly in a namaste and Satish Uncle and Shruti followed her.

Swamiji blessed us with his raised palm as we sat on the floor. He then fixed his gaze on me. It had been a year since I'd seen him. 'So, Siddharth, you missed our Himalayas so much that you decided to return again this year?' he said. 'And I see you've got your sister with you.' He glanced at Mala and Shruti. His eyes had their old playfulness, and I could tell he was about to begin his game of twenty questions. 'So, who can tell me,' he said, looking to the girls. 'Does an egg taste sweet or bitter?'

Pat came Mala's reply. 'It is sweet. It's definitely not bitter.'

'No, it's not. An egg is neither sweet nor bitter. It has an eggy taste,' I said, and Swamiji clapped his hands.

'Ha! There. Caught you!' he said. 'You eat eggs. But your sister, here. She doesn't even know the taste!'

Shruti giggled. I glared at Mala and looked back to Swamiji red-faced. 'But Swamiji, how did *you* know the taste?' I was tempted to say. But I'd never dare.

He slapped me affectionately on my back. 'Siddharth, I was only teasing you. Still, I want to ask you for one small thing. But you have to promise me that you will say yes.' He raised his eyebrows. 'Yes?'

I had a sinking feeling in my stomach. 'What is it, Swamiji?'

'Will you give up eating meat?' He paused. 'Forever.'

As a teenager, I'd given up non-veg several times, but all my moves had been temporary, their duration conditional on very *unspecific* bargains I'd struck with God: 'Please God, if I pass my chemistry test, I'll become vegetarian for a week,' or 'Please God, if I score better than Arjun, I'll go veggie for two years-ish.' As it happened, I was contemplating another such deal: I'd give up meat for a while if I did well in my Economics exam.

I scowled at Mala and mummy scowled at me. 'Don't be foolish,' she said. 'Say yes! Swamiji, Siddharth says yes!'

Mummy had been vegetarian since forever. She had grown up in a vegetarian home, had tried meat through friends at school, and subsequently given even that up at university after making a promise to God to do so if she got a first division, which she did. And save for very rare slips into *eggitarianism*, for which she passed through bouts of intense guilt, driven in part by things Swamiji had said to her ('To cancel out your sin for every egg will take you twelve years of pooja, Shashiji!'), I'd never seen her eat anything other than pure vegetarian food. For her, non-vegetarianism was a vice. And it belonged squarely to the Kapilas, my father's side of the family.

'Swamiji,' I finally said. 'I'll give it up for some time. But I can't promise forever.'

Disappointed, Swamiji didn't press me. But he didn't humour me further either, something I secretly enjoyed. He glumly licked his lips and turned towards the Mehtas, and now Ritu Aunty and he went over the nitty-gritty of the upcoming wedding ceremony at Badrinath.

The following day, after we'd taken a dip in the Ganga, Mala and I accompanied mummy to what used to be Maharajji's room. Tucked away at the rear end of Shivsagar Ashram, it was a place of which I had only a few memories; from back when I was little and Maharajji was an old and bedridden man paralysed from the waist down, his legs rigid, blue and still. I remember touching his feet at one end of the bed and him blessing me from the other end with his palm raised faintly.

One time when an elderly devotee saw me tiptoeing nervously to the back of the room, he said, 'Don't be afraid, beta. Maharajji is like this because he has absorbed all our sins. All our diseases.' I remember finding the man's explanation morbidly fascinating. Maharajji had taken on my problems so that I could live problem-free. I did like that part.

I remember also that Maharajji's cheeks were red and his smile broad. But what I remember most of all is not Maharajji himself but the effect he had on his devotees. For everybody who met him—aside from the occasional exceptions like papa—looked like they'd been transformed. And I don't mean physically altered—although some people such as Sehdev Uncle have said that they were bodily cured, too—but rather 'mentally reprogrammed', as it were.

After people had sat for some time with Maharajji, they were different. They had what I as a teenager called the 'trance look'. It was a feature that was easier to spot than describe and it was passing across mummy's face just now. Her eyes were closed, and her eyelids pulsated like she was in REM sleep. It was as though she was there, but not fully.

My mother, who had seen Maharajji's brilliance from age nineteen, used to say that when he walked on roads, dogs would follow him, and when he stopped, they too stopped. Once, a wasp got stuck in the folds of a curtain in this very room, and he let it out the window saying, 'In here someone might harm you, dear Lord, so it's best you fly away.'

You see, Maharajji saw something special in every strand of life. In every person, each of whom he considered unique but a related microcosm of the one Brahman: the Supreme Eternal Ineffable Infinite Divinity.

I strove to invoke the sensation I sensed mummy was feeling. But I drifted back to the here and now. To what I was seeing. Was I seeing the real, or was she?

Swami Shraddhanandji said he would not be able to join us this time. But he was sending in his stead two pandits. Pandit Mahesh was to minister the wedding on behalf of Lord Vishnu, the groom, and Pandit Sachidanand was to direct prayers for Shruti, the bride-to-be. Pandit Mahesh was about twenty years old and had a pencil-thin moustache. He proudly announced that he had recently completed his Vedic studies at Varanasi. Pandit Sachidanand, on the other hand, was a pot-bellied middle-aged man who said he had nigh on three decades' experience as the supervisor of poojas at Rishikesh's Shivanand Ashram, a nugget of information he presumed wouldn't be lost on the two mothers, and he presumed right.

When I entered the minivan, I saw that the two priests had taken my favourite long seat at the far back. The seats at the front, one a double-seater and the other a single-seater, were also taken by the Mehtas. So I sat down behind them. And as I did, Ritu Aunty rose. She padded to the back of the van.

'Panditji,' she said to Pandit Sachidanand, 'can you move to the front? I need to lie down from time to time. I have a back problem.' And the two priests got up.

But before either one could make for the front single seat nearest to the driver, I occupied it, and with no Swamiji to counter me this time, I slipped him my mixed tape. He was to play only this, I said. 'But don't play it too loudly.' The music began and I slung my head back, closed my eyes.

No Doubt's 'Don't Speak' was followed by Def Leppard's 'Love Bites'. '*When you make love, do you look in your mirror? Who do you think of? Does he look like me?*

There was a faint interruption: 'Driver.'

'*Do you tell lies and say that it's forever? Do you think twice...*'

'Driver!' It was Pandit Sachidanand.

'Yes, panditji?'

'What is this noise? Are we going to Shri Badrinath or a madhouse?'

Ritu Aunty burst out laughing, and the driver hit the stop button with a relishing smile.

'When our gurus played music to the gods the baked earth sprang fresh water,' Pandit Sachidanand said. 'But with this noise, even young trees will die.'

Then everybody began the *Hanuman Chalisa* and my music was forgotten for the rest of the way.

We stopped for lunch at a noisy Vaishnav Dhaba, and it was here that I saw that Shruti was neither as gloomy nor as big of a behenji as I'd previously imagined. We were seated at a long wooden table and Satish Uncle and Shruti were joking about something.

'So what will you have, beta?' Ritu Aunty asked her daughter.

'Nothing. Chai is fine,' she said.

Chai? I was starving. When the food arrived, Ritu Aunty placed a parantha before her, but Shruti looked away. Satish Uncle shook his head at his wife, but she ignored him.

'Ghee is good for you,' she said, holding the plate in place and Shruti stood up. Her face was screwed up in knots.

'Why don't you eat it yourself, then?' she said. 'I've agreed to this ridiculous marriage. Isn't that enough for you?'

Satish Uncle opened his mouth to say something, but Shruti stormed out. The two pandits exchanged an embarrassed look, which mummy doubtless noticed. As she apologized on the young woman's behalf, Ritu Aunty turned to Mala.

'Beta, would you be a nice girl and bring her back?' she said. Then she placed her hands over her head. 'This girl...! Shruti was dating this boy. This British boy, Mark, she met in London. She thought they would marry, but he broke it off. She doesn't tell me anything.'

She threw her hands up in the air as if to say her daughter's fate was up to God now.

'Oh,' mummy said, and the two pandits exchanged another look.

We spent the night at a derelict guesthouse in Rudraprayag at the confluence of the Alaknanda and Mandakini. Here, mummy, wearied from the bumpy drive uphill, asked for a massage lady to be sent to our room. When an hour passed and nobody showed, though, she oiled her hair herself but could not wash the grease off for there was no water in the taps.

On the road the next day, as if she were determined to punish herself further, she announced that since it was Ekaadashi, the eleventh lunar day during the waxing phase of the moon in the Hindu calendar month, she would be on a fast of only nuts and fruits. She said she had enough not just for her but for another person, too, if anybody was interested. Shruti said she was, and Ritu Aunty put her hand on her head again.

I sought to distract myself by conversing with Pandit Mahesh sitting beside me. 'Panditji, what are all those rings on your fingers for?'

'This one,' he pointed to his forefinger, 'is the *Pukhraj*. It represents the planet Jupiter. It brings good fortune. This one is the blue sapphire. It removes obstacles. And this...you should know what it is. It's a ruby. It brings glory and recognition. Why don't you wear any?'

I owned a sizeable three-stone pendant that I was meant to always have around my neck. But my first day of wearing it to school, hidden beneath my shirt though I'd kept it, had resulted in me being teased by classmates and told off by a teacher for breaking school uniform rules. I'd since kept it safely locked away.

My attempt to change the conversation was going nowhere, so I eventually put my headphones back on and tilted my head towards the colourful world outside. The terrain fluctuated with every hairpin bend and changing slant of light as the lushness of pines gave way to the barren world of the upper Himalayas. We passed a precipitous crag, then a waterfall. Then a peak across the valley, red as blood. As we turned a corner, climbing higher and higher, the red mountain dimmed to orange, then to chocolate brown, before going totally black.

There was a drop in temperature and the wind was gathering speed. But this didn't stop Satish Uncle from keeping his window open. 'It's so fresh,' he said with his head out when Mala asked him to shut it, and she went quiet the way teenagers sometimes do when they are dismissed by adults. Shruti chimed in: 'Papa, please.' But he ignored her too.

'Oooo! Oooo…!' This was mummy. 'Did you see that?'

'What?'

'You know, I was just thinking, all of Vishnu's durbar lives here. Garuda, Lakshmi, Shesh Nag. That's how you know we are in his dham. I've never seen anything quite like it. This massive white bird flew past. Did you see?'

I turned to Mala. She giggled. Was mummy seriously saying she saw the mount of Lord Vishnu up here? 'Don't tell me you saw Garuda?' I said, my voice dripping with sarcasm.

Ritu Aunty let out a grunt. 'Sid! Don't speak to your mother like that.' She was flat on her back with that nest on her head tucked into a pillow, the lot of her swaying with the turns of the van.

'Mom, you also said you saw Ashwathama in Kedarnath. Remember?'

Yes, people said that Ashwathama, the great warrior and son of Guru Dronacharya who fought on the side of the Kauravas in the battle of Mahabharata, was alive. But people also said that Santa Claus lived in the North Pole.

Mummy was quiet. She wasn't listening to me. She was sinking mind-deep into the here and now. But rather than the here and now in which we were in the minivan, she was *back* in another epoch, and her voice took on what I can only describe as this profound, timeless quality. It was the sort of voice I imagined Brahmin pupils had reserved for their gurus since time immemorial. 'Panditji. Pandit Sachidanandji,' she said. 'Can you tell us more about how Shankaracharya came to Badrinath? How he established it?' And panditji, knowing well that precisely answering such questions was what earned him his keep, re-wrapped his shawl and cleared his throat.

He had barely begun when Ritu Aunty let out a yowl. 'Satishji, what are you doing? Please close your window. I got my hair made just this morning.'

Satish Uncle rolled up his window, and Shruti winked at Mala, and Mala spontaneously asked, 'You got your hair made here, aunty? Where? Rudraprayag?'

'Yes, beta. This woman made it for me,' Ritu Aunty said. 'She came to give me a massage last night also.' And finally, mummy swung her head around and Ritu Aunty stared at her, uncomprehending.

Badrinath. That evening

I was told that thanks to a Shivsagar Ashram contact, we'd have a room with cable TV. So by the time we got to Badrinath, there was only one thing on my mind and it was catching the next episode of *Friends*. I got off the van, found out which our room was at the reception desk, and went straight up to it and switched on the TV. The first channel was playing *bhajans* dedicated to Shri Badrinath, so I changed to the next one, which also had lectures on the history of the dham. There was no third channel. So I tossed the remote aside and returned to speak to the receptionist, which proved to be a thoroughly futile exercise.

When I got back upstairs, a mere five minutes later, I found that the TV had been turned back on and the sound turned to the maximum. Satish Uncle was sitting on our bed. He was on my bed, and his suitcase was placed on the dressing table, unzipped and flung open.

I fumbled for words. 'Uncle, I think…'

'Sid, your room is downstairs,' he said evenly.

I was still stuttering when mummy walked in. The others were behind her.

'I hope it's okay if we take this room, Shashiji,' Satish Uncle said. Ritu Aunty stayed silent. Caught unawares, my mother went silent too, but I saw anger taking root in her eyes.

'Good, you're comfortable,' she said as squarely as she could and turned around and strode out.

'Leave it, na.' I caught up with her. 'The TV was showing nothing interesting anyway.'

'Nothing interesting for you,' she said. 'Anyway, that's not the point. It's not good to come on such a big yaatra and cheat people. It's not right.'

If in Kedarnath the air was suffused with tributes to Shiva, in Badrinath I was carried away by bhajans ('*Shriman Narayan Narayan Hari Hari*' and '*Om Namo Narayanaya*') and prayers (the *Vishnu Sahasranaam* and the *Sahasranaam Dhyanam* and the *Ganjendra Moksha*) dedicated to Vishnu. Instead of lingams and portraits of a dreadlocked Shiva I saw in Kedarnath, the shops here contained paintings, small and large and of varying likeness, of Shri Badrinath, and of Lakshmi, Kubera and Garuda. And rather than bel leaves, mounds of tulsi, holy basil leaves that are earthly incarnations of the goddess from whom they get their name, covered the tops of shop counters and carts.

While the parents had all gone to attend the evening aarti at the temple, Shruti, Mala and I took a stroll down the town's chilly lanes bustling with activity. Mala hummed along to the Bollywood hit 'O O Jaanejaana' which could be heard playing somewhere nearby. Shruti broke the ice.

'I'm sorry,' she said, meeting me in the eyes. 'My father gets overprotective.'

'Oh, don't worry, didi,' Mala speedily replied, then asked: 'So, what is it like in London? Was it difficult for you, being a vegetarian and all?'

Shruti grinned. 'Not really. Nobody can make you eat something you don't want. I managed fine.'

'And did you keep all your fasts over there also?' I said cheekily.

'I kept the *navratra* fasts, Sid,' Shruti said easily. 'Keeping a weekly fast wasn't practical, though.'

'Did you hear that?' Mala let out a giggle. '"O O Jaanejaana". They've made it "O O Hare Rama,"' and Shruti flickered a hint of a smile.

We later accompanied the two mothers to a jewellery shop and here Ritu Aunty latched on to poor Pandit Mahesh. 'Tell me, panditji, what should I get for the growth of my family?' she said with a sidelong glance at Shruti. 'And what about constipation?' she said with another look at Satish Uncle.

Pandit Mahesh said Pukhraj was generally a good choice. Ritu Aunty was dissatisfied with the young man's brief answer but not discouraged, and dived mouth-first into haggling with the shopkeeper, an exercise that involved her walking out of the store only to be called back inside, and which ended some ten minutes later, with her buying for herself a pair of diamond earrings as sparkly as they were fake.

Mummy, always an admirer of thriftiness, also bought the same pair, and as we exited the shop, as if forgetting all that had transpired earlier, she cheerily proclaimed: 'I'm really so lucky to have you, Ritu!'

At dinner time, Ritu Aunty sat at the large centre table of our resthouse's dining room, and Satish Uncle and mummy joined her. But Shruti, who had spotted an empty two-seater at the far corner, was already sidling the other way, taking Mala by hand. And seeing her the two pandits also took the opportunity to excuse themselves, although they took care to not sit too far from their sponsors.

Satish Uncle got up to find a pay phone, and Ritu Aunty gave me a quizzical look: *Don't you also have somewhere to go?* I shrugged my shoulders: *Where should I go?*

She then held mummy's hands. 'It's normal for children to get into relationships, na?'

This was the window of privacy she'd been waiting for and she would not waste it. She withdrew her hand, stroked her bun and leaned forward.

'In the last year, that boy Mark stayed with us twice,' she said. 'The last time, I gave him so many gifts assuming that, Okay! now he's going to be a family member... He was so fond of my daal. I even gave him my pressure cooker to take back with him. Never to be seen again, of course... I mean, relationships are normal. But what is this depression? To not eat properly? To not sleep? And she now says she doesn't care whether she marries or not. Does she want to be a sanyaasin?'

Ritu Aunty's bun shook through the five minutes of unconstrained talking, after which she fell back in her chair, out of breath. Mummy allowed for a minute's quiet to pass.

'Look, Ritu,' she then said, 'Shruti will be fine! We both know that. But what's important now is that you dilute the adverse effect of her planetary positions. And getting her married to God is the best thing you can do, no?'

'But she's unappreciative of it,' Ritu Aunty said, shaking her head in that way parents sometimes do when they can't fathom what their kids do or why. 'I'm telling you, she's changed. She told me yesterday that she doesn't understand the point of this wedding. She called it playing with dolls! Can you believe it? And I have been trying to make her see the logic. The reason for our poojas.'

By enacting the wedding, my mother's reasoning went, you imbue it with meaning. Every being has positive and negative qualities. We have good and bad periods emanating from properly and adversely placed planets. And to neutralize the bad planets, you have to take positive countermeasures.

'And Shruti can see you're doing the right thing,' mummy consoled her friend. 'Otherwise, you tell me, would she have come here?' She drew in a breath. 'Wait. Let me call panditji... Panditji, could you please tell us the importance of this wedding?'

I felt that my mother was arguing with an urgency she only ever used for the courtroom, so I also made my voice forceful. 'Maybe you do all this because it makes you feel good you're doing *something*,' I said, but was obviously ignored. When I look back now, though, I see that even if my delivery was frivolous, my words were not. I was venting too. Venting feelings for which it was neither the right time nor the right place.

Pandit Sachidanand took his seat at the head of the table, and looking pleased to finally be accorded the courtesy he'd been denied so far, he began his sermon in highly Sanskritized Hindi:

'You see, after a Manglik girl marries Vishnu, when the next marriage occurs, the adverse effects have been cancelled out. Otherwise, a Manglik girl carries the risk of becoming a widow.' He let the prospect of the horror sink in. 'Why do we do our poojas? To purify ourselves. We take a bath to clean our bodies, no? Just like that, we clean our speech by reciting shlokas, and in the process, we also wash our environment. We imbue it with good energy. This is why we light lamps and incense. This is why we do havans... At every stage, we are energizing ourselves and our atmosphere...

'What is marriage? Marriage is the one relationship where the planets of two strangers come into alignment. And in our *sanskriti*, a girl's destiny depends on the boy she chooses to marry. *Hai na?*

Panditji carried on eloquently for ten minutes, then handed the baton back to my mother. 'See, Ritu,' mummy squeezed Ritu Aunty's hands, 'the most powerful emotion in the world is love. And the spiritual principle is that if you want something badly, then you should first give it. So, to focus your love on specific points, ritual is essential. Our idols, our poojas, they help us focus our love.'

When Satish Uncle returned, he found Ritu Aunty and mummy locking eyes. Both were close to tears. Ritu Aunty wiped her face with her dupatta. 'Satishji, please eat well today,' she said. 'You're fasting tomorrow, na?' Satish Uncle nodded. Then he edged towards his wife and took her into his arms. And Ritu Aunty rose and embraced mummy. As the three grown-ups embraced each other I got up and left the table.

At the girls' table, the air was correspondingly tense.

'... Didi, do you believe this will help? How do you really feel about it?' Mala said. And the self-assurance with which my younger sister put forward her question made her sound suddenly mature.

Shruti saw me, took a bite of her apple and averted her gaze. 'You're still young, but prayers work from what I've seen. I know their power,' she said. 'The main reason I've come here is'—she inhaled deeply—'to pray that something work out. I was seeing somebody and something happened... As for this marriage, this wedding, I mean...'

Shruti was stalling. But why? If she found both religious fasting and prayers sensible, why did she have a problem with this wedding to God? Wasn't it also just a kind of prayer?

'I mean, do you believe in it or are you just doing it for your mother?' Mala pushed a little more.

'If it has a positive effect, then great,' Shruti said. 'I'm not against it. But I do find it a little...' and she let her answer trail away into the night.

6:30 am, the next day

The Neelkanth Parbat that rises above Badrinath like a steep 'A' with its tip dipped in a morning golden was, according to Pandit Mahesh, once not there. There used to be a *pagdandi*, a trekking route, connecting the Vishnu and Shiva dhams of Badrinath and Kedarnath, that the fervent would use to pray at both temples on the same day. But then due to a sin committed by a worshipper, Lord

Shiva got angry and placed this mountain in the path, permanently blocking the way.

Bathed in an ethereal glow, the Neelkanth Parbat looked so near, I thought. And yet, it was so pristine, so unreachably far. Maybe when people said that Lord Vishnu lived here in the Satyug, they meant that the place looked so perfect that it seemed to belong to another age. To a time when haloed gods and goddesses sailed languidly between clouds on mythical birds. And that somehow, by some odd stroke of fate or prayer, it had slipped through the cracks in the space-time continuum to the present day.

We crossed a bridge beneath which the Alaknanda, trailing white jets and eddies, surged with forbidding ferocity.

I could fly with this logic, I thought. Why, just the previous night, I'd seen yaatris from Nepal setting 108 *diyas* afloat in the river, and as the lights rushed down the waters, bobbing and surging against the current before each faded to black, I felt as though the swirling lights were fireflies dissolving into the night. And when somebody on the bridge said, 'Isn't this divine?' I said, 'Yes. It is.' But what I really meant was that it looked spectacular.

There was the temple before me, with its blue gate and a long line of people waiting to get inside. But before I could join them, I was meant to take a dip inside the tapt kund, the hot sulphur springs. Vapours wafted up in the air as the icy water gushed down below.

Pandit Mahesh said jubilantly, 'Just look at this gift of God. On one side, the water is so hot that my hand can't touch it, and on the other side, it's so cold that my hand can't even go inside! Isn't it *adbhut*, unbelievable?'

I got that there was something soothing about how faith worked. The way it struck an inner chord. Faith was your personal engagement with the shifting ropes of nature. It was the nurturing of a connection with the numinous movements of the universe. And when I tried to view reality and my place in it in this way, poojas and rituals began to make sense. Believing was like dreaming, I thought. It pulled you in. It inveigled you to let go. It propelled you to another time and place.

But the constant problem was that I could never get fully sucked into the vortex. Because there was another part of me. And this part was not dreamy. Steeped in another school of logic, he was hard awake and continually tugged in the opposite direction. And he just now said: These diyas and flowers, they'll just muddy this river. Why bother with this waste? Why do this pooja? It's so pointless. So senseless. And no, there's nothing godlike about these hot springs. They are a natural phenomenon. The emergence of geothermally heated groundwater that rises up from the earth's crust.

And because this other me was gaining an edge in this moment, I said to Pandit Mahesh, 'I'll wait outside, panditji. I've already had a bath.'

One moment I was at the edge of the sanctum sanctorum, and the next, I was swept in by the pull of the intoning and impelling throngs. At the far back, beside Ritu Aunty, Shruti and Pandit Mahesh, I found myself at a spot where I could just make out the tops of mummy and Mala's heads. They were bang in the front, pressed against the railing beyond which stood the idol of Shri Badrinath and the other deities. Then they were lost, like sand taken away by a wave.

'Jai Badri Vishaal!' 'Jai Badrinath!'

Pandit Mahesh sent his hands into the air and closed his eyes. He was retreating into himself. To somewhere near to where Shruti already was, with her eyes closed and her palms joined together. I stood on my toes, craning my neck to the left and right, but couldn't manage even a glimpse of the deity. So, I did what everybody about me was doing. I closed my eyes and pictured as whole an image of the Lord as I could. For being collectively in the presence of God is significant enough, moving enough. And so I prayed:

Om Namo Narayanaya. Om Badri Narayan. Om. Dear God, I promise you if I get 65 in Economics, I'll go vegetarian for two years. I won't even touch eggs. And I'll come here again for sure. I promise you, dear God. I want nothing more. I… I felt an elbow in my chest. 'Watch it!' I pushed back.

It was uncanny how Pandit Mahesh and Shruti were swaying with the crowds. If the lot reeled to the left, they moved left, and if it pitched forward, they moved forward. If I was a boat fighting the tide, they were one of its currents—currents which they were themselves swayed by, standing as they were trance-fixed.

Transfixed and ferried away to some faraway place, they weren't here. Here where now Ritu Aunty hit Pandit Mahesh hard on his shoulder.

'Panditji, I can't see anything. Do something!'

The ruffled young man turned to me. 'Why don't you lift up your mother?'

'She's not…' I began, but Ritu Aunty cut in: 'You heard panditji. Aren't you like my son?'

Was she serious? I looked into her eyes. They were sharp. Her bun, dead-still.

'Lift me up, baba. No time now.' Ritu Aunty pinched my hand.

And so I bent down and put my arms around Ritu Aunty's hips, and imagining myself a lighthouse in a battering sea, I raised her above the other devotees. She took a moment to steady herself, craning her neck this way, then that. 'Just wait. Just wait, Sid!' And suitably locked in place as I was by the crowds, I waited.

Then came the upward boost, '*Jai…*' and then the bellow, '… *Badri Vishal!*'

'Repeat after me, Sid! Repeat!' she said, and I happily repeated the Lord's name after her. For I knew as she did that if she saw God then being physically attached to her meant I did too.

With the auspicious *muhurta* for the wedding—beginning at 10:41 pm and lasting until 11:30—being only twenty minutes away, I took a peek inside the little Narayan temple at our resthouse. From inside I could hear the singing voice of Pandit Mahesh. He was getting the Lord ready as he recited the *Vishnu Sahasranaam*. First, he bathed the deity with a fresh cascade of Gangajal; then he robed him, pleat by painstaking pleat, in a red dhoti lined with a golden border; and finally and adoringly, he skimmed God's forehead with a red tilak. Then he carefully brought the idol, a miniature Lord Badrinath, up to his shoulders with both hands.

I tried to lope past mummy, Ritu Aunty and Pandit Sachidanand, standing in the corridor embroiled in a final tête-à-tête aimed towards perfect ceremony execution.

'Where do you think you're going, young man?' Ritu Aunty said.

'Huh? To your room, aunty.'

'You knew this would be a proper wedding. Please put on some proper clothes.' This was my mother whom I could contradict.

'This is what I have.' I continued on. What was wrong with my sweatshirt and jeans? But before I went inside I turned to look at the ladies. They were dressed in their best sarees, pink and magenta with shimmering patterns, and despite the shining artifices on their ears, they did look good.

Three mattresses had been spread out on the floor in the shape of a 'U', enclosing a steel receptacle filled with firewood. Mala was sitting in a corner in a colourful salwar-kameez. I hunkered down on the floor beside her and crossed my legs. Out of a CD player came streaming indistinct and shallow beats, which at 10:39 pm, turned up by Pandit Sachidanand, intensified into the drumming of a wedding *dholak*. At which point mummy came and sat down and the bride appeared at the door.

Flanked by her parents, Shruti bore all the trappings the occasion demanded, and she bore them admirably. Sareed-up in red and bejewelled like the wife of God she was to be, Shruti looked beautiful. She was beautiful and her bearing, too, was becoming, for she remembered to keep her gaze lowered entering the room, taking short demure steps, and even managed to keep a straight face as her mother rained marigold petals over her from behind. But then it seemed like her resolve cracked, for as she sat down, she giggled.

'This is just ridiculous, ma, I can't...' she said, and Ritu Aunty placed an assuaging hand over her shoulder. Satish Uncle, too, who was dressed to the nines in a cream-coloured sherwani, raised his palm in a calming way. Then Pandit Mahesh came in and sat at the *mandap*, cradling the Lord in his arms, and Pandit Sachidanand signalled that I stop the music. Which I did.

When the room went quiet, compelled by some curiosity, I had to ask, 'Who will take the circles around the fire with Shruti? Pandit Mahesh?' and Pandit Sachidanand produced a squawk.

'Do you want Shruti to marry God or Mahesh?' he said, and Shruti's giggles swelled to shakings, and I realized it was perhaps the first time I'd seen her laugh so openly and fully.

Satish Uncle placed Shruti's hand over the petite hand of the Badrinath idol, and Pandit Sachidanand lighted the fire, and the wedding mantras began.

It was time for the seven nuptial circles, and Pandit Mahesh gingerly entrusted the Lord into the hands of the bride. But what he didn't see was that Shruti was still laughing. And so it happened that Shruti took hold of the deity but went on shaking for what seemed like five minutes but must have been at least two.

'Come, beta,' Ritu Aunty tried to persuade her. But to no effect. Then Satish Uncle put his arm around his daughter, and, well, another minute passed in exactly the same way.

But then, after another minute, Shruti began to yield. And after a fourth minute of simpering, in a flash, a shade of her old self crept into her eyes, and as this shade of tranquillity arrived it grew to become a shadow that spread and deepened across her face so that by the end of the fifth minute she was scarcely giggling. And after the sixth she was still.

Shruti had grown as stiff as the statue in her hands.

Was she rising to the reality of the ceremony or fortifying herself to the moment's urgency? I don't know. But it was clear that Shruti had descended into a depth of being I hadn't seen in her until now. And yet, it was now, in this instant, when she'd voyaged deep into herself, that I got to know something of who she really was.

No. It was more. It was in this moment that in this virtual stranger, this foreigner, this behenji, I saw a mirror, and in it, I could see myself.

Just the previous summer, I was stricken by a nasty bout of jaundice that had rendered me bed-bound for a week and unable to eat junk food for three torturous months. By the end of the ordeal, I'd lost so much weight that Mala said I'd started looking like a crow, which at a time when I was used to being called fatty, was oddly wounding.

When I regained my weight, Swamiji suggested I do a pooja for my health. The yagnya would involve a thousand recitations of the *Maha Mrityunjaya Mantra*, the Great Death-Conquering Mantra.

'A thousand recitations?' I said, my jaw dropping.

'Oh, don't worry,' he said. 'The pandits will do the chanting. You only have to sit at the sacred fire for some time.'

The *Maha Mrityunjaya Mantra* was originally a verse in the Rig Veda attributed to a Rishi Markandeya. The boy's parents were great devotees of Shiva and had implored the Lord for the boon of a son.

To which He had agreed, but with a catch. The positioning of the planets dictated that the parents had to make a choice: they could either have a righteous son with a short life or a child of low intelligence who would live to grow old. They chose the former and were blessed with Markandeya, an exemplary son, but who was destined to die at sixteen.

Markandeya grew up to become a great devotee of Shiva himself, and on the day of his destined death, he composed this mantra. Shiva was so impressed with the boy that when Yama, the God of Death, arrived on the scene and sprang a noose around the young sage's neck, by accident or fate, it mistakenly landed around the Shivalingam in front of which the boy was offering his prayers! Shiva then emerged from the rock and attacked Yama with all his fury, defeating him to the brink of death, only to leave a warning: 'You are being let off on one condition,' Lord Shiva said, 'and it is that Markandeya should live forever.'

Later, Chandra, the moon, cursed to fade into obscurity by his father-in-law Daksh Prajapati, also recited this mantra. The moon was diminishing rapidly, losing his vitality and sheen. But when Shiva heard him recite this prayer, he appeared straightaway and stopped him from disappearing. And so it happened that the moon now fades only for fifteen days in the month and waxes for the remaining fifteen. A pleased Lord Shiva then placed the crescent moon's shape upon his head, bestowing it with honour, while simultaneously demonstrating that he, the Lord, was in complete control of his own emotions. For, you see, the moon represents control over the mind.

'Cases of cough, cold, poor mental health are related to the misalignment of the moon, which is why you must do this pooja.' Mummy went on and on.

'Okay. But not now. Later,' I said.

Then a month later, when I accompanied her to the Mahakaleshwar Temple in Ujjain, she asked again if I wanted to do the pooja here, for Ujjain was not just the site of the most sacred of jyotirlingams, it was also where Shiva took on his most impressive form as *Mahakaleshwar*, the Great Controller of Time and Death, and I refused again.

But this time, there was a catch in my refusal. This time my 'No!' was more in speech than spirit. This time, I gave in. This time

I recited the *Maha Mrityunjaya Mantra* sitting cross-legged by a fire in forty-degree heat for nearly four hours. And like Shruti, I did it without protest.

After Shruti had completed her rounds of the sacred fire, she stood by wordlessly as the two pandits reached the last of their incantations. Satish Uncle tried once again to put his arm around her, but she inched away.

'I'm fine,' she said. Her eyes stayed flaming for a long while, I recall.

That night as my mother, sister and I lay awake in bed, mummy broke the silence:

'Now do you see?'

'Hmm?'

'You tell me. It's so obvious.'

'Shruti?'

'There is a change in her.'

'Oh. Come on,' I said.

'If after seeing everything you want to be naive, it's your choice. But before there was an unhappy girl. Now, you have a happy bride. And there is only one reason for this—God.'

'That's because all this song and dance is quite fun!' I said. 'I don't know if it has any meaning, but it's definitely entertaining.'

'Exactly,' Mala said with a strange and new emphasis in her voice. 'It lifts your spirits. And if it adds meaning to your life, then it's worth exploring.'

'No. That's a ridiculously simple way of looking at it.' I would have gone on, but a knock on the door saved our conversation from moving into fight territory. I opened it. There was Shruti again. She was back in her pyjamas and giggling. She gave me a grin and looked over my shoulder. 'Can I stay here for some time, aunty?'

'Of course. Come. Come.'

Shruti lay beside Mala and stretched her hands into the air as if reaching for some lost thing. She giggled. 'I must be the only bride in the world who has to go to bed with her own mother on her wedding night,' she said.

Delhi. July 2000

There was a phone call from Arjun. 'The website is stuck. But it's out! I've had the mouse in one hand and Ganeshji in the other for like ten minutes now.'

'I'm going there now.' I hung up the phone and left the house.

There was a scrum of classmates and parents pushing and shoving in front of our school's notice board. I wormed my way in. My Class XII results were out, and this revelation I had to get a view of. After a little struggle, I got to the front. This was the moment of truth. The answer to my prayers. I ran through the names once but couldn't spot mine, so I went again slower. Yes, there I was. I'd scored an 85% overall, but in Economics, my main worry, I got a dismal 58% and was suddenly crestfallen.

When I got home later that evening, my depression gave way to anger, and as I had to take it out on somebody, I did on my mother. 'After all that pooja, not even 60? It's crazy,' I said. 'I don't know who checks these papers. Even Arjun scored better, and that's just not possible.'

Papa rolled his eyes and took a sip of his whisky.

'Doesn't matter,' mummy said. 'Your overall grade is decent, na?' Then more soothingly: 'Maybe you didn't pray sincerely? See, Shivji is easy to please, but Vishnu is discerning. He has to be. He is the preserver of the cosmos, of the laws of dharma. Of—'

'Oh. As if Ritu Aunty is so sincere!'

'Where does Ritu come into this? Anyway, Shruti has got engaged, to Mark. Did I tell you? The wedding is in January next year.' Mummy sounded pleased.

'Whatever.'

But January 2001 came and went, and Shruti didn't have a wedding. And then the whole of that year went by and there was still no word of it. Shruti did marry, of course. But it was three years later, and it was not to Mark. By this time, I'd advanced from being a sporadic non-vegetarian to what mummy calls a 'hardened carnivore; a true Kapila.' (I did not turn vegetarian even for a day since this Badrinath yaatra over twenty years ago. Will I again? Who knows?)

The man Shruti married was a Delhi businessman who owned a

sprawling villa in Delhi's Sainik Farms. I've met him only a few times, so I'm presently forgetting his name. But I remember that: (a) he too was a Manglik, because a Manglik should only marry another Manglik, the pandits said, and that (b) he was of Ritu Aunty's choosing.

PART II

Orders of Flow

October 2016 & October 2015

Orders of Flow in Badrinath

Under the shadow of the Neelkanth peak and sandwiched between the Nar and Narayan mountains, Badrinath (3,100 metres) sits on the banks of the Alaknanda River. While traditionally, the Garhwal Char Dham Yaatra begins at Yamunotri, before moving on to Gangotri and Kedarnath and culminating at Badrinath, according to many Hindus it is this last stop of Badrinath that is the most pivotal, the absolutely un-missable, of the four sacred Himalayan abodes.

What I said to you earlier, Dear Reader, is true. I *was* interested to learn about how faith shaped people's lives. But you'd be right to ask: *Was something else going on?*

By the start of 2016, I had more or less stopped practising law—something I had invested a lot of time in. I was single with no prospect of marriage on the cards, or on my mind. And to top it all, as if on a whim, I now announced to the world that I wanted to write. When relatives probed, 'What about, beta?' I couldn't say.

I didn't fully know 'what' myself. *Could I even write?* I wondered. My mind was like a hall of mirrors looking in, reflecting nothing. My feet were itching to break loose.

During a road trip from Delhi to Darjeeling in July 2016, my friend Sumeet asked, 'Where are you going with your life, Sid? Do you know?' I was taking in the sights of towns and villages of UP and Bihar. The rice fields and flooded plains. The misty hills and gleaming grasslands. The goats, bulls and stray dogs. The cows. The people. I noticed how every village had at least one large temple, and many had a scummy pond abutting the outer limit in which plastics, sewage and pigs mingled and rotted.

I am going into the heart of India, I was tempted to joke. But I stayed quiet. Sumeet was an engineer. He didn't love his job, but he got on with it. He was married to my friend Amrita. She was climbing the career ladder in the world of academia. They were both getting on with their lives. All my friends were.

'I'm figuring it out,' I said.

And I was figuring out, I told myself, too. In my early thirties, I went travelling to places far and wide. In Israel, I found myself wandering in the old quarter of Jerusalem, talking to Hasidic Jews, devout Christians and Orthodox Muslims. In Japan, I was captivated by the great stone Buddha statue at Kamakura and the bronze Buddha statue at Todai-ji. And in Athens, I absolutely fell in love with the Acropolis. Closer home, the temple ruins in Bagan, Myanmar left me speechless, and the clusters of crumbling Shivalingams at My Son, Vietnam made me wonder about the intersections between religions and geographies.

And while I explored all manner of places with great keenness while away, I continued attending dinners and things at home.

Life went on. I watched Netflix. I surfed dating apps. I went on dates. Many in fact, through which I sometimes sought comfort in casual sex. But after these acts of quick gratification were over, I went home all alone to long spells of emptiness and brooding. I was lonely and drifting, and I was unable to deny it.

And yet, thinking back, those couple of years wallowing weren't all bad. Some good did come from them because it was during this time that I began to seriously self-reflect. I began evaluating my strengths and weaknesses.

I read a lot. I read books that took me far (*A Short History of Nearly Everything* and *Sapiens: A Brief History of Mankind* and *The Communist Manifesto*) and books which brought me home (*A Fine Balance* and *Giovanni's Room*, and for the third time, *Catcher in the Rye*). I read Spinoza and Plato. And for the first time, I picked up an abridged version of *The Upanishads*.

I followed my passion for food. I cooked a lot. And eventually, I began writing. And the more I travelled, the more I wrote.

By 2014, my sister Mala had got married and moved away. Arjun had been busy with his family business for a long while too. Many of my friends, lawyers at the old firm I used to work at and friends from school, had relocated to other cities. Everybody was chasing new pastures. I told myself I am travelling around hectically so my life too is moving on. But I knew this was just feel-good talk.

I was stuck and the one person who saw this more than anybody was my mother. Mummy was busy with her lawyering and poojas as usual. But we lived in the same house and she was growing worried about me. 'Why don't you help me draft this appeal?' she would say. And I'd produce a half-arsed product for her and walk away.

She decided to take matters into her hands. 'I am going to Rameswaram next Sunday,' she said one day. 'You have to come.' I had no real excuse not to go. So I went. I remember we had to wake up well before dawn for the darshan. So, I got up on time and went into the bathroom for a shower.

'Don't bathe now,' she called out. 'We have to bathe in our sacred rivers.'

'What rivers?' Rameswaram is by the sea coast.

'Wait and see.'

What my mother meant was that we would have water from twenty-two sacred wells, each one named after a holy river, flung in our faces, bucket after bucket, by twenty-two pandits. As I stood there all wet, visibly amused at what I'd just experienced, mummy said to me in a vindicated voice, 'I knew it. Only coming to God could pull you out of your slumber.'

Between 2014 and 2017, mummy and I made over twenty-five yaatras together.

After paying our respects at Rameswaram in Tamil Nadu, going all the way down to the tip of Dhanushkodi town, only twenty-four kilometres away from the coast of Sri Lanka, from where it's believed Lord Ram and his army of monkeys made their passage to rescue Sita, we went to the Krishna Dwarkadhish Temple on the western shore of Gujarat. And finally, in 2015, we went to the Jagannath Temple in Puri, thereby completing the nationwide Char Dham. We topped off this yaatra with a trip to Ganga Sagar in Bengal where the Ganga merges with the sea.

2015 was also the year that I started going to holy centres all on my own. And whether this was because of aimlessness or actual belief didn't matter. I kept going. And I kept writing about my experiences.

I would often tell people the tired old cliché: 'I'm on a kind of *Eat Pray Love* journey. Except my journey is to Question, Investigate and sometimes Pray.' To others, I said I was a spiritual seeker. But what exactly it is I was seeking I couldn't quite articulate, even to myself. Not for a while, anyway.

In retrospect, a sliver of an answer presented itself to me in April 2015 when my family and I joined Swamiji and 107 of his devotees on a yaatra to Ganga Sagar in Bengal. For it was on this yaatra that I began to seriously ask believers about their experiences. I began to wonder why they believed in God so sincerely despite the abundance of proof to the contrary. And it was here I began reflecting on their answers.

Some months later, in October 2015, I attended the Kullu Dussehra Mela in Himachal Pradesh. The Himachal Pradesh High Court had banned the temple practice of *bali*, or animal sacrifice, that year on the grounds that it was barbaric. I wanted to witness the festival for myself. Here I sought out the Raja of Kullu, Maheshwar Singh, and asked to take his interview, to which he agreed.

'These traditions are important to us,' he said when I asked him about their practice of bali. 'We will honour the High Court's verdict. But how is what we do any worse than what a butcher does?' Well, animal sacrifice *is* a barbaric practice is it not? I wanted to say. It is also irrational. But the more I heard the Raja talk, the more his arguments made sense to me.

'We offer the animal for sacrifice to the Lord first, after which we consume [the meat]. Does it become so bad just because we offer it to God first?'

I can just as well say that I undertook my journey because I was looking for a distraction to avoid getting back into the messy business of *living*: getting a wife and having babies, finding a proper job. Or maybe I was searching all along for what Armaan—whom you shall later meet in these chapters—called my 'connection with the Universe'. Or I was just at that point in life when I saw routine things—sipping my coffee while staring at the computer screen in the morning, returning drunk from a club late at night—as an affront to myself. *Should I go on as before or should I live differently? Do I make my own way or allow others to make it for me?* I guess these are eternal questions of superfluity or meaning. Which is just as well. Because I still don't have clean answers to any of them.

But in October 2016, as I went up to Badrinath with Pandit Hemant from Rishikesh and Theo, the backpacker from Germany, I finally saw one thing as clearly the Alaknanda River we were driving alongside: I was finally on track. Of this, I had no lingering doubt.

En route Badrinath. October 2016

'This is Pandukeshwar village, bhaiyya ji,' the driver Sanjay said, rousing me from my reverie as seemed to be his habit. He parked the car on the side of the road. I rolled down my window and returned to a cool, still-bright evening in the Himalayas.

Pandukeshwar was a quaint village with narrow lanes lined with small brick houses from whose windows Garhwali children smiled at you with that shy curiosity so many rural folk have for their better-off city cousins. Pandukeshwar was established by King Pandu, father of the Pandavas, Sanjay said. It was where the Pandavas were born. And so we had to pay our respects at the Yog Dhyan Badri Temple, where the *pratima*, or festival images, of Lord Uddhava and Lord Kubera were brought down from Badrinath in the winter months. As in Kedarnath, the Badrinath temple closes from Diwali to Chaitra Poornima, for which time devotees bring the pratima of Lord Badrinath to Joshimath forty-five kilometres below, the northernmost of the four cardinal institutions established by Adi Guru Shankaracharya.

Panditji, Theo and I followed Sanjay down a path alongside the Alaknanda arriving at two ancient stone temples. Both had identical rectangular fronts and a dome towering up at the rear. Both I realized, as we walked back to the car, were smaller replicas of the temple at Kedarnath.

Our next stop was at Hanuman Chatti. Panditji told me a sacred legend about this place:

The strongest Pandava, Bhim, had become so full of arrogance that he'd started going to all temples backwards. Bhim had his back turned to God and everything in his path would fall away. Then Lord

Hanuman said, 'Let me do something to break his ego,' and he came down to Earth in the form of an old monkey and blocked his path with his enormous tail. When Bhim collided with it, he fell to the ground. He tried to lift it many times but just couldn't. Then Bhim said to the old monkey, 'Buddhi Bandar Maharaj, please remove your tail!' And Hanuman replied, 'O Bhim, you are so strong. I'm old. Why don't you lift it for me?' But when Bhim once again tried, it wouldn't budge! Bhim then fell at Hanuman's feet. 'Please forgive me for my arrogance, Lord,' he said, 'But remove your tail. Let me have a darshan of God.' And that was when Lord Hanuman assumed his real avatar and allowed him to pass.

'From that day, they say every yaatri shall first do your darshan, Hanumanji, and only then shall they have darshan of Badri Vishaal,' Panditji said.

Sheets of ice blanketed the mountainside. And then the road turned into a rushing stream. Then it was entirely swept away thanks to a landslide, and we had to take a detour. The sky was darkening, too, from a clear white to a deep blue, and as our Innova bounced along a broken road in a cloud of rubble and dust, Panditji began the story of Badrinath.

'In the beginning,' he said, 'only Lord Shiva lived on Earth while Lords Vishnu and Brahma lived high up in the heavens. Shiva used to live in the mountains in this very place, and at that time, this area was called Kedar Khand. There used to be a forest of Badri trees here.

'Then, one day, Vishnuji came here as a child. Shivji and Parvatiji were leaving their cottage then, and Parvati saw a boy crying in the cold. She said to her husband, "Look, we can't leave him out here! Should we take him inside?" But Bholenath understood that this could only be Vishnuji, nobody else. "Let's go," he said. "We'll see about him later." But Parvati was adamant. She said, "No, the boy will die in the cold. Let me first put him inside the house."'

'Because,' Sanjay added from the wheel, 'ladies have a soft heart from the beginning, na? ... Now, of course, in this Kalyug, ladies' kindness is becoming less and less, and their clothes are also becoming less and less.' He guffawed at his joke.

Panditji cleared his throat. 'So, Parvati put the baby to sleep in her cottage, and the couple went off. But when they returned, they found they could not get back inside. "See, I was telling you, don't take this boy in," Shivji said to his wife. "He is a magical child. He may put us in trouble."

'Then he revealed to Parvati that the boy was none other than Lord Vishnu. He said that Vishnu had come for tapasya, and now that he was here, it was their duty to vacate this spot. Right then, Lord Vishnu revealed himself atop Neelkanth Parbat. And so Lord Shiva decamped for Kedarnath.

'Lord Vishnu began his tapasya, and whether there was rain, sleet or snow, he did not stir. His wife Lakshmiji then took the avatar of a Badri tree to give her husband shelter.'

'And in time,' Sanjay said, 'other goddesses like Tulsi also took root here to keep the Lord company.'

Panditji turned to Theo and switched to English. 'Yes, that is why we calling this place Badri-nath. Nath means husband.'

But the young German had wrapped his face with his scarf and was staring out the window with a bored expression. I've to say, though, that after six hours driving through the mountains, Panditji and Theo had established something of a friendly rapport. If nothing else, they had learned to tune in to and out of the other's views without causing offence. It helped that they both appeared to have some interest in the world of the other. But if curiosity prompted a conversation between them, incomprehension inevitably collapsed it, and I was left to step in as the interpreter.

Panditji switched back to Hindi. 'One could get the Lord's darshan here in the Satyug, Treta and even the Dwaapar Yuga. But then Nar [man] Narayan [Vishnu] took the avatar of Arjun and Krishanji, and from then onwards, the Lord's darshan here was impossible. People then went to Lord Brahma and asked for help and Brahmaji placed the image of Vishnuji here. But this was also destroyed by *Boudh log*—the Buddhists.

'So people then went to Shivji and that was when the Lord came here in the form of Adi Guru Shankaracharya. It was Shankaracharya who found Vishnuji here and re-established Badrinath dham.'

By the time we got to Badrinath, with both the day's lights and my energy waning, I was feeling pretty bleak. And to top it off, the first image which caught my eye was entirely unholy: streaks of vomit on the sides of State Transport buses parked outside town, which Theo pretended not to notice and Panditji, who looked like a boy just landed on the moon, would not have anyway. But then my next vision was absolutely sublime: the Neelkanth Parbat, shimmering in the evening moonlight sliced right through a thick cumulus as well as my exhaustion.

As in Kedarnath, newer accretions had tacked onto the older base structure in Badrinath also, so that at first glance, the town looked nearly as vast and sprawling as Rishikesh, straddling both sides of the Alaknanda River, connected by a pedestrian bridge. But here, too, the town's core was instantly recognizable. The old temple with its blue and red painted gate beckoned you from across the river like some sage protector, and the steep 'A' of the Neelkanth Parbat and the Nar and Narayan peaks gazed down from above like gargantuan druids with mystical beards.

We threw our bags inside our tent, erected by the state-run Garhwal Mandal Nigam, Theo and I, and decided to go for a walk. Panditji said he'd meet us later at one Vaishnav Bhojanalaya by the river. It was October, so the bazaar in town was devoid of its usual commotion, but even so, the place was twice as crowded as Kedarnath. No matter how far God's gates are, the boon of a fully paved road cannot be understated.

I could hear the tinny melody of a bhajan from a shop nearby, but then it was overpowered by the bells and song of the evening aarti from the Badrinath temple above. Only the gush of the Alaknanda drowned everything out, if you let it...

In a shop selling Lord Narayan paintings, I got chatting with a young trio from Bengaluru. The two boys and a girl, who looked to be in their twenties, wore smart windcheaters and hiking boots. They were here for the trek up to Satopanth Lake. The Satopanth glacier was the source of the Alaknanda River. But what the girl made me aware of was that the lake was where it was believed Lords Brahma, Vishnu and Shiva all bathed on the auspicious day of Ekaadashi.

'Which is why it is triangular in shape,' the shopkeeper pitched in with a knowing smile.

'But God,' the taller of the two boys said to Theo, 'is not our thing.'

'But we will still go to the temple, na?' The girl gave him, presumably her boyfriend, a reproachful glance and met the shopkeeper's eyes, embarrassed.

A dozen or so yaatris came walking uphill from the river bank. The lot was swaddled in shawls, and one man was breathing so hard that Theo couldn't help snigger.

'We are not used to this cold,' the man said with a self-deprecating smile. He was a middle-aged Bengali from Bardhaman.

Had he had a good darshan? I asked.

'Oh, yes,' he said. 'We Bengalis are Durga worshippers. So, we must come here at least once to see the home of her Lord, na?'

The Neelkanth peak was still obscured by that thick cumulus, but its steep contours glistened in the moonlight. The same light which in the river below floodlit a swirl of diyas and made me stop and stare. The oil lamps made an '8' in the water, then vanished into the darkness.

'Wow, did you see that?' I said, suddenly high on adrenaline. Theo stayed quiet. When we got to the middle of the old bridge, though, he turned around.

'Sid, can I ask something?' He looked pale.

'Sure.'

'What's this temple going to be like? In Kedarnath, those people were going crazy around that rock. Is this place also going to be crazy like that?'

For a second I was taken aback by this young man's gall. Did he need help understanding where we were? Where his mind ought to be? But then the absurdity of the situation hit me and I smiled. The young German had said he was interested in learning about Hinduism, and probably was. But I had yet to appreciate just how out of his depth he was.

I'd been so caught up in my talks with Panditji that I'd forgotten about Theo. I saw him more clearly in the moonlight now. With his blue eyes, track pants and German-made jacket, he looked like one of those fancy St Bernards walking around in the summer heat of Delhi. It was plain he was putting on a brave, inquisitive front. But his insides were strained.

After some light banter at dinner, I egged Theo on. 'Why don't you ask Panditji what you asked me?' I said. I was curious to observe an exchange between a Hindu novice and Hindu priest. Of course, I felt like being amused, too.

Theo looked at Panditji tentatively. 'Panditji, when I went to Gaumukh, I really felt a connection there. There were no people anywhere and'—he took a bite of his dosa—'I really felt like I could see God in the mountains. I felt I could touch God. But in Kedarnath, those people were being crazy over that rock when the real God, the mountains, were outside.'

Theo spoke in English through me, but Panditji got the general import of his words. Especially the 'crazy'. He turned to me and raised his eyebrows.

'It is how we see God,' he said before returning to his food. I thought he would begin a sermon on how a Shivalingam was a form of Shiva-Shakti. The seed of creation. But he said: 'In their religion, don't they see God as a man on a cross or something? Ask him, what's the difference?'

'Well, it is not really like this,' Theo said swiftly. 'And anyway, I'm not Christian.' And Panditji held out his palms in a gesture that said, '*Do relax.*' Which Theo did. But then he presented his next question: 'Is Shiva superior or Vishnu?'

'Both are like your mother and father. Can you say who is more important?' Panditji said. 'Even now, when I pray in the morning, I first thank my parents. I say to them, it's because of you I'm here.'

I told Theo about how Panditji had left his parents when he was only eleven to follow a spiritual path and never returned, and his probing eyes sobered down a level, appearing now almost reverential. He took the final bite of his dosa. 'You know, Panditji,' he said with a grin, 'this is the best dosa I have had in my entire life.'

Later that night, as I lay in my sleeping bag, my thoughts were a mangle of past and present. Who was superior? Shiva or Vishnu?

In July 2007, soon after my Nani died, I accompanied my mother to Kankhal in Haridwar to scatter her ashes in the Ganga. This was where our family, like many North Indian families, went for Hindu funeral rites. Mummy and I stood on the banks of the Ganga in mournful silence as the pandit looked through the urn containing my grandmother's ashes. He slid his hand around a few times until his eyes widened with an *aha!* He then pulled out a small stump of bone. This was the *aatma ram*, he said. It was the one bone fragment of my Nani in which her aatma, her soul, resided. And in which God resided, so it could not burn.

'If you look closely, you may even be able to see her face in it,' he said, and mummy leaned forward.

'Which part of the body does this come from?' I said.

And the pandit touched the base of his rib cage just above the stomach. 'Here. This is where your soul resides. In only the most spiritual people does it stay solid like this after the body is cremated. In most of us, it burns away. Your Naniji must have been a very special lady. Very spiritual. I can see that.' And he was not wrong. Like many women of her class and time, Nanima spent her mornings and evenings steeped in prayer.

Then the pandit recited a shloka and tossed Nanima's aatma ram into the Ganga with a soft plop.

It was at Kankhal that Lord Shiva's first wife Sati, considered by some Hindus to be the ideal wife, jumped into a fire. Sati's father, Daksh Prajapati had held a huge yagnya for which he had invited all the *devtas*, or gods, and rishis. But he deliberately excluded Shiva, whom he never liked. When Sati learnt that everybody she knew was attending this ceremony, she told her husband that she had to go. But Shiva said, 'Even a daughter should not visit her parents' house without a proper invitation.' Sati insisted. She went. When she got there, however, she saw that not only was her father unwelcoming towards her, he was openly hostile towards her husband, Shiva! Unable to bear her father's insults, Sati jumped into the fire of the yagnya kund.

This yagnya kund, now called the Sati Kund, was not far from where we stood that morning, and my memory of this story, which the pandit was relishingly expanding on, was only adding to my overall state of unease.

When Shiva learnt of his wife's death, he was gripped by such anguish and fury that he pulled one lock of hair from his head and flung it to the ground from which emerged the warrior Veer Bhadra. Veer Bhadra then destroyed the yagnya and cut off Daksh Prajapati's head.

Shiva went running around the world with his wife's charred corpse in his arms. He was like a madman. But He wasn't a man. Shiva was a crazed God capable of destroying *every single thing*. Lord Vishnu realized that the Destroyer of the Universe had to be controlled, or everything would be annihilated. So now He, the Preserver, stepped in and unleashed his *sudarshan chakra* from his right hand. Lord Vishnu cut Sati's body into fifty-one pieces, and wherever a bit fell to the Earth became a *Shakti Sthaan*—a forcefield of raw divine feminine energy.

'As many, nearly twenty-five body parts, fell in Eastern India, it was no wonder that Bengali people worshipped Devi so much,' the pandit said. 'The toes fell at Kalighat, the lips at Attahas, the left leg at Trisrota.' Mummy nodded along.

As we took a dip in the Ganga at Har ki Pauri later that day, I casually said, 'So tell me. Is Shiva superior or Vishnu?'

Mummy didn't answer. 'There is one spiritual power,' she then said abstractedly. 'It manifests itself in different ways. It can become Brahma, the creator. It can become Vishnu, the discriminator. And when the karmic cycle needs to start over, it becomes Shiva the destroyer.'

'Hmm.'

'But the fundamental trinity remains,' she went on, a spark returning to her voice, 'and it's actually one force. One Brahman. In its purest form, it is Shiva and Shakti. And when the force starts discriminating between right and wrong, it becomes Vishnu... But Shakti is raw energy. She can go up, down, any which way. You can have Bhadrakaali and Chandalika or any goddess in raw form. She becomes Lakshmi when you distil this energy in favour of wealth and Saraswati when you pray for knowledge.'

I suppressed my urge to smile. 'Are you getting my drift?' I heard her say as I submerged my head in the water.

At 3 am, I stepped out of our tent into a cold dark night full of thousands of stars. The sky was pitch black except for straight ahead where a cloud still hovered over Neelkanth Parbat looking like a *rakshas*' head stuck on the end of a sword. I peered hard at the mountain, almost into it, and I did this for a long time. I stared stupidly and wilfully, totally unselfconsciously, as if this act would force out from the Himalayas their hidden mysteries.

I kept staring, and after three or four minutes of foolishly gawking, something happened. Something bizarre. For an instant, for a microsecond, I was seized by a sense that the Universe was looking into me as much as I was looking into it. It was an eerie feeling. It was a wonderful feeling. And you would know what I am talking about if you've ever experienced something like it.

In fact, I'm sure you have experienced this. I'm positive. Because I know I've encountered this same thing far away from holy places, too. I've felt this same spirit while admiring the sunset over the sea in Goa or watching the moonrise on a clear night in Delhi. I felt like I was becoming one with the One as I drowned in the sunset in Santorini or rose with the sunrise over low brick houses while traipsing drunk in the streets of London. It's a feeling that defies logic and verbalization and what in plain English is called an *epiphany*. A word which initially referred to the manifestation of Christ.

Why is it only the pious who see in these universal moments evidence for the truth of *their* faith?

At 6:30 am the following day, it was all cloudy, cold and drizzling. And from where we were standing, Panditji, Theo and I, the stairs leading to the temple gates appeared full of yaatris. In truth, there were only about fifty people ahead of us. But because the line was static, and more notably because I was less than enthused about the whole praying business then, this little thing of having to wait in line seemed impossibly difficult.

Maybe I had had my fill of faith at Kedarnath, or it was the earliness of the hour. But compressed as I was between yaatris, all leaning on each other for warmth, I could find in myself only impatience and a bundle of distractions, the topmost of which ironically was the architecture of the Badrinath temple itself.

The building's design seemed so intriguing, with its wide arch, detailed carvings and bright colours. It was so similar to Buddhist temples I'd seen in Himachal Pradesh and Ladakh. I guessed that this was to be expected. Panditji had said that the Buddhists had desecrated an earlier Hindu shrine which Hindus later revived thanks to Adi Guru Shankaracharya. But what exactly had happened so far back in this remote corner of the Himalayas, did anybody honestly know? To the faithful, does an uncomfortable account of history even matter?

What I did know from my travels, however, was that in much of the Indian Himalayas—in much of South and Southeast Asia, actually—what constituted Hinduism and Buddhism was often undefined. The divisions between the two faiths were often blurry, their ideas now mingling, then branching off like incestuous relatives at a party.

Of all the religious sites I visited, if there was one which best brought out this blend of Hindu-Buddhist traditions, it was the Kinnaur region of Himachal Pradesh that sits between the districts of Shimla and Spiti. During my visit to Kalpa, a village in the Sutlej River valley, in October 2019, I had a glorious view of the majestic Kinnaur Kailash range from my hotel room. As the name Kinnaur Kailash suggested, the mountain range facing me looked every bit like the hallway to Shiva's abode at Mt Kailash one could imagine. Moreover, I could even see a vertical stone column atop one of the peaks through binoculars—*a natural Shivalingam!* And indeed, this is what one of the boys at the hotel said it was.

But the hotel receptionist, an older man, disagreed. He said that the rock was originally a local deity. But would say no more. Thankfully, a shopkeeper in town, Rakesh Kumar, was more forthcoming.

'Look, people here are not religious like you're thinking,' he said in a frank no-nonsense manner. 'First, everybody had their own *griha devtas* [home deities]. Then somebody got Lord Ram from the plains, and others started copying him. And slowly, when more and more people came from the plains, more gods came too. This was maybe five–six hundred years back or something. But the Brahmins never had control up here like in your Badrinath and all.'

I sought out the local lama at the local monastery in Kalpa, the Hu-Bu-Lan-Kar Gompa, said to be founded by Rinchensang-Po (950–1055 CE). I smiled as I saw him offering his prayers. He went prostrate before the Buddha as I would in a sashtang pranaam. He joined his hands like we did when he recited mantras, his lips quietly mouthing ancient verses. The difference was that his prayers were in Tibetan whereas mine were in Sanskrit.

'My Hindu name is Dev Kumar, and my Buddhist name from my Sangha is Nawam Kunga Mulam,' the slender forty-something-year-old red-robed monk said. 'It is a mixed Hindu-Buddhist culture here.

For some customs, we follow Hindu ways, and for some, Buddhist ways.'

'Buddhism came here from Tibet, yes?' I asked.

'Buddhism went to Tibet from Hindustan first. *Hai na?*' Lama Dev Kumar gave a grin.

'What about the Shivalingam on top of Kinnaur Kailash? Some people say it used to be a local god before.'

'Yes, earlier people called the god Radang. Only now do people call it a Shivalingam. But before, people here would do a Radang pooja.' Lama Dev Kumar studied my face. Was he prising out a latent feature of Hindu arrogance? 'In our Kinnaur culture, Radang means a place where not everybody can reach,' he said. 'First, people did a Radang pooja. Then when they started calling these mountains Kinnaur Kailash, they started calling the pooja Kailash pooja.'

Back in the line, a family of three, a father, mother and their young son of around ten, was ahead of us. The parents were viewing Theo with that curious eye so many of us have for white people in our midst.

'Where you from?' the father finally asked. He was a big burly man with a massive tika across his forehead. From his accent I guessed he was either Punjabi or Himachali. His wife, a large, broad-shouldered woman, seemed especially curious about this foreigner. But their son, a small-framed bespectacled boy, was rubbing his eyes as if he wanted to return to bed.

'I want to learn about Indian spirituality,' Theo began. 'You have a rich culture here.'

I rolled my eyes, but the mother slapped her son on his back. 'Did you hear that?' she said. 'Now we will learn about our culture from foreigners, *haan*?'

The father placed his hand on Theo's shoulder. 'Very good. What you are saying is very true. We are forgetting our culture. My son has no interest in our history. He is on his phone all the time.'

The boy looked at me embarrassed and Theo gave me a sideways sheepish grin as if to ask, *Am I being mocked or praised here?* But I was preoccupied with my own irritations and I looked away.

The drizzle was turning to a fat-dropped rain and Panditji was on a loop ('*Badri Narayan, Narayan, Narayan… Shrimad Narayan,*

Narayan, Narayan'), while the yaatris behind me, many from Gujarat, were going on about how the presence of such a hot spring in the middle of these freezing mountains could be nothing but a gift of God. The Bengaluru trio from the previous evening stood behind them, and they still wanted nothing to do with God. At least the boy didn't. 'Let's just leave, da,' he whined to his girlfriend.

I wiped my face with a sodden sleeve and caught a whiff of body odour. Was this myself or my surroundings I was smelling? It didn't matter. Because I knew I was going to leave the line right away. I wanted a darshan of God, but I didn't want to stand in the rain to get it. Luckily, my eyes fell on a young pandit striding past just as I was about to tap Panditji on his shoulder. He was going towards the temple and his confident gait could mean only one thing: he was a local pandit of Badrinath dham.

I stopped him. 'I have come from Delhi, panditji. And this is our family pandit from Rishikesh. This is my friend from Germany.' I repressed the urge to laugh when Theo produced the most perfect namaste I'd seen. 'We have been waiting here for a while. Is it possible to get us inside sooner, please?' I took Rs 500 out of my pocket and pressed it into the pandit's palms. And I did this so shamelessly that it embarrasses me to think about it now. But the truth is that back then I couldn't care less about proper behaviour. (In our temples, sometimes *this* actually is proper behaviour.)

The pandit assessed my face, then said, 'Come with me.' I followed him with my two companions at my heels. As we entered the arched temple's arched gate, I could hear competing with the thunder the collective chant of '*Jai Badri Vishaal!*'

'I often come to Delhi. To Vikaspuri. I have relations there,' the pandit said. 'So, what pooja will you do? Have you brought your wife with you?'

I wiped myself under an awning. 'I am unmarried, panditji.'

'Then you must do this special prayer to get married. Abhishek pooja, or maha abhishek. It is only for Rs 4,000.'

'It's okay, panditji,' I said. 'I just want a simple darshan.'

Allow me to pause here for a slight expansion on certain key beliefs surrounding the Badrinath temple, Dear Reader. It is believed that the *Rawals*, as Badrinath pandits are locally called, are descendants of the Namboodiri Brahmins from Kerala who Adi Guru Shankaracharya had brought with him when he (re)established Badrinath dham.

Sometime in the eighth century, Shankaracharya was born in Kalady, a village in Kerala, to parents from this same Brahmin community. Shankara was attracted to a spiritual life from childhood, but his mother disapproved of his ways. She feared what the lack of a safe conventional family life would mean for her son. One day, when Shankara was eight, he went with his mother to the riverside for a bath and was caught by a crocodile. As he was being pulled away, he said, 'Give me permission to become a sanyaasi or let this crocodile take me!' What choice did his poor mother have? She agreed.

People say that it was after this incident that Shankara left home. He studied the Vedas and in due course became one of the greatest philosophers and logicians India has seen. Shankara went to Gujarat and Bengal and far and deep into the Himalayas, and all along the way, he participated in debates with different schools of Hinduism as well as with Jains, Arhatas, Saugatas, Charvakas and other sects. But it was with the Buddhists in particular that he emerged victorious.

One account that Swamiji liked to give was that after Shankaracharya established his victory over Buddhist scholars through sheer intellectual and spiritual prowess, they shamefacedly left India. This was the price of defeat. This was why until today Shankaracharya is credited with the revival of Hinduism in the country. As Panditji would later say: 'He saved this ancient area from the *vidharmis*'—the faithless, the Dharma-less.

Given this backdrop, perhaps it was no surprise that in an almost Buddhist fashion Shankaracharya himself established Hindu *mathas* (or monasteries) in the four corners of the country—Jyotir Math, also known as Joshimath (which lies at a distance of forty-two kilometres from Badrinath) in the north; Sri Sringeri Sharada Peetham in Karnataka, in the south; Kalika Matha in Dwarka, Gujarat in the west; and Govardhana Matha in Puri, Odisha in the east. So went this version of the story, anyway.

What's more, Badrinath was also where it is believed the sage Ved Vyas wrote the Mahabharata. Badrinath was where Ved Vyas classified the Vedas into four parts. And Badrinath was where he composed the Puranas, including the great *Bhagavata Purana* dedicated to Lord Krishna, which mummy loved most of all.

But if Badrinath was so ancient, there must be a mention of it in our scriptures, right? Swamiji said that it was definitely mentioned in the *Bhagavata Purana*. As goes Swami Prabhupada's translation of it: '*There in Badrikashram [Badrinath] the Personality of Godhead [Vishnu], in His incarnation as the sages Nara and Narayana, has been undergoing great penance since time immemorial for the welfare of all amiable living entities.*' (3.4.22) But about the place's mention in the Vedas he gave no clear answer.

The Badrinath temple has three main structures. The outermost one is the *sabha mandap* (the hall where devotees assemble) which leads to the *darshan mandap* (the hall where devotees offer their prayers) and the *garbha griha* (the sanctum sanctorum). The garbha griha houses the *Shaligram*: the one-foot black stone idol of Lord Badrinarayan that stands in a gold canopy under a Badri tree.

'Only the temple's pandits can enter it to do *seva*, abhishek, aarti,' the pandit said. Meaning: we devotees had to content ourselves with a darshan from afar. He pointed at the idol of Lord Badrinarayan. 'As you can see, God has four arms. He holds a conch shell and a chakra [discus] in two hands, and his other two hands rest in his lap in *padmaasana* [the lotus posture of deep meditation]. Beside him is Lakshmiji. The sage Naradji is at his feet; Lord Kubera and Uddhava are on his one side, Nar and Narayan on the other. And Garuda is also here. The Lord's complete family.'

'You have ten minutes to pray,' he said, then dipped under the railing to join the other priests in the inner sanctum where he busied himself in handing out prasad and moving worshippers along. Most yaatris couldn't linger in front of God for longer than thirty seconds. Unless, of course, they also offered cash.

The darshan mandap where I was standing, squished up against the metal barrier separating the worshippers from the priests, was brimming to capacity. I was wet and cold, but I had to find in myself the muscle to pray. And fast.

'Whenever Rawaljis do pooja of God, they must bathe properly,' Panditji said. 'But another rule is that nobody can touch them before they enter the temple. Rituals here are very strict. You, I, nobody can touch the Lord here like in Kedarnath.'

'Why not?' Theo asked.

'Because Vishnuji is not like Shivji, in that any Aghori or cripple can go to him and he'll just accept him blindly.' He shook the notion away with a rude wave of the hand. 'No! Vishnu protects Dharma.' Panditji regarded the Rawals with misty eyes. 'I have heard that they're born with their *janeu* scarred on their torso. It's like they are born for this very purpose. To please God.'

A janeu, for those who may not know, is a sacred thread tied across the body of traditional Brahmin, Kshatriya and even Vaishya boys—or those from the priestly, warrior and commercial classes in the caste order—during a rite of passage ceremony marking the commencement of adulthood.

My main concern at the moment, though, was what I ought to ask God for, and there was no escaping it. So, along with Panditji, I closed my eyes: *Dear Vishnuji, why am I returning to you again and again? It is so you show me the way. It is so that you give me 'stability' and 'structure'. So you show me the path of 'normalcy'.*

Why was I putting inverted commas around my wishes to God? I opened my eyes as I let out a sad laugh. Theo was looking about the hall nervously. Building on the previously mentioned metaphor, the poor guy was now like a lost St Bernard in an enclosure of meditating cats.

I don't mean to be snarky about Theo. In fairness to him, he had been following my moves as best he could. But I also felt that he was miming me in that overly-cautious European way that is oh-so-very-polite yet also betrays a trace of disdain. (But was I really seeing contempt for the un-Christian in this young German, or was I imagining it?)

I closed my eyes again only to go down another diversion: *Why am I praying to God in English and not Hindi?* I've struggled to work out from where I've inherited this superstition—that English is an improper language for my prayers. The quick answer is that it's something I heard once, long ago, in Rishikesh. The slightly longer one is that Sanskrit is Hinduism's liturgical tongue so I suppose it makes sense to pray in one of its offshoots. But here's the other thing: our faith also stresses that God is beyond language, beyond comprehension. So, why do I persist with these falsities?

Nonetheless, I carried on:

Dear Vishnuji, the Bhagavad Gita says it is better to follow your own dharma, howsoever imperfect, rather than another person's way. So, you tell me, what is perfect? Is it following the staid way? The normal way? And what is 'normal'? Having a wife? Making babies? Is this what makes a man fulfil his dharma?

You know me, dear God. You made me. You know I can't be a blind electron circling around this nucleus of faith. But the fact I'm in your Universe, must mean something, no? And if you're the Ultimate Preserver, must you not preserve me, too?

Vishnuji, if you want me to fulfil my dharma, I should ask you to fulfil yours.

So, show yourself to me. Yes. God, if I'm a part of you, then you must also be a part of me. So, show me the way.

Was I straining too much? I guess. Because when I opened my eyes, I saw Theo regarding me with a look of such perplexity that I felt a flash of heat. But I continued:

So, show me, Vishnu Bhagwaan. Show me your voice. Show me what to do…

A minute passed this way. Then two. And three. And then something happened: God actually showed himself to me. Lord Vishnu spoke to me, and He said, '*You, Siddharth, will do something creative with your hands. Do you really need me to tell you this?*' His voice was so reassuring and loving, so instructive yet so non-judgemental, that I had no reason to believe that the entity I was speaking to was anybody other than God.

Lord Vishnu was self-evident. *He was beyond self-evident!* Lord Vishnu was as tangible as the feel of my palms joined together. But even as I grew more and more elated that God was speaking to me I heard another voice. It was a tiny voice, a niggling voice, but it was there, and it said that the person I was speaking to was none other than myself.

You know you like to write, this smaller person said. *You've been devoting more time to writing, have you not? And you like to cook, too. And is cooking not another boon of the hands? Really, do you really need God to tell you this?*

And now I began to laugh. I laughed a big, open laugh that arose from the pit of my gut and which I felt spreading throughout my body like fire. The heat was seizing me and I couldn't stop it from burning everywhere. I couldn't stop shaking, maniacally shaking. Theo was staring at me like I'd gone mad—and I had. But then Panditji met my eyes and smiled. He smiled just briefly. But his smile said, *I know what you're feeling*, and it permitted me to carry on laughing and praying, praying and laughing, believing and disbelieving. And believing all over again...

Under an arch in the courtyard outside, a group of about twenty Rajasthani women was sitting on the floor clapping to the rhythms of a bhajan. Their yellow and red sarees spilling in cascades from beneath their baggy sweaters, they looked a picture of delight. The woman singing praise to the Lord into a microphone, however, wasn't one of *them*. She was a blonde European, and she was singing so mellifluously that you almost didn't notice her foreign accent.

'*Badri Narayan, Narayan, Narayan*,' she offered, and '*Shrimad Narayan, Narayan, Narayan*,' the women returned. Her voice rose higher and higher, and the clapping grew louder and louder, and after climbing to some ecstatic bend in the river of song, it brusquely stopped.

A wiry elderly man now spoke into the microphone, his voice all crackly and ostentatious:

'*Praniyon mein sadbhavana ho*,' he said. May all life be bestowed with good energies. And the women repeated after him, as they did after each line he spoke next:

'*Jagat ka kalyan ho.*' May the Earth be blessed.

'*Gau Mata ki raksha karo.*' Protect the Mother Cow.

'*Aatankvaad ka naash ho.*' May terrorism be crushed.

'*Gyan ka prakash ho.*' May knowledge shine bright.

And then: '*Har Har Mahadev!*' to which everybody returned a thunderous '*Jai Badri Vishaal!*' A call to Shiva had to be matched by an equal cry to Vishnu.

One of my favourite childhood God stories was about Lord Brahma, the creator of the Universe. Very early in Time, the self-born Brahma had the exalted status as the Supreme One in the Hindu triad of Lords Brahma, Vishnu and Shiva, although this position was lost somewhere along the way.

The ascetic Brahma, the story went, had started longing for female company, so he split himself into a form called *Satarupa*, or the one with a hundred beautiful forms. In fact, Satarupa was so beautiful that Brahma himself started chasing her. And poor Satarupa, what could she do? She tried running in various directions to avoid her father's lustful gaze. But how could she? Lord Brahma had created the Universe. So when Satarupa went west, Brahma grew a head facing west. When she went south, he grew a head turned to the south. And likewise, he chased her in the east and north too. When Lord Shiva saw what was happening, he was appalled. It went against the Laws of Dharma for a father to behave in this way. So, when Brahma started chasing Satarupa upwards, growing a head racing towards the heavens, Shiva cut it off with his trident. Shivji decided that Brahma had to be punished, so he cursed him that nobody would worship him from then on.

'That's why save for the famous Brahma temple in Pushkar, we ignore Him,' an old pandit sitting by the Alaknanda said.

Panditji and I (with Theo watching) were standing at the Brahma Kapal Ghat. 'It was here that Brahma's fifth head fell to the ground. And why did Shivji cut off Brahmaji's fifth head?' Panditji said. 'It was because he had moved away from the path of dharma. And it was also here that Brahmaji's head came away from Shiva's trident and Shivji himself was freed from his sin. Shivji had committed *Brahma-hatya*. He had killed the biggest Brahmin… Why do we pray here? For the salvation of our ancestors, so that their souls also get *mukti*'—liberation from the cycle of birth and death.

The old pandit nodded. 'Your mother and father want their children to pray for their souls' salvation. Why do they give birth to you? So that when they grow old, you can look after them and this and that. *Hai na?* And this is why we must pray here.'

'*Ji*,' I said, thinking, 'Another pandit trying to fleece me.' 'Where to now?' I said, turning to Panditji.

To the edge of civilization

As Theo remarked, the place looked 'like something out of the Flintstones'. And it wasn't just the surrounding barren red mountains that lent it this air either. The locals, too, had a bucolic otherworldly charm. For one, their appearance was more akin to Tibetans than people from the North Indian plains; and second, their traditional dress was exotic even for me. The older women—their eyes so warm and maternal, the skin around them so wrinkly—wore long black robes, long bead necklaces and a headscarf and looked, I thought, like the locals of Spiti valley.

A sign at the village's entrance said: India's Last Village. And underneath it: Indo-Tibetan Border Police. Army camps and signs dotted these slopes as conspicuous reminders of Nation and Land in what paradoxically seemed so much like no man's land.

We had come to Mana, three kilometres away from Badrinath, because it was from here that the Pandavas began their *Swarg Aarohini*, their journey to heaven. From this off-the-beaten-track village in what seemed like *Almost India*. Yet, as we started climbing the village's arterial lane, lined with stalls selling woollens and bags, I noticed that the others going up this track alongside me were people like me. By which I mean they were Hindu yaatris from mainland India and not the region's locals.

As I huffed and puffed up, a boy of about ten overtook me at a peppy pace. He was in a white dhoti and mouthing a shloka. I thought he had the austere aura of an old pandit, which made me feel bad for him. But then I heard his father call out from behind. 'Wait for us also, Maharaj!' There was so much pride in his voice.

An old local lady came up to me in her majestic black gown. 'Will you have chai? We have Maggi, or our local food, if you want.'

I looked to Panditji. I knew food would be the last thing on his mind, but as we'd had no breakfast it was foremost on mine. 'You both eat *araam se*,' he said continuing up the hill. 'I will see you at Ganesh Gufa.'

'We'll catch up,' I said, and asked the old lady to give us her speciality.

In a few minutes, she brought out a plate of hot fried rice spiced with cumin and garlic, a dish called *bhumla*, and two chais spiked with mountain tulsi. It was a delicious combination that warmed my throat and head, and as good food tends to do, it also opened up a point of conversation.

The old lady said she belonged to the Rongpa tribe. Assuming that I needed further explaining, she added, 'Some people say we are like Tibetans because of how we look. But our sanskriti is very different. It is very ancient. We are older even than the Ramayana and the Mahabharata.'

Theo, who was eyeing our exchange with fair attentiveness, also chipped in: 'How come the people here look so different to you?'

I could hear my voice ring with false pride as I answered. 'What is the Indian look anyway?' I said. 'We have thousands of communities here. You must know that.' But even as I said so, I knew just what the young German was getting at. It was incongruous, wasn't it, that in a place regarded as the wellspring of the most mainstream of Hindu scriptures, the Mahabharata and the Vedas, there now lived a fringe community which people mixed up with Tibetans?

'I get what you're saying,' I said. 'This place is a bit weird. It's like'—I considered for a moment—'the case of Jesus. I mean, we know Jesus lived in the Levant and was a brown-skinned man but his image as a white man has come to dominate in the West. I mean, it is the same-same here. But different.'

Theo adopted a slightly guarded expression.

'We build God in our image, right?' I said. When I saw a family chanting prayers in Tamil walk past, I added, 'Of course, Hinduism is from this soil and not from someplace far away.'

I should be honest with you here, Dear Reader. My Hindu mind has a superficial impression of Christianity. For sure, the religion is attractive with its grand churches, beautiful hymns and its message of compassion. But because Christianity is mainly a *Western* faith, a world I associate more with material things and values, I've come to view it as—how shall I put it?—*lacking in depth*. The thing is, I've found several practising Christians to be much more particular about their approach to God. Somewhat dogmatic about it, actually. (Is this also why so many Westerners are equally dogmatic about their atheism?) And as I tend to believe that any faith that regards itself as superior to another is limited for this exact reason—deficient, as it were, in the competing strings of self-doubt that deeply inhabit both Hinduism and Buddhism—I was never drawn to it more than in a that-Cathedral-is-stunning! sort of way.

In the valley below, the Alaknanda wound around rocks and islands in her path—*Still worlds in the Cosmos of the river!*—then disappeared behind a mountain. The sky was burning a harsh blue and the Himalayas seemed to dig deeper into it, like children's legs at the deep end of a swimming pool. Undaunted by dogma and piercing the depths of space and time, these brown-red ripples of the earth cascaded on. From India to Tibet. From my world to another.

'It's weird,' I said. 'It's like we're at the edge of civilization.'

'Chai? Shawl?' A bunch of boys ran up to us, selling their wares. They were all under ten, one snotty, another devilish, and very high on energy.

'Can you tell me the way to the Ganesh Gufa?'

'Follow me,' the biggest of the posse said and charged forward. 'It's this way.'

A signboard gave the ways to the main sites at Mana: the Bhim Pul, the Saraswati Dham, the Ganesh Gufa and the Ved Vyas Gufa.

The Bhim Pul was a natural bridge made of two boulders converging over a stream. Bhim had created it so that his wife Draupadi could cross over easily. The Saraswati Dham referred to the Saraswati river—or stream—that flowed beneath it. The Vyas Gufa was the cave where the sage Ved Vyas composed the Vedas and the Mahabharata, and the Ganesh Gufa was the cave slightly downhill, where Lord Ganesha transcribed them.

But Theo wasn't listening to me. His eyes were fixated on the boy skipping ahead. Who now stopped and held out his hand. 'Here is our Ganeshji's gufa,' he said. 'Now give me twenty rupees.'

Theo laughed. 'He makes Ganesha sound like his neighbour.'

The notice board outside Ganesha Cave read (in Hindi):

'Here, in this place, the Puranas and Mahabharata as conceived and narrated by Shri Ved Vyas were transcribed into text by Shri Ganesha.

'Lord Brahma told Shri Ved Vyas to pray to Shri Ganesha to help him transcribe his poetry into text. Hearing Vyas's prayer, Lord Ganesha agreed to be his scribe. But on one condition.

'"Oh Vyas, when I put pen to paper, my ink should not dry even for a moment. Only then can I be your scribe," Lord Ganesha said.

'And Ved Vyas said, "Fine. But you must not write even one word without first understanding its full meaning."

'So with the blessings of Lord Ganesha and Shri Ved Vyas mankind has received this epitome of wisdom and guidance.

'Darshan of Lord Ganesha at this place removes all obstacles.'

We united with Panditji and arrived further uphill at the Ved Vyas Cave, above which was written (both in English and Hindi): *This Holy Cave is 5,324 years old.*

As I took my shoes off, I felt a hand on my shoulder. 'Hello, bhaiyya.' It was the shy, bespectacled Himachali boy and his overbearing parents. The father smiled and opened his arm for Theo to enter the alcove and Theo and I ducked our heads and stepped inside. The nook was cold and dark but alive with small echoing chatter. Straining to cross my legs, I sat down in one corner.

As my eyes adjusted to the dimness, I saw a slender pandit sat on one end. He appeared to be in his fifties and had a thin *shikha* on his crown, while the rest of his head was clean-shaven. By him stood the black stone idol of Ved Vyas, the author of the Vedas, who was draped in the orange hue of a sadhu. On the opposite side sat a group of village women. From their talk, I gathered they were either from UP or Bihar.

The pandit was saying, '… And who all do not have the right to read the Vedas? Women, Shudras and Brahmins.'

A woman at the back interjected, 'Can you say that again, panditji? I can't hear you.'

'Women after the age of fourteen. Members of the fourth caste. And Brahmins,' the pandit said. His voice took on a more resounding tenor. 'Women after fourteen have no right to read the Vedas, we accept this. The fourth caste has no right to read the Vedas, we accept this. But why did Ved Vyasji stop us poor Brahmins from reading the Vedas? Have you people thought about this?'

'There must be a reason,' said one woman.

'Aren't you the one who will tell us?' said another, and her friends giggled.

'So, why did Ved Vyasji write this? I will tell you. Ved Vyasji meant that only those Brahmins don't have the right to read the Vedas who leave their Brahmin caste and marry somebody who is Kshatriya, Vaishya, or Shudra... And if you think about it, today, exactly this is happening.'

'*Bilkul, aisa hi ho raha hai,*' the Himachali mother concurred.

Theo stood up to take a picture and the pandit raised his voice. 'This is not a picnic spot that you take a photo and then go home and show it to your friends: Look how lovely these Himalayas are! No. This is a pure dham.'

The poor guy sat down and put his hands in his pockets. The pandit continued:

'When did Ved Vyasji write this? He wrote this 5,324 years back. And it is coming to pass today... So, all those who have no right to read the Vedas, how will they get *kalyaan*? Have you people thought about this? In front of God, everybody has the right to be blessed, no? No matter which caste they're from. No matter if they're man or woman. So, which is that text which contains the secret of our Shaastras and the essence of our Puranas, and by imbibing which anybody can get kalyaan?'

The word 'kalyaan', I told Theo, meant 'benediction'. But then I said, no. There was no exact translation. At best, it meant the total welfare and good of a person—with God's added blessings.

'Brahmaji told Ved Vyas that such a text is the Mahabharata. As only in the Mahabharata is all the knowledge of our scriptures contained... But now there was another problem. The Mahabharata contained one lakh shlokas and the Kalyug was fast approaching. So, who could write it down so fast? Who was capable? Then Brahmaji told Ved Vyas to pray to Ganeshji. And that was when Ganeshji presented himself.'

As the pandit lapsed into a round of bhajan-singing, the women burst into applause, and I rose to leave. Panditji sat me back down.

'One time, when Ved Vyasji was sitting by the banks of the Saraswati River, he saw Naradji and the first thing he did was a proper pranaam in the proper aasana [posture]. Vyasji touched Naradji's feet and did his pooja. He asked him about his health. This is our Hindu Dharam *sanskaar*, people. This used to be the way back in those days.

But today if some guest enters the house, then you see how upside-down everything is. You all can imagine it…

'And how you eat and drink is how you behave. Why did God make our teeth small? So we can eat rice and *roti*. A lion has big teeth so he can eat meat. But what's happening today? Nowadays big-toothed animals are not eating meat and small animals are…

'After 84 lakh life cycles, we are blessed to be born in this human form, a form in which God can see his own image, and to move towards God is the objective of human life, isn't it? …

'So yes, Ved Vyasji then said to Naradji, I've written down all the holy texts. The Vedas, the Brahmasutras, the Puranas, the Mahabharata. But still I'm not at peace. Still my mind is restless. And Naradji said, "Until you describe Lord Krishna's qualities to the people, describe his *rasa* in its fullest glory, until then you won't be at peace, O Ved Vyas." And that was when Ved Vyas composed the Eighteenth Purana, the *Bhagavata Purana* in honour of Lord Krishna.'

An enormous bird with outstretched wings was circling the afternoon sky. It cruised the winds—effortlessly, gracefully—like, I thought, chuckling to myself, it was an incarnation of Garuda and an unconstrained Theo and I took photo after photo.

The three of us had come to Mana's famous *The Last Chai Shop in India*, and Panditji was on another story. When Ved Vyas composed the Mahabharata, the mighty Saraswati River passed by his cave. But so loud was her current that it disturbed the sage's concentration and he cursed her to go unseen. This is why she, now a mere stream, merges with the larger Alaknanda River and in so doing loses her identity.

But then I stopped listening. The image of those village women was still in my head. What I saw was such a caricature of my faith, I thought. But was it, though? Was I so blinded by my privilege that I couldn't see my people for who they were? Only the previous year at Ganga Sagar, I'd come across a similar sight: a group of women huddled on the vast beach, laughing and nodding among themselves as they heard the words of a sadhu.

'Don't you find this sad?' I said to mummy.

'You'll see things in your way,' she said. 'Can't you see how content they are?'

The reason I was outraged, of course, was because my pride was hurt. Because I knew what I'd seen was the picture so many Westerners had of India, and because it was something I'd long resisted. 'What you see on BBC is a gross misrepresentation!' I'd once said to my English friend Paul. When an American colleague said, 'Religion is why India will never develop,' I had shot back, 'That's such a generalization!'

And yet, the personification of backward India had appeared before me in flesh and blood. Theo and Panditji were there too: one who couldn't resist taking snapshots of the 'Orient', and another who himself embodied its antiquated ways.

'...and so Shankaracharya meet Ved Vyasji here,' I heard Panditji say.

'But didn't Shankaracharya come here only in the eighth century?' Theo asked.

I cut in. 'Did you believe him? What that pandit said. About women and Shudras not being allowed to read the scriptures?'

Pandijti, who'd been sipping his chai dreamily, raised his eyebrows. 'But it is written, Siddharth. The pandit wasn't making anything up. It is written in our Shaastras. Do you want me to make up things for you?'

The man sounded so accepting of what was *written* that I momentarily considered if there really were some truths to life this pious man had figured out and which I was only now coming to see. Yet, Pandit Hemant was also the man who sought religious guidance from my mother. Who knew she had read all the scriptures. Who had himself learnt some portions of the *Bhagavata Purana* from her. But not only this. Panditji knew mummy was unconventional in other ways. She didn't worship my father. She was a practising lawyer. (And a terrible cook.)

And what of me? Panditji knew I ate meat. He knew I didn't do pooja regularly, and now he also knew something he probably already suspected: I disregarded many of his sayings.

And despite this, we—mummy, Panditji, I—accepted each other, didn't we? We held our judgements, but privately. Wasn't this the beauty of how our faith worked? By accommodating everybody. By subsuming all our contradictions and customs into this one umbrella called Hinduism.

Panditji elbowed out these unexpressed moderating voices in my mind. 'Now see,' he said, 'even dogs and cats have relations only during their mating season. It is only we humans who break all rules... Now see, you're writing this book and you have come here for your research.' He used the English word 'research'. 'Why? It is because our ancients have already done all the search for us. You are just re-searching what they have already done!'

I was tempted to laugh, but I was still angry. So, I gulped down my tea and ended up burning my tongue.

'What about those sweepers in Kedarnath you were telling me about?' Theo said. 'What does Panditji say about them?'

Caste was tricky territory. But I took the bait. 'Yes, Panditji,' I said. 'On the way up to Kedarnath we saw so many sweepers. They clear all the horse shit for us, all the rubble when there is a landslide. They clear the snow in winter. And all they ask for is money for chai. They chant Bhole Baba's name morning and night. But will they be allowed inside the temple? You tell me, will you people let them in?'

It was clear from the sweepers' submissiveness that they would never be let in. Not in this lifetime. But what was also becoming equally clear was this note of false injury in my voice. Here I was, this Kshatriya Punjabi man suddenly talking like the defender of the downtrodden. I must have sounded very absurd.

'That is their dharma,' Panditji said easily. 'That is how they get darshan of God. By performing their duty. And this is also their karma.'

'That is such nonsense! They are in that position because we've had them stuck there for thousands of years. Pandijti, you are an educated person. I thought you should be able to see that.' I looked to a lost Theo for affirmation and back at Panditji. 'Can't you see that?'

Panditji glanced at Theo. 'But Siddharthji, his case is different. You can't compare foreigners to us. Their system is different. Their ways are different.' He switched to English and said to Theo, his eyes unblinking: 'Your culture—different.' This time, I did laugh.

Then he bore his eyes into mine. 'You speak about yourself. Why did you give money to that pandit outside the temple this morning? Why not to anybody else? Why have you brought me here with you? Would you get a pooja done by a sweeper who has studied the scriptures from beginning to end? Or by me, a real pandit? Tell me. Would you?'

Panditji's voice was breaking, and a film of sweat had appeared on his forehead. We were at that point where an argument could turn into a fight and I had to rein myself in. After all, Pandijti was my guest on this yaatra. He had come with me as a favour. He was simply a pandit performing his duty.

I lowered my voice and mumbled something irrelevant. Then I placed my hand on his shoulder. 'It's okay. We'll talk later,' I said. 'Can I get you another glass of tea?'

I see the silliness of our argument. I do. What was I expecting, really? I'd seen how differently Panditji's mind was constellated from mine. But still, I'd be lying if I didn't also say I was a little disappointed by how predictable he was. By how visceral he was. By how true to his caste and profession he was. 'There is order in the Universe no matter where you look,' Panditji said. 'Our Dharmashaastras say this.'

As I tossed my empty glass into the bin, I glanced back at the sky. The Garuda-like bird did one last somersault in the blue, then slipped behind a mountain. Wasn't the universe, at its core, random? Isn't order a meaning we attach to the innately stochastic?

Inside our tent later that night, I shot out again into the darkness: 'These ideas of dharma and karma, don't you think they depend on the time and place? Things are so different now compared to thousands of years back when people wrote these rules.'

Panditji swallowed in the silence. 'I will tell you one thing I have not told anybody,' he said. 'Like I said, I hadn't seen my mother for many years after I left home. But one day, when I was twenty, she turned up at Shivsagar Ashram. Don't ask me how she knew I was there. She just did. She had found me. I remembered the day I left my village very well. It was exactly nine years and four months since I'd seen her, but I remembered her face like it was just yesterday…'

He collected himself. 'When my mother saw me in my new clothes—I was wearing the clothes of a pandit—tears came to her eyes. The evening aarti had just finished and everybody was just staring at us, mother and son. One by one everybody was then forming a queue to go do pranaam to Swamiji, and my mother…you know what she did? She was staring at me, and I don't know what came over her, but she bent forward as if she was about to touch my feet. She was about to touch my feet! My own mother! I shook her by her shoulders. "Don't you ever do that," I said. "Only I'm allowed to touch your feet." … Then we both went up to Swamiji, asked for his blessings.'

Panditji laughed lightly. 'Swamiji recognized her instantly. He said, "So, your son's journey is complete, mataji? I hope you're proud of him." And my mother smiled sadly. But she was proud. I could see it.

'Our *vansh*, lineage, is carrying on so easily. Have you wondered why? It is because our *pitra log*, ancestors, had given it great thought. How are you able to carry on without any big needs and wants? It is because of your parents. Your ancestors. This is because somebody in your family generations back did good karma for you. They did all the work. And you're reaping the benefits. This is why I say that if a son doesn't do enough for his parents he becomes *dushta*…rotten, redundant.' He said this with force. 'And that is when the elders curse them. And the curse of your parents is worse even than of the gods.

'The Pandavas also had to remove the debt of their ancestors. They'd killed so many in war. And this is why I was telling you to pray properly here, Siddharth. Because over here your sins get erased completely.'

After we completed our darshan of Lord Narayan early the following morning, Pandijti went into ecstasies of thanks.

'You are like my saviour, Siddharthji,' he said. 'For so many years, I planned to come here but nothing worked out. So many times yaatris who passed through Rishikesh asked me to go with them, and my plan always fell through. But you insisted. You've really come like some devta.'

It was a glorious morning, and with yesterday's clouds all gone, the Neelkanth Parbat shone like a silver arrowhead holding up the firmament.

'Oh, please stop, Panditji. You're embarrassing me.' I held Panditji's hands.

'No, no. I could come to see God only because of you.' He squeezed my hands. 'I only have one small final request.'

I'm ashamed to say I said, 'What now?'

He pointed to my iPhone. 'Can you take some photos of me?'

On our descent, Panditji expanded further on the story of Badrinath. I was full with faith by now, but I let him speak uninterrupted.

He looked over at the gushing Alaknanda outside the car window. 'When the Buddhists came here, it was with the intent to establish their rule and kingdom. So, they took the main statue of God, the Shaligram and put it in this river.

'When Shankaracharya came to Badrinath, he saw that the Buddhists had completely spoilt this place. But he saw there were signs of God everywhere. The statues of Garudji, Naradji, Kuberji... indeed Narayan's entire family was here. So, how could it be that God himself could not be found? Shankaracharya then decided to do tapasya. In his mind he saw something beneath the river was pulling him to itself. So, he immersed himself in the river and a black stone came into this hands. He wondered, *Can this be God?* And to test whether it was, he threw it back in the water. He then went to a different spot and immersed himself again. But again, the same stone came into his hands. So, he put it back into the river and went to a third spot. And again the same stone came into his hands! It was then that he realized that this stone was none other than Lord Narayan himself.

'Shankaracharyaji placed the idol in the cave where the hot springs are, and in the sixteenth century, a Garhwal raja placed it inside the temple where it stands today.'

Later, I'd learn that shaligrams are fossilized shells found in the riverbeds of the Himalayas that once made up the seabed of Tethys, a water body that covered much of what later became Eurasia more than 190 million years ago. Sudipta Sen writes in *Ganga: The Many Pasts of a River*: 'The proto Hindu scriptures pit human finitude against eternal creation (*kala* and *akala*); stories of how the world came to be have always straddled the divide between god and nature, cosmology and ecology. Vishnu, the keeper of all creation, took the form of the fish (*matsya*) avatar during the great deluge to save the world. Many of his insignia are aquatic: ammonite, conch shell, lotus. The River Ganga in Hindu mythology is the purest emanation of Vishnu in fluid, natural form.'

As for the Hinduization of sacred sites, S.N. Sadasivan notes in *A Social History of India*: 'Whenever a Buddhist institution was seized by the Brahmins, a confusing variety of legends were woven round it to establish the divine ownership over it and the common people gullible enough to believe at least in one or more of them. All over the country the Buddhist shrines were captured and converted into Brahmanic places of worship. In the forceful takeover of the temples of Amarnath in Kashmir, Kedarnath and Badrinath in the Himalayas, Sankara [*sic*] had played a leading role.'

And according to Ramchandra Guha, in his book *The Unquiet Woods: Ecological Change and Peasant Resistance in the Himalaya*, Shankara expelled all the Buddhists in the region with the help of the Parmar ruler king Kanak Pal and it was he who erected the temple. The hereditary successors of the raja governed the temple and endowed villages to meet its expenses and the income from a set of villages on the route to the temple was used to feed and accommodate pilgrims. In time, the Parmar rulers came to hold the title 'Bolanda Badrinath', meaning speaking Badrinath, and the king enjoyed ritual obeisance by devotees before proceeding to the shrine. This practice continued until the late nineteenth century.

Theo asked Panditji, 'Do you ever regret becoming a pandit, Panditji?'

'*Arre*, you boys don't know how happy I am to have had my experiences,' he said. 'Most people never get to have these in their whole life. I am so thankful to God. I am so thankful to my parents for this life…' He then asked Theo, 'In your country, you can take a year to travel the world; what about your work? What about your marriage?'

'They can do that. They save money and they have the luxury of travel. It's not the same for the average Indian,' I said.

'So, if I want to go to his country, how expensive will it be?'

'Quite a lot,' I said. 'You will need a visa and air tickets. You need to show that you have enough money to support yourself there.' I sounded a little superior when I explained all this. As if I wanted to remind Pandijti that he was the expert in the world of faith, but in the real world he was nobody. I realize the pettiness of this sentiment now.

Panditji inhaled deeply and studied Theo's expression one last time. Theo was admiring the view outside where in the valley far below the Ganga throbbed and blazed in the sun like some primal being winding through obstacles. 'Well, it's good we have everything in our India,' he said.

A Taste of Faith in the Valley of Gods

Kullu Dussehra Mela. October 2015

Glistening calmly, ensconced in a wooden palanquin before me was the metallic idol of Chamunda Devi. The goddess, dressed in red and garlanded in marigold, was not alone. Also present in these teeming grounds was the devta Ghatotkach, who fought on the side of the Pandavas in the Mahabharata, and Devi Hadimba, mother of Ghatotkach and wife of the Pandava, Bhim. Indeed, in attendance was a constellation of divinities from the Mahabharata and the Ramayana. Each interrelated and morphing into another, swirling in a great bowl of mythological soup.

The cry of a conch pierced the crisp morning air, cutting even through the sonorous calls of bugles, the buffalo-horn *narasingha* trumpets among them. Drums beat out their *dhadak*. And the *rath*, a palanquin-chariot bearing Chamunda Devi, was raised aloft. Hefted upon the faith-hardened shoulders of devotees, the Devi then quaked to life. She began to sway, watched keenly by the mass of believers, trademark *pahari topis* on their heads. The village elders rushed to her, the Devi, pleading for pacification. They cajoled and implored her to move, to pay her respects to Lord Raghunath on whose *bulaawa*, divine calling, she had come here in the first place, before eventually making the return journey to her home, the village of Jhadag Chachoga.

Minutes passed before the goddess showed any sign of acquiescence.

Then her bearers lurched forward before they again came to a shuddering stall. It seemed to me as though they were competing to see who could make the best show of throwing the idol off balance without actually letting it fall.

'Why are they shaking the goddess?' I blurted out.

'Shaking?' An elderly man standing beside me laughed. 'Nobody can shake the gods. *Bhagwaan pravesh karte hain...*God enters them. Why don't you take the palanquin on your shoulders and discover for yourself?'

I did not know what stimulant was at work but the sceptic in me went silent. I was seized by what I was seeing.

I had come to Kullu, in Himachal Pradesh, to immerse myself in the annual Dussehra Mela, a massive festival with four to five lakh visitors. The devotees here believed that the idols came alive during this time, injected by *shakti*, the power of God. But for me, there was another lure to visiting, too: the custom of *bali*, or animal sacrifice, at the Mela—which was all the more significant because this was the first year of celebrations after the Himachal Pradesh High Court had banned the practice.

I went to meet Maheshwar Singh, the Raja of Kullu, in his palace. The living room walls held on to the faded portraits of deceased royals, their grandeur long gone but not forgotten. He told me the story of how the Dussehra Mela came to Kullu.

A Raja Jagat Singh, who reigned over the then flourishing kingdom of Kullu from 1637 to 1672, had brought the Mela into existence. Jagat Singh had heard that a Brahmin, Durgadutt, was in possession of unique pearls. Convinced that they had been stolen, the Raja ordered that the Brahmin return them at once. Durgadutt was incensed at the accusation, and feeling dishonoured, he set himself and his family ablaze. But not before he cursed the Raja.

Soon afterwards, Jagat Singh's kingdom fell to penury. Desperate for a way out, he undertook a pilgrimage to Manikaran, located about thirty-five kilometres from Kullu, in the Parvati valley, where he was told of a solution. He would have to bring the idols from the Tretanath Temple at Ayodhya to Kullu and dedicate his kingdom to Lord Ram-Raghunath.

So, Jagat Singh sent a Brahmin named Damodar to Tretanath to pose as a sweeper. And one day, when the path was clear, Damodar stole the idols and fled. He had not reached even halfway when he was stopped by the protesting residents of Ayodhya. They seized the idol of Lord Raghunath from him, determined to restore Him to his rightful seat. However, when they attempted to lift it, the idol wouldn't budge. It was as if it was stuck to the earth!

But when Damodar retook the Lord upon his shoulders, He became lighter and lighter with every step he took. 'So you see,' Maheshwar Singh said cheerfully, 'Raghunathji came on his own to Kullu.'

Jagat Singh then dedicated the village grounds to the devtas, and placed a duty on all surrounding villages to bring their gods here every Dussehra. Since then, Lord Raghunath has loomed large in the consciousness of Kullu.

When in December 2014, the idol of Lord Raghunath was stolen from the temple in the Raja's palace, the entire valley was desolate. *For whom would the gods gather on Dussehra now?* Happily, though, the idol was soon found, and the thief caught.

It was afternoon, and my ears throbbed with the beating of drums. Overhead, a hoarding called for an end to animal sacrifice. The Dhalpur grounds were a sea of people with deities bobbing around the island tent, inside which stood the festival's chief deity, Lord Raghunath. Additional bearers were employed to steady the flouncing palanquins here and a group of women broke into dance there.

I was taking in the spectacle when a heave of bodies pushed me to the side. Out-of-control trains of palanquins went zigzagging into the crowds. These were the *Nag-Bhoomi Devtas*, the serpent-gods entrusted with clearing the way. On this last day of celebrations, there would be a final procession of the gods that would culminate with the offering of bali.

Typically, five animals were slaughtered on Dussehra: a buffalo, a goat, a rooster, a crab, and a fish, each representing one of the five weaknesses of lust, rage, selfishness, attachment and ego. When I questioned Raja Maheshwar Singh about what he thought about banning of bali, he recounted the story of a sadhu who, pained after learning of the practice, had searched him out.

'If it is so necessary, then cut me before you cut any animal,' the sadhu said.

'If I cut you, I will have sinned,' the Raja replied. 'Plus, you will be useless to me because I can't eat your flesh.'

Maheshwar Singh believed that the *parampara*, tradition, was important to uphold because it was bound up with his people's belief in Shakti.

'Is it also a parampara to make a show that the idols are possessed?' I said.

'Some people might like to show off, but I have personally witnessed the force of Shakti,' he said. 'The people here have total belief in the gods whereas you people from Delhi might doubt all this.'

Thousands had gathered on the path of the procession. On balconies, on rooftops, on top of buses. A man near me, his tongue lolling, shook like he was possessed. Raja Maheshwar Singh then strode into the sacrificial compound followed by his entourage and somebody shouted, 'Phones off! *Sab band!*'

'Is the bali really going to happen?' I asked.

'*Bilkul*, but it will happen covertly. If you take a photo, it will be a problem for you and us, but if they do it in *pardah*, in hiding, then you're happy, and we're happy, and the gods are also happy,' a man said.

The horde pushed forward and I was thrust to the rear of the pack. I craned my neck to get a peek, but it was pointless. There were expectant faces. Murmurs. Then, silence.

A thunderous crack.

Was it a goat?

Through a gap, I could see that Maheshwar Singh's face was flushed. His cheeks were slick with tears. Men leapt up to hold him for he was so spent that his legs could at any time give way. Slowly, with great effort, he began walking, still needing support.

The passage opened up. I hurried ahead towards the sacrificial site. Only to find on the floor traces of vermilion, flowers and a smashed coconut.

PART III

The Revelation of a Glacier

May 2007

Revelation in Gangotri

After I finished high school, I got my BA in Economics at Delhi University, where college was a time of bunking classes and discovering the new freedoms conferred by instant text messaging and alcohol. It was also a time when my sister Mala and I fought with our mother a lot and hardly went on a yaatra. Not when it didn't suit us anyway.

Then in 2003, I left for the UK. I had an offer to study law at Cardiff University, and law was the most obvious thing to do. My Nana was the grand old lawyer in our family, and my parents were tax lawyers. I was sure I didn't want to pursue Economics further and that I liked playing with language. After all, I had the lineage, I thought. What I didn't appreciate back then was that the Law and Religion are very different in theory and practice. But let's not digress.

When I was twenty-one, I wasn't thinking so much about building a career. What I was most looking forward to was flying away from home and exploring a new world. And so, naturally, I found the student parties at university exhilarating, the pubs and the new meaty foods so very satisfying.

In short, my time abroad was both wonderful and edifying. But now, at twenty-five, after having lived away for four years a part of me was beginning to wonder whether freedom, *real freedom*, was something of a myth. I mean, certainly Western culture had major upsides. For starters, there was no honking on the roads, no pushing and shoving during Church service (a few of which I attended), and no preaching of dos and don'ts through Swamiji. Yet, for all of its orderliness and wealth, I sometimes felt that the West was a little *too efficient*.

I don't know how else to explain my sensitivity other than to say that getting used to Western structures can be challenging when you've been raised in the hot chaos of India. I missed the ringing bells from our pooja room in the mornings. I missed the muezzin from the mosque behind our house in the evenings. I missed the afternoon warmth of Delhi's winter and, yes, even the searing heat of our summer. I missed our household help, I did. I won't lie. I missed even the strays and filth in the streets. And so, like a beetle crawls back to its old ball of dung, in the May of 2007, I returned home for good.

One sweltering evening that same month, mummy asked if I wanted to go with her to Shruti's son's birthday party. I said yes.

May 2007

Shruti's husband's farmhouse was just as I'd imagined. In the enormous living room, paintings with bold borders stretched up to the ceiling, where the sunlight came through a glass shaft. Outside, young parents stood on the lawns making small talk in sex-segregated clusters. While the men talked of business and the government's economic failures, the women spoke about their kids' talents and the government's appeasement of minorities. Shrieking children ran around chasing giant bright balloons propelled by mist fans.

The food looked good. I walked over to the counter and piled my plate high.

'There you are!' Ritu Aunty spotted me. She looked the same, except her old bun was now absent. Her hair was jazzed up in a wavy style, but her head still shook energetically as she spoke. 'Look at you!' She smiled. 'I see that living in England has made you both fairer and fatter.' She poked my beer belly.

Let's stop with Ritu Aunty here, though. I remember this evening well. Not because of her, but because it was the day I first met Ritu Aunty's distant cousin, Rupa Attwal. Or Rupa Aunty.

Mummy was chatting with a plump woman who had the curious combination of dark skin, which looked even darker in her bright pink salwar-kameez, and moss-green eyes. I plodded over. She was speaking in Hindi with a heavy Punjabi accent.

'Sid, this is Rupa Aunty,' mummy said.

'Namaste, aunty.' I turned to mummy. 'I think I'll be leaving.'

'Rupa and I used to meet all the time as children,' mummy said and went back to regaling her old friend about the innumerable benefits of Pranic Healing.

Just as she'd fixated on yoga and homeopathy in the decades before, Pranic Healing was my mother's new fascination. And what a serious fascination it was, too. In just two years, she'd become one of South Delhi's core members. Her group, primarily women over fifty, would have regular healing sessions over Skype.

Out of curiosity, I accompanied her for one meeting for beginners at the Chinamaya Auditorium on Lodhi Road. A loud portly woman was on stage. 'The method we will practise today,' she said brightly, 'has been handed down from Saint Francis of Assisi. He gifted the world with the divine methods of inner alchemy and transformation. Just like ancient alchemists could transform lead to gold, bending God's laws of chemistry, Saint Francis taught us how to change our negative auras to positive ones by using our minds and bodies as channels.'

The auditorium was about three-fourths full and while most attendees were people in their forties or over, I was surprised to see a handful of college students present too.

The portly woman said, 'Now, for those who don't know, Saint Francis of Assisi was a Christian saint, but his powers are as deep as any of our gurus. So, please remember, God is one. Don't approach healing with your biases.'

She closed her eyes, and the auditorium blacked out.

'Now, repeat after me:

Lord, make me an instrument of your peace,
Where there is hatred, let me sow love;
Where there is injury, pardon;
Where there is doubt, faith;
Where there is despair, hope;
Where there is darkness, light;
Where there is sadness, joy.'

Mummy's hands stayed quivering in the air above her lap for a whole minute after the lights had come back on.

'We will have enough time to discuss this next week, behenji. I'm counting on you,' Rupa Aunty said, smiling as freely with her eyes as she did with her mouth. As freely, I thought, as the pink smiley balloon behind her.

'*Ji*,' mummy said vaguely, annoyed at being cut off.

'Will Siddharth come too?'

I looked up from my phone. 'Come where? Lunch?'

'Oh, you must come!' Rupa Aunty laughed. 'Why don't you come to our house tomorrow? It's a Sunday.'

Unlike her wealthier cousin, Rupa Aunty's (husband's) house lay in the congested bylanes of Delhi's Shahadara. Two-storey houses with shared walls squeezed the narrow road in from either side while tangles of electric wires pressed down on us from above. I was behind the wheel, honking our way past a mesh of auto rickshaws, cycles and scooters, and I was losing my patience. I rolled down my window to yell at a rickshaw puller.

To be honest, driving through overcrowded neighbourhoods still tests my nerves. But back then, when I was in my twenties and had just tasted clean Western living, I lacked even the semblance of sensitivity.

'Girl Impregnated by Father. Mother Blames Black Magic,' was a headline I had read in *Hindustan Times* only some days before. That sordid incident had happened right here in Shahadara. I narrated the story with all its lurid details to my mother. 'Did you read about it?' Mummy was narrowing her eyes at the road.

'Surely, the only solution is education,' I went on. 'That's the problem here. Just look at this traffic.'

'Stop here,' mummy said.

'What?'

'Stop the car.'

I pushed the brakes.

'It is just a small detour.' She had a glint in her eyes. 'Come.'

To my right stood a wide gate above which, on a blue board, was written in Hindi: *Radhe Krishna Gaushala*. Radhe Krishna Cow Shelter. My mother looked so pleased with herself that I considered: When it comes to blind faith, even good schooling can do only so much!

'Feeding a cow is one of the foremost good deeds you can do,' Maharajji had once said. 'For a cow has everything, and feeding it is equivalent to pleasing 84,000 devtas. Indeed, a cow is everything, for its every part is useful. From its dung which becomes fuel to its urine which is medicinal. And is there any better nourishment than mother's milk? Feeding a cow is like feeding your mother and we've known this for ages. Even in the *Katha Upanishad*, there's one story about the proper manner of donating cows.'

While I didn't quite share my mother's staunch reverence for the bovine form, I realized I'd come to respect the creature in my own way. Back at university, I'd debated with my Greek flatmate, Jonas, one evening over the Hindu prohibition on beef. It had seemed illogical to him.

'Why not also stop eating chicken, then?' he argued.

It was not so much the substance of his argument but his condescending tone that made me bristle. 'Firstly, vegetarianism is integral to Hinduism,' I said. 'But the cow has a special status in India with good reason.' For effect, I said, 'She's given us so much for millennia.'

Jonas rolled his eyes.

'Now, would you eat your horse?' I said. My defensiveness had surprised me.

Rupa Aunty was waiting for us in an auto by the gate, and with her was her son, Prince. She was in another pink salwar-kameez, and Prince was in a white kurta-pyjama. Prince was a thick-set guy with a slight belly and looked to be in his early thirties. Two things about him stood out. First, he had countless red pooja strings on his wrist, and second, though he had his mother's green eyes, his skin was a Punjabi fair.

He dived to touch mummy's feet. 'Bless you, beta,' mummy said and nudged me to reciprocate. 'Namaste, aunty,' I merely said to Rupa Aunty.

Inside the gate was a large grass enclosure ringed by a wire mesh screen inside which hundreds of cows were mooing away. Mummy stuck her hand full of fodder through a hole in the screen. 'Come, my darling. Come.' Her voice was soaked in honey. A gaggle of cows approached, tenderly bobbing their heads. 'You must feed a hundred at least,' she said to Prince.

I was standing at some distance, making small talk with Rupa Aunty in the shade. She was out of breath from the walk from the gate. She had found a chair. I told her I'd fetch her water from the car. I was going over when mummy said, 'And what do you think you've come here for?' I sighed and trudged over.

'See. Like this,' she said as she fed a cow straight out of her hands. My mother made the exercise look so easy that I also gingerly stretched my hand forward. But then a cow licked me, and I recoiled and wiped the goop off on my jeans. Prince and mummy laughed.

A caretaker led us to a shed in which cows tied by weak ropes were staring blankly at an empty furrow. And here mummy bounced ahead, her hands full of hay. I really didn't mind her lack of restraint so much. But when I saw her moving towards a massive cow—Oh wait, no. It was a bull!—with pointy red horns, I had to yell: 'Stop!'

Mummy ignored me and extended an assertive hand to the animal's mouth. When the bull bobbed its head forward, she thankfully retreated. But then an ebullient Prince hopped ahead of her and dropped fodder into the furrow, and now her voice grew louder. 'Here, son!'

I ran over. But it was too late.

The beast lunged forward and Prince grabbed mummy and yanked her back. Mummy was stunned, but the shock on her face lasted only a few seconds as she willed her features back to their usual sprightly proportions. She got up, dusted herself off.

'Why do you never listen to me?' I was shaking her by the shoulders.

'I'm fine, I'm fine,' she said, laughing.

'Show me your arm.'

'Leave me. I'm fine,' she growled.

Only when we reached Rupa Aunty's house did I see that mummy was certainly not fine. The little dot of red I'd seen on her sleeve was now blooming.

I parked our car beside an open sewer full of black foaming water, and we went down a trash-choked gulley and then up a *paan*-stained stairway. Rupa Aunty sat us down in her living room and disappeared into her bedroom.

Save for an old TV set which stood against a blackened wall on which a torn calendar with a painting of Lord Krishna was awkwardly hung, there were only a couple of plastic chairs and a chipped coffee table before me. Prince hurriedly covered the table with a newspaper and gave my mother an apologetic look, and I felt suddenly depressed.

By 2003, my parents had moved back to my grandparents' house in central Delhi. For me, Delhi didn't exist beyond Connaught Place on the one end and South Delhi, where my friends' homes were, on the other. On the few occasions I ventured outside my comfort zone, my outings were brief and with specific intents in mind. To meet my friend James from London for lunch at Karim's by Jama Masjid, for example. Or to go along with mummy to Mangolpuri, where she claimed to have met the best astrologer in a decade.

By this time, my father had retired from the government and started his own tax law practice. And not just him; my mother, too, was making frequent appearances in the Delhi High Court and the Supreme Court for high-stakes tax matters. I'd tagged her on a few occasions and was dazzled by her tax knowledge and oration. She could reduce complex interlinkages between rules of accountancy and rules of natural justice into nuggets of wisdom that left the judges smiling and me at a complete loss as to who this person was. Really, in the courtroom, mummy was electric, and I was so proud. Logical and shorn of all traces of faith, she was a totally different person.

Considering this, I'd later tell her that what upset me about the Attwals' home was not so much its abject state but the irrationality I associated with it. We had seen a small degree of scarcity growing up, so it wasn't that. My point was, 'Why must you still hang out with these Sehdev Uncle types?' But I think I wasn't being truthful. The Attwals' home depressed me because it was indeed depressing. But now I also wonder: Did I spontaneously associate irrationality with poverty because it is what I expected of the poor?

Rupa Aunty returned with a mug of hot water, some strange pink solution, cotton and a torn cloth. When she saw my horrified expression, she said, 'It's new! Don't worry.' She turned to mummy. 'Roll up your sleeve, didi.'

'I think we should go see a doctor,' I said, fuming. 'She needs a tetanus shot.'

'Beta, don't worry. It's a scratch. Now, will you have *achaar* with your food? We have lots.' A young girl who looked about my age emerged from the kitchen and set three jars of pickles before us (carrot, mango, garlic). She did a quick namaste to mummy who, shoddily bandaged, was now chatting with Prince, and retreated to the kitchen, and soon the aroma of frying food shrouded the room.

Prince's wife Charu had an oval pretty face and large dewy eyes, which she kept shyly lowered as she ferried plates and glasses from the kitchen to the table. When Prince ordered her to serve us, she complied noiselessly, so I assumed she was like one of those deferential daughters-in-law you saw in Hindi TV serials.

The poori-aloo she served us was delicious, too, and forgetting my irritation I ate heartily. As did mummy. But when Charu emerged with the fourth batch, I gently told my mother, who'd recently learnt she was diabetic, it was time she stopped. She glared at me and asked for another helping, which Charu graciously brought her. But as Charu lifted the empty tray off the table now, her eyes briefly met mine and she produced a mischievous smile and Prince, who was munching his food noisily, stopped and frowned. Charu didn't seem to care, though. She skipped off to the kitchen, smirking. And I knew then I would get along with her as much as I wouldn't with her husband.

Only after we were full to the brim did the two ladies of the house begin to eat, and that was when Rupa Aunty came down to her main business with my mother. 'Didi, the problem started with Indrajit Singh,' she said placing a morsel of roti to the side of her mouth. 'He was that moneylender I told you about earlier. His brothers had all died before him. So, when he realized he was the only son left, he got their widows to sign all their wealth in his name. He cheated them, and those women, they would curse him all day long. When he'd pass them in the village they'd say may your children die and things like that.' She bit down on a green chilli. 'Then, a year later, untimely deaths started occurring in his family. The first to go was Ranjit. He was Indrajit's favourite son. And then a year later, another of his boys died. Indrajit went on to have three more sons but they say he was never the same man again. One of these sons was Jagmohan, Prince's great-great-grandfather. He became a father at twenty-eight. But by the time he was thirty-three, his first three children had also died.'

'Wasn't this common in those days?' I said.

Mummy grimaced, but Rupa Aunty carried on. 'Yes, but listen. Finally, Jagmohan had three sons and a girl—Prince's great-grandfather Kuldeepdas was one of the boys, but their mother died in childbirth also. So, Jagmohan, a totally broken man, decided to go to a Muslim fakir in his village. That man told him an evil spirit had trapped his family, and he gave him a black *tabeez* to wear around his neck. After this, Jagmohan found a new wife, a new mother for his children, and things got better for some time.

'But then some thirty years later, Partition happened, and the killings began. Prince's grandfather, Harcharandas, he had no choice but to leave his house, his properties, everything behind, and the three brothers and their wives, they all moved to Jalandhar. Their family was lucky to have a home there. But their old family haveli, their land in the village, everything was lost. Prince's father, he says even now, at least Kuldeepdas was lucky to have died before witnessing all this.

'We were a rich family once, but what was there now? Three brothers, their wives and children—but no money. And all of us living in that small house in Jalandhar.'

Prince went over to his mother and took her neck into the hook of his elbow. 'Aunty,' he said, looking to mummy. 'Our kismet began to change when my mother came to the house. Even papa says, when your mother came, it was like a pure spirit had entered our world.'

A tear crept out of the corner of Rupa Aunty's eye and she slapped her son on his thigh. 'Oh, you stop,' she said. 'So, there's strong *pitra dosh* in our family, and it all started with that Indrajit Singh.'

Pitra dosh, or the debt of your forefathers, was a defect in one's astrological chart. You see, when a person takes birth in this world, their past good and bad karma carry over into this life.

What are the symptoms? Money would not come into the house, or if it did, it would slip out and away. Your home would become joyless, dark. If a bride came, an heir might not come. Miscarriages would occur. The family would grow small, from fewer and fewer brothers and sisters to none at all. In a house afflicted by pitra dosh even animals wouldn't stay long: birds, dogs. The cow. *But what caused it?* If, in a home, a cow had died due to some fault of the family, three generations would suffer. If women had been dishonoured, five generations would suffer.

Swamiji had told this to mummy, and she to me: the old game of Indian murmurs.

So what was the remedy? Oh, there were several. But bathing in a river, especially on a moonless *Amavasya* night, was most advisable. Giving food and water to the needy would help too. 'You must tie a little bit of ghee mixed with cow dung in a little ball and keep it on your person at all times.'

Rupa Aunty had a Guruji who belonged to an ashram in Brindavan, the town where Lord Krishna spent his childhood years. Her Guruji had passed on five years back, but he'd recommended that she make the yaatra to Gangotri, for that was where Raja Bhagiratha had brought the Ganga down to the Earth to right the wrongs of his ancestors.

The story broadly went thus: When Bhagiratha learned of the awful end of his 60,000 great-uncles thanks to the curse of a Rishi Kapila, he handed over his kingly duties to his minister and went to the Himalayas to do tapasya. He prayed for thousands of years asking God to release the Ganga and free his great-uncles from Kapila's curse and eventually Lord Shiva granted him his wish and the goddess Ganga came down to Earth as a river. This was why the headstream of the river originating at Gangotri is named after him: Bhagirathi.

It was a given that mummy would accompany the Attwals on their yaatra. And if she was going, so was I. If nothing else, I didn't like the idea of my mother journeying deep into the Himalayas on her own. What if she decided to trek up to Gaumukh? She would! What if she then got stuck in a landslide? Besides, I didn't like the idea of her going up alone with Prince. And if both mummy and I were going, so was Mala. Because, apart from her own motivations, this is what my family did: go on yaatras.

But when mummy said, 'You both *must* come. It's important,' I had to say: 'Rupa Aunty obviously wants to see results. Charu and Prince have been married for three years, and there's no baby. She wants to lift her karmic debt or whatever. But why must *I* go?'

'Because,' mummy said, 'there is pitra dosh in your chart also.'

Rishikesh. May 2007

Swami Shraddhanandji had moved out of Shivsagar Ashram a year earlier. He now lived across the Ganga in a quieter part of Rishikesh, in a little cottage, with only a sole helper to look after his needs. There had been a falling out over the running of Shivsagar Ashram, and the resident sanyaasis had split into two opposing camps. While one group was loyal to Swami Vairagya Teerath, or Maharajji, the other was faithful to the present ashram *mandaleshwar* (or head), a Swami Atmanandji.

As we, mummy, Mala and I, made our way over the Lakshman Jhula, I looked over the side of the bridge. The Ganga here never failed to pull me into its depths. On the one side, the river broadened and greyed as it turned a bend going off towards Haridwar and the wide flat plains beyond, while on the other side, the side of the Himalayan foothills, it narrowed and elongated, streaming greens of lime and grass and rumination.

A boy of about five was wailing uncontrollably. 'Bad monkey!' his mother said, pointing to the bridge's rails where a horde of macaques was scuttling away. One monkey grabbed a suspension cable, and just when I thought it would fall into the river it jumped back on the bridge and skipped off, Frooti in hand. 'Look, Hanumanji has taken it. So why cry?' the boy's father said, and the boy looked perplexed, then wonderstruck, but then started bawling again, full-throttle.

Through a haze of marijuana smoke, which mummy didn't notice, we passed a row of cafes full with foreign tourists. There was Little Buddha, famous for its Nutella crepes, and Hare Krishna, which had the best veggie burger in town, and a little further came Ananda. It served amazing waffles and lemonana.

Lemonana is a mint lemonade of Middle Eastern origin incidentally, but many Western backpackers had come to associate it with India. *How did I know this?* Simply because as more and more Western cafes had started springing up along the Lakshman Jhula these past few years, the more I'd sneak away to these parts from Shivsagar Ashram for a bite. Even if the food in Rishikesh was customarily vegetarian, eating here somehow always had a touch of the illicit. Plus, of late, I'd begun to find conversations with Western tourists much more stimulating than the predictable talk of ashram devotees.

It was just my luck then that Swami Shraddhanandji had sided himself with the old guard.

'Swamiji believes Shivsagar should preserve traditions,' mummy said. 'Frugality was always our strength. When you commercialize our institutions you ruin them for good.'

Swami Atmanand, however, favoured change. He wanted to admit Western guests into the ashram. He wanted to build a brand new yoga centre in the space where Maharajji's room stood and was still visited by his old devotees.

'All this Mandaleshwar cares about is money. He wants to charge Rs 1,000 a room for a night, like a hotel. His open-mindedness is just *bakwaas*, totally self-serving.'

Despite her objections, my mother was, after all, a lawyer and so she'd struck up a compromise: out of loyalty, we would stay only at Shivsagar Ashram. But for advice she would turn to Swami Shraddhanandji and nobody else.

We got to a dirt track on the hillside and with the town's car-honking a distant cry, the deep natural quiet of the Himalayan foothills engulfed me. Amid the warble of the Ganga, you could hear the rioting of crickets and tweeting of iridescent birds. The trees were darker here, too. They were *jungle-ier*. And nestled in this jungle, like someplace Lord Ram probably took shelter in on his long journey away from his kingdom, lay Swamiji's cottage.

I opened a small rusty gate, walked over a weedy patch of grass, and knocked on his door. It was open a crack, and I could hear him from inside. I pushed it open. The room was dark, with no sign of electricity. But I recognized the old smell: Swamiji's smell. Of yellowing books and incense. Of just-sung shlokas and old cobwebs and fresh ghee. The Rishikesh of my childhood.

Swamiji was sitting on a high bed with his back to the wall, and his attendant, crouched on the floor, was massaging his feet.

'Om, Swamiji,' I said, and he smiled brightly and gestured for us to sit on a mattress on the floor.

Swamiji had aged considerably. His black beard was now a patchy grey, and there were deep stress lines on his forehead. But he still licked his lips as he spoke, and his smile was still warm. Even if Swamiji was a little admonishing, a little judging, he always remained genial and inviting.

Swamiji's attendant turned around. He looked familiar. Mala squeezed my arm and leaned closer, but it had come to me. It was Sehdev Uncle. He seemed suddenly so haggard it came as a shock. It was not just how much his face had gone loose and wrinkly. What struck me was how badly stooped his back had become. Sehdev Uncle looked wretched. He wasn't the sprightly old penguin at all. He now looked rather like a weathered turtle, carrying in his murky eyes a life of hardships and untold secrets.

The old man staggered over and held mummy's hands. 'How have you been?' she asked. Despite herself, she was happy to see him. The last time they spoke, a few months earlier, Sehdev Uncle had told her he was in desperate need of money. After working at MDH, Sehdev Uncle joined his brother's Paharganj grocery shop as an assistant. But the brothers had had a fight, and he'd decided to leave the family house and return to his 'real home, among the sadhus of Rishikesh'. But my mother suspected he had little choice. The brothers had a property dispute and she believed he'd been kicked out. 'His brother could bully him because Sehdev has no wife, no kids; no money or backbone,' she said.

'How long have you been staying here, uncleji?' I asked.

'Some months.' He was still staring stupidly into my mother's eyes.

It was ironic, I thought. Sehdev Uncle *was* actually living the life of a sanyaasi after all and I felt sorry for him. Of course, I didn't know then that thanks to a few tricks of fate and the stupendous commercialization of religion, Sehdev Uncle's fortunes would see a momentous change in the coming years. He would grow to become richer than his three brothers—combined. In 2010, Sehdev Uncle would become the manager of Swamiji's new ashram in Gurgaon. And by 2014, this little ashram would have over a hundred resident sadhus. Sehdev Uncle's brothers would come asking him for loans then. With his buoyancy returned, he would say then that his luck had changed 'Only because of God. Only thanks to Maharajji's blessings and Swamiji's help.' But today, this future was not imaginable.

Swamiji was yelling into the phone. 'Sonipat and Gurgaon? Are they your only options?' I noticed he had the same phone as I did. A Nokia

N95. 'No. What are you saying, you idiot! We can get acres of land over here for that amount.'

Sehdev Uncle dropped mummy's hands, hurried back to Swamiji and opened a ledger and pointed at some detail.

'I'll talk to you later,' Swamiji said and hung up. He stepped off his bed. 'Shashiji, it is so good to see you. I was just telling our manager, what we need is a good lawyer and here you are. God really plays his games.'

Mummy tittered. Swamiji laughed. And Sehdev Uncle gave his old oily smile.

I felt like I needed some fresh air, or a cigarette, and I stepped out of the cottage. In the warm gloam, the Ganga looked even richer, swarming with old fish and older stories. A man dressed like Lord Hanuman walked down the dirt track. His face was painted red and his plastic tail swished vivaciously from side to side. Then he disappeared into the jungle, like a spirit stepping into another dimension.

I could hear Swamiji. 'These are some of the other locations available,' he said. 'Still some time away, but I was just discussing with Sehdev here if you might be interested in becoming a trustee of the ashram? You can take your time to consider this. No rush. But we would be absolutely delighted if you join us. We will name it Vairagya Teerath Gyanpeeth, after Maharajji.' As if mummy needed this clarification.

I didn't need to look inside to know my mother's answer. 'It would be my honour, Swamiji,' she said.

It's no secret that irrationality and religion are close associates. But if you must go down the religious path, if you really, unequivocally must, should you not still draw a line somewhere? If you have to feed the poor to gain good karma then do so by all means. But why must you further spoil those overfed pandits? Consult Swamiji if you feel you should, but must you fund all his whims and excesses?

These thoughts were stewing in my brain, and after a half hour, at the gates of Shivsagar Ashram, they came out like steam from a pressure cooker. 'Swamiji has a pretty cool phone. Did you see? … He keeps talking about our ancient achievements. Why does he use Western gadgets, then?' This was my new tact. Hitting the matter head-on had proved pointless over the years, so I decided to fight unreason *with* unreason.

'Don't tire me now,' mummy said.

'In fact, Maharajji refused even to speak in English. You used to say he considered it an unclean tongue. Used for subjugating millions!' I realized I was sounding rather foolish now. And yet those things had been said to me in all seriousness once, hadn't they?

Mummy was fiddling with the lock to the Lotus Room. She clanked it against the door. 'You know what Sehdev told me just now?' She looked exhausted.

'What?'

'He said your son doesn't listen to you. And whatever else, about this he's right. Sometimes I think I never should have sent you abroad.'

At 2 am that night there was a power cut and the creaking Lotus room fan finally died. I waited for either sleep or the electricity to come, but when neither did, I joined mummy and Rupa Aunty out on the verandah where they lay on charpoys under a hot dark sky.

Rupa Aunty was fanning herself with a folded-up newspaper. 'I still get much better sleep out in the open,' she said dreamily. You could literally smell the grass around and the riot of crickets and the buzz of mosquitos was making my head spin.

'This is how we grew up,' mummy said.

'How romantic,' I said, struggling to unfold my charpoy.

'Oh. You've no idea what Maharajji taught me,' mummy said.

'Yes, what my Guruji taught me. Except for Prince, these youngsters don't appreciate it,' Rupa Aunty said.

Though Rupa Aunty was a patron of an ashram in Brindavan, her conduct at Shivsagar Ashram's evening aarti had been nothing short of exemplary. Not only had she followed mummy's every move down to the tiniest detail, she'd also readily taken on the role of Guru Ma, correcting a Sanskrit pronunciation here, suggesting a prayer there.

I told Mala that Rupa Aunty probably saw mummy as an Italian chef might see an Indian one. It was not her kitchen, but it was a kitchen all the same. After all, cooking is cooking.

'What did your Guruji teach you, aunty?' I said.

Rupa Aunty considered her answer a while. 'One time, I had

horrible pimples on my face,' she said. 'I went to so many doctors. I was in so much pain. Then I decided to tell my Guruji my problem. He said, "Will you do as I say? I will only give you the solution if you agree to do as I say." I said, "The pain is so bad, Guruji, even if you tell me to jump into the Ganga, I will."' She swallowed at length. '"Okay, listen carefully to me," he said. "Leaving aside the first one of the day, take your urine and apply it to your face. Do this for three months, then come to me." I thought this is so difficult. How could I do it? But Guruji had said it, so I had to try. My first week was terrible. I felt like vomiting all the time. Even my husband started to curse me. He said, "You silly woman, you will die like this. I can't stand beside you." He'd walk away from me. But I was determined. I continued. Then after two months I started seeing changes. New pimples stopped appearing, and then the old ones also started to clear. And after four months, my husband said, "You look like a young girl!"'

An extended silence followed and I found that even though I was grinning widely in the darkness, I could not bring myself to laugh. Rupa Aunty's straightforwardness, the way she laid herself bare, was so refreshing and heart-warming that my overwhelming feeling was not disdain but affection. 'Tell me more stories,' I wanted to hug her and say. But for now, enough mosquitos had bitten me, and all this urine talk made me want to pee. So, I picked up my charpoy and went back inside the seething Lotus.

Uttarkashi, meaning Varanasi of the north, is a large town (1,158 metres above sea level) by the banks of the Bhagirathi. We stopped here for lunch at one of Shivsagar Ashram's smaller branches. The dining hall was similar to what I was used to, with the signature uneven sticky floor and the Brahmin food bearers. But the food they ladled out here was rather different. Devoid of any masala it was unbearably bland.

Prince kept asking for more salt, and Rupa Aunty seemed to be putting more chillies than rice into her mouth. At the same time, Charu ate silently, scooping up tiny morsels with her fingers like a bird, while Mala chewed mechanically as if the food was fuel. Only mummy, sitting three spaces away from me, was mashing her dal-rice with the abandon of a labourer at the end of a day of back-breaking work.

I turned to Rupa Aunty. 'How old were you when you met your Guruji, aunty?'

'It was 1970. So, I must have been twenty. He had this glow. Totally reddish. He really was unlike anybody I'd seen before.' She pulled a packet of *makhanas* from her bag and handed it to me. 'Guruji once asked me, "Where were you before this life? Do you remember?" I said, no, and asked him, "Do you know this Guruji?" and he smiled with his eyes. I did not have to speak at all. Before I could answer, he knew everything. And I *knew* that he knew. That was the beauty of our relationship.'

A server came around and dropped a laddoo each into our plates. I took a bite of mine: hard as a rock. I placed it in a corner.

Rupa Aunty was galloping now. 'Guruji had a…how shall I tell you…yes, a mental ultrasound. When he would put his hand on my forehead, there would be this wave rising from inside me. Cooling, peaceful. I felt like I don't belong in this world. I felt like I was in heaven. I—'

'Yes, yes, aunty… Mom, that's enough!' I burst out when I noticed mummy asking for an extra laddoo which she stashed away in her purse. Both Prince and Charu stopped eating and stared at me.

'Will you stop?' mummy snarled. I'd crossed an unspoken line of propriety, and I immediately regretted it. But then my mother was used to me as I was to her, and so she followed up her words with a salve. 'This is prasad.' She lowered her voice. 'Look how you've made yours into shreds.'

'You can have mine if you want,' I said, to which she responded affectionately with: 'As if I'll have anybody's *jootha*.'

This was our way of dealing with our differences, mother and son. So, why the hell did Prince have to butt in with his holier-than-thou 'You should not stop your mother while she's eating; it's a sin'?

It was only the second day of our yaatra and I hated Prince. He was the guy who went down to a road crossing on a moonless night to have evil spirits bashed out of him by a fakir for—it was clear from his mother's retelling—an attack of migraine. He was the kid who dressed up as Lord Krishna at a Krishna Leela play while his mother played the part of Mother Yashoda. And he spoke about his deeds with such a sense of smugness—about not keeping a copy of the Mahabharata at home (for it leads to clashes within the family); about not cutting his hair on Tuesdays (because Mangal, the planet Mars, who rules on Tuesdays lived in your blood, and it is from your blood that your hair grows); about never having jootha (because eating food sullied by another's mouth reduces your brain power)—that it made my blood boil.

Unlike his cousin Shruti, who had at least grown to question things, Prince, I told Mala, was a fool. My sister asked why I was more forgiving of Rupa Aunty's irrationalities, and I said this was because people of her time and background weren't educated. But even as I said this I knew I wasn't being truthful. Mummy was educated and could be the very definition of illogical. Speaking of logic, then, there was little when it came to my dislike for Prince. It was an emotional thing. I can say now I disliked him not so much because of his silly ways, but because mummy seemed to like him precisely for them.

When we got to Gangotri that evening, we retired to our rooms at the Garhwal Mandal Nigam guesthouse—the Attwals in one, and we Kapila-Malhotras in another. But no sooner did a half-hour pass than Rupa Aunty was back in our bed with her bag of makhanas opened up for me along with her heart.

'You know, Shashiji,' she said to mummy, but looking at me, 'my in-laws wanted me to have a son. I had already had an abortion once, and after that, the AIIMS doctor said if I wanted another baby, I would need an operation. He said there was a problem with my tubes. When I told Guruji about this, he said, "Devi, do you want pain? In this path, I see only sadness. You won't be able to bear it. Don't do it."'

'He said no?'

'He said, "If you want, in one second I can change your fate"'—she clapped her hands—'"but there is sadness." But I still had the desire to have a child. That desire just wouldn't go away.

'One day, my sister-in-law asked if I wanted to adopt her son. But Guruji said, "No. Whatever your fate is, it will happen." Then that same boy died in a motorcycle accident when he was just twenty. And when this happened, I understood that Guruji was actually saving me from a horrible fate.'

'No parent should see their child go before them,' mummy said sympathetically. 'And you're right, behenji, whenever I disobeyed Maharajji, there was pain. Otherwise, he knew everything straight.'

'Yes, Guruji was like a laser.' Rupa Aunty took a long swallow. 'Then, when I was twenty-five, one day, early in the morning, my husband came out of the bathroom and said he had just vomited. He couldn't stand. I called the doctor, but by the time he arrived, he had gone. He had a heart attack.'

An awkward silence followed for a minute after which mummy cut in with an optimistic tone.

'I will tell a story now,' she said. 'I used to be a naughty girl in my teens, and once I thought I'd made a big mistake somewhere. So, to apologize to God, I stayed up late into the night in our temple in Shivsagar Ashram. The next morning, when I went to bathe in Ganga, where in front of me I would usually see the sun rising above the hills, I saw something peculiar. I'd been bathing in this spot for years, but that day I saw a brilliant image of Ganeshji. A beautiful statue. It was as though God was there himself. My friend Susheel was also with me, and I turned to her. I splashed water on my face. But when I looked up, Ganeshji was still there! I asked her, can you see something across the river? She said she couldn't.' Mummy's eyes shone. 'I started to laugh and tears came into my eyes. I said, "See, Ganapati! Can't you see?" But she looked at me like I was mad.

'I went to my Maharajji. I said, "I saw a beautiful statue of Ganapati across the Ganga this morning." I was so happy. I said, "I've never seen anything like this before." He was reading, and he didn't look up. Then after a minute he stared at me with his full intensity. I thought he'd say, how wonderful, that he would be happy for me. But he said, "There must have been some shortfall in your prayers, devi. Had you prayed sincerely from your heart, Ganeshji would have come down to you Himself. Have you wondered why he sent only a statue in his place?"'

'*Hai Bhagwaan!*' Rupa Aunty cried. It was a cry of longing braided with some weird, impenetrable joy.

What had happened to Rupa Aunty in the past exactly? So, she had a previous husband? So, Prince was her son from her new husband?

Mummy shrugged off my questions. But she did say that, like Prince's father, Rupa Aunty also once belonged to a well-to-do family. And like him, they, too, lost everything in the Partition. When their family moved to Jalandhar from Lahore, her father opened a garments shop with what little money they had. But the man had no head for business and soon ran into losses. It was left to Rupa, the eldest of three daughters, still in her teens, to keep the family afloat and she did what she knew best: making pickles. Mango, jackfruit, garlic, ginger, chilli, *dela*. She made them all.

'It was Rupa who put her sisters through university, and in the end they all married well. One even lives in Toronto. The fact is, she lost out. She didn't study further than school. It was her marriage prospects that suffered.'

At 6:15 am the next day, it was time for a dip in the Ganga. At Gangotri, a mere eighteen kilometres downstream from Gaumukh, the river is like liquid ice and you can't stay in the water for long. Just a quick dip and out, that's the way to go, I thought.

But the *ghats* were swarming. Men with their turbans, *dhotis* and trousers kept to a side, clad chiefly in underwears and vests; the women still in their sarees, petticoats and salwar-kameezes (although many rural women felt no shame in exposing their bare chests); and children wearing whatever took their fancy were all swishing in and out of the water. Merrily, methodically. With thumb and forefinger clasping the nose shut, everyone was immersing themselves in the Ganga. Then again, and again.

I knew the routine well. But when you're expected to bathe in sub-zero temperatures, life plays out in *slow* motion. So, like Rupa Aunty, all I could muster the strength for was a face splash and a head sprinkle.

Charu and I stood diffidently at the top of the ghat's steps while the others were knee deep in the water, readying to immerse themselves. Prince waded to us, splashing water jauntily like he was Akshay Kumar. Then he took Charu by her hand and led her, step by step, deeper and deeper, into the Ganga.

The couple offered Gangajal to the sun, dropping the water down in a thin stream from a namaste high above their heads, after which they drank in several palmfuls of the river. Mummy brought a coconut out of a plastic bag. She made a circle around their heads with it three times, her eyes blinking fervently. Then she came to where I was standing—vermilion, diyas, flowers lapping at my ankles—and cracked it open with a squelch. 'Come, come.' The bag caught a current and sped off downstream.

'How cold is the water, Mala?' I yelled. But my sister couldn't hear me.

'C-cold. Come, na,' Charu said, her teeth clattering.

Holding Charu by the hand, Prince was going 'One-Two-Three,' preparing to go under for the fifth time. Charu stole a sideways glance at me. A barely perceptible smirk, a glint of mischief, through which she said: *What can I do? He's like that.* Yes, we shared a moment, she and I, like two daydreamers meeting eyes in a class upright with attention. But then the moment passed and Prince gripped Charu's hand, and the couple submerged their heads in the Ganga.

The Cow's Mouth

After paying our respects at the Gangotri temple early in the morning, the lot of us (save for Rupa Aunty who stayed back because, she said, 'These knees have done their life's exercise') were trekking up to Gaumukh glacier under the cover of thick pines. Our guide, a lean Nepali chap named Yashpal, had the agility of a sportsman, but the deep wrinkles at the corners of his eyes made him appear much older than his thirty years. It was only when he started talking that his naughty side came through.

'What's his name?' I asked of his pony.

'He is my Babu,' he said. 'He is my son.' After which he proceeded to bear poor Babu down with all our bags.

'How's life up here?' I asked him later.

'Way better than your Delhi,' he said. I liked him.

Within half an hour, the shaded track opened into a thin strip along the mountainside under the sun's glare. The foliage was a deep green to my left while in the valley to my right the Ganga was more alive than ever. The river was churning and moaning, jumping and circling, crashing against rocks and stilling my mind like some angry avatar of the goddess she here really was.

'One misstep and Ganga Ma will swallow you up!' Yashpal warned, so we listened and walked in a single file. I was in the front.

At one point, I stopped to admire a little whirlpool that appeared and then disappeared like a dream and Prince overtook me. We eventually came to a spot where loose stones were held together by a fragile wire net. Yashpal crossed over it in two swift steps, then hopped back to lead each of us across by hand. Prince rejected his offer and crossed over alone, and I did the same. Well, I almost did. Because I slipped and froze bang in the middle of the wobbly spot. Yashpal gave me a mortified look and I willed my legs to carry me over.

At Cheerwasa, a tiny encampment near the halfway point, we got to a little chai shop where Mala collapsed on a long wooden bench, dramatically throwing her arms away from her body as if she were dead.

Apart from the chaiwaala, a white trekker was the only person present. The man had on trekking shoes, sunglasses and a knapsack. He had very white skin and that long unkempt orange beard one associates with European mountaineers. He nodded us a hello.

Mummy pulled Mala to herself. She placed a hand on her forehead and asked Yashpal to hand her her bag. Then she stuck a thermometer under my sister's tongue. Mala had a fever of 100 degrees F. Mummy rummaged through her bag again and pulled out four little glass bottles from its outer pocket. She held each one against the sunlight, narrowing her eyes to read the labels.

'Open the hatch,' she said and dropped four pills of Gelsemium sempervirens under Mala's tongue.

Predicated on two revolutionary principles: (1) the notion that a disease can be cured by a substance that produces similar symptoms in healthy people, and (2) the notion that the lower the dose of the medication, the greater its effectiveness, homeopathy is a system of medicine that was developed in Germany two hundred years ago. According to broad scientific consensus today, however, it is pseudoscience. But its popularity in our country is so immense that I sometimes wondered if its association with the 'rational West' had ended at birth itself.

Mala and I had grown up on the stuff. At home, a large cabinet stocked with homeopathic pills and potions was always kept under lock and key, away from the hands of an imaginary fevered kleptomaniac. When we were little, mummy used to look up a book, *Materia Medica* by William Boericke (which now sits on the bookshelf between *The Origin of Modern Pranic Healing and Arhatic Yoga* by Master Choa Kok Sui and *Kundalini Tantra* by Swami Satyanand Saraswati), and decide which medicine to give us—Nux vomica for high fever, Bryonia for a cough, Aconite for a headache. But by now, she believed she understood the combinations and dosages instinctively. Homeopathy was not just a system of medicine, she'd say. Administering it was an art, and as with pooja, you had to understand what specific remedy the moment called for. Instinctively on my part, I now rejected my mother's doctorly advances. Rhus tox and Aconite had done nothing to cure my asthma, whereas my Asthalin inhaler always worked like a charm.

'Please just give this Dr Chatterjee a chance,' she said one day.

He was meant to be the best, so I reluctantly agreed. I described my symptoms to him.

'Any disease can generally be traced to some deep-seated underlying issue. So, it's important I ask you some questions,' the doctor said. He looked up. 'Personal questions.'

'Okay.'

'Have you had any love troubles recently? Any heartbreak?'

I've never taken homeopathy seriously since that day. Even if the sugar pills are still soothing.

Prince stepped forward with a plastic bottle. 'Aunty, try this also.' The bottle had familiar Hindi lettering on it. Yes: *Triphala*. Deceptively named 'three-fruits', the mix was a bitter-as-hell Ayurvedic powder. It had done nothing to cure my asthma either. I considered intervening, but decided against it.

'Open the hatch.' Mummy opened her own mouth as she now placed a heaped spoon of triphala on top of (not under) Mala's tongue.

My sister gave a start and spat the glob onto the floor, her eyes suddenly wet. 'Give me some water!' she said, and the white trekker in the corner started to laugh.

'You know you children really make me nervous.' Mummy was going through her purse for the third time when she abruptly stopped and looked at me wide-eyed. 'I'm so silly.' She put her hand to her forehead. 'I should've waited. Now the Gelsemium is all neutralized.'

That was when the white trekker came up. 'This might be what you want.' He handed mummy a strip of pills. 'It's Paracetamol.'

'Oh, thank you. I was just going to…' mummy said, her eyes now squinting in gratitude.

'I was watching you and thought, what is this lady doing?'

'Oh, no,' mummy said and launched into a brief discourse on the wonders of homeopathy. How it worked like magic. How it was a German medicine. But Greg, who was Austrian, seemed unimpressed and skilfully steered the conversation to himself and his travels.

This was his third trek in Uttarakhand, he said. He had trekked all over the world, from the Alps to the Andes, but trekking in the Himalayas was what he enjoyed most. 'Because the snowline is much higher here than in Europe. When you get so high in the mountains, nature seems wilder. The snow is pure white in the Alps. But here, it is mostly covered in mud. You've to go very high to see the purity of snow.'

'Oh yes, these mountains are pure. Raw. Wild,' mummy said absently as she checked Mala's temperature for the third time, and Greg slurped his chai noisily as if he was really enjoying partaking in this wildness they were speaking of.

'You know the difference between the mountains in China and India?' he said. 'In China, the food is amazing, but the people are disgusting. But in India, you people are amazing, but the food is all f—ing Maggi noodles.' He guffawed at his joke and lit up a beedi.

Mala opened an eye, and she and I exchanged a look. Did this man just use the F-word?

Just then Prince exclaimed, '*Arre baap re!*' and we turned in his direction.

Perhaps two hundred meters away, three men, one at the front, two at the back, were carrying something of a stretcher downhill. The thing was fashioned out of a couple of bedsheets, and it drooped like a ragged hammock. As the trio neared us, one person's extended whine grew to a wheezing cry. The man in the front, I saw now, was just a boy, probably no older than sixteen, and he was wailing like a wounded animal. In the sheet-hammock lay a lifeless man. His head was wrapped in a white cloth, stained mud-brown at the forehead. His lips were open just a hair. *Was he dead?*

'*Har Har Gange!*' the men said, slogging on.

'*Har Har Gange!*' Prince said softly.

'*Har Har Gange!*' we repeated.

Greg turned to mummy, who was now fussing over Mala with a renewed vigour. 'Poor bastard…he won't make it,' he said.

His manner was frank and inoffensive, but something in me was appalled. So, when out of nowhere, Prince said, 'Please don't say bad words here. This is a pure place,' I found that, for once, I agreed with him.

'Sir, you know why we worship the Ganga?'

'It is a holy river. I know.'

'She is not just holy. She is a goddess. Do you know her story?'

Greg was cornered, and Prince was determined to teach this *firangi* a lesson. So, mixing Hindi freely with English, he started with Ma Ganga's story:

Bhagiratha, a great devotee of Shiva, brought the Ganga down from the heavens after a deep tapasya asking God to right the wrongs of his ancestors. And after a long, long time, Vishnu answered his prayers. Only the pure waters of the Ganga could help him, He said. But he would have to pray to Shiva to bring the Ganga down to Earth.

'However,' mummy said, 'the Ganga came down with such force that there were fears she'd wipe the Earth out. So, Bhagiratha then implored Lord Shiva as only he could absorb such an onslaught. And so Lord Shiva took the entire brunt of Ma Ganga on his head and she got lost in his matted locks. Bhagiratha then asked Lord Shiva to release the Ganga in a measured form and this is how we see her now.'

Prince broke into an ode to the river:

jata joot shivji sar sohae, ho gayi jai jai kaari
shri mata gange, main tere charan kamal balhaari

Mummy translated: 'It means, from the matted hair of Lord Shiva the Ganga came down. Glory to her, victory to her. Oh, Dear Ganga, we bow to your lotus feet.'

'How far back did you say this happened?' Greg said.

'5,500 years,' Prince said.

'No, no, Bhagiratha *prayed* for 5,500 years.' Mummy clicked her tongue. 'But the Ganga came down long before. Don't go by these Western measurements of time.'

Greg laughed, took one last pull on his beedi and put it out under his boots.

The way between Cheerwasa and Bhojwasa (3,775 metres) was a thin thread with unforeseen knots and curves stitched into the mountainside. The pine trees were far below us now, with only a line of green visible if I turned around to look back. Across the valley, little rocks rose from the base to become sky-kissing crests; and as Yashpal started naming them—the white dome at two o'clock was Mt Shivling, and far ahead, beyond that curve, was Mt Bhagirath—I imagined them as dollops of ice-cream. *Chocolate, hazelnut, butterscotch, their tops dipped in cream.* Now a mountain with a gash and at its base lay a heap of rubble. Now a rock on which was written in Hindi: 'Baba Shivgiri lives in Tapovan.'

I'd heard Tapovan (4,463 metres), a lush grassland at the foot of Mt Shivling, was the seasonal home to sadhus who lived in caves and huts. 'What do those babas eat up there?' I asked Yashpal.

'*Jadibooti*,' he said. 'For months, they eat only these shrubs.'

'Have you met any?'

'Some.'

It turned two, then three, and the sky darkened. I felt a drop, then a drizzle.

I was tired, and bored. I yelled at the top of my lungs, '*Har Har Gange!*' And from somewhere above, an inert rock sprang to life. It began a slow descent. Then gaining momentum it bounced on our track ahead of Prince, sped downhill and disappeared into the lathering Ganga.

Yashpal was shaking me by the shoulders. 'You mad boy! You must respect these mountains. Even the slightest sound can make these rocks come crashing down. Always remember, the Himalayas can turn at any time from devtas to Yamraj. From God to your Death.'

I turned to Mala. She'd come this last stretch bestride Babu, the pony. She had her head on the animal's neck. 'Are you sleeping? Are you crazy?' I said, and Mala mouthed some incoherent reply and fell back on her mystical pillow.

By the time we reached Bhojwasa, the base camp for the trek to Gaumukh glacier, it was past 4 pm. The place was nothing but a rocky riverbed with a handful of structures—a one-storey building stood here, a few red tents billowed in the wind there—in the wilderness. Bhojwasa looked, I thought, like the first camp humans might set up on a newly discovered planet in some remote galaxy. Or someplace out of the Treta Yuga.

Still, there was the usual state-run Garhwal Mandal Vikas Nigam guesthouse. And it was miraculously operational. In a large dormitory a dozen beds were lined up alongside a wall while an equal number lay on the opposite side. I collapsed onto a bed in one corner and mummy tucked Mala into a blanket beside me and slipped her another dose of Gelsemium.

My last memory of that evening is two sadhus sitting on the bed opposite, drinking chai. They smiled at mummy, and she smiled back. And then, I fell into a deep sleep.

I awoke in the middle of the night to fierce whistling and rattling noises. Gales were whipping against the thin window above my bed and I feared the glass would break. I looked at my phone. 4 am.

And then I saw a *ghost.*

Somebody was standing over Mala, its hands trembling, its body shuddering. I switched on my phone's torch. It was mummy, in her Pranic Healing mode.

Quivering frantically, mummy sashayed down from Mala's head to the pit of her stomach. Once, twice, a third time. Then she balled her hands into fists and hurried towards the window above me and released towards the Ganga all her daughter's ailments, all her toxicities, all her fevers, all her infections. All the warmth from my chest!

Coughing, I took a puff of Asthalin. 'Please close it. I'm dying here.'

'Oh, sorry,' she said, giggling and returned to bed.

But after twenty minutes, she was up again. She stuck the thermometer into Mala's mouth and waited, her eyes blinking in the darkness. Her gaze moving from her daughter to the Ganga coursing outside. She took the thermometer out. 'She's fine,' she said.

When I got up, it was 6 am. Prince and mummy were both absent, and Charu was sitting on her bed drinking chai with her windcheater and sneakers on.

'They'll just be back,' she said. 'They've gone to the Ganga.'

I ran to the bathroom, brushed my teeth, and threw on my shoes and jacket. Mummy came through the door. She had four empty plastic bottles with her.

'Oh, you're awake? Good. I need you to fill these up. Do it right at Gaumukh. Two are for Minna Masi and Rashmi Masi. Don't forget.'

I stared at her. 'What? You're not coming?'

Mummy eyed Mala who was snoring gently. 'No.'

'Don't be silly. It's only a few hours,' I said. 'Come! She'll sleep right through. You can't miss Gaumukh. It's the most important yaatra.'

The two sadhus from the previous night were watching us from the door. Their boots, obviously hand-me-downs, were torn, and their scraggly beards needed a thorough washing. But then I met their eyes. They were morning-fresh and trenchant and peering straight at my mother's.

Prince strode into the room. 'Mataji,' he said to mummy. 'If you want Gangajal from the source, I will bring you as much as you want. But you stay with Mala.' And he relieved the bottles from her hands.

Mummy looked from the sadhus to Prince, to Mala, and back to Prince again. She rearranged her vacillating features into an expression approaching certainty. 'You're right, beta,' she said. 'If this is what Ma Ganga chooses, it's what she chooses. But don't forget my Gangajal. I need it straight from the cow's mouth.'

'You don't worry, mataji,' Prince said and touched mummy's feet.

Early in the morning, the Himalayas rule over even the sun. It is almost as if the mountains are saying to Him, 'Yes, your moment to shine will come. But later. So let us protect you like the towering parents we are, because after 9 am, only you will bring us glory.'

Through the boulder-strewn shadowy valley, we—Yashpal, Prince, Charu and I—began our trek from Bhojwasa to Gaumukh glacier. At this height, the way was just scree, and how the earth zigzagged, then dropped down and curved up, before plummeting freely again, left me breathless in no time. To my right, the top of Mt Shivling burned yellow even as the rest of it lay wreathed in darkness, while Mt Bhagirath, straight up ahead, was growing steadily brighter as if emerging from a boundless eclipse.

I imagined I was on the back of a dragon. But then I felt a tinge of disloyalty at this outside thought and willed my mind to picture myself on the back of Garuda, ascending to Heaven.

Charu stumbled on a rock and grabbed hold of my arm. We stopped for a drink of water, and I took a puff of Asthalin. My throat was cold and dry but also hot and burning from the exertion. 'Can we rest a minute?' I called out to Yashpal.

'*Challo*, just a little more,' he shouted back. Both Prince and he were pushing on unimpeded.

So, panting madly and using up the last reserves of my inspiration, I went on. At this last bend, the Ganga seemed much different from her avatar even down at Bhojwasa. Frothing and seething, the river was a wild grey python. With chunks of ice speeding by on her surface, she was a rope of water in a mammoth tug of war. One berg crashed against a rock, splintering into a thousand pieces such that even the rock looked afraid. The Ganga was livid. And yet she was also handsomely calm. An arrogant calmness of a queen in her palace, as it were. The calmness one has on their turf, their terms.

And then it was before me: a wall of ice as high as a building of four storeys. Gaumukh glacier was not white but a murky brown. And from its depths, out of something like a cave—Did it look like a cow's mouth? *Maybe*—emerged the Ganga.

Greg was by the water's edge taking pictures with his long-lensed camera. He was right, I thought. Gaumukh was nothing like those pristine white glaciers you saw on the National Geographic channel. Gaumukh was grimy. And maybe you had to look past the grime to see her beauty?

The two sadhus from our dormitory were by the edge, too. One man had untied his hair and his tangled locks fell to his waist. He picked out a brass *lota* from his satchel and plunged it into the river, filling it to the brim. Then he chucked the towel around his waist to reveal an orange cloth tied around his crotch. Pubic hairs crawled out of his groin like insect antennae. Charu grimaced, looked away.

'*Har Har Gange!*' the baba said, pouring the icy Ganga over his head. And Greg clicked away.

Charu and I joined Prince at the point nearest to the glacier and I offered Gangajal to the rising sun. After scanning for sediment, I drank glacier-fresh Gangajal from the cup of my hand. I recited the *Gayatri Mantra*.

Then I was done. Then I was jumping back across the rocks toward the two babas.

'Wait!' Charu called out as she clambered over to join me. And Prince stopped his prayers and let out a grunt.

'How do you tolerate this cold, babaji?' I asked one baba, sounding more naive than intended. Having towelled himself dry, the man was fretting with his hair now.

'When you live here for so long, you start having a different relationship with two things,' he said, shivering. 'One is God. The other, the cold.' He bent down and splashed water on his face again for good measure. 'We live in Uttarkashi. But there are babas in these mountains who can withstand cold like nobody you can imagine.'

As we turned around, Charu said in my ear, 'It's just practice, Sid. What a stupid question. If you ask me, these babas are all fakes.'

Gaumukh glacier didn't look so much a point of origin as a medium that the river passed through, so copious was its discharge, so powerful the water's rush. That Gaumukh was a potent gateway was plentifully clear. But how could the birth of something so splendid, so ever-changing and nourishing be so…*ordinary*? No, it wasn't just ordinary. It was messy. Dirty, even. It was a muddy, rocky, cluttered mess of a wonder. *Like a mother giving birth?*

I heard an unexpected voice: *Can you not see where you are? Do you even realize what you're seeing, you fool? Do you know how many would die to see this?* And then: *Did you not see that somebody just died to see this?*

Charu gave me a quizzical look as I rubbed my eyes. 'Nothing,' I said.

Then the sun came up from behind Mt Bhagirath, and the dark shadows around us lifted. For an instant the sky was such that Gaumukh turned a scintillating snow white.

Greg now clicked a bunch of pictures in rapid succession. First stooping, then standing, then hunkering down, eternally locking this moment. It was a time when my dream turned real and graspable. But then a cloud came and the gloss vaporized. My trance dissipated as quickly as it had come.

Why did I see only two extremes of people at the birth place of our most sacred river? The outsiders who cared only for mud-brown snapshots and the devout who seemed not to question anything. And to which camp did I belong? Was I moved? I was, indeed. No matter how rational I thought myself, like Kedarnath, Gaumukh had stirred in me something intense, something preternatural. Gaumukh was a place where the cold facts of Logic collided with the icy wall of Faith and shattered into thousands of pieces. Was this what holy men meant when they said certain places could trigger an inner awakening?

Equally, I now wonder: Had I been free of all guiding pressures would I have been so moved by what I saw? For I also remember cheekily thinking: 'This glacier is just rock, ice, snow, mud. It does look like the mouth of a cow… But perhaps one sick from eating plastic.'

Back in Bhojwasa, I thought mummy would be depressed but I couldn't have been more wrong. Her eyes were shiny, and she was skipping around the dormitory. Her hair was shiny too. *Was it damp?*

'I just had the most amazing bath of my life,' she said as she saw me. 'Come with me. I've to make you meet somebody.'

'You took a dip here?'

'Don't be silly. I very carefully poured water over myself three times. Then I wiped myself fast.' She simulated her bathing actions with an imaginary lota and a big smile. 'You're forgetting. It's not my first time here. Now come with me.'

So, back out we all went, this time with Mala included, and tripping over rocks and boulders, we reached a large wooden shed by the Ganga. The building looked shaky. About a hundred metres away, bright red tents swelled and deflated in the wind. An old baba in white robes was standing at the entrance. He had coarse skin, bushy eyebrows and red veins webbing the whites of his eyes. His long, silver, flowing beard went regally with the rest of him to give him the appearance of an old shaman.

'Sid, touch Babaji's feet,' mummy said breathlessly, and as I did, the man's spell broke. His feet were cracked around the heels, and his blackened toenails curved inwards.

'This is Lal Bihari Baba. When I came here last in '76, he was here.'

As Lal Bihari Baba placed a grandfatherly hand over my bowed head, I saw another man sitting on the floor further inside the shed. He had a neatly trimmed moustache and looked to be in his forties. He stepped forward to shake my hand. His handshake bespoke officialdom.

'Your mother and I were just having a great conversation with babaji,' he said in English. 'I'm Rajeev. I work for the Indian Meteorological Department.'

'Rajeev here is gathering data on the Gaumukh glacier,' mummy said. 'His team is camping in those tents there. He says the Ganga is drying up so fast that by the time you're my age, it might even be gone.'

Rajeev laughed. 'Well, not that soon, Shashiji. But yes, we should be very concerned about our ecology. The glacier's rate of recession is a matter of concern for everybody.' He looked mock-gravely at Mala and me. 'Especially our younger generation.'

'Babaji, do you find that the weather has changed?' mummy asked Lal Bihari Baba. 'I think it was colder when I came here thirty years back.'

'Maybe it's even colder now that I'm older,' Babaji said, laughing.

A helper from our dormitory came through the door bearing a tray with a thermos of tea and steel tumblers. When he came to me I declined, and Lal Bihari Baba chided me affectionately. 'Leave your fussiness down in the plains,' he said. 'Up here, you have to drink to keep warm.'

I used this opening to say, 'Babaji, do you live here throughout the year?'

'In the summer, yes. In winter, I go down to Gangotri,' he said. 'But this is my home.'

'How do you manage here?'

'With Ma Ganga, one always manages.' Lal Bihari Baba laughed again. Then he sobered his voice. 'This is *tapo bhoomi*. The land of penance.'

'Babaji, please tell my son why we worship the Ganga,' mummy said. 'Why she is a living goddess. He thinks I'm foolish and keeps doubting me.' I had the brief urge to shake my mother, but Lal Bihari Baba slapped me gently on the back.

'Is that so, son?' He laughed. 'See, it is like this,' he said. 'If you do a pooja at home, it's a good thing, but if you do the same pooja in a cow shelter, you get ten times the fruits because you are rewarding somebody who has blessed you with so much. If you do this pooja by a river, any river, the reward is ten times that. Because a river is a giver of life. And if you do the pooja by a *pure* river, particularly at its source, you will get ten times that. If you pray in a temple in the Himalayas, you get ten times that. And if you pray in a Char Dham temple, the reward is endless—the fruits are so great.' He drew in a breath, chuckled. 'And where are you now? You are at Gangotri Ma's temple at the source of the purest river of all!'

I should say I was impressed by the baba's incremental-benefit line of logic even though it didn't strike me as new. I turned to Rajeev.

'What Babaji means is that water is an energy source,' the meteorologist said. 'It is rivers that lead to life and civilization, yes? So, in this sense, a river is a representation of God. No?'

I must have appeared dubious because Rajeev went on. 'There are five elements—earth, water, air, fire, ether. You accept this? Aren't they all manifestations of God? If you look deeply, you will see that spirituality asks the same questions as us scientists.' He gave a short laugh.

'This mythology is fascinating, sir,' I said. 'But is it true that the glacier was once down at Gangotri?'

'Definitely. And Bhagiratha's reference to the Shivling peak, moraine ridges and the waterfall at Gangotri also clearly tells us that at the time of his visit, the snout of the Gaumukh must have been around Gangotri.'

The shed was making frenzied howling sounds, and the tents outside had swollen up to the point of bursting.

'Look, everything has a context,' he said. 'The Gangotri glacier system has a glacierized area of some three hundred square kilometres. And the Gaumukh glacier itself is about thirty kilometres long. We also know this area was more glaciated before than it is now... In fact, in the *Skanda Purana*, Bhagiratha said, "*Then came down from the sky, Ganga the daughter of the snowy Himalayas, and Mahadev received the Ganga on his own head.*"' He paused, took a sip of tea. 'Bhagiratha's description of this place is so accurate that it can't be dismissed.'

I clung to my tumbler for warmth. 'How fast is the glacier receding?'

'Given that Gaumukh was at Gangotri about 5,500 years back, we can guess it has retreated a distance of around forty to forty-five kilometres in about 10,000 years. This glacier is going to end one day, and here we can look again to Bhagiratha. He said, "Ganga one day shall be recalled to the heavens." This means that Bhagiratha knew thousands of years ago that this glacier would retreat. So, if we assume that it will continue to retreat at this present rate of fifteen metres a year, even then it will take almost 1,500 to 2,000 years for it to go away.'

Outside, I heard a chunk of ice smash against a rock.

'I met you before in 1976, Babaji.'

'Yes, so many groups have come over the years.'

'There was nothing here back then. Just your hut. I think it was much bigger in those days. We were three girls and maybe fifteen boys.' Mummy was warming up for a big story, and Rajeev, Prince, Charu and Mala were all riveted.

'I had come with my IAS group of trainees back then…' My mother had visited Gaumukh as part of the Bharat Darshan tour young government officers went on to get familiarized with different parts of the country. 'The previous year, there had been a huge landslide here. And at that time, only Babaji lived here with the barest essentials. When we landed up, I remember he was so furious at us. He said, "You people disrespect our tapo bhoomi. Why do you come here?"

'I, of course, had my Rishikeshy background, but the others couldn't care less. These youngsters were full of contempt for faith, and some had even brought meat and liquor with them.' She paused. 'Yes, tinned tuna meat,' she said with a relish that made even Rajeev chuckle.

'At the time, there was only Babaji's shed here, and you had to sleep on mattresses on the floor. But he'—Lal Bihari Baba was listening closely—'was so angry with us. He said, "You stay wherever you want, but I won't let you in. You *Englishwaale*, you misbehave in our country. You throw meat into the Ganga and this is what causes accidents. Over here, we pray to the Ganga night and day, and in one second you spit at it. You pollute it. Go away."

'That was the first time I saw these oversmart boys cower and turn to us girls for help. We three girls came to Babaji and begged him to let us stay with him. I mean, there was nowhere else to go. And he said, "You three, Ganga, Jamuna, Saraswati, you can go inside." And he fed us such good food.' Lal Bihari Baba looked positively delighted. 'It was simple watery dal and rice, but it was so delicious. Then when he saw we were full he said gently, "Now, devis, go call the boys in."'

Mummy switched to English. 'The next morning, I stepped outside the shed while the others were sleeping. It was a bitterly cold morning, and I saw that Babaji was taking a bath. He did it very neatly. In that freezing state, he was in just a *langoti*. There was a huge drum filled with water, and from the top, icicles drooped down to the ground. I saw him pour water over his head, once, twice, thrice, all the time saying, *Har Har Gange!*'

Mummy mimed Lal Bihari Baba's bathing actions as she'd done her own earlier. 'He looked so happy.' She giggled. 'I ran inside before he could see me.'

By the time we got to Gangotri the next evening my legs were noodles so I was more than glad Rupa Aunty offered to knead them back into shape. I refused her offers of massage, obviously. But when she insisted, I didn't resist, and before I knew it she'd uncapped a bottle of almond oil and had begun pressing into my soles.

Rupa Aunty's presence was so warm and maternal that once again I did what felt like a natural thing in the circumstances. I asked her to tell me more of her story.

'... You said your husband had died, aunty. Then?'

'Then what?' she said. 'I got married to Prince's papa. What else?'

Mummy popped her head through the door. 'What are you making aunty do? And that too after yaatra. You should be the one pressing her feet.'

I shushed my mother and bolted the door and Rupa Aunty began talking. 'Our Guruji used to have a *pravachan* for us unmarried girls every Sunday morning. He would tell us girls about life, about marriage, about how to be a good wife and mother. You understand, na?' She pulled her hands away.

I nodded.

'Sometimes, after his sermon, Guruji would go around and drop an almond or sweet into the hands of a girl or two who were gathered there. The girls who received almonds always had a boy and the girls who received sweets had a girl. It was always like this. Always. Once, I even took Ritu with me and Guruji put a *mishri* in her hands and within a year she had Shruti.'

Rupa Aunty saw a smile begin to form on my face and she slapped my leg. 'Really! I am not lying.' She smiled. 'Anyway, like I told you, by this time I was a widow and I'd gone back to live in my father's house and he just wanted me out. He wanted me to remarry and I was also desperate to leave. I would have gone at the first opportunity I got.'

Rupa Aunty allowed some silent moments to pass. 'It was a year since my husband's death, and I had gone for Guruji's pravachan one morning. He came to me after he was finished. I was sitting on the floor and he looked into my eyes from above for a long time. Then he dropped an almond into my hands. I kept staring at him. I still remember, I kept staring. And without realizing it tears started rolling down my cheeks. My Guruji knew everything about me. He knew about my abortion; my husband's death. He knew how much I wanted children. He knew everything. So what was he saying? He'd himself told me earlier not to do the operation.'

Her eyes moistened. 'I felt very angry. But then I thought, if Guruji is saying this then there must be a reason. So, I silently ate my almond and went home.' She capped the bottle of almond oil and motioned Prince through the window to wait a moment.

'One month later my father said a match had come for me. I was so relieved. I would've married anybody.'

At 6:30 the next morning we were ready for the final darshan of Ma Gangotri.

School summer holidays were on and there was a heavy rush of yaatris in town. The ashrams and guesthouses were so full that some had had to spend the night in their vehicles. Amid farmers and engineers, roadside vendors and big businessmen, housewives like Rupa Aunty and lawyers like my mother, we were stuck in a scrum outside the temple. It seemed as if all of India had arrived to do a pooja of the Ganga that morning. But here too, as in the rest of the country, the proportion of people of each group varied widely.

I've come to realize that like our trains, our temples too are a microcosm of India, and we, the *elite*, through contacts or money, always manage a space in the First Class. And it was this privileged position Prince and mummy were negotiating for with the priests up ahead as I stood behind in the crowd with Mala, Rupa Aunty and Charu.

A pandit came up. 'What is your *gotra*?'

'Kaushal Gotra,' I said. 'We're from—'

'Pakistan,' Mala filled in. She was bored and tired and looking to amuse herself.

'From Lahore?' the pandit said. 'We have pandits who look after families from all over Punjab.'

Rupa Aunty suddenly grabbed Mala's arm. 'Don't take those filthy *Musalmans'* name here, Mala,' she said. Sweet Rupa Aunty had such severity in her eyes that even the pandit backed away sniggering to himself.

Flustered, she then held my arm and pulled me to one side. '*Challo, mandir ki parikrama lete hain...* let's circumambulate the temple.' She began elbowing her way through the mass of worshippers. The temple courtyard was packed and I didn't want to lose our spot in the line.

I said, 'No, let's just wait here, aunty.'

Just then another pandit made his appearance on a pulpit. 'The doors will open in ten minutes,' he said and instantly the pushing and shoving began.

'*Araam se, araam se...* relax,' he said. 'You will all get darshan. Be calm.' He laughed. 'It is always the ladies who do all the pushing. We men are always more relaxed.'

'What nonsense,' Charu said, but Rupa Aunty laughed aloud.

With my mind still up in the Gaumukh clouds, I was sandwiched between yaatris when I heard a shriek to my side: *Mala!* I tore my way through the people between us.

My sister's face was red. 'What the…? Are you okay?' I said.

'No. I'm not. *I am not okay!*' She kicked me in the shin.

I grabbed my leg. 'What the…?'

'*Aaah!* You're just standing there dreaming…' Then, 'Sorry, sorry. I am so angry. This guy… He was just here.'

'What?'

'This guy… He felt me up. Right here. Here. In a place of God of all places. I can't…'

Rupa Aunty put her hand around Mala's shoulder. 'How shameless these men are. Come with me, beta. Let's get some air.'

'*Ek minute. Ek minute.* We just need to go out,' I said as we made our way out of the gathering.

We had just made our way out in the open, near the steps leading down to the Ganga, when I sensed a commotion building to the side. A brawl had broken out and there was a lot of clamouring. There was a man yelling, a man whispering, and another man encouraging somebody. Then, slicing through it all there came the sound of a slap and instantly everything went quiet.

All eyes were fixed on two men. At the centre of the clearing stood a thin, dark, short man. Going by his earrings and turban, I guessed he was a young farmer from Rajasthan. He had his eyes to the ground and bearing down on him was a much heavier guy. He was light skinned—Prince.

'It was this man who misbehaved with you, Mala, wasn't it?' Prince barked.

My sister couldn't quite believe this sudden turn of events. Rupa Aunty, Charu and mummy, and hundreds of people, were mutely watching.

'Erm, I don't know, bhaiyya,' she stammered. 'I didn't see. But it's okay. It doesn't matter. It's fine. Let's leave it. I'm fine.'

'Of course it's him. He has it written on his face.'

'I didn't do anything,' the poor man said, his voice barely audible.

'Wait. Let's not create a scene,' I ventured, but then allowed my words to fade into the Ganga, which was now louder than everybody else.

Prince's lower lip twitched. 'Do you even see what's happening? Your sister was right behind you. Where were you?' He let his words sink in.

'What?'

'Where *are* you?'

I turned to Mala and Rupa Aunty, my face now cold, now hot. 'What? I…I didn't see anything,' I said.

Prince gave me a look of pity. After which he proceeded to slap the poor guy a few more times before he released him back into the crowds, but only after Charu and his mother begged him to stop.

Mala regained her composure in a couple of hours ('This happens all the time. But what angers me is how they have no shame in a place of God. In a place of God!' she said again and again), but I felt like an outcast for the rest of the day. It was Charu who took me aside to comfort me ('He's hot-blooded, ignore him,' she said). Rupa Aunty showed her concern for Mala by massaging her shoulders and for me by passing me packets of makhanas and bringing up more stories of her Guruji ('One time, Guruji told me that in my past life I was a deer…'). But I rebuffed her overtures.

I heard her say that that her next yaatra would be to Ganga Sagar in Bengal where the Ganga merged with the sea, for that was where Raja Bhagiratha's journey ended. But then I lost track. Angry and hurt, I was in a deep sulk. It was not just that my pride was hurt. I think it was the latent realization of something deeper. Something cruder and truer.

I may have been English-speaking and had a Western education but this meant nothing to Prince because deep down he knew he had the upper hand. For Prince, I was an effete man ignorant of my role in the order of things.

That day I wondered, *Who am I?* Yes, I got the lilt of the shlokas from the temple. And yes, I knew their rhythm. But could I decipher their logic?

Maybe I was the odd one, not Prince. Prince, who knew just how to sway his head to our prayers even if he, like me, didn't get all the words. Prince, who knew just when to touch the feet of elders while I constantly wanted to break away.

For mummy, Prince was the Gangajal bearer. It didn't matter that he'd got back not four but three filled bottles of water from Gaumukh, filching the extra one for himself. And that I, despite not being told to get one, had brought one anyway.

Cardiff, UK. July 2008

I was in Gassy Jacks, a noisy pub in Cardiff, having lunch with my friend Paul one afternoon when my phone vibrated in my pocket. Mummy's voice was breaking up and I had to place a hand over my ear to block out the music. 'What? I can't hear you. Hang on.'

'Today…! There is a lunar eclipse today. No meat!'

I stared hungrily at the plate of fish and chips in front of me. *Too late.* 'Yeah, okay.' Paul was enjoying roast beef. At least I wasn't having that. I always avoided that.

'Another thing. I don't know how to say this. But please also avoid sexual things right now.'

'Will you stop?'

Mummy laughed an evil laugh. 'So, anyway,' she said, thankfully changing the topic of conversation, 'Prince and Charu have had twins. Girls.'

It took me a second to shift my mental gears back to another world, another time. 'Oh, nice. But didn't Rupa Aunty want a boy?'

'No. Rupa is very happy. In fact, they were having no luck so I think they opted for IVF treatment. Both Prince and Charu are over the moon. Especially Charu. She was sort of sneering of the poojas, like you. But now she's making a plan to take the family to Vaishno Devi.' Mummy laughed happily.

My old conversations with Rupa Aunty came flooding back. 'Really? Isn't it ironic that Rupa Aunty also had to have an operation to get pregnant once? It's like history is repeating itself.'

'What?'

'Rupa's Guruji,' I said. 'He stopped her from having an operation earlier. But then she later had Prince, so she must have had some procedure.'

'I don't know what you're talking about,' mummy said. 'Prince is not Rupa's real son. His biological mother was his father's previous wife. She died when he was less than a year old. Didn't you know that?'

I never met Prince or Charu again. But around 2011, I learned one afternoon from Ritu Aunty that Prince had joined politics. He owned a garment export business and was doing very well. The Attwals now lived in a spacious house. I smiled.

'Certainly there was luck involved,' Ritu Aunty said. 'But I tell you, Rupa's faith paid off.'

Ritu Aunty sounded so convincing when she spoke in this way that I couldn't help grinning. And as I did, a new thought entered my mind: certainly religion kept people from questioning old ways. It made us conform, like pieces on a chessboard, its boundaries defined. But was it possible that it also achieved a demonstrable end? Like homeopathy's placebo effect, could faith work if you *wanted* it to? This was a new and terrifying thought and I pushed it aside.

But then some nights later, like a dandelion sailing in still air, it came back.

Believing in God was like falling from a great height. It was only when you fell off the earth that you actually felt gravity's force. You could *understand* belief only when you allowed God to get into your bones. I realized then that I was indeed asleep, and dreaming, and falling. I was lucid dreaming, falling deep down and I wanted badly to touch the ground. But it kept receding, it kept extending deeper.

It was the Princes of the world who never offended their parents. It was the Princes who were the first to marry, have kids and grandkids. It was they who seldom left their turfs; seldom questioned.

If religion was a kingdom, who was I? Maybe I was the privileged visitor. I got far away from it because I could. But also because I knew I could go into the *inner sanctum* when I wanted. I enjoyed the pomp of faith and even defended it on impulse. But I could never be that person all the time. The air would become too stagnant, too suffocating.

Maybe most people understood something deep down I was only now beginning to see. Most seemed to think it was all right if you sidestepped reason and overlooked hypocrisy because the important thing was that the game of faith had to go on. Perhaps for believers, religion was their stability. It was their mooring, an inescapable duty. It protected you from the dangers of nihilism. *Was this the unspoken logic?* Did people believe because of fear? Was it a fear of loneliness?

That if you went too far overboard you risked falling into a void in which women didn't have babies and men couldn't find wives. Was it this fear that made mummy bow her head to Swamiji, and me bow mine to her? Was this why Charu married Prince?

Perhaps some were afraid that us rule-breakers would question them too much, even end up making our own rules.

Even if I didn't always adhere to the nucleus of faith, that I was present in the universe meant something, didn't it? At times, I resisted, and at times I gave in, but if I existed, I had to fit in somewhere, didn't I?

I was the privileged visitor continually wandering around old structures. Still, was there a way back *in*?

Gaumukh glacier. The melting and breaking of the glacier is a matter of grave concern. Wikimedia Commons/Gauravkaintura1234.

Approaching Bhojwasa from Gangotri town.

Bhagirathi Massif as seen from Gaumukh.

(Right) Ganga at Harsil, 25 kilometres shy of Gangotri.

(Below) Gangotri town. When I visited with Armaan in May 2018.

Front view of the Gangotri Temple.
Wikimedia Commons/DipankarSen68.

(Left) Baba Updesh Giri for whom I bought a shawl. (Right) Baba Songiri, who wanted to share his food with me. Gangotri, May 2018.

Communal bathing and washing in a stream flowing into the Ganga at a village between Uttarkashi and Gangotri. May 2018.

(Right) At Gaurikund. The base town for the trek up to Kedarnath. On my October 2016 visit to Kedarnath.

(Below) Pandit Hemant can be seen in pink kurta as yaatris make their way up to Kedarnath.

Horse porters going up to Kedarnath.

Pandit Hemant at the Kedarnath Temple.

The leopard-print-skirt-wearing baba
who I spoke to in October 2016.

The entry point to Mana, 'India's Last Village'.
Pandit Hemant posing for the photo.

Devprayag, where the Alaknanda and Bhagirathi rivers meet.

The Badrinath Temple. Wikimedia Commons/Kinkhab.

The *tapt kund*, hot springs, alongside the Alaknanda River at Badrinath.

The Ved Vyas Gufa at Mana village when it was 5,321 years old (in 2013).

At 'India's Last Tea Shop' at Mana, October 2016.

Kullu Dussehra Mela, October 2015. (Top) The procession of deities in Kullu's streets.

(Right) Bearers carrying deities on palanquins.

The Lakshman Jhula at Rishikesh crowded with pilgrims.
Wikimedia Commons/Dherwalstudio.

Kanwariyas at Rishikesh.
Brothers Kuldeep and Vikas.
August 2018.

T-shirts on sale for kanwariyas.

Smoking pipes being
purchased by kanwariyas.

Pilgrims disembarking at the Haridwar Junction railway station. October 2016.

Pilgrims taking a holy dip in the Ganga
at Har ki Pauri, Haridwar. June 2014.

A hoarding at the Kumbh Mela stating the collective resolve of pilgrims: 'We will pray at the banks of the Ganga, not brush our teeth or gargle.' Mahakumbh Mela, Allahabad, 2013.

Yaatris making their way to and from the Sangam at the Mahakumbh Mela in Allahabad, 2013.

The mudflats surrounding the Sangam at Allahabad.
The Mahakumbh Mela 2013.

Boy selling flowers at the Mela, 2013.

The procession of the Naga sadhus. Prayagraj, Kumbh Mela, 2019.

(Left) Sadhus being fed at a maha bhandaara public feast at the Mahakumbh Mela in Allahabad, 2013.

(Below) Pilgrims making the holy dip at the Sangam on Makarsankranti, Mahakumbh Mela, 2013.

Pilgrims disembarking a boat at Varanasi ghats.

The queue at Kashi Vishwanath in November 2018, before the renovation of the temple complex.

The Dashashwamedh Ghat Road all spruced up after the construction of the Corridor. July 2022.

A postcard from 1905 showing the Kashi Vishwanath Temple. The white domes of the Gyanvapi Mosque are visible in the background. The original caption reads: 'The Golden Temple. Held by many to be the oldest and holiest temple amid the 1,000 temples of Benares, the holiest city in India. Covered with gold plates, set on copper, it really dates from the 18th century and was built to replace the one razed to the ground by Aurangzebe.' Wikimedia Commons/Raphael Tuck & Sons, London.

Pilgrims carrying Gangajal for abhishek pooja on Mahashivratri at the Kashi Vishwanath Temple. Varanasi, February 2020.

The 'Holiyana mahaul' in Varanasi. Boys partying on the eve of the Mahashivratri in February 2020.

The Shiva Baraat procession in Varanasi in February 2020.

Some of the more morbid sights one might see in Varanasi.
(Above) A man bathing at the ghat as a monkey's corpse floats in the river.
(Below) A dog chewing on a human skull near a ghat in Varanasi.

Babas sleeping in alcoves set into a wall in the streets of the old city in Varanasi.

A woman beggar with a trishul sleeping at the Varanasi ghats.

Sunrise in Varanasi.

A baba somewhere in Varanasi.

A pandit performing a family pooja under one of the ubiquitous chhatris on Varanasi ghats.

Me with some kids who wanted their picture taken. August 2022.

(Above) Baba Lingaraja Aghori meditating at Manikarnika Ghat, Varanasi. July 2022.

(Left) The Aghori who agreed to pose for a picture but refused to talk.

Mr Dubey, the former taxi driver.

The Kapila Muni temple which houses the idols of Ma Ganga, Kapila Muni and King Sagar, at Sagar Island. We were unable to do a darshan here since it was closed at that time of the year. Wikimedia Commons/Sourav Bapuli.

PART IV

Dives into the Deep End

January 2013, May 2018, August 2018 & January 2019

A Ray of Light in Gangotri

I think it's time I provide a fuller context to these existential metaphors I've been salting and peppering throughout my account. It's time I spell it out for you, Dear Reader. It is something I'd long kept a secret and separate from the rest of my life. And it was both the secret and the fact of it that caused me to feel rootless, then adrift, and eventually very depressed. It is why I knew in my bones that no matter how much I changed my gait, I'd still end up walking outside every old order. It was what made me fundamentally divergent from all ideas of dharma. And it was why in my darkest moments I thought, *Man, I must have accumulated some really bad karma to be born this way.* And seeing as it was the culmination of all this angst that set me on my course down the Ganga in the first place—digging into all my avatars from my past even as I sought God in the present—it is germane not just to how my journey began, but everything that followed.

So, in the interest of full disclosure: it was on a cold January morning in 2008, about six months after our trip to Gangotri, that I decided to tell my mother about my sexuality.

Granted, this was the 2000s, and I belonged to an educated Delhi family. So, coming out of the closet was not the end of the world. But that is not the point. The thing is, like many gay men, I carried in myself tons of shame and a world of foreboding about my future. It would take me years to feel entirely comfortable about my gayness in the presence of heterosexual friends, for instance, and that it has taken me this long to write about it should tell you something about how fears continue to plague my mind even now. But at twenty-five, at least at home, I'd had enough. I'd had enough of poojas and yagnyas and yaatras ordering me to conform. I had to come clean.

It was morning time, I recall, and my mother was running from room to room looking for a book or wi-fi. She had a call with her Pranic Healing group or Gita classes with her Gita Paath group. Or something else. I told her I had to speak to her.

'I'm in the middle of something important,' she said.

'Well, this is important.'

She sat down, her eyes still elsewhere. 'Okay, tell me.'

I wanted to be done with this awkwardness and my words tumbled out idiotically. 'I'm seeing somebody,' I said. 'Shobhit.'

My then-boyfriend Shobhit was sociable and chatty and mummy was rather fond of him. It helped that he always touched her feet when he greeted her and enjoyed talking about temples and their divine auras. In fact, she even suggested him as a match for Mala, causing my sister much amusement. I hadn't told Mala about Shobhit either, but she knew me well enough. Sisters somehow always know things.

What I remember most distinctly about my mother's reaction is how long she kept silent, how swiftly her face passed through a gamut of adaptations. At first, she seemed to think, *What? What did he say?* Then, *Oh Dear God, What?* Then, *It's Fine. Don't look worried because it'll worry him.* Then, *I think I knew this…* Then, *How could I not have known this?*

And finally: *WHAT did he just say?*

But it is to her credit that at least outwardly she was composed. As dramatic as mummy was about God, I knew there would be no drama from her about me. We loved each other and nothing could change that. But I also knew that mummy was a woman of her time and even if a part of her had divined this part of me somewhere along the way, she'd buried it away under decades of poojas asking God to bestow me with a good wife and beautiful children; to place me on track.

Honestly, mummy had once said that it was all because of *me* that she turned to God. My birth was the catalyst. I'd been born eight weeks premature and was in intensive care for two torturous months. At one point, I went into cardiac arrest and nearly died. 'So, it was after you came…and boy, how you suffered. That changed me,' she'd said. 'And you came out of it whole and look at you now.'

I guessed it was only a logical extension of her faith that when I suffered from asthma in childhood, she sought comfort in homeopathy.

It's true, I also learned a lot of practical yoga and pranayama from her. But she never quite gave up her penchant for those sugary pills and bitter potions of dubious origin.

That I was my mother's primary reason to seek God was, no doubt, flattering to hear, but I was now seeing that this was just a self-serving mirage. Why, Minna Masi once said, 'Even in college, Shashi would hop on the bus to Rishikesh every month.' And, 'Even in school, your mother was a seeker,' Ritu Aunty said. And even now, when Mala and I no longer live with her, she continues to make temple runs at the riskiest of times—aged seventy-one, she was, in fact, one of the thousands of faithful who managed to reach the doors of Lord Venkateswara at Tirumala in December 2020, in the middle of the Covid pandemic while I was locked up in my flat. So, I'm more inclined to believe that she was always this sort of person.

But at this moment, like millions of mothers in that position, her world had been upended. In a sentence, I'd reduced her reality to dust, and she was staring at me blankly. *What is happening?* her eyes said. *How could this happen despite everything?*

I almost wanted to say, *Well, it did. Despite God, shit happens.* But I felt guilty, and I said, 'Mummy?'

Her eyes smouldered for a while. But the heat was ebbing away, and it was now being replaced by what I feared most. A creeping sadness.

'You mean to say you don't like girls?' She looked confused. 'But you look normal.'

I resisted the urge to laugh or argue. 'I just feel a connection with people like myself most,' I said and left it there.

A few words about Hinduism and homosexuality here: I tell you, it's weird! And I'm not being glib for the heck of it. It's true that there's no central authority at the top passing decrees to execute gays. And we indeed have a long history of literature and imagery rich with representations of gender fluidity, from the Ardhnarishvara avatar of Shiva represented as equally half-male and half-female, to the character Shikhandi in the Mahabharata who is born female but raised as a man, and even married to a woman. And yes, there are chapters on the bending degrees of sexual expression in the Kamasutra. But make no mistake. We Hindus are a prudish bunch. We like to pretend that things that appear different from the 'normal' don't actually exist. What exists in our minds in bucketfuls, however, are notions of dharma and karma and the attendant ideals of manhood and family.

Dharma stipulates the four stages or *ashrams* in a man's life. In the first, *brahmacharya*, a man is a boy and student. In the second, the *grihastha*, he has a family and takes the mantle of a householder. This is followed by the *vanaprastha*, during which, after having fulfilled his family obligations, he begins to extricate himself from attachment to both people and things. And in the fourth and last stage, *sanyaas*, man undertakes complete renunciation.

What I was saying to my mother was that I'd unequivocally left the Order of Dharma and decided to play my own game. A game in which there were no rules and a thousand perils. I'm saying that although I never believed that this old format applied to me, I got it. I got where my mother was coming from and felt terrible about it.

Mummy was looking at the shelf of homeopathic pills behind me as if she were afraid to meet my eyes. As if she wished she could pull some potion out of it and make everything return to normal. She gave me a guarded look. 'I'll still talk about you being set up with girls, with others.'

'Sure. Whatever.'

There was a pause and I saw a glimmer of hope in her eyes. 'What?' I said.

'Nothing. I'm not so worried. Swamiji has said that you'll have a very good wife. And the best son.'

It would take mummy years to come to terms with the truth. And in some ways, she's still dealing with it—through poojas and consultations with Swamiji. By suggesting a prayer here or a fast there. By sometimes hearing me out respectfully and sometimes getting frustrated with everything. But all the while always wanting nothing but complete happiness for me, her firstborn and only son.

So why are you telling me this now? you ask. One reason is I was dodging putting this fact out in black and white earlier. (And because, as in Physics, in Faith too, the perspective of the observer can not be separated from what they observe.) The other more amorphous reason is that nowadays I wonder if Swamiji's son prophecy did come to pass in some twisted way after all. It's because I've no logical way to explain certain things that happened on my journey down the Ganga other than to ascribe to them big ideas like 'determinism'—or God.

You see, during my yaatra to Kedarnath in 2016, as I stood with Panditji before Lord Shiva in the form of a bull-shaped Shivalingam, I prayed hard, very hard. And what I prayed for above everything else—above things like 'structure' and 'normalcy'—was that I find a partner.

At the time, I was lost and drifting, and my foremost and most intense desire was to find a companion. To find somebody who *got* me.

So, before Shiva, the *Vairagi*, the wanderer who lives outside the bounds of society, I joined my hands together. Before the Ardhnarishvara, the embodiment of all genders, I did a sashtang pranaam. On the One Who Destroys Old Worlds, I poured Gangajal. Again and again. And in my way.

Dear Shivji, I'm a part of you, I said. *I'm in you. If you have placed me outside the limits of dharma, then there's a reason, no? If I'm the result of some cosmic karma, you must guide me, no? So, Shivji, please give me direction. Please show me the way. Shivji, find me somebody like me. A confection of male and female energies. An elemental rule-breaker. An old gene lost in this world of Order. A string from another Universe…*

No sooner did a month pass after I returned to Delhi than I met Armaan. Sure, we met on a dating app, the lucky convergence of internet signals at the right instant. But a few months after we'd started to date, I thought: *Was it God who'd answered my prayers?* Only to push this irrational thought quickly aside.

But then, a year later, a pandit on Dashashwamedh Ghat in Varanasi made another prophecy. The old man examined my palm with his magnifying glass, then stared at me. His right eye was cloudy with a cataract. 'You're not married, are you?' he said. I shook my head. He said, 'I see in your future somebody much younger than you. Maybe a son.'

When we met, I was thirty-four, and Armaan was twenty-two. And although he's my partner and nothing like a son, given how symbiotic our relationship has felt from the start, I do wonder, *Was the crossing of our paths a design by God?*

Yes, my rational brain is still around. And it says, *There are books written about this, you know?* Books on psychology and neuroscience. *The Future of Illusions* by Freud and *The God Delusion* by Richard Dawkins and *The Moral Landscape* by Sam Harris. Why do you insist on linking disparate parts of your life to fit what *you* want to believe? To which, my believing side responds: I get what you're saying. But I also get that, for better or worse, the seeds of both doubt and faith will continue to grow in me for as long as I live. I think I'm just this sort of person.

May 2018

It was 6 am, the door to the pooja room was open a crack and mummy was deep in the *Shiva Mahiman Stotra*. It would take her fifteen minutes to finish. So, I bowed my head before Ganeshji, Shivji, Lakshmiji and Maharajji's picture and signalled I was leaving. Mummy rose, still chanting mantras, picked up a plastic bottle of water in the corner and uncapped it: Gangajal. She handed me a steel glass and filled it halfway.

How many years had it been sitting there? I thought. But I swallowed my hesitation along with the water and touched my mother's feet. She took a pause.

'Are you going alone?'

'No. Armaan is joining me.'

'Armaan? Okay.' She frowned. 'Please don't eat any meat on yaatra.'

I rolled my eyes and picked up my bag and turned around. As I descended the stairs, she said, 'All the best, beta. May God always be with you.'

Armaan was Afghan and had sought refuge in India after his family started receiving threats from the Taliban. Born to a devout Muslim family, he said he used to pray five times a day as a child, but a deeper study of Islamic scriptures had got him so disillusioned with his religion that he said he was now a non-believer. So much so that he'd purged all Islamic words from his speech and refused even to celebrate Eid. A rather extreme reaction, I thought.

Still, I didn't believe Armaan was actually a non-believer. At the very least, he was a seeker. It takes one to know one, I guess. The two of us had had numerous discussions on religion, many of which adhered to this broad pattern:

'Your religion is very different, Sid. It is not absolute. It is not political.'

'Of course, it is political. It just works differently.'

'Okay. But at least different communities can coexist here. Islam is only about fear.'

'I think fear is a component of all religions, all faiths.'

'Leave it. You don't know Islam.'

'And you don't know Hinduism.'

And Armaan didn't. As an outsider, I didn't think he understood how Hindu mores seeped into our psyche. How the idea of something being *jootha*, for example—that particular Hindu food fixation that translates to 'defiled' rather than leftover, for food may be leftover but perfectly unsullied (*sucha*); or freshly made but spoiled forthwith by somebody savage enough to have a taste and put the tasting spoon back into the serving bowl—was a reflection of the rigours of caste and ritual purity. He didn't get how vegetarianism, for all its noble roots in non-violence against animals, made some vegetarians uncomfortable in the presence of meat-eaters at *their* dining table.

Yet Armaan wasn't a Hindu newbie either. By his own admission, his three years in India had changed him. He had raced through not only the abridged versions of the Mahabharata and the Ramayana but also become vegetarian after gleaning what he called the 'calm look' on the faces of Buddhist monks during a trip to Dharamshala.

Whenever we would go out for meals together, he'd have a boring pot of beans or dal as I'd tear into a leg of chicken or goat. Mind you, he was the same guy who used to adore Nando's chicken. Over one dinner, I recall, Armaan asked if I felt any guilt about eating the flesh of another sentient being as a Hindu. Rather than respond with a lecture about how not all Hindus were vegetarian, how each community had its own dietary rules, I said, perhaps not untruthfully, 'If I feel guilty, I just say a little prayer.' Armaan made a Swamiji-like face.

Yet, I should admit that I was secretly flattered by Armaan's talk, too. Because no matter how liberal I liked to believe I was, there was something bolstering about a Muslim-raised person praising my faith and berating his own.

I knew it would not take much to convince him to accompany me to Gangotri.

Somewhere outside Gangotri. May 2018

When I looked up, I saw a sea of white crests cutting through grey clouds, and when I looked down, switchback after switchback extended down to the lower reaches of some netherworld. I rolled down my window to take it all in but was instantly seized by a coughing fit as black smoke from the truck in front floated into our car. The Uttarakhand state government was broadening the roads from Rishikesh across the Char Dham sector, as a result of which an awful traffic jam extended for some five or six kilometres outside Gangotri. We were stuck.

'Roll it up, Sid,' Armaan said, covering his nose.

He had two books on his lap. There was *Old Path White Clouds: Walking in the Footsteps of the Buddha* by Thich Nhat Hanh. And there was a Persian one, *The Upanishads, translated from Sanskrit by the Mughal-Shahzada Dara Shukoh, son of Shah Jahan*, which paradoxically looked more Islamic than Hindu and so not the ideal accessory for a tirath yaatra.

During my yaatra to the Lord Venkateswara temple in Tirupati earlier in the year, I had to pass through a checkpoint before my car could ascend the sacred Tirumala hill. A notice board above read: 'Only Hindu books allowed.' 'As if Christian missionaries will come here,' I said to the driver. After all, Tirupati is one of India's most sacred (and richest) Hindu temples. But he took my words literally. 'It has happened, sir,' he said. 'Of course, it has happened. And only traditional Indian dress is permitted inside the temple. For men, dhoti or *veshti* and for ladies, only saree or salwar-kameez.'

Armaan was from the land of salwar-kameez, I thought. Or, in any case, nearer its place of origin than Tirupati. While Armaan has light green eyes and light skin, he could easily pass for a Himachali or Kashmiri Pandit. Just so long as he doesn't open his mouth, because his foreign accent gives him away. Still, I was glad his name was an ambiguous Armaan Sepehri, and not an eyebrow-raising 'Mohammad' or 'Abdullah'.

Down at Uttarkashi, as the government clerk entered our names as yaatris into the computer, he hadn't even bothered looking up. 'S-E-P-E-H-R-I', he repeated as he routinely punched the letters into the system. As though this Persian name were no more alien than, say, Balasubramanian from Tamil Nadu.

In our rapidly developing country, new technologies are seen as a sign of progress and with good reason. Yet sometimes the spread of computers also makes me sad. *Are we losing our old ways in this global rush to modernize?* But then, *Is this feeling nostalgia for some imagined grand days of yore, or does it have a basis?* These fuzzy, somewhat loose thoughts were bubbling in my mind since leaving Uttarkashi.

In January 2013, soon after my Nana died, I accompanied my mother to Pehowa, a small village in Haryana on the outskirts of Kurukshetra, the town where the battle of Mahabharata was fought. According to belief, Pehowa sits on the banks of the mythical Saraswati River, the present manifestation of which is a large water reservoir, the Saraswati Ghat, in which many devout take a bath. It is at the edge of this ghat that families from across Punjab and Haryana flock to do *pind daan*, a pooja for the liberation of the souls of your departed ancestors so they can be freed from the cycle of rebirths and merge with the Creator.

Although traditionally it is the son who does this pooja, my mother performed it for her father that warm winter morning. The pandit prepared seven balls, each made of rice flour, wheat flour, oat flour, dried milk, honey and sesame seeds as offerings. One was meant for the soul of my Nana while the rest were meant for our forefathers who had passed before.

I noticed the other men performing even more elaborate rituals. A Sikh man had a charpoy and a bundle of clothes beside him. And another man had a bunch of utensils stacked up on the floor, all of which would end up in the hands of the local pandits, mediators, through whom alone these material possessions could reach the souls of the deceased.

When we emerged onto the main street, pandits, sadhus and beggars milling about us, mummy announced that I would now see something fascinating. And on this occasion, I have to concede she was right.

'I'm looking for the pandit who keeps the records for Malhotras,' she said to a man and three pandits within earshot ran up. 'Which Malhotras?' one asked. 'From Lahore? From Ludhiana?' asked another. My mother said her father had roots in a village called Maachiwara. She thought a moment. 'And also in Bairsal Kalan.' At which the men launched into a lengthy discussion among themselves—the old game of Indian murmurs—whereby one pandit spoke to a second, who spoke to a third, who spoke to a fourth. So that a half hour later, we found ourselves standing in the dusty office of a fifth pandit, a serious-looking middle-aged man with a grey beard and a calm but insistent manner. He said that he was the keeper of our family's records.

The pandit's room was large but jam-packed, full of what looked like twenty little tables on top of which mounds and mounds of large scrolls, yellowing, dusty, primitive things, stretched into the distance where they met the wall at the back and grew into a mountain of paper. A couple of old wooden almirahs with spotty glass fronts and falling-off handles stood against the wall to the side.

From this mildewed disorder, the pandit fished out a scroll, which he glanced through and rolled back up. He then brought out a large register from one of the almirahs and, licking his fingers, began carefully leafing through its pages until one detail gave him pause. After a few minutes of opening and rolling of scrolls he returned to his desk with a big a smile and a bundle under his arm.

As he ever-so-gently unfurled a scroll, I saw that it was not one but many papers rolled up together, the parchments fraying at the edges like fraying paper I'd never seen. He beckoned. 'Ah, yes. Look.' And there I saw it. In Hindi, my Nana had written: 'Shivsharandas.' My great-grandfather's name. 'Time of death: 6:25 in the evening, 7.12.1977.'

On the next page, Shivsharandas had made an entry recording his wife's death. She had died in childbirth in 1919.

'Show me more,' I said, unable to contain my astonishment. And the parchments went on. My great-great-grandfather was a Mathuradas. His father was Bhagchand. And his father, Kishanchand.

The pandit said that our family records could be traced back to the 1700s, after which things got hazy. I didn't have reason to doubt him; before my eyes, the records went back to the early 1800s. But I asked why. 'Because,' he said, 'even though this system goes back to the time of the Mahabharata, many records were burnt by Muslim rulers.'

Not wanting to get pulled into controversial talk, I nodded silently. Nowadays, one hears about wealthy Americans going through genetic testing to learn about their ancestry. And here in India, inside this musty room in a town whose name I hadn't heard of before, I'd found proof of my roots going back four hundred years and more! I was all Punjabi Indian and I didn't need a blood test to prove it. I knew it from our dust. I knew it in my bones. *Seeing is believing!*

Having just recounted this episode to Armaan, I said, 'So what do you think it means? Doesn't it mean that despite our messiness there's something deeper at work?' What I meant was: India is a hot anarchy, yes. But how could our culture have survived so many incursions unless we carried old worlds of order with us? Weren't these ancient structures precisely what the defenders of religion, the pandits, sadhus and mothers, were so keen to protect?

But Armaan's answer took a different line. 'I think what you call the messiness of India is your strength,' he said. 'It's because everything goes, that so many cultures coexist here… In your religion the rocks are gods, the trees are gods, the rivers are gods, and animals are also gods. This is why you can't just rip them out. If you believe there is consciousness in everything, there is the Brahman in everything, then you can't just kill it… And I think this is a much more logical way of seeing things.' He laughed. 'Otherwise, I know people who think God made chickens just for them to eat.'

'Yeah,' I said. 'I get that. But I think maybe our religion has the opposite problem. We worship nature so much that we end up taking it for granted. We bathe in the Ganga because she's pure, but we don't think twice about polluting her. It's almost like we're thinking to ourselves, *How can you not take liberties in your home? In your own body? If you can't take liberties with your mother, with whom can you?*

The air outside was thick with smoke and the honking of cars. The traffic was getting unbearable so I told the driver we'd see him later at the car park, and got off. It was only a kilometre to Gangotri from this point. A few metres ahead, a Garhwali chap, probably around twenty, approached us, pushing an empty wheelchair. It was meant to transport older pilgrims to their lodges but he was using it as a luggage trolley.

'Put your bags here, bhaiyya,' he said, baring that warm unpretentious smile that some people in the Old World still retain.

The sides of the road were lined with babas of all hues of skin and shades of robe. There were young babas and old babas. There were babas in white, babas in orange and babas in black. There were babas whose skin was swarthy and one whose skin had gone all pink-white with vitiligo. Some clanked their metal bowls against the ground for alms and sang bhajans so unselfconsciously that it made you stop and actually listen. Some had no clothes on other than a loin cloth around their crotch.

One such baba, no older than twenty-five, with ash smeared on his torso and face, said his name was Baba Songiri. He had an orange satchel by his side in which he kept his meagre belongings. On his other side lay a sack of grains somebody had slung his way only yesterday. He was simmering khichdi on a wood burner and invited me to taste it.

'No, thank you,' I said, rather moved by the young man's generosity. 'I'll come meet you tomorrow.' This was the India I loved. The India of open-hearted kindness, in which even those who had nothing wanted to share their food with you.

'You have booking, na? Everything is sold out,' Sanju the porter said when we got to the town's one and only arterial lane. 'School holidays rush has started. First, the Punjabi families came, now from Himachal and everywhere. You want to go on a trek to Gaumukh? You need a permit.'

'No. Not this time.'

Past shops selling pooja items and dhabas offering chowmein and samosas and Oreo milkshakes, we were now passing the resthouses and lodges. I looked at the booking on my phone: *Hotel Mandakini*.

The building was split between two blocks. One was on the side of the mountain and the other stood across the lane with its willowy pillars plunging dangerously into the torrential Bhagirathi. By the time we walked up to the reception, it was 5:30 pm, and the cold and altitude hit me in a sudden wave of dizziness and exhaustion.

A rather lost-looking Garhwali chap of around my age with bad teeth but that same warm Old World smile greeted us. 'You are lucky,' he said. 'We have only one room left.'

'Yes. I booked it,' I said.

'You did? We have no booking.' He picked up a register lying on the table and flipped through it before slamming it shut. 'Yes, no booking.' He smiled again.

'But I've paid 3,000 rupees for the night,' I said. 'Here, look.' I showed him the confirmation on my phone: *Booking is all set! Team Yatra wishes you a pleasant stay at Hotel Mandakini for 2 nights. Happy Yatra to you!*

'*Nahin hai*,' he said. Not there. He then rang the hotel owner who lived down in Uttarkashi. But the network was spotty, and we had to wait over ten minutes before he could get him on the line. Only to be told, *No.* Definitely no booking had been made because the lodge didn't even have a website so I was probably the victim of a scam. But I needn't worry; a spare room was available and only for Rs 500 a night.

Thoroughly drained, I was in no mood to argue. Armaan and I dropped our bags in our room, a veritable icebox on stilts immersed in the Bhagirathi, and went down for a stroll by the river. I took a seat on a rock.

Mountain shadows elongated before me like creatures that drew their strength from the night as the sun slipped behind a mountain across the water. The air's chill was growing acuter with every passing minute, and beneath a bridge over the river I saw four sarees stuck in the rocks. Red, yellow, green, blue, shivering with the currents like ghosts. What did these poor women wear after their clothes were lost to Faith?

Rupa Aunty distributed food packets to babas squatting down in a line at the end of this same bridge, I remembered. One gaunt man with sunken cheeks and stumps for fingers said, 'Behenji, please give me one more. I haven't eaten in two days.' But sweet Rupa Aunty held out a firm hand. 'I have many to feed,' she said. 'Just sit quietly and eat what I've given you.'

It had made me smirk. 'You must feed as many needy people as you can,' Rupa Aunty's Guruji had said. 'Only then will you get the benefit.' But now I just felt sad.

I turned to Armaan. 'People have come here to pray. So, don't come in their way. Okay?' And Armaan put his finger to his lips and rose. He hitched up his pants and went, first ankles in, then knee-deep into the night-silver Ganga. And I went back to fuming about the money I'd lost. I never would have got scammed like this if I were in a developed country.

7 am, the next day

I was standing at the Gangotri Ghat in front of a wide one-storey building. This was where I was told I'd find the *purohits*, the head pandits, of Gangotri Dham. I climbed up the stairs with Armaan close behind me and took a peek inside. The door was wide open. In a large hall, carpeted from wall to wall, a lone pandit, perhaps in his mid-forties, was sitting cross-legged at a low table, poring over a text. The hall's expansive windows were flung open, and the voices of bathing yaatris came streaming in with the cool air.

'Namaste, panditji,' I said. 'Can I speak to you?' He didn't look up so I raised my voice. 'I wanted to ask you some questions about tirath sthaans. I'm a writer.'

The man assessed my face from above the rim of his glasses, then asked me to take a seat. 'And you?' he asked. Armaan said he was from Delhi which for the moment proved sufficient.

'Which newspaper do you write in? I have a patron from *India Today*. And the editor of *Jan Satta* also comes to me. You must have heard their names?' he said.

I nodded, then said that I was a lawyer, at which he trotted out the names of a handful of Delhi lawyers he knew. I didn't just come from a family of lawyers. We were old devotees of Shivsagar Ashram at Rishikesh. Had he heard of Swami Vairagya Teerathji? Or of Swami Shraddhanandji? The pandit said he hadn't, but my credentials had piqued his interest, and so, without wasting time, he got down to retelling me Ganga's old story:

'You can call it history or our stories, but according to our Puranas, Gangotri is a mool sthaan, a place of origin,' he said. 'This was where Raja Bhagiratha did tapasya for 5,500 years. It was Satyug then, and people lived thousands of years, so 5,500 years only sounds a lot.

'Of this time, Bhagiratha prayed for 5,000 years to Brahmaji alone, and Brahmaji said he could release the Ganga, but who could contain her force? Her current was so strong that she would go directly to the *paataal*.'

Paataal is the most mysterious of the three worlds mentioned in Hindu scriptures, I told Armaan. Lacking sunshine and illuminated only by the glow of jewels, it is an enchanting place somewhere beneath the ground.

The pandit nodded. 'Brahmaji told Bhagiratha, you should do Shivji's tapasya. He's the only one who can do this job. Nobody else is capable. And that is when Bhagiratha, standing on one foot, did a further five hundred years of tapasya of Shiva. Only then did Brahmaji release the Ganga. But now she got lost in Shiva's *jataayein* for a while.'

'What is jataayein?' Armaan asked.

'You know, hairs?' the pandit said in English detecting a foreign accent. 'But on Earth, it is these Kailash mountains you see here... So, Shiva kept the Ganga locked in his hairs, and then Bhagiratha implored him to release the Ganga. Don't keep her confined with you, he said. She has come down from the Heavens but she is stuck in your hairs. Then Shivji broke a lock of hair from his head.' The pandit broke an imaginary lock from his nearly bald head. 'And the Ganga came rushing down to the Earth in the form of a river. What does Gangotri mean? It means from where Ganga *utri*.' From where the Ganga descended.

'Gaumukh glacier was originally down here at Gangotri, yes?' Armaan asked.

'Yes. And melting, melting, melting, melting, it is going back, back, back.'

'When was that?' I asked.

'In the Satyug.' The pandit looked annoyed. 'Then after that came Treta Yuga and now we are in Kalyug. This was thousands and lakhs of years back.'

Pandit Madhav Semwal belonged to the Semwal gotra of the Bharadwaj clan, and only members from his gotra could become pandits at Gangotri. Just as the head priests (Rawals) of the Kedarnath temple trace their extraction from the Veerashaiva Lingayat community of Karnataka and the Badrinath Rawals are Namboodiri Brahmins from

Kerala, the Semwals, too, originally belonged to Southern India. But when I asked Pandit Semwal if his family also came from Kerala (as it was the Malayalee Adi Shankaracharya who is credited with establishing the Char Dham in the eighth century), his answer was imprecise.

'Yes, in these mountains, all the pandits came from the south. That's what our elders told us,' he said. 'Many generations ago, they came from a village near Kerala or somewhere nearby and settled here in Mukhimath village.'

In the winter months, just as the idol of Lord Vishnu is brought down from Badrinath to Joshimath, and the Kedarnath idols are transported to Ukhimath, Goddess Gangotri descends to Mukhimath. A replica of the Gangotri temple is present in the village where the pooja takes place for six months in the year.

'And what about this temple?' I asked, referring to the main Gangotri temple just twenty steps away. 'How old is it?'

Pandit Semwal said that while the present structure, a small white-domed temple, unimpressive compared to Badrinath and Kedarnath, was only one hundred or so years old, a smaller wooden shrine stood in its place before, which had been built in the early eighteenth century by a Gorkha Commander, Amar Singh Thapa. Before that, an even smaller structure went 'back, back, back' in time.

Talking of development, he said that it only happened in the last fifty or sixty years. Earlier, when the region was under the control of local kings there were no proper roads and it would take people six months or more to walk up from Rishikesh. 'But then the attitude of yaatris was different, too. People used to think, "It doesn't matter if we come back down or not. It is a blessing to go up to God's abode." Our elders said only a few people came here earlier. A hundred pilgrims in the whole year. And they always brought their own pooja *samagri*, *bhog* and *batti*. For the last twenty-five to thirty years, there has been so much development that in just in the last year, some four lakh people came… My grandfather would tell me it used to snow a lot here in his childhood. And each snowfall would cement what had fallen before. So, the glacier would not melt so easily.'

'*Ji*. Global warming is ruining our planet,' I offered.

'*Ji*. But I'm saying that now so many people come and just their presence produces heat and because of this the glacier is melting, melting, melting. It is going back, back, back.'

When we came down to the ghat, I took a seat on the top of the stairs and said a little prayer to the rising sun after which I drank the waters of the Ganga. A large joint family of a mother, father, children, grandparents and a few uncles and aunts had squatted down in a circle for a pooja a few feet away. The pandit asked everybody to place Rs 10 in the centre and the father promptly pressed a note each into his boy's and girl's hands. But no sooner had he done this than the wind carried the little girl's money away and deposited it into the river. She ran after it, and her brother went after her. And the next second, brother and sister were laughing and screaming, splashing in the water, their money lost and forgotten.

Their mother appeared before them then. She slapped the boy and yanked him and his sister by their arms back to the pooja. Back to reality.

'Where are you lost?' Armaan said. 'Why did you touch that pandit's feet? And you gave him five hundred rupees. My god, Sid! You said you weren't religious!' He shook his head.

I wanted to laugh because Pandit Semwal had smeared a red tika across Armaan's forehead so that he suddenly looked like a pandit himself.

'But I'm not!' I said, a tad unconvinced of my words. 'Anyway, come, let's go for darshan.'

The queue at Gangotri temple, not too long as yet, was made up mostly of farmers from the northern plains. I popped out my phone recorder. From my interactions with temple-goers over the years, I've learnt that the average rural Indian views his urban English-speaking counterpart in much the same way we view relatives visiting from abroad. There is an initial trepidation, but if you're friendly, if you show that you're more like the other than not, people open up.

Ahead of me was a handsome dark-skinned rustic man with a big moustache and a large turban. He appeared in his forties. His name was Shyam. He was a farmer from Chittor in Rajasthan. We exchanged pleasantries about the weather at first. But then I asked him if he had got what he asked God for.

'Our dhams are heaven,' he said. 'Two years back, I went to Badrinath, and I can tell you that whatever I asked for, I got double. Why, I got more than double. So, I decided to come back again this year.'

'And where are you from?' I asked the thin, shivering man behind me. He appeared to be in his fifties and had wrapped a shawl around his shoulders. But around his waist there was only a cotton dhoti.

'I am from Morena,' he said, and seeing my clueless expression, he added, 'It's near Gwalior… I have come for the first time. First, we went to Yamunotri, and now we are here. From here, we'll go to Kedarnath and Badrinath.'

'You city people ask for proof of God?' Shyam said. 'I got my proof in Badrinath. Have you been there?'

I nodded.

'Over there, there are hot springs surrounded by cold mountains. Is that not proof enough for you?'

'You just said my thoughts,' the man from Morena said.

I remarked as we chatted that I'd heard that in the olden days people would come to the Char Dham at the end of their lives, after they had taken care of all their worldly duties. But how, today, with so many buses anybody could come at any time.

To this the man from Morena said, 'Technology and all is a different matter. But for us it is possible to come here because there are buses, na? In the end only those whose bulaawa has come will reach here. Others can keep making plans their whole life but their yaatra will get cancelled for one reason or another. This is their karma.'

'*Bilkul*,' Shyam agreed. 'In Kedarnath they have a helicopter to go up, but they say you have to book in advance online. We also tried to book. We can also go on the computer. It is not like we can't. But it wasn't possible because they ask for your dates of travel… You tell me. You're an educated man from the city. How can we give our dates? What if our bus breaks down? It took us four days to get here. Stop. Start. Stop. Start. That is how we've made it here, dealing with so many problems. How can we give our dates?'

'Yes. Who plans these things? If it's God's way, it is our way,' I said, Armaan looking at me like he didn't know who I was.

Inside the temple, the placid queue like the Ganga at Varanasi now turned into the rushing river fifty metres away. 'Stick behind me,' I said to Armaan pushing my way forward. Inside the inner sanctum, I thrust myself to the forefront before Gangotri Ma and began to pray. There was no time.

I asked Mother Ganga for my health, happiness, and stability. (Not for 'direction' or 'normalcy' this time.) And then, unwittingly, I prayed for mummy. I prayed for her health, but also that she live less in faith and more in reality. That her reasonable mind win over her superstitious one sometimes. And that our connection, hers and mine, have less to do with faith and all the insidious ways in which it glosses over real life.

I was just about wrapping up when the pandit before me held my folded hands and gestured to a spot behind me. The old priest's eyes were hard and unrelenting and I spun around. Armaan had extracted himself from the incoming rush and was standing aloofly in one corner. He'd crossed his arms at his chest and appeared somehow both repelled and engrossed by what he was seeing. He looked like a man ogling at a parade of fools. He met my eyes and sighed.

'*Ganga Maiyya ki Jai!*' '*Har Har Gange Ma!*' '*Jai Gange Maiyya!*'

The crowd was moving over, and the old pandit pouring spoonfuls of Gangajal into our hands was pushing me along. He hurriedly dropped the sacred water into the cup of my palm, and as he did, he shot Armaan a scowl and shook his hand in a hostile question mark: *What are you doing here?*

He turned to me. 'Is he with you?'

'Yes,' I said apologetically.

A few years before, a pandit at Jagannath Puri had said to me that he could tell if a non-Hindu had entered the temple. 'I can tell by their *attichude*,' he said. At the time, I replied irreverently with, 'As if this was what non-Hindus spend their free time doing.' But now, I felt an uneasy knot in my stomach. I hissed at Armaan, 'Please go outside. I'm right behind you.' And the poor guy stirred from his daze.

Out in the open, he said, laughing, 'That man didn't like me there at all.'

'But why didn't you follow my moves? You just had to fold your hands, like this.'

'Sid, can you calm down?' Armaan's tone was casual, but the hurt was palpable. 'You know I don't believe in all this pooja. I just came to see this place with you.' He shook his head. 'And really, I had no idea *you* were so religious.'

Babas and babas. 10 am

On one side of the town's main arterial lane squatted babas as yaatris hurried past them, while from the other side came the hum of shopkeepers and *dhabawaalas* calling out to prospective customers. '*Rudraksh mala, sphatic mani [quartz crystal] ki mala, special mala, panch mukhi [five-faced] mala, crystal mala. Take it with you and do Bhole Baba ka jap,*' a man said. 'Come eat *chhole bhature*, samosa, noodles,' said another.

The aroma of food frying in ghee mingled with incense in this Ganga-sprayed Himalayan air. Amid this Hindu world, a handful of white trekkers to Gaumukh stood out with rucksacks on their backs.

I stopped to admire a prayer book, *Garhwal Tantra Mantra Sadhana*. On the cover was the drawing of a man with a lion's head tearing his claws into the stomach of a rakshas. This was Narsingh Dev, an avatar of Vishnu. He came down to Earth to kill the demon Hiranyakashyapa. When Lord Brahma granted the demon Hiranyakashyapa a boon of immortality—that nobody he'd created could kill him; that he could not die inside the house, nor outside it; that he could not be killed either during the day or the night, and not by any human or beast—Lord Vishnu, taking the avatar of this half-man and half-lion, which is neither a man nor beast, and at twilight, which is neither day nor night, killed him with his bare claws at the doorway to his palace, which is neither inside the house nor outside it.

Armaan pulled me away though. 'Come, let's go speak with some babas, Sid,' he said. 'Isn't that what you came here to do?'

Baba Updesh Giri from Lucknow appeared a desperate man. Vitiligo had made his face and hands a whitish pink and his dirty toes stuck out the fronts of his broken shoes. He said he was sixty, but the manner in which he squatted on the ground, subserviently though with much dexterity, made him seem innocent as a child. A child with an old man's face and a lost man's soul.

'Can I get you anything?' I said.

'Can you get me a shawl?' He pointed to one hung in a shop across. 'I'm staying at a *jhuggi* [slum] at Gaumukh Mor. That's where all the babas are.'

Gaumukh Mor was near the car park outside town and I remembered seeing him there yesterday. I gave Baba Updesh Giri Rs 150. But when he approached the shopkeeper, the man rebuffed his offer. '*Dedh sau, haan?* Do I want to make a loss?' he said. He poured tea into an earthen cup from a kettle on his counter and handed it to him. 'Just drink this and be quiet.'

I went up to the shop, paid the shopkeeper Rs 250 and handed a grateful Baba Updesh Giri a bright red shawl which he wasted no time in wrapping around himself.

'Come, madam. Shawl, saree, samagri, I have all. Come, come,' the shopkeeper called out to an old woman being pushed down the lane in a wheelchair. She glanced at his shop, then looked ahead. When Updesh Giri stretched out his red-cloaked hand, she swatted him away like a fly.

Armaan held my shoulder. 'I know what you're thinking,' he said. 'It's not a waste. It's better to spend Rs 250 on this man than to waste a rupee on that pandit, if you ask me.'

Nagari Baba, from Akola district, Vidarbha, Maharashtra, was an awe-inspiring man. The seventy-six-year-old sat in orange robes on an orange carpet inside a cave (or what was more like a cavity) in the mountainside. His skin was wrinkled and leathery and his white eyebrows were thicker than the scant threadlike hairs that made up his beard. Behind him was hung a torn calendar with Shiva's painting. On it was—aptly—written: 'Shiva and Co.'

'I am here in the summer and winter. All twelve months, I'm here,' he said. 'Maybe 100-150 mahatmas live in this Gangotri area. And maybe twenty-five to thirty winter here. The Haridwar department and the police, they know about us.'

'And what do you do for food in winter, babaji?' I asked.

'Well, you yaatris are always there to help us, *hai na*?' he said with a chuckle. 'You bring us grains and I cook it myself. Somebody brings gas, somebody clothes. Somebody from Punjab or from Delhi.

And some yaatris come after Diwali just to give us food. Forty kg *atta*, forty kg rice they gave me last year. It lasted me a long time. My needs are not many.'

'My hut,' he pointed to some mysterious spot downriver, 'is there. And my cave also. So, six months I am there, and for six I sit here.'

'It must be horribly cold in winter,' Armaan said.

'Yes, it used to be very cold before 2000. Now, less. But I've been living here such a long time, it has become a habit. I've been here since 1993.'

After Nagari Baba left his village in Vidarbha he stayed in Shirdi near the Sai Baba temple for a few years. 'I used to live with Him before,' he said of Sai Baba. 'He is the one who sent me here.'

Everybody knew who Sai Baba was, I told Armaan. The most revered of babas, many believed Sai Baba was born to a Muslim family. But nearly all his devotees today are Hindu. He had passed on almost a hundred years back.

'God takes you on the track you are meant take,' Nagari Baba said wistfully. 'Now, if there are five brothers, one a lawyer, one a doctor and so on, it means that every person is following his destiny, *hai na*? My destiny was that Sai Baba sent me here, to heaven. I first came here for Morari Baba's Ramayana *katha* [story telling] in 1993 and I liked it so much that I stayed on. Now I go just till Uttarkashi, at most for a couple of days. Never beyond that.'

A draught of wind blew over and Armaan rubbed his hands together for warmth. 'But babaji, how do you spend the winters here?' he said again.

'Time passes very well in winter. I keep singing bhajans, and I don't know how the day and night go. From behind that mountain'—he pointed to a peak behind us—'the sun comes up at nine, and at about 1 pm it passes over that other mountain over there. Then at five, it starts getting dark.' He grew quiet. 'You get so immersed in the sun's movements that you really don't think about anything else.'

Two years earlier, as I took in the Shiva aarti at Kedarnath, my vision had wandered to four babas gathered around a fire. The most striking of the lot had a tousled bun of matted locks on his head and a leopard-print skirt around his waist. The rest of him though was bare, covered in ash. He was the same baba who had told Pandit Hemant and me that he'd witnessed the devastating flash floods of 2013.

The evening aarti was on its final leg, and the pujari stepped out of the temple with the *jyot*, the sacred flame. He held it aloft for everybody to take in. Some devotees extended their arms forward so their palms could touch the fire while others pointed their phone cameras in his direction. And why wouldn't they? It was a splendid image: A fire in the hands of a pandit framed against an ancient stone temple with snow-clad peaks as the backdrop.

The leopard-print-skirted baba then punctured the air with his two-headed drum, and in what struck me as a practised manner he revved up his drumming to match the clashing cymbals and bells from the temple. I went up to the four babas for a chat. The youngest, only sixteen or seventeen, was blowing air into his hands for warmth and laughing. 'I just need charas,' he said, and the leopard-print-skirted baba passed him a joint. The boy then brought out a phone from between the folds of his orange robes. Probably to film the aarti, I thought. But instead he played a video. And now a scantily-clad Rakhi Sawant was shaking her bosom and belly to the beats of the aarti at Kedarnath.

'Do you think these babas are fakes?' I asked Pandit Hemant.

'No, you can't say that,' he said. 'Shiva is a vairagi, a hermit. He doesn't follow the rules. So, the sanyaasis who go off society, they are the ones who worship him most ardently.' He looked at me sharply. 'But does this make all waywards into Shiva devotees?'

'Did you notice one strange thing about him?' Armaan said.

'About whom?'

'Nagari Baba. He didn't move his hands once while talking. They stayed totally still in his lap. Like he is at complete peace with himself. This is the exact same calm look I was telling you about that I saw on the faces of Buddhist monks in McLeod Ganj.'

Baba Songiri beamed a smile I could spot from afar when he saw us walking in his direction. Like yesterday, his eyelids were ash-smeared and droopy, but today he looked happy. He looked stoned. Squatting down on his haunches in nothing but a cloth tied around his crotch, he was again cooking wood-fired dal and rice for lunch.

'Will you have some?' he cheerily asked, and I politely declined.

As if he'd been preparing to tell me his life story, he leapt into conversation. 'I am from UP, District Jalaun,' he said. 'I've been here for thirty-six days. As you can see, these are my things. My atta, daal, rice… It's been some fifteen–sixteen years since I have been here in Uttarakhand. I am twenty-three years old. I stay here for six months in the summer, and in the winter, I go down to Dhumakot. It's not as high, but it also gets very cold in winter. On May 25, I'll go to Kedarnath.'

I smiled at the young man's spirit but for some reason he thought I doubted him. 'Yes, yes, I'll go walking,' he said. 'There's a shortcut.'

An older baba sitting beside Songiri cut in when I asked him how long it would take: 'We leave in the morning and reach in the evening.'

'No, it will take three days,' Songiri said. 'Yes, there is a one-day route also, but it's filled with *riks*.' He met Armaan's gaze and abruptly broke off. 'Where are you from, bhaiyya? You're not from here. I can tell.'

'I'm from Afghanistan,' Armaan said and Songiri clapped his hands.

'Yes! I knew it from your eyes. Very good.'

He turned to me. 'So yes, bhaiyya, if you want to jump into a well, knowing all the *riks*, it's foolish, na? If you know that prodding a snake will make it angry then why poke it on purpose?'

'Why did you spend your whole life in this path of faith?' Armaan asked him, changing the subject.

'We are three brothers. Two are married. They have a family. There is no problem with them at all. I decided to take a different path and it has been fifteen–sixteen years that I've been roaming around Uttarakhand.' He looked into Armaan's eyes. 'Is there anything wrong with that?'

'*Bilkul nahin…*absolutely not,' Armaan said, 'I really liked talking with you,' and gave Baba Songiri two crisp hundred-rupee notes from his wallet.

We walked back to town, Armaan and I. Crossing the old bridge, we each sat on a rock at the edge of the Bhagirathi. It was a bright, clear afternoon, and the bustling ghats were bathed in sunlight across the rushing waters.

A rustic woman on the stairs, wet and shivering, was coughing, and her husband handed her a syrup. She dropped it into her mouth from a height so as to make no contact with the bottle's lip. Then she plunged her freezing self into the Ganga. She ticked all the right boxes, I thought. The medicine was sucha, and it was definitely Ayurvedic or homeopathic.

I took off my shirt and slid into the Ganga. With the cold water lapping my waist, I began breathing fast, as if doing pranayama, and Armaan laughed. 'Like this,' I said and submerged my head. I came up for an instant, the sun blinding my eyes, and then went under again. And again. And Armaan eventually joined in.

'So? What did you think of it all?' I asked him.

'It's nice. It's beautiful here,' he said. 'I like these mountains. I like the babas.' His voice took on a funny tone. 'The lamas in McLeod Ganj could teach me how to fly on a carpet. What can your Hindu babas teach me?'

'Be serious, na.'

'Your babas have something deep in them. I can see that,' he said. 'But I don't like your pandits. Didn't you see how that man's face changed when you gave him money? And then he had to show off and say that he knew so and so and all that.'

To my right, from behind the snow-capped peaks, the sun's rays cut into the sky in vivid straight lines, as in children's drawings, and the picture ahead appeared just as captivating: The Ganga. The bathing yaatris. The sliver of Gangotri town. The pine trees. The brown band of mountainside. And the ceaseless blue above.

'Don't you think this is like a six-layered sandwich of reality?' I said.

'Maybe.'

Armaan sat back up on a rock, closed his eyes. 'Okay, now let me meditate,' he said. 'I get energy from concentrating in the moment. This is one thing I am learning from Buddhist monks and your babas. They have both learnt how to still the mind.'

I tried to copy Armaan, invoking techniques mummy had once taught me. But my eyes returned to the external. Yes, I thought, these holy men had grit and determination but there was something acuter about them, too, something harder to articulate. Were their mysteries as old as these mountains? Was their toughness more than a result of practice? Could it be that there was something truly divine about this place? Perhaps some places on earth were actual spiritual centres that had gathered energies from prayers carried out at the same spot by millions over generations? *Maybe.*

Certainly, though, I can say that it was my search for answers to these shapeshifting questions that led me next to interact with the *kanwariyas* in Rishikesh and the Naga babas in Prayagraj and the Aghori babas in Varanasi. And it was my interactions with these men that propelled me to dig deeper into Hindu and Buddhist philosophy. To become, so to speak, less concerned with the world of organized religion and more interested in the mysteries of Vedanta, Buddhism and deep meditation.

When I opened my eyes again the sun was so intense that I had to shield my face. The Himalayas dazzled. The trees above Gangotri town soared. And the Ganga was so immense, so mighty, its current so decisive. Only the people, *only we people*, looked small.

A couple of nights later, back in Rishikesh, Armaan and I were having another of our discussions on faith at the famous Beatles Cafe over a couple of veggie burgers. The view was spectacular from here where the Ganga made a brooding curve widening into something like a lake before again narrowing to its organic shape and flowing on, deeply, placidly, anciently.

'If I can be honest,' Armaan said, 'for me, the monks in McLeod Ganj were more attractive. These Hindu places seem commercial. Real spirituality is missing for me.'

'You can't compare the two!' I said, laughing. 'Maybe it's a cultural thing. You've been bombarded by images of Buddhist monks. *Seven Years in Tibet* and all that. As for India, all you know is Bollywood. I really think we need to make a high-quality *Game of Thrones*-type series and sell our epics abroad.'

A man from the table beside us called out to us. 'Excuse me.'

He was white and middle-aged but in a white dhoti. The style of tika on his forehead gave him away as a Hare Krishna devotee. 'Sorry, I couldn't help but overhear your conversation,' he said. His accent was English. 'Sorry to interrupt, but I disagree. I have to say that there is something very pure about the Ganga and about the air in Rishikesh in particular. I've been coming here for a decade.'

The man's original name was Paul, but he had been *reKrishan'd* as Govind. Armaan and I introduced ourselves.

'Oh! You're from Afghanistan,' Govind said, a little surprised. 'Oh. Very interesting.' He pondered this a moment. 'Things are very difficult in your country, aren't they?'

'The problems are plenty,' Armaan said. 'Poverty...tribal values... Women's equality also has a long way to go.'

'Oh, yes, yes,' Govind said. He took a momentary pause. 'But the real reason your country is in a bad way is rather more straightforward, I think.' He shook his head. 'Wherever they cull cows in big numbers, there will be problems. The cow is like your mother.'

Walking with the Kanwariyas in Rishikesh

Haridwar is a merger of the Hindi terms 'Hari', meaning Lord Vishnu, and '*dwar*', meaning 'door'. 'Rishikesh' is the merger of the words '*rishi*', meaning sage, and '*kesh*', meaning hair. Situated in the Uttarakhand foothills and only twenty kilometres apart, both towns are gateways to Devbhoomi, or the Himalayan Abode of the Gods, and have for ages been home to many saints, temples, ashrams and legends.

Delhi. Many moons ago

Whenever Swamiji stayed with us, he took dinner alone in the master bedroom upstairs with mummy personally serving him out of stainless steel utensils untainted even by onion and garlic. But tonight, he decided to eat dinner with the family. Tonight, mummy seated Swamiji at the head of the dining table—papa's spot. And while she ensured that no meat had been cooked in the house, papa made sure to fortify his nerves with a large peg of Black Label.

As mummy scurried between the kitchen and dining table bearing hot ghee-smeared rotis, Swamiji went on about the depth and scope of Vedanta philosophy.

Very early in their marriage, my parents had reached something of a truce: papa would never broach the subject of religion with mummy and she would not meddle with his food and drink. But tonight, papa's eyes were glazed over, and his lips were closed tight in a scowl. Tonight, he was in one of his moods and the pact was at serious risk of breach.

'Swamiji, can you define God for me?' he said out of nowhere.

Swamiji swallowed his food at length. 'Well, it is like this,' he said. 'If you need to ask me, you might never understand Him.' He exchanged a knowing look with mummy. 'Buddha even said that God is nothing. But I personally don't agree with this view. Our Shaastras say God is eternal and indefinable. He resides in everything.'

Swamiji went on in this charming opaque manner referring liberally to the Vedas and the Upanishads before he came down to the more accessible gods.

He was talking about Lord Shiva and the Ganga when papa said, 'But why the Ganga? What is so great about this river?'

Mala put her hand on his shoulder and I felt a twist in my stomach.

A bit about my father here: He's not just a man who kept out of temples. He's a man who made it a point to keep out of them. Back in the '70s, when he'd trekked up to Badrinath and Kedarnath, he stayed out of the shrines in both places. He had never once come with us to Shivsagar Ashram because (1) he had no interest in religion and (2) because mummy showed no interest in getting him interested. Although, in her defence, the one time she did take him soon after their marriage he got so bored that he spent all his time smoking cigarettes in his room.

And yet my father is also the man who, in some peculiar way, seemed unbothered by my mother's embrace of faith. I sometimes thought that he secretly even agreed with her, just so long as she spared him of her ways.

'I don't think atheism is any more rational than a belief in a God,' he once said to me. 'It doesn't answer the only real question.'

'Which is?'

'What the hell are we doing here?'

As I mulled over what I took as a rare moment of self-doubt in my father, he slapped me on my back and enlarged his eyes. 'It's still all bunk,' he said.

'All rivers are sacred,' Swamiji was going on, 'but our Ganga has more depth. It is not for nothing we have been praying to her forever.' His hand went into the air as if he was about to make some profound disclosure, but then he quietly returned to his food. 'Sometimes the faith of millions can't be understood from the outside,' he said.

The rest of the evening thankfully passed without incident, but sure enough, my father's anger came spilling out the next morning. 'You bloody well can't tell me what to eat in my own house,' he yelled.

'Can you show respect to my guests for once?' mummy yelled back.

And things got heated but then cooled down as my parents reverted to their old and separate ways.

But one barb papa threw at mummy returned to me as I scrolled down my Facebook newsfeed one day in August 2018. 'The bloody kanwariya goonda season has started,' a friend commented. 'Stay safe,' wrote another.

Papa had said: 'You better not put my ashes in any filthy river after I go, dear lady. I'd rather you put me in the gutter.'

Rishikesh. August 8, 2018

A couple of kilometres before Rishikesh, I stepped off the taxi onto a hilly road buzzing with motorcycles and fluttering with orange flags and the national tricolour. It was a muggy morning, and to better fit into my surroundings, I put on an orange T-shirt and shorts. My shoes—Skechers, I noticed—stood out in my milieu. This was because the kanwariyas around me, carrying on their shoulders a *kanwar*—a bamboo pole with water from the Ganga hanging from a brass container at each end—had only chappals or nothing at all on their feet.

It was the day before *Shravan Shivratri* and I had joined the throngs on their yaatra from Haridwar to the Neelkanth Mahadev Temple, thirty-two kilometres ahead of Rishikesh. Just like in Delhi, nine out of ten yaatris were male. Maybe 9.5.

Over the past decade, the monsoon swell of kanwariyas has grown and grown, and with it, so has the ire directed against them from my peers and myself alike. I, therefore, came to Rishikesh as a challenge. I wanted to partake in this Hindu phenomenon that had grown to become India's largest annual religious gathering with an estimated twenty million participants—even if for two days.

Swami Shraddhanandji, now white-bearded and sage-looking, was back in Rishikesh on one of his long stints away from Gurgaon. After greeting him, I asked: 'Why do you think the kanwar yaatra became so big? I don't remember so many yaatris when I was little.'

'The crowd has increased, hasn't it?' he said jovially. 'Before, there were no amenities. But today, there is free food and lodging. So they come.' He chortled. 'This custom is ancient. To lift water from the Ganga and take it to a Shiva temple. But this yaatra, the way it is now, this is new.'

He said several NGOs and local trader committees stepped forward to provide for the yaatris. In addition to water, food and tea, people collected funds for first aid and medicines like painkillers. It was the community's way of vicariously participating in the pilgrimage.

I ran into Pandit Hemant afterwards and asked if he would like to join me on my journey, but he declined. 'These boys are *bhrasht*, corrupt,' he said. 'They only want to dance and smoke.'

At noon, though heaving with pilgrims, Rishikesh was empty of cars. The main road was split in two by a wooden fence going down its length, along one side of which yaatris were going up to Neelkanth, while on the other side many more were returning. On the roadside, there were all manner of clothes stalls. The T-shirts ranged from orange to blue and black and each was blessed by Lord Shiva either pictorially or in words. While the God Himself was primarily shown in a posture of deep penance or coolly smoking a chillum, there were a fair few images of him adopting the hirsute avatar of a new-age gym-man in possession of a fierce brow and six-packs, but with a trident in hand.

I heard the chime of *ghungroos* on the ankles of the boys marching beside me and then saw legs wrapped in cloth bandages. To prevent blisters, I was told.

Then came an array of smoking pipes of distinct shapes and sizes, from fat earthen ones to thin loopy brass cursives. The cheapest was ten rupees apiece and teenagers from Haryana made the purchase.

'In the olden days,' Swamiji had said earlier, 'only the very devout made this journey and always by foot.'

In fact, the word 'kanwar' is a coming together of the terms '*kam*' and '*var*': *kam*, meaning water, and *var*, meaning pure. It is considered so holy that a kanwariya should never even place it on the ground. 'So these boys who carry it on bikes, they are following a fashion.' He laughed. 'Before, people would take water from Gaumukh in the

Himalayas to their homes. Then it became water from Gangotri, which later moved down to Haridwar and Neelkanth.'

The Neelkanth Temple is where Lord Shiva ingested *halaahal*, the poison which originated from the churning of the ocean when the gods and demons joined hands to obtain *amrit*, the divine nectar of immortality. Lord Shiva arrested the poison in his throat, neither imbibing it nor leaving it out in the world, and as a result his throat went blue, and he came to be known as Neelkanth, or the blue-throated one. 'So, water is put on Shiva to cool him.'

But I was more interested in the present state of affairs, and I pressed, 'So, you believe it is a fashion, then?'

Swamiji laughed again. 'Well, what is a fashion? As people's wishes get granted their *aastha* [faith] also increases. Now see, Ganapati pooja was originally practised only in Maharashtra. Now, we see it all over the North also. And so it is with this yaatra.' He grew thoughtful. 'But yes, many boys copy others,' he said.

Threading through thousands of yaatris, I crossed the pedestrian suspension bridge Ram Jhula, going over the Ganga. The walk uphill from here was some fourteen kilometres, and the sheer implausibility of spending the night away from Rishikesh hit me. It wasn't the climb that daunted me. My shoes were hardy and I wasn't likely to tire if I took breaks. It was the growing prospect of having nowhere to sleep that was becoming increasingly distressing.

A little uphill, I got chatting with a young bunch smoking ganja. 'Will you *lagao dum*? Do you want Bhole Baba's prasad?' the gang-leader asked me, wide-eyed, and I politely refused. He said the group was from Badaun, UP, and this was their third yaatra to Neelkanth.

'Have the yaatris from your town increased?' I ventured.

'Yes. Increasing, increasing,' he said, pulling on his chillum. 'All have belief in *parmaatma*.' He was in his mid-twenties and had friendly, if mischievous, eyes.

'Do people come more for *bhakti* [belief] or *masti* [fun]?'

'They should know that themselves. How should I know?' He grinned. 'We have belief. I think seventy per cent must come for bhakti. We have to spend our own money and Rs 4,000–5,000 is a lot. I only have a small barbershop. And…'—he took another pull—'the journey is tiring. Last night we stayed at Swarg Ashram, but tonight we will have to stay on the road because there's no place available up.'

I glanced at my phone: 3 pm. I would trek up another hour, then turn around.

As I got up to leave, the gang-leader called out. 'And bhaiyya,' he said. 'Why can't we do mauj masti and also have bhakti?'

Rajesh Kumar Choudhary was a fifty-three-year-old lean but solid-looking farmer, from Muzaffarpur district. He was descending the slope using his kanwar as a walking stick. 'Its job is done,' he said smiling. 'I've put Gangajal on Mahadev. Now, I will bathe in Haridwar, and from there I'll take *jal* back home with me.'

After some polite small talk, I asked some pointed questions.

'See, before, three–four people used to come from my area, then it grew to five–six,' he said. 'This time—it's my third time—we are twenty-two of us. We usually go to Baidyanath Dham in Deoghar. So, we decided to come here for a change.'

Shravan Mela, a major festival at Deoghar, Jharkhand, is where thousands of yaatris bring Gangajal from Sultanganj, covering a distance of 105 kilometres, and offer it to Lord Baidyanath. Kumar believed that this yaatra dates from the time of the Ramayana. When Ravana decided to lift Lord Shiva from the Himalayas and carry him to Lanka, Shiva said to him: 'Don't you make the mistake of placing me on the ground, because if you do I won't budge.' En route, Ravana had a strong urge to urinate, so he asked a cow herder passing by to hold the Shivalingam for a moment. But when he returned, he saw that, unable to bear the immense weight, the herder had put the Lord on the ground. Where He'd joined inseparably with the Earth!

So, it was Ravana who first offered Gangajal to Shiva to ask God for forgiveness. 'This is the story from our area,' Kumar said. 'All this is aastha.'

When I asked him how come there were no women in their group, he said, 'It's difficult for them. There are few provisions here. In Haridwar, there is a Kali Kamli Mandir. We used to stay the night there. But this time the police didn't let us. And if it's raining or hot, we manage.' He gave a genial laugh of resignation, turned to his companion. 'It was raining, and we slept on the road because there was nowhere else to go. But if we have ladies or kids with us, they might have a problem. So, we leave them at home.'

'You look like a true believer,' I found myself saying. 'But many come for fun, yes? I believe there are troublemakers too.' This came out more as a statement than a question, and Kumar's friend, who'd been quiet thus far, spoke up.

'No,' he said. 'We all have aastha. Otherwise, you tell me, we are poor people. Why should we spend so much? I can have masti at home. Why come this far?'

'We spend so much on *Dharam* that we don't like to have things for free,' Kumar said, with a touch of pain in his voice. He looked as though I'd accused him of a minor theft. 'We spend on the train, on food and all this.' He pointed to his kanwar and a sealed metal container in his hand. 'On this alone, I spent Rs 2,000. And it is almost Rs 10,000 with the train tickets and everything.'

He met my gaze again. 'The troublemakers make it difficult for everyone. Some boys become excited when they are in big groups. But we are *kisaan aadmi* [farmers], so why should we spend so much money? We spend in the name of Dharam.'

While most kanwariyas said they were driven by faith, I felt it was perhaps of a style that sat uneasily with those aspiring to a more austere of its varieties.

For a trio from Bareilly, aged eighteen, nineteen and twenty, the yaatra was a matter of bhakti, but it was as much an outing with friends. But for Padam Singh from Uttam Nagar, Delhi, it was purely a matter of belief. While this fifty-year-old put up a stall of chappals back home, he came here barefoot. He said he had trekked through the night without even a drop of water, and going by his wearied face, gaunt body and swollen feet, I had no reason to doubt him.

'You know why you don't see many girls and families around?' he said. 'It is because if these boys bring their wives and sisters, they can't smoke and drink. Do you see any of them carrying a kanwar? Only twenty per cent carry it. The rest walk with their plastic bottles or go *brrrr-brrrr* on their bikes. They've made this mela into a party.'

He shook his head. 'This is a fashion,' he said.

On the last couple of kilometres during my return, I met brothers Kuldeep and Vikas, aged nineteen and seventeen, respectively. They had made the journey from Laksar, near Haridwar. Their bare and callused feet tinkled with ghungroos, and their frail shoulders each bore a kanwar. It was their fourth trip to Neelkanth, and their reason for undertaking the yaatra was simple. They had come to thank God, for were it not for Him, they wouldn't be here in the first place.

Their mother had pleaded Lord Shiva for the birth of a son, and after years of prayers, she had got not one but two boys. However, her deteriorating health prevented her from making the yaatra herself, so Kuldeep, the elder of the two, stepped up when he turned fifteen. He promised her that he would make a total of five yaatras on her behalf. That was four years ago when she was still alive. Now, it was just the brothers and their father, a labourer, at home.

'The yaatra was fine,' Kuldeep said. 'There is a *langar*, but the line is very long, so it's good we got our own food. The problem is that it gets tiring and the expenses add up. When we get home, we will have to spend another Rs 5,000 on pooja and a *bhandaara* [feeding Brahmins].' But he smiled easily and moved to lighter matters. 'Our friends will come after the fifteenth,' he said. 'They will come for masti.'

'Won't you come with them?'

'Not this year. But after our final yaatra, I will.' He pointed over his shoulder. 'I won't have this load with me then.' As I admired the duo for their stoicism, I remembered that my hotel was approaching, and I bid the brothers goodbye.

'We'll just keep walking,' Kuldeep said, marching on. 'It will take another four hours to Haridwar. We'll take the train home from there, if we get one. Otherwise, we'll lie down where we can.' He smiled again.

August 9

Today was to end in Shivratri: the night of Shiva, when yaatris rush to put the Gangajal, lifted from Rishikesh or Haridwar on Shivalingams in temples in their villages and homes. The crowd had thinned out substantially and the main road had opened partially to cars. No sooner than I'd gone a hundred metres down it, though, I was stopped by a sight: A kanwariya running hard as bystanders cheered him on. A couple of motorcycles, on which additional kanwariyas rode, moved alongside. The runner was barefooted and bare-chested and his head was wrapped in an orange *gamchha*.

He passed the baton, a bag of Gangajal, to the next runner some hundred metres ahead, whose arm was stretched backwards in anticipation. But not before he made a flourishing juggle with his hands behind his back. Then the second runner relayed the baton to a third, and the race continued.

I spotted Pandit Hemant observing the spectacle from the sidelines and went up to him. He had the air of somebody who appreciated what he was seeing but couldn't be bothered to do the thing himself.

'These boys are what they call the *dak kanwars*,' he said. 'They move non-stop. They've made a promise to complete the yaatra within twenty-four hours...or thirty-six, or forty-eight hours...it all depends on how far their home is!' He let out a hoot.

And it struck me: this race neatly captured the soul of the kanwariyas, didn't it? *A rousing show of both bhakti and masti.* A performance in which focus meets fun and sheer grit combines with an unabashed display of pomp and masculinity. Weren't these the core impulses of the kanwar yaatra? Or at any rate, the essential ingredients of what it had in this day and age become.

'Last year, these bikers caused some accidents and people became unfavourably disposed towards them,' Pandit Hemant said. 'But now look at this, all this effort they put in. I even saw one boy carrying his grandmother on his shoulders all the way up to Neelkanth.'

The road between Rishikesh and Haridwar was jammed with trucks carrying armies of dak kanwars booming with dance music. There was a Mahadev DJ truck and a Bhole Baba DJ truck. And a while later, I even saw a 'Fire Gym' truck. Its side had been painted over with the blue-hued back of Shiva, the shoulder blades sculpted, the spine taut, the hair flowing down jet-black. A song blared: '*Har-Har! Bam-Bam! Jeetega bhai jeetega* [We will win].'

It was a veritable open-air nightclub, except that it was afternoon, not night, and only boys were in it. Boys merrily dancing. Boys smoking. Boys clapping.

I asked the taxi driver to pull over. 'Hey!' I said to one particularly intoxicated guy dancing without a care in the world. 'I'm interested to learn about your yaatra. Can you tell me why you play this music?'

'*Utsaah* [excitement] hai,' the dancer replied, all sweaty. '*Bas.*' There was excitement, indeed. 'You are writing about us?' he said. 'Please also write that since Yogi Adityanath has come to UP, he's allowed us to enjoy fully. Every Hindu supports him. He is a great person! I say there should be more DJs! Many DJs! We should be free to enjoy ourselves. When Akhilesh Yadav was chief minister, he would not let us enjoy. He only promoted Muslims. Please write this.' He collapsed into the back of the truck as his friends went into a tizzy of laughter.

I was unfazed when, a while later, I heard the lyrics of another song. It went: '*DJ bajwa diya Yogi ne. Rang jama diye Yogi ne.*' Yogi allowed DJs. Yogi injected colour into our celebrations.

That evening, the train going to eastern UP was like a bloated orange snake. And even after it lumbered out of the platform, the station air felt just as hot and humid as it did when it was standing, filled up with yaatris.

I'd changed my clothes now. I was back in a staid grey from the festive orange and this small act had produced a shift of disposition in me. I'd been so comfortable with all the madness a couple of hours back, but now I was tired. Now, all I wanted was an air-conditioned room, some quiet and proper food.

Inside the Shatabdi, I was greeted by light chatter in English, the rustle of newspapers, the smell of brewing coffee. And cool air.

There was a newsflash on my phone: 'Delhi: Outrage Over Kanwariya Vandalism', read one headline. 'Kanwariyas engage in violence in Delhi, UP: It's time to stop unruly "pilgrims" threatening people's safety', read another.

And a funny thing happened: I felt a pang of defensiveness. This was highly unusual given the distance between myself and the persons referred to on the screen. But my mind surged.

Indeed, there are some hooligans, but this news shows such a lopsided picture! What about Kuldeep and his brother? Or Kumar? Why do we never read about their stories?

If the kanwariyas blocked vehicular traffic then isn't it also true that we car owners came in their way as they trod down the highway, barefoot and thirsty? And whose right of way is it? Of the millions of pedestrians or the SUVs and cars?

Outside the window, a group of boys waiting to go home had gathered to play cards while another lot was tapping away on their phones. *These were like boys anywhere, really!* Boys looking for a sports ground, a nightclub, a gym. Boys in search of a higher calling. *They wanted to have fun!* And when their circumstances could not give them what they desired, they went ahead and got it anyhow—in the form that was available to them, in a way that they understood. I would do the same if I were in their shoes. *If my shoes weren't Skechers.*

I turned to the popcorn on my tray. *So much of my judgement stems from my position of privilege, doesn't it?* I stretched my worn legs and ate a fistful.

Yes, I'll think more deeply about this later, I thought. I reclined my chair and closed my eyes. Right now, I'm just happy to be back in an air-conditioned room.

A Brief Immersion in the World of the Naga Babas in Prayagraj

The Kumbh Mela is a major yaatra held four times over twelve years, with the Mela rotating every three years between four sites situated along holy rivers: (1) the confluence of Ganga, Yamuna and the mythical Saraswati at Prayagraj, (2) the Ganga at Haridwar, (3) the Godavari at Nashik and (4) the Shipra at Ujjain. At every mela, millions of Hindus congregate on auspicious dates for a *Shahi Snaan*, or royal bath, seeking mukti (freedom from sins) and moksha (salvation).

The Mahakumbh Mela of 2013 and the Kumbh Mela of 2019 were both held in Prayagraj (still Allahabad in 2013). Drawing an estimated 120 million and 220 million believers, respectively, each festival was cited in India and abroad as the largest human gathering in the world.

One day in January 2013. 9 am

'Oh my God!' Mummy rubbed her eyes as she opened the door. She smiled a big smile. 'How did you find me?'

'I have my ways.' I smiled back. But I could see dark circles under her eyes. Having woken up at some unearthly hour, she was probably catching up on her sleep. Behind her, spread on the floor I saw only a thin mattress and a fusty blanket. That's it. That's all there was.

Already I could feel anger growing in my veins. 'Is this what you call VIP treatment? Please, let's find a hotel.'

Mummy laughed. 'Good luck with that.' Yaatris were sleeping in tents, she said. They were camping out on the streets, staying in buses. There were dormitories along the river banks where people were renting beds by the hour. 'That I've got this room really is VIP treatment!'

From my taxi, I'd seen a sea of grey tents stretching up to the Old Naini Bridge. And far, far beyond it. *A temporary settlement reaching the horizon! A testament to human ingenuity and resilience!* I had to concede.

Swami Shraddhanandji had invited my mother to attend the Mahakumbh Mela in Allahabad in 2013. It was the ideal place for the sadhus and trustees of Vairagya Teerath Gyanpeeth to meet.

Swami Atmanand and several other sadhus from Shivsagar Ashram were also going. 'Sehdev, Prahlad, Saroj, everybody's going,' mummy said. And she was too. Because this was not just the Kumbh Mela, but the Mahakumbh Mela, and it came only once every 144 years.

I had to dissuade her. Not just because it was hard to shake off stories about people getting lost in the crowds but because there lay the very real risk of a stampede. There lay a certainty that my mother would drink the water in which millions had bathed and fall violently ill.

Mummy naturally began her side of the argument by retelling one of the most well-known Hindu legends, the *Samudra Manthan*, or the Churning of the Ocean of Creation between the *asuras* (demons) and the devtas (gods).

As I've mentioned, Dear Reader, first, the ocean expelled halaahal *vish*, the poison Lord Shiva trapped in his throat. But finally, from the sea's depths emerged the physician of the devtas, Dhanwantari, holding a pot of amrit. And as he appeared, the devtas grabbed the pot and ran, and the asuras began chasing after them. During this chase, drops of amrit fell to the Earth at four sites, instilling each place with numinous properties: Haridwar, Prayagraj, Nashik and Ujjain.

The other, less mythical, origin story I'd see championed by many sadhus was that Shankaracharya began the Kumbh Mela to arrange regular meetings of ascetics for discourse and deliberation—a way to consolidate the Hindu sadhu base.

But my own reading on the Kumbh said differently. While it certainly was beyond doubt that river bathing festivals in India had an ancient history, it was far from certain that the Kumbh had commensurately started at these four sacred sites. As per the

Encyclopedia of Global Religion, 'The earliest historical account of the Kumbha comes from Hiuen-Tsang, a Chinese Buddhist pilgrim who visited India in the seventh century… Although four locations are mentioned in the mythology of the Mela, early historical accounts of its occurrence refer only to Prayag and Haridwar.' According to the Indologist Kama MacLean, Allahabad's religious Mela prior to 1760 was an important yaatra, but it was not a Kumbh Mela. And according to an essay titled 'The Kumbh Mela festival processions' by James G. Lochtefeld: 'The Kumbh Mela's contemporary importance is belied by surprisingly scarce historical data, much of which points to a relatively recent formation—at least as a single festival celebrated in four places. Yet historical records clearly reveal large, well-established bathing festivals. Some were annual such as Haridwar's Baisakhi Mela and Prayag's Magh Mela. Others were determined by Jupiter's twelve-year cycle—Haridwar's Kumbha Mela and Nasik's Sinhastha Mela whose differing charter myths clearly point to independent origins.'

Not that I expected such analyses to make the slightest difference. My mother went. And now I'd joined her.

12 pm

Mummy and I shared that same basic room at Brahm Vidyapeeth, an Allahabad ashram loosely affiliated with Vairagya Teerath Gyanpeeth. And as I was with her I fell into her tempo of activity.

As sadhus were the chief guests at the Kumbh Mela, the Brahm Vidyapeeth and Vairagya Teerath Gyanpeeth joined hands to organize a maha bhandaara feast for them. As the ashram's trustees and patrons, it was our duty to feed them; and so, carrying large steel buckets, I ladled out daal, rice and sabzi onto dried leaf thaalis set out on the floor in a long line behind which the holy men sat down to eat.

There were easily over five hundred sadhus at the bhandaara that afternoon. About three-fourths wore orange, but the rest were ash-smeared semi-naked men: the Nagas. There were austere babas who ate only one roti and hungry ones who wanted more than three servings. There were gracious babas who thanked me as I offered them a token of Rs 10 and put a tilak on their forehead and others who went through this routine perfunctorily. There was even one doped-out Naga who fell asleep while eating. And another with sunglasses and a fancy handbag which looked like it could have been purchased in Sarojini Nagar Market.

And in one corner, I saw a cluster of female sadhus. *Sadhvis.* I told mummy that maybe she should join them, and she laughed delightedly.

Later in the afternoon, I went for a stroll to the *Sangam*—the confluence of the Ganga, Yamuna and the mythical Saraswati. The mudflats surrounding the riverbanks are an expansive tract of sand equalling some 3,000 football fields and the entire place was teeming with makeshift tents stretching into the wintry haze. Poles supporting streetlights, linked by long drooping cables, had been erected everywhere, and kiosks selling refreshments were set up at key junctions.

On the sand's fringes came the flimsy tents of the poor.

Here, a woman was cooking on a stove powered by cow dung. She flattened a roti with the palm of her hand before putting it to cook on a *tava.* A boy dressed up as Lord Krishna offered yaatris blessings in return for a few coins. Behind, his mother, stretched out on the sand, was breastfeeding his nude infant brother. An old beggar sat inside a wooden cart fashioned into a shaky wheelchair. It had a secret compartment where he'd stashed away peanuts. And further on came a teenager selling flowers. His bright roses and marigolds spread out on a plastic sheet was a red oasis in the grime.

Nearer the river came the prominent, fancier tents set up by the myriad sadhu *akharas,* or orders. Each had a bright image of a head sadhu displayed outside. Here I saw clusters of well-off patrons drinking tea, having samosas, chatting. Here were chubbier kids, chubbier adults. A group of tall white devotees were laughing aloud. They had on white kurta pyjamas and dark sunglasses. An India suddenly gentrified, I thought. The Kumbh Mela certainly showed you the *real* India. Or at least an India I hardly ever ventured into and which some foreigners came only to see.

At the site of the Sangam itself, though, were few people. 3 pm was indeed an odd time for a bath. Still, the sparseness was probably because it was Makar Sankranti the next day, and everybody was saving up on their zeal for the Shahi Snaan.

Fearing unsanitary conditions—fears being borne out on my walk—I'd again been discouraging my mother from taking the holy dip on Makar Sankranti after lunch when Swamiji briefly addressed the day's importance.

Falling on January 14, Makar Sankranti marks the transition of the sun from the zodiac of Sagittarius (*dhanu*) to Capricorn (*makara*). Also called *Uttaraayana*—a term that combines the Sanskrit words '*uttara*' (north) and '*aayana*' (movement)—the day indicated the northward movement of the sun. But what this meant in religious terms was that it marked the precise time when the doors of the devtas opened up for us mortals.

'In the Mahabharata, Bhishma Pitamah'—also known as Gangaputra, the son of the Ganga—'was pierced by thousands of arrows by Arjun,' Swamiji said. 'As he lay thirsty on his deathbed of arrows, Arjun shot an arrow into the ground, and Gangajal sprang up to quench his thirst. But despite his horrible injuries, he did not die. Why? Because he had the boon of *ichchha mrityu*. This meant he could choose exactly when he wanted to die. When Bhishma Pitamah fell on his bed of arrows, it was *Dakshinaayana*'—the six-month period preceding the Uttaraayana—'a time when the devtas' doors are closed, so he decided to wait. He tolerated the pain for another fifty-eight days.' He clapped his hands. 'But as soon as Uttaraayana came he left his body. He knew the devtas were waiting.'

4 am, the next day

Roughly two hundred sadhus and about fifty devotees were gathered at the ashram gates. Mummy and I were among them. The sadhus began chanting *Om Namah Shivaaya!* and we repeated after them. And still chanting '*Om Namah Shivaaya! Om Namah Shivaaya! Om Namah Shivaaya!*' we started our walk towards the Sangam.

As we made our way through the sandy streets, the rivulets of yaatris began to swell into a tide, and within twenty minutes, the entire expanse of the mudflats turned into a sea of humanity. It was an endless carpet, an effervescent organism, unfurling itself, as it were, towards the source of all life and rebirth. And being one with this primeval force it was hard to resist its current. It was hard to resist feeling like I was going to witness something exceptional.

At one point, the tide split into two streams, and now we were moving alongside a road on which chariots were coming down with much pomp and celebration. Scores and scores of chariots carrying *mahants*—head sadhus—and sadhvis, and their followers.

Cries of '*Har Har Mahadev!*' came from the Naga babas up ahead. They had been given the honour of taking the first bath. But now they were returning and it was our turn. The turn of the Niranjani Akhara, the order to which both the Vairagya Teerath Ashram and Shivsagar Ashram belonged, and which was headquartered in Haridwar.

The head of the Brahm Vidyapeeth, a Swami Pragyanand, ascended a chariot, as did Swami Shraddhanandji. And as he did, he called out to my mother, '*Aa jao. Jagah hai*...hop in, there's space.' And so, she climbed atop it. As did I. And riding among sadhus, we went forward.

'*Har Har Mahadev! Har Har Mahadev! Har Har Mahadev!*'

When we reached the river banks, light had broken. We had only twenty minutes to bathe and had to be quick. So, without wasting a breath, everybody—the sadhus to one side and the devotees to the other—rushed into the water.

'*Har Har Mahadev! Har Har Mahadev! Har Har Mahadev!*'

Dithering at the shore, I spotted a Hindi banner overhead that read: '*Ganga tat par hum jap aur tap karenge, kulla aur manjan nahin.*' We will pray at the banks of the Ganga, not brush our teeth or gargle. And it was true. As far as I could see, everybody, thousands and thousands, was praying. It was an unforgettable sight, and not wanting to forget it I took several photos.

I heard a man calling out the names of the elderly and children who'd been separated from their families over the loudspeaker: '*Beena Mataji khambe number char par intezaar kar rahi hain. Unke parivaar waale aa kar le lein.*' Beena Mataji is waiting at pillar number four. Her family may come and fetch her. A funny sensation ran down my spine. A frisson of excitement, but also absolvement.

I have to say though that despite everything, despite this churning rush of millions, the holy bath was well organized. There was a wooden fence in the water that ensured you couldn't swim into the deep so everybody was standing in the shallows and offering water to the Uttaraayana sun. Drinking it in. Taking dip after holy dip. There was room for everybody and there was no pushing or shoving.

I later thought that being in the Sangam felt like being in a vigorously thronged bazaar in which every vendor knows their role, every shopper knows the way.

By the time the Ganga and the Yamuna reach the plains, they turn from rushing torrents into sluggish bodies of water. But here at the Sangam the water wasn't slow, it was stagnant. The Ganga was no longer the Ganga of Rishikesh. It was a bog and everybody was submerged in it. Suffused in it. Taking it in in fistfuls.

A part of me had thought that when the time to bathe came, I'd join the others, but now that I was here I couldn't do it. It was all too much, it was too intense. Why, I even tried to hold mummy back, but my pleading came out as a whimper. *As if she'd listen, anyway!* But as she just now brought a handful of water to her lips, I shouted, 'Don't!'

'Hah,' she said and gulped it down.

I fumed all the way back to the ashram. I fumed throughout our train journey to Delhi. And I raged for a good week after we'd got home. And when, mercifully, mummy didn't get so much as a tummy ache, I said, 'It was just luck.' And she scoffed again.

Sadly, many others weren't so lucky. On February 10, 2013, a stampede broke out at the Allahabad train station, killing forty-two people and injuring at least three hundred.

Prayagraj. January 2019

A middle-aged man with a mop of matted hair and intense black eyes stood outside his tent, covered from head to toe in only ash. Behind him was another man, proudly austere, squatting by a fire, smoking hashish. Dense clouds rose from his lips, hung briefly in the air, then merged with the enveloping smog. But the image lingered: a naked man with a beehive for a beard, his mesh of untold mysteries.

Neither person wore his nudity as an affront. It was simply there like some avatar meant to reveal a lost primal state of incarnation. And once I adjusted my eyes, as I earlier did my feet to the dark-cold waters of the Ganga, the picture fit.

Here at the Prayagraj Kumbh Mela 2019, everything looked primal. While I lived in an India with one leg in the digital race, the limb here was dipped in our rivers of faith. On the mudflats surrounding the confluence of the Ganga, Yamuna and Saraswati, it was not smartphones but tridents, rudraksh necklaces and uncovered phalluses that contended for conspicuity.

January 15, 2019. 9 am

It was Makar Sankranti, the Mela's first big bathing day, and the pop-up 'Tent-city'—a panoply of bright camps stretching out in all directions separated by pathways spilling with sadhus, pilgrims and sand—was throbbing. Built in under two months, the tumult would revert to a lull after Mahashivratri on March 4, the Mela's final day.

Vinaygiri, a youth leader of the Bharatiya Janata Party, had told me earlier that this tent-city was unlike any he had seen. For one, there was a laser show, and everything was digital. I told him that when I was here last for the Allahabad Mahakumbh in 2013, I'd read that the Mela was the subject of a case study at Harvard University. Scholars were interested in learning about the logistics behind the city's swift popping up and winding down.

'It was Allahabad then,' Vinaygiri said. 'Now it is Prayagraj. Before foreigners came to see our poverty. Now, they'll see our greatness.' He pointed to a row of plastic toilet stalls to one side. 'All this wasn't here when you came before, was it?'

I didn't mention that at my camp, wi-fi was available only on the booking site, and when I'd complained about this to the manager, he'd jovially but also self-righteously said that no Kumbh pilgrimage would be complete without incurring some hardship!

Having passed the camps of a Lakshmi Narsingh Khalsa from Brindavan and a Sadhguru Sai Ma from Varanasi, I stood among a crowd seeking blessings from Mathura resident Naga Baba Shyamanandgiri. His stand was one of many belonging to the Joona Akhara, the Old Order, which with over 400,000 sadhus as members was among the original thirteen orders of Hindu spiritual learning at the Kumbh.

On the bridge alongside, a procession of orange-clad sadhus plodded past me. The gurus sat on thrones on chariots and their disciples followed by foot. A helicopter whizzed by and down came a shower of rose petals trailed by a roar of *Jai Shri Ram!* Then came the parade of nude and semi-nude Naga babas, all barefoot, and the incantations to Shiva rose to a fever pitch. One baba had dreadlocks so long he clutched his coils in his hand like a bag.

An observing old woman joined her hands in prayer. A child's jaw dropped open. A tourist brought out his fat-lensed camera. And the police pushed the onlookers back.

Above, a hoarding with the pictures of Chief Minister Adityanath and Prime Minister Modi read, '*Padhaaro Sant aur Sajjan.*' Welcome, saints and gentlemen.

These Nagas were saints, but were they gentle? What spurred them to live as they did? How did they live? I wanted to know. I told myself I was an inquirer rather than a pilgrim. But when you're in the thick of the world's largest religious congregation, such distinctions matter little. Everybody who was here was here to find some meaning.

The baba spotted me. 'Come, beta,' he said, beckoning with a peacock feather. I was too old to be his son, but his bearing showed candour, so I asked, 'Babaji, can you tell me about yourself?'

He answered swiftly, as though my query were routine and his life was as bare as his body. 'What do I want? I want *jagat ka kalyaan. Parmaatma ka chintan*...the good of the world. To immerse myself in God. First, we toughen ourselves in the Himalayas. Any place where man—where *you*—cannot live. Then, after two years, five years, or ten, our guru orders us to return to the world, and we come here for our induction. At dawn, we sit on an empty stomach and have our *dhooni*. We chant *Om Namah Shivaaya*. We take 108 dips in the Ganga. We do our pind daan.'

The ritual Hindus carry out when a family member dies—pind daan—to return to the Universe what was fleetingly yours, the body, sanyaasis did for themselves. From this moment, they were meant to renounce worldly life and commence a path free of attachment. But for the Digambar—or sky-clad—Nagas, nakedness was an additional mode to approach Truth—it necessitated a life of seclusion, away from carnal distractions. They said this state enabled them to penetrate the *maya* that made up the material but illusory world of the senses.

Shyamanandgiri, however, unlike many of the other sadhus around—who it seemed to me were drawn to devoutness due to their dire circumstances—said he was spiritually inclined since childhood. He had a master's degree no less, which he obtained after taking up sainthood. 'Who says I should stop studying?' he said. And when I inquired where he lived, he said serenely, '*Brahmaand mein.*' In the universe. A response that might have elicited amusement coming from somebody else, from him—a man with no home and who led a peripatetic life, spending a night in a cave near the Ganga's source or on the beach at Ganga Sagar where it merged with the sea—seemed sage.

To a man who had abandoned all desire and extracted equal joy from singing bhajans by a stream in the jungle or beside burning corpses in Varanasi, a sense of belonging scarcely seemed important. *Or did it?* For he did say that wherever he went, he never missed the Kumbh Mela.

In the beginning, however, the Nagas, literally mountain dwellers, were not benign wanderers. They had a clear purpose: to protect Sanatan Dharma, the Eternal Path, from outside threats.

Of the four monastic orders established by Adi Shankaracharya (the *Hans*, *Paramhans*, *Dandi* and *Naga*, and of which the thirteen Kumbh Akharas were living branches) in the eighth century, the Nagas were warriors entrusted with the faith's tridents and spears. And we needed them because 'if all sadhus busied themselves in sermons, who would protect our Dharma?' Vidyasagar Saraswati, a Joona Akhara spokesperson, explained to me. So, while most sadhus preserved our *shaastras*, sacred texts, the Nagas carried *shastras*, weapons. Ever ready to fight, 'in one hand they held a *mala*, and in the other, they carried a *bhaala*,' spear.

When they were confronted with adversaries, they would first cite divine reason. And if this failed, they could hit. But could these naked fakirs really fight? Who did they fight? Gaunt and drug-addled, with eyes that seemed more dazed than determined, many more held chillums than tridents in their hands. Even the sturdy ones had bellies and a look of blithe unconcern about them.

It was plain they had zero regard for their appearance. But did their skills in combat amount to anything more than a nod to the gods? Sureshpuri Baba, a saffron-robed sadhu from Ujjain, said they undeniably did. The fifty-two-year-old lean man with lucid coal eyes was an enthusiastic talker so I was happy he agreed to give me a camp tour.

We passed a Naga who had a bell hanging from his penis, which pilgrims rang one at a time to gain his blessings as others bowed in reverence. And one who rolled his foreskin around a metal rod like a wrapper, then proceeded to stretch the thing in various ways, all painful to watch. When he took the lot from between his legs to his back and twisted his wrists as if turning a lock, he smiled. I grimaced and Sureshpuri chuckled.

'This is his *linga kriya*,' he said. 'Some of them can lift weights with their lingams also. Want to see?'

'No.'

He laughed. 'You asked me to show you things, so I did. But don't get the wrong idea. This is not what makes Nagas saints. These are tests of tapasya. The reality never stays hidden forever. It can only be like that for some time. There are fakes here also but they have no religion. They don't belong to any akhara.'

Sureshpuri went quiet. 'Have you seen the ocean?' he said. 'Does it keep anything toxic with it for long? It doesn't. It throws it back out. Just like that, our akharas also throw the fakes out. These chillums also, like their sunglasses, came later. But it takes more. A lot more. You must look deeper.'

And so I looked. Inside one camp, I saw two men sparring with swords. *Was it a mock joust?* Then I saw one baba who drove his wooden staff through a stack of bricks placed over another's head as spectators gasped in awe. And then another, a barrel-chested Naga in a loincloth, rotating a wooden staff in each hand like a pair of motors as he propelled his legs jauntily forward.

A baba Vashisht Giri, still in his twenties, had his arms and neck covered in rudraksh necklaces. The beads towered over his head rising like a crown pyramid capped by a crescent moon. He said he spent half the year meditating in caves near Kedarnath and his lot of necklaces weighed fifty-one kilos. Another, Lakkad Baba, also from Kedarnath, claimed he had been silent for twelve years. He communicated solely through handwritten notes. He left his job as a policeman to serve God, he wrote.

Apparently, some Nagas could stand on their heads for hours. They could put their bodies through intense heat and cold and went without food and water for days.

'Can your commandos show this kind of hardiness?' Sureshpuri searched my face. 'Things change with time. But these things remain. What do you think this means?'

Like many religious folk, sadhus liked speaking in riddles. But still, what did he mean?

Sureshpuri said that the thirteen Kumbh Akharas were divided into fifty-two regiments called *Madhi*, and each one practised a different discipline. While one Naga clan trained in swords, the next turned to the *gada*, the mace, the weapon of Hanuman. While one invoked fire, another prayed to *Surya*, the sun. But the God who stirred every Naga was Shiva, the Lord of Destruction who was also the summation of cosmic energy. 'It was Shiva who made the Naga sadhus one force.'

Was it a coincidence that our army regiments' war cries echoed the age-old sadhu calls on the gods? I said aloud. '*Bol Bajrang Bali ki Jai!*' and '*Jo Bole So Nihal, Sat Sri Akal!*' were the battle cries of the Rajput and Sikh regiments. Even the term akhara, which I associated with wrestling clubs behind Hanuman temples, appeared to have a connection with these shadowy seers.

Sureshpuri said such links were only to be expected and the reason was simple. 'The Nagas were our army at a time when we had no nation, no force.' The Nagas might seem an inscrutable bunch of shy, intimidating men today but everybody at the Mela knew who they were. 'The Nagas were the ancestors to the Indian army.'

I must have appeared doubtful because he said, 'Why, do you not find what you see familiar?'

As bewildering as the sights were, I had to admit that I'd just been on a walk down a hidden memory lane. I recognized the Nagas' battle cries. Their chants were embedded in our prayers. Their metre was borrowed from our mantras. The Nagas' clothes were nothing, but their invocations—they were reaching for something.

Perhaps this was one design of the Kumbh Mela? To breathe into me vague feelings of nostalgia. To enliven lost memories. To vivify them and give them God's shape. To root me to the ground. To my identity. To my faith and country.

I gave Suresphuri a nod and he beamed.

Yes. At the Kumbh, folklore rather than historical facts held sway. And I had more questions.

I was starving. So, I grabbed a leaf plate and joined a line at a camp where food was being served at a nominal price. I sat down to eat with a family from Punjab who had come to the Mela with their guru: Swami Madhavanand from Haridwar. The sadhu had a greying beard and a slight belly draped in rich silk pleats. It was his sixth Kumbh pilgrimage.

I said I would like to ask him a question. 'Many sadhus cite the Mughals and the British as outsiders whom the Nagas resisted. Is this correct?'

That the Nagas had organized themselves so during the Islamic rule in the subcontinent was an oft-told account of history here. One man even said that a band of Nagas resisted the very armies of Aurangzeb who went on to destroy the Kashi Vishwanath temple at Varanasi.

'The Nagas were Dharma's defenders,' Swami Madhavanand said, 'constantly safeguarding it from attacks from "*Mlechchhas*".' Barbarians. The word 'mlechchha' incidentally initially occurs in a Vedic text and is used for people who could not speak clearly. Given that Sanskrit was confined mainly to upper castes, 'mlechchha', scholars surmise, might have been used to connote people who fell outside the caste structure.

Swami Madhavanand scooped sabzi onto a section of roti and took a bite. 'Islam and Christianity came later,' he said. 'But even when the Nagas were born many centuries before, Sanatan Dharma was close to disappearing. We were the minority, and the country had lost its mooring in the Shaastras. At that time, atheism was spreading fast everywhere.' He chewed over this. 'In those days, it was the raj of the *Boudhwaale*.' The Buddhists. 'People can say anything. But can you believe them all?'

While Swami Madhavanand neither confirmed nor denied what was implicit in my question—that the Nagas had resisted Islamic invaders—he reiterated what was common knowledge: that it was when a boy named Adi Shankaracharya came on the scene that things began to change in Hinduism's favour. It was thanks to his efforts that Hinduism was revived.

'Did the Naga Sadhus make the Buddhists leave India, then?'

Though how and why Buddhism left the subcontinent is the subject of scholarly debate, with experts citing reasons ranging from the reascendancy of the Brahmins to the mismanagement of monasteries and the arrival of Islam, I was in search of the principal currents of belief rather than historical fact.

'The Buddhists were made to leave through knowledge, not by force,' Swami Madhavanand said. And to buttress this point, he narrated the story of Kumarila Bhatta, a philosopher of medieval India who was a staunch believer in the Vedas.

The Buddhists had been unable to defeat Bhatta in debates, so they put to him a challenge: 'If your Vedas are the Truth, you should survive a fall from a hill,' they said. And Bhatta accepted their test, proclaiming, 'If the Vedas are the Truth I will survive.' Thus he was pushed down a hill and survived the fall, but lost an eye. When he questioned Gayatri, the fount of Vedic knowledge, about why this had happened, she said, 'You must have had some doubt in the Vedas' truthfulness; otherwise you wouldn't have attached the word "If" before their Truth!'

Swami Madhavanand placed another rotiful to the side of his mouth. In the end, Sanatan Dharma prevailed, and the Naga babas were instrumental in making this happen. Shankaracharya founded the mathas in the four corners of the country—Govardhan Matha in Odisha, Sringeri Sharada Matha in Karnataka, Dwarka Matha in Gujarat, and Jyotir Matha in the Uttarakhand Himalayas. And as sadhus went about preaching Dharma between these far-flung corners, the Nagas protected them. Indeed, 'they played so key a role in winning Hinduism back, that we honour them as mandaleshwars [leaders of sadhus] at the Mela even today. And the Nagas, too, go around chanting Shankaracharya's name whom they consider an avatar of Shiva as they roam from place to place. *Hai na?*

Swami Madhavanand gestured the sole woman in the group to fetch him water, and I realized that despite talking continually, he'd nearly finished his meal, whereas I hadn't even begun mine. I had been just as caught up in his storytelling as the Punjabi yaatris were.

'When the Kumbh Mela finishes, they will go back to their mountains and caves,' he said.

I weaved through a patchwork of tents on an empty river bank later that evening. Most pilgrims had retreated to their camps and the bright blue lights alongside the mudflats gave the Ganga a silver sheen.

Had any battle between the Nagas and the Buddhists or the Mughals ever been recorded? If any had, I hadn't heard of it. On the other hand, I had heard rumours of internecine battles *between* sadhu akharas.

I was to later read an article by historian David N. Lorenzen, entitled 'Warrior Ascetics in Indian History', in which he speaks of a prolonged sanyaasi-fakir rebellion in Bengal against the British that occurred in the latter half of the eighteenth century. Lorenzen writes, '[T]he precise historical beginnings of warrior ascetics in India are not clearly known… Most if not all the known groups of warrior ascetics were…founded only after the Muslim conquest and evidently were not the result of a gradual evolution of previously existing institutions.' However, he clarifies, 'This does not mean to say that violent confrontations involving ascetics were not known before this time. Religious conflict, one of the basic preconditions necessary for the rise of warrior ascetics, was present in India at least as early as the sixth century BC. Most often this conflict took the form of sect competition, usually capped by theological debates and miracle contests between rival schools or sects… On the part of the Hindus, we hear as early as in Panini of ascetics who carry an iron lance. Nonetheless, there is nowhere any clear indication that early sect competition ever led to the formation of anything resembling military orders.'

Later he writes, 'The earliest well-documented armed clash involving warrior ascetics in India occurred in the presence of the emperor Akbar near Thaneswar in about AD 1567. *The skirmish was not between Hindus and Muslims, however, but between two different Hindu orders.*' And: 'The evidence regarding the founding of the six akharas or "regiments" of Dasnami nagas, so-called from their habit of going about "naked" (nagi), is uncertain and conflicting. *This lack of historical data tends to support our belief that the Dasnami naga akharas were created to defend local interests such as the lands and treasure of temples and monasteries* since such defence would be unlikely to attract the interest of Muslim historians in the same way as did the Sikh and Satnami rebellions. The earliest source on the founding of akharas is a Hindi manuscript of probably the nineteenth century which was loaned to [Jadunath] Sarkar by the Nirvani Akhara. This document, as summarized by Sarkar, purports to give the spiritual genealogies of the heads of the six akharas and to describe some of the more important battles in which they took part… *Two of the more interesting events mentioned in the manuscript are a battle between the Nirvani and some bairagis, i.e. Vaishnav ascetics at Hardwar…in about AD 1254 and another battle between the same akhara and a sultan, possibly Aurangzeb, in 1664. Unfortunately, none of these dates and traditions can be corroborated from other sources.*' (Emphases mine throughout.)

A mother and son were walking back from the river bank after a bath. *Was it their second one of the day?* How many pilgrims would return on Mauni Amavasya? It was the next big bathing day, marking the start of the Hindu month of Magh. My neighbour at my camp, a retired professor from Ranchi, had said the crowds were expected to be the heaviest then, followed only by Basant Panchami, the last big bathing day that marked the onset of spring.

'Careful, bhai,' I heard a man's voice and looked down.

I'd nearly walked into a cluster of babas. There were four men hunched around a fire, chatting and smoking. One was robed in black and the other three wore the more ubiquitous orange. I took out my phone and turned on the recorder. Acquainted with the sadhus' direct-but-dense style, I felt less inhibited this time. 'Can I talk to you?' I said. The man in black asked me to buy him tea first, which I did.

'Why do so many Nagas look so angry?' I then asked him. This aspect of the sadhus' deportment had impressed me deeply.

It can be difficult to visually reconcile the Hinduism of non-violence, vegetarianism and accommodating pandits—my faith—with images of bloodshot eyes and waving tridents. I appreciated that these images played out in real life, of course. But in my mind, these things happened far away: in the sky where good fought evil and won, or in distant places on the ground where Hindu–Muslim riots occurred.

The baba turned towards the Ganga. The river had turned a reflective white, and wisps of white gulls raced over it to their homes. He tilted his head to a side in the way I'd come to learn babas typically do, took a long pull on his chillum and exhaled a plume of smoke into the cool air.

'What is Shiva without the *maatra*?' he said. His lips were cracked. His eyes were yellow.

'What?'

'See this.' With his chillum, the baba wrote *Shiva* in Hindi in the sand. Then he wiped out the 'i' *maatra*—here, vowel—clean, so that what remained was '*shav*': dead body.

'Do you understand me?' His eyebrows converged into a snake.

When I returned to my camp, the Ranchi professor was furious. 'Let me tell you what happened here,' he said. 'These people are criminals. I paid for my tent in advance, but now they want me to share it with somebody. Just now, this nice lady from New Zealand left after fighting with the manager. They took full payment from her on the internet, but when she came here he said they are booked out. She told him straight, "You say you treat your guests like gods. But this"—he opened his arms to the smoggy sky—"this is the reality."'

The man stared sadly at his shoes. 'These people really make us look bad.'

I slept briefly under a warm (but unwashed) blanket that night, but at 1 am I was up. My train to Delhi was at 3 am, but given that most roads in the city had been closed off, I was relieved I could get to the station in time.

I stood on the platform with my thoughts swimming inside, my earphones in. The train tracks stretched on interminably into the night.

Shiva without anger equals death. Did he mean the death of belief? Or the end of culture? Death of Self or Identity? What kind of death? The only answers that made sense at this moment posed further questions. *What was faith without teeth?* I thought. *What was the phallus without blood?* Nothing. *What was attachment without jealousy?* Maybe this was what the sadhus meant by Shiva-Shakti. That God was a confection of all emotions and all energies. God was a summation of all dimensions, all scopes, all realities… I realized I was beginning to sound like a sadhu myself and laughed aloud.

Somebody tapped me on my shoulder. I turned around. 'Are you waiting for the Rajdhani?' a man said. He looked roughly my age. He spoke like the sadhus. Pious and whole, like a sugar cube. He'd come with his guru, he said. He belonged to the Mahanirvani Akhara. What about me? I said I was on a material gathering trip, that I'd spoken with many saints, and he let a moment of silence pass between us.

'Whatever work you have in life, it won't get done until you find your guru,' he said. 'Believe me.' And the way he said this, at once sincere and searing, made me want to turn my face away.

'I know from experience,' he said. 'I bathed in the Ganga at 4 am yesterday, with the Naga sadhus.' I could tell he was very proud of this feat. As though he had experienced a state of bliss for which only a select few had been chosen.

I was there too, I didn't interrupt him.

I boarded the train, climbed silently into my berth and lay down but my eyes stayed open. Around this time yesterday, the Nagas from the Mahanirvani Akhara were the first to run into the Ganga. After thirty minutes, it was the next akhara's turn, the Atal Akhara. While some Nagas posed for photographs like models, their sunglasses turning a kaleidoscope of lights, others bared their teeth as if they wanted to be left alone. Others still retained an air of refined insouciance, as if they'd descended to this world of mortals only because they had to. Only so they could immerse their bodies in the Ganga. For their souls already belonged elsewhere.

I could feel the rumble of the train's engine growing faint now.

That other train I saw yesterday, the human one made up of charging Naga babas with its horn blaring *Har Har Mahadev!*—when it leapt headlong into the Ganga, was it a mere spectacle to admire as one would a special effect in a movie, or was something deeper at play? Had something inscrutable come out from the churning of the ocean between gods and demons and settled in Prayag along with the droplets of immortality, so that even now serpentine dreadlocks splashed about alongside river-bathing software engineers?

The mortals and the immortals, drawing on different heads of the many-headed snake of Truth, took a dip at the Sangam yesterday. When the sadhus came out of the water, the yaatris rushed in. There were people from everywhere. From Nepal and Tamil Nadu, Gujarat and Bengal, Mumbai and Azampur. From Germany and Russia and Brazil, too. The foreigners mostly stood outside as the locals rushed in. The rich and the poor, everybody submerged their heads.

I was one with them. I went into the water. I took it all in. But I could go no farther in than ankle deep.

PART V

Loops of Clarity

November 2019, March 2022, June 2022:
Before, in between & beyond

A City in Flux: Varanasi

As one of the twelve jyotirlingams, the Kashi Vishwanath is the most revered temple in this holy city of over 3,000 temples and counting. Records show that it has been destroyed and rebuilt many times. It was last disassembled by the Mughal emperor Aurangzeb in the late seventeenth century, who built the Gyanvapi Mosque in its place. A century later, the Queen of Indore, Ahilyabai Holkar, erected the new temple in a spot adjacent to the older site.

Most recently, in 2019, the BJP government under Prime Minister Modi's stewardship, undertook the Kashi Vishwanath Corridor project to further remodel and enlarge Ahilyabai's temple. The Corridor was completed in June 2022.

Once, on a flight from London to Delhi, a too-candid Australian backpacker said that for him India was 'the three Fs of Food, Faith, and Filth' and that these three things converged best in Mumbai. Such generalizations are silly, I know, but if I had to apply this adage to one place it would have to be Varanasi. Where else will you get the delicious *tamaatar ki chaat*? Or sight so many yaatris? Or such splendid squalor?

But my facetiousness aside, I've seriously wondered what it is about Banaras that makes it so unique. It is not the dirt, even though it is dirty like nowhere else. Or its beauty, even if it is beautiful like no place else. And after over a dozen visits, I think I'm zeroing in on at least one thing that pulls me back to it again and again. You know how foreigners sometimes say that India is 'an assault on the senses!' At some base level, I think Varanasi also has this draw for me. Where else will you see a woman chasing a cow down the street to collect its urine? Or a stray dog filching a human skull from the hands of an

Aghori baba? Or a butt-naked white tourist getting a body massage on the ghats while pious sadhus take a dip in the Ganga, and you spot nearby floating in the water the corpse of a monkey? All in the same day!

And just when you start getting nauseous with the dirt everywhere and think you've had enough of this shit, the next morning, you see the most uplifting sunrise in years. First, the sun is a little red ball rising from the edge of the dusty plains across the Ganga, wooden boats breaking the river's silken surface like rousing dreamers. Then, it is a big halo to which the devout offer ablutions in solemn *surya namaskaars*. And then it is a blinding fireball powering a manic city. And if you admire this scene long enough, you might even spot the odd bird impressed by it as it lifts its head out of the water, a wedge of carrion in its beak, before it flies on and away...

At 7 am for me, though, this Varanasi spell was fading.

I was sitting scruffily cross-legged at Assi Ghat and had been meditating, or trying to, and had just achieved a relaxed state of mind. But the overall effect was such that rather than arrive at a point of mental acuity, my mind, running from the river to the sun, to the birds, had produced in me a stiff erection. I've never been turned on by nature before, I thought. So, at least this is a first. But now I'll have to wait before getting up.

And this brings me to the other thing about Banaras: In order to appreciate it, you have to wait. You have to be patient. You have to soak in it, even if like me, you never dip in its soiled waters.

You have to observe it, and fight it. And finally, let go to it. Let go to its crowded roads and its warren of sinuous streets. To its assortment of sadhus, snake charmers and Aghoris. To its aarti, the Mahashivratri, the Dev Diwali. To the aloo-poori! The paan! The chaat! To its thousands of temples. And to the Ganga. And when you tire of it all, what do you do? Yes. You wait again for the quiet to return in the afternoon when the ghats wind down to a snooze under the sun and you can hear pandits snoring under those giant umbrellas by the river that the city is famous for. And as you walk through its lanes, amid temple-bells, you hear students practising musical *raagas*, and tweets of squirrels and sparrows jumping through old trees rending even older walls. And sometimes, when you open a bright blue temple door out of the darkness, a bat comes flying straight at you!

It's so multifaceted a place that even the city's three names, like the three Gods of the Hindu Triad, sear different impressions into the mind.

Varanasi is Hinduism hardcore. Banaras is India in 10D. Kashi is Bharat on *bhang*.

So, if nothing else, I promise one thing. Even if you dislike it, you won't forget it. Because Kashi, this crumbling ancient city where so many Hindus go to die, will make you feel more alive and thoughtful, like nowhere else I know I can.

And so, here I was again, sitting on Assi Ghat, gazing at the Ganga for the third morning in a row. Determined to arrive at a breakthrough in my *dhyaan*—a term both Buddhists and Hindus use to describe mindfulness—I was set on keeping myself free of all thought for a half hour. Or fixated on one thing: my breathing.

You might think it strange that having spent so long in the Himalayas, I chose Varanasi, this swarming, raucous *city*, as my spot for deep introspection. After all, the Himalayas are full of caves made by God just for this purpose, right? And to this, I'll only say that Varanasi has its particular alluring effects and many a seeker would agree on this. Whatever else they disagree about.

As Diane Eck writes in her book *Banaras: City of Light*, Hindus believe 'Banaras stands at the centre of the earth as the place of creation and gathers together the whole of the sacred universe in a single symbolic circle, a *mandala*. Yet it is not an earthly city. Kashi is said to sit above the earth as a "crossing place" (*tirtha*) between this world and the "far shore" of the transcendent Brahman'.

Our Puranic lore, too, seems to have recognized the site's pensive potential. According to one story, when the goddess Ganga asked Lord Shiva if she could go past his holy city, He said to her, 'No, you are too noisy. You will disturb my tapasya. Go some other way.' But she assured Him not to worry. She said, 'In Kashi I will be my quietest. My most placid.' And so, travelling against her original course, the river took one last meandering loop north. Turning limpid and sheer, she opened herself up as if to drink in the sun, before moving east to join the sea.

Over the years, many well-meaning folk had pushed me to try a Vipassana Meditation retreat. But since an enforced form of *anything* has only ever generated an allergic response, these encouragements never gelled into any real determination on my part. I realized if I genuinely wanted to approach Truth, the only way to do so was myself. And by now in my journey, there was this other thing I felt almost duty-bound to account for: my growing conviction that I *could dig* deep into myself if I wanted. I found I *had* the willpower to follow through with things I set out to do. I had the grit. And vitally, as you know, I believe I possessed both my rational mind and my religious soul. Plus, I'd seen before the silvery contours of something indescribable, even if not godlike, hadn't I? So, all I had to do was keep piercing this moh-maya, this veil of Reality, with my arrows of concentration and mindfulness, and finally, I'd be able to see coming through the clouds a beam of light from the Vast Oneness: the Eternal, Supreme, Unchanging Brahman! (Oh yes!)

Which, let me forewarn you, never happened.

Still, after a week of returning to the Ganga every morning and observing my breath rise and fall and rise and fall, something not insignificant did. God knows these esoteric experiences are hard to describe. But here's a go:

For a few short moments, I reached a place I could see myself seeing myself. Where I was so outside myself that I felt like somebody not like myself. But it was an *outside-ness* that was also a fine-tuned *inside-ness*. I mean, even though I'd moved somewhere outside my core, I'd also toured so deep within it that I felt I-was-not-and-yet-wholly-was-myself like I'd never experienced before. (I know this sounds bizarre. But bear with me.)

At the end of my physical journey, even though I didn't entirely swallow mummy's over-ritualized style of faith, I eventually found my own 'trance state'. Forgetting my padmaasana-numbed legs and beeping phone, I managed to still my mind for over half an hour. (*Actually, I became a phone sending and receiving signals into the Multiverse!*) Here in Varanasi, I arrived at a point where the two tireless competitors, Faith and Logic, united briefly in a parachute pull of the mind and subtly changed the Reality I saw.

I'll return to my loops of clarity, but for now, let me just say that it was in Varanasi that I came somewhat close to understanding what the bald kid with paranormal powers in the film *The Matrix* told Neo. He said, '*Do not try and bend the spoon, that's impossible. Instead, only try to realize the truth...there is no spoon. Then you'll see that it is not the spoon that bends, it is only yourself.*'

Sadhus would later tell me that what I'd experienced was a small shadow of the *nirguna* Brahman. At the same time, Buddhist monks would say that this was but a glimpse of the true nature of things, the *non-self*. They'd both say, 'Oh, this was only the beginning, son. You have to go deeper.' And maybe they are right. But I didn't care any more for finding *their* Truth. I was happy I was constructing my own. As of course I'd been doing all along.

My rational mind told me that this flickering light I saw in my mind's eye, which seemed to go just beyond my confines, was the result of an 'awareness' that could come to anybody with deep meditation. Besides, my new-found understanding was akin to what many seekers, Hindu, Buddhist or whoever else, had all experienced before. So, what I was seeing was not my soul linking up with Shiva's third eye. Or my Kundalini awakening. I was only seeing things a little newly, that's all. (An outcome of maturity? A fruit of a prolonged cultural habit?)

But I simultaneously considered: Aren't you also seeing what you're capable of? Aren't you seeing again and again what faith can achieve, psychologically, if not mystically?

And so I thought, Why not continue digging deeper? And even as I asked myself this question I knew that I would. Because you see, like Neo in *The Matrix*, I'd swallowed the red pill. I'd picked a certain way. And there was no turning back.

Varanasi. November 2019

But right now, it was 8:15 am, and sitting in some flux between transcendence and arousal, I was petting a stray dog with the ghat's morning stir filling my ears. A bunch of sadhus were doing aarti here. A woman was reciting a shloka there. A motorboat cut through the water ahead. And somewhere behind me, boiling chai scented the air.

I got up. My friend Samar and his friend Palakh were waiting for me back at the hotel. We had decided to go to the Vishwanath Temple for darshan at 9:30 am.

A forty-four-year-old from Jaipur, Samar Singh Solanki belonged to a traditional Rajput family, and with his impressive handlebar moustache and diamond studs on his earlobes he looked traditional, too. I would tease him that he was quickly turning into a middle-aged uncle because he would send me flowery *Good Morning!* texts every morning, and his WhatsApp display picture changed to a new Hindu god every week. What's more, Samar did pooja without fail every day, stayed vegetarian during the navratras, and even though he lived alone, he somehow always had in his house the requisite sweetmeats and pooja items for every big festival, all of which he celebrated with aplomb. Still, my friend was not rigid about his faith. He never bothered with purity-focused concepts like *jootha-sucha*, for instance; he enjoyed eating meat without any sense of guilt; and like me, he often lamented the sweeping politicization of faith that had become ubiquitous in our country in recent years. Like so many Hindus—*why, people of any faith really!*—Samar bent his religion to his personality rather than let dogma bend him.

Still, my friend's conformist tastes could only go so far. Because all things considered, he was a closeted single gay man who'd never expressed any interest in marrying a woman. As a result he suffered from what he called a sense of 'listlessness'—a not-uncommon affliction, I think, among those of us who find ourselves outside old orders, whether by circumstance or choice.

Samar's parents, however, *did* still have expectations of him. As the only son, the pressure to marry remained strong, and Palakh Shekhawat, the daughter of Samar's parents' friends, was the prime candidate for a wife these days.

A pleasant single girl in her mid-thirties, Jodhpur-born Palakh also came from a similarly traditional Rajput background. But having spent the previous decade working a corporate job in Mumbai, not least being the product of Ajmer's elite Mayo boarding school, she kept whatever orthodox leanings she might have had wrapped inside a glossy coat of English-speaking cosmopolitanism.

While Samar was essentially a laidback, take-a-half-hour-to-shave sort of guy, Palakh struck me as driven over the half-a-dozen times I'd met her. At poojas at Samar's house, although she took care to cover her head with a dupatta, close her eyes and join her palms together,

her manner was mechanical. While Samar was just the guy to take in the temple prasad and sacred fire with a big gulp, Palakh, as she herself said, was 'not the pooja-doing type'.

One time, after a Ganesha pooja at Samar's house, I said aloud, 'Is there something to eat here? I'm starving,' and Palakh said smoothly, 'We will serve the food in some time.'

I didn't miss the look of barely hidden annoyance on Samar's face then, mixed though it was with flattery. It was clear Palakh was fond of Samar. And although Samar enjoyed this female attention, this facade of 'normalcy' he sometimes thought the world had thrust upon him, he usually pulled away.

Samar and Palakh had both come with me to Banaras—their first time—to see the city's famous Dev Diwali celebrations. But if either one had ulterior motives about something they wanted from Lord Shiva in his home city, I didn't know. Nor did I ask.

The non-couple's old pattern of exchange was playing out before me at the door of our hotel room: 'Which is better?' Palakh was holding up a pair of salwar-kameezes. But Samar, who had spread on the bed a white dhoti and a cream kurta, was engrossed in his own options for dress.

'Either is fine.' He glanced up from his suitcase from which he now pulled out a pair of Rajasthani *juttis*. 'The pink one is good.'

He saw me smirking at the door.

'Oh, good, you're back.'

'Totally useless this man is, Sid.' Palakh went past me. She stopped before going on to her room. 'We should wait, by the way. My mother has arranged for a pandit to take us to the temple.'

Some ten minutes later, Pandit Vimal, a young man in his mid-twenties, showed up at the hotel wearing jeans, an orange scarf and a checked shirt, in whose pocket he'd shoved his sunglasses, and despite the big red tika on his forehead, he looked more like a Bhojpuri film actor than a priest.

'You'll take us?' Palakh asked him, openly amused. 'You're a real pandit, I hope?'

Pandit Vimal produced a boyish grin baring teeth tinged pink with paan. 'My father sent me today,' he said. 'I wear jeans sometimes. But don't worry, in my knowledge of Kashi, I'm *bilkul* first-class.'

Dear Reader, I've been going to Varanasi for such a long time now that even I can tell you how things were in 'the olden days'.

To get from the ghats to the Vishwanath Temple in the days before the construction of the Kashi Corridor, you had to first pass through a tight warren of lanes, some so narrow that if a cow blocked your way, you had to turn around. The other more straightforward route was to walk along the ghats to Dashashwamedh Ghat, the most famous one of the eighty-four, where Lord Brahma once sacrificed ten horses, but is now the site of the daily evening Ganga aarti.

The main pedestrian road, the Dashashwamedh Ghat (DG) Road linked the Ganga to Gowdolia Chowk, a Banaras landmark traffic square. Along the stairs leading from the Dashashwamedh Ghat to DG Road crouched begging widows (which brought Deepa Mehta's film *Water* to mind), sadhus and lepers. And as you came up on the road, you saw a snake charmer, an ear cleaner, a baba whose leg had gone ginormous from elephantiasis, an Aghori with lice-ridden dreadlocks and multitudes of other abject wanderers.

All day long, thousands of yaatris from all corners of India and the world continually walked up and down this thoroughfare, with the locals typically heading first to the Vishwanath Temple and the Westerners making straight for the ghats. Through these throngs swirled motorcycles, scooters, cycle rickshaws, cows and dogs amid cow dung, incense, paan-laced spit, balloons, sarees, dhotis, heaps of garbage, heaps of flowers, earthen cups, plastic waste, grime, sweat, perfume, vermilion: you name it, every beautiful and ugly thing under the Indian sun. So much so that the first time I came here, aged twenty-five, I said to my mother, 'Now this is the Great Indian Highway!'

Of course, the DG Road is still there, and as before, it is still lined with the old clothes shops (Laxmi Saree Ghar, Santushti Sarees, and New Liberty Tailors, from where Samar bought his clothes), eateries (go to Keshari restaurant for a North Indian thaali and Ayyar's cafe for South Indian fare), rest houses, ashrams and what have you. But as this road leads both to the Ganga and to Gate No. 1 of the Kashi Vishwanath Temple—atop which fittingly sits the statue of Adi Shankaracharya—since I first saw it in 2007, spruced up with new street lights and its shop fronts all painted in a uniform red, it has undergone a radical makeover.

Yet when I last visited Varanasi in January 2024, the *Great-Indian-Free-for-All* was as spirited as ever, with shop stalls spilling onto the pavement and hawkers calling for your attention as we temple-goers walked past wretched beggars, many of us, as before, streaking the pavement red with paan.

In the olden days, a labyrinthine maze of hundreds of lanes stretched on either side of DG Road, from hectic ones chock-full of food stalls to tranquil nooks enclosed by old homes with a Shivalingam set into a niche in the front. And as you stopped to wonder if some of these were actually temples with a small house at the rear, as monkeys leapt across the tightly-packed roofs overhead, a passing sadhu would offer you advice.

'In Kashi's lanes, you must keep moving,' he'd say. And somebody else would say, 'Kashi makes even some desis into tourists.' To which a local woman sitting on the steps of her house cleaning rice would add, '*Videshi ke bina Kashi Kashi nahin*...without foreign visitors, Kashi isn't Kashi.'

'I'm from Delhi, bhai,' I'd say. 'I just like taking photos!'

This entire web of lanes—which Diana Eck describes as 'a palimpsest, an old parchment that has been written upon and imperfectly erased again and again, leaving the old layers partially visible'—was nourished on one side by the Ganga. And still is.

Just as the lanes of Chawri Bazaar surrounding the Jama Masjid put the 'Old' back into Delhi and Marine Drive preserves some 'Bombay' in Mumbai, it was Varanasi's lanes as much as the ghats that continually led me from Banaras to Kashi. Or brought me back to Kashi from Banaras.

And I'm not alone in thinking this way. The ghats and lanes have stirred travellers' imaginations for hundreds of years. In 1890, W.S. Caine, in his *Picturesque India*, described the riverfront in a manner that could hold just as true today: 'Up and down the ghats, all day long, but especially in the early morning, stream the endless course of pilgrims, ragged tramps, aged crones, horrible beggars, hawkers, Brahmin priests, sacred bulls and cows, Hindu preachers, wealthy rajas or bankers in gay palanquins, Fakirs, pariah dogs, and scoffing globe trotters from Europe and America.'

About the Great-Indian-Free-For-All, James Kennedy wrote in *Life and Work in Benares and Kumaon* (1885): 'Everything you see is wild, grotesque, unnatural, forbidding, utterly wanting in verisimilitude and refinement, with nothing to purify and raise the people, with everything so fitted to pervert their taste and lower their character…' But with Indians and foreigners alike, for every excoriating account there is a breathlessly glowing one, as of Count Hermann Keyserling, who left Europe shortly before the First World War to journey the world, and who said:

'Benares is holy. Europe has grown superficial, hardly understands such truths anymore… I feel nearer here than I have ever done to the heart of the world; here I feel everyday as if soon, perhaps even to-day, I would receive the grace of supreme revelation… The atmosphere of devotion which hangs above the river is improbable in its strength: stronger than in any church that I have ever visited. Every would-be Christian priest would do well to sacrifice a year of his theological studies in order to spend this time on the Ganges: here he would discover what piety means.'

Perhaps the most famous such adage is of Mark Twain, who as you've probably heard once said: 'Varanasi is older than history, older than tradition, older even than legend and looks twice as old as all of them put together.'

But in truth, even though Varanasi is old and its legend primaeval, going back to the Satyug, as Madhuri Desai writes in her book *Banaras Reconstructed*, 'no significant building on the riverfront can be dated to an earlier date than the year 1600'. In fact, 'the Kashi that contemporary visitors experience largely evolved after the twelfth century, as pilgrimage routes and a growing city were configured around the principal Vishveshwar shrine'.

But then history is one thing and belief another, because as per Hindu lore set out in the *Kashi Khanda*, a set of verses found in the *Skanda Purana*, the Kashi Vishwanath Mandir, also known as the Vishweshwar, or the Temple of the Lord of the Universe, has been the beating heart of the city to which Hindus have been flocking through Kashi's winding arteries for ages and ages. And it is precisely these arteries, precisely these centuries-old lanes, that were now being eviscerated. Or, as some said, *transplanted*. For the Kashi Vishwanath

Temple, with its long and intricate history, was once again getting a new burst of life.

When I was here only the previous year, in November 2018, I'd witnessed the buildings around the temple being brought down with great zeal. Heaps of brick and cement lay strewn around as labourers picked away at the remaining structures standing with their basic hammers and chisels. 'The area is too narrow for a bulldozer to come in,' a man said. 'So, the demolition has to be done in the old way.'

Homes and shops with miniature Shivas and Ganeshas set in their walls were pulverized to dust before my eyes. Then the debris was carted away on the backs of donkeys. One donkey owner said to his friend, 'Before in Kashi, we would say *Bam Bam Bhole!* Now they will say *Bam Bam Modi!*'

And in a way, he was not wrong. For this pandemonium sweeping through the old city was thanks to the implementation of Prime Minister Modi's Kashi Vishwanath Corridor Project. Newspapers said that Modi's aim was to create a wide pathway directly linking the Vishwanath Temple to the riverfront. But one could see that his larger, arguably his main purpose was more ambitious. Modi wanted to beautify Banaras. He wanted to modernize it. And he had decided to do this by first cleaning up the crowded, narrow lanes around the Vishwanath Temple.

Modiji wants to 'give Kashi back the grandeur it has lost through Muslim invasions,' mummy, one Varanasi old-timer, said. To which papa added: 'Yes, he is following the Kyoto model. So, from the modern viewpoint, he's developing it fine.'

Now, a year on, in November 2019, 47,000 square metres of lanes around the temple had all but gone. Old buildings, their temples and gods with them, tracing back to the nineteenth, eighteenth, and even the seventeenth century, if locals are to be believed, were ripped down and cleared away. And from the rubble emerged even older temples. These were '*bhavya*' temples, some said, using an adjective which means 'grand', but is also the name of the goddess Parvati. But many residents around the main shrine disagreed. They said that these temples were 'Always there!' Nothing new was found, they said. 'You just didn't see them before because of all the old buildings clustered around.'

Nonetheless, I couldn't help but marvel at the full baring of these once-concealed shrines. With their square bases and long conical spires, the central spire encircled by several similar though smaller spires, each temple had the appearance of a temple hamlet unto itself, such that when the whole lot was viewed together, the entire area around the Vishwanath Temple appeared like a resurrected ancient temple city. *A reminder of a more aesthetically refined age?* Certainly. But also of the contending histories and upheavals that Varanasi, like so many holy cities, had passed through…

'Kashi is Kashi because of its lanes,' I said to Pandit Vimal, repeating words that had been said to me the year before.

'*Yeh devnagri hai. Agar mandir hata doge to kya rahega. Kuch bhi nahi. Yeh Dilli-Mumbai ki tarah udyogic nagri phir rah jayegi*,' a shopkeeper had said. '*Yahaan log kyun aate hain? Bhagwaan Shiv ki araadhna karne, log moksha ke liye aate the*.' This is God's city. If you remove the temples, then what is left? Nothing. It will become like Mumbai and Delhi—like any commercial city. Why do people come here? You come for Lord Shiva. To attain moksha.

A restaurant owner two lanes away from the temple meanwhile was more concerned about the compensation he'd receive from the government if his house came up for demolition. 'See, for this house even if we get a good rate, so what?' he said. 'They say they will give us some thirty lakhs, but we will still have to divide it between everybody. My father has two brothers, and they don't even live here. What will we do if they relocate us to someplace far away? Our business depends on the temple.'

And then there was the elderly owner of a well-known cafe who said that nobody in the area was happy about what was happening. 'They've broken down thousands of Shivalingams and people are just silently watching. It saddens me to see our culture being destroyed like this. When Aurangzeb attacked the city, we are the people who saved it. Our ancestors, they have lived in these lanes for centuries, safeguarding Lord Vishwanath, always. And how are we being rewarded today? By being thrown out. *Wah ji wah!* This is Kalyug indeed.'

When I returned to this same man's cafe in March 2022 after visiting the refurbished Vishwanath Temple, I was happy to find his place unscathed. 'What would I have done without your dosa?' I said to him.

The man smiled weakly.

'So have you been to see the new temple?' I said. 'People are coming from everywhere.'

The old man shook his head. 'There's a Shiva temple in my own house also. Those who want to find God can find him within themselves. I'm not interested in this new building.'

Seeing me taken aback, he softened his tone a little. 'Look, these new buildings are made for you visitors,' he said. 'You people talk about our narrow and dirty lanes. But before, there was a *thandak* [a coolness] in this area. Because of the buildings, the sunrays couldn't reach the ground. Our gullies were always lined with flowers, with bel leaves. Everywhere was sprinkled with Gangajal. With milk.' He gave a bitter laugh. 'Now I've heard the temple courtyard is so wide that your bare feet burn just from the hot marble floor.'

The more I spoke with townsfolk through November 2018 and November 2019, the more a pattern emerged. One's position on the Kashi Project hung naturally on whether you lived in the temple's proximity or some distance away. People whose properties and livelihoods were being toppled were against the demolition. But others spoke of the imminent construction in glowing terms. This latter set believed it was high time the place changed, and they wanted to build something new and magnificent befitting both Lord Shiva's majesty and the present political dispensation, which had, as Swami Shraddhanadji said, 'at long last chosen to revive Hindu grandness'. But there was a third category of people. And they were those like the old cafe owner, who loved Banaras *just as it was*, with its soot-covered lanes shrouded in incense and dusted with marigold and cow dung.

Of all the people I spoke to, one man, Rajendra Tiwari, a *mahant* at the Vishwanath Temple, whose own house had been demolished in the city's makeover, stood out for his outspokenness.

At the time of the refurbished temple's inauguration in December 2021, he said to me: '*Banaras ki pauraanic pehchaan thi. Ek aitihasic pehchaan rahi hai jise vartman sarkar ne tod kar vyavsaic nagari banayi hai. Banaras saadhana ki nagari hai. Aur yeh dukh ki baat hai ki inke pramukh ek aise vyakti hain jo apne udyogpati mitron ke prabhav mein aa kar pure Varanasi ka bhes badal rahe hain.*' Banaras had an old Puranic identity, he said, a historical identity, which the present government has completely destroyed. They are converting our city from a spiritual centre into a commercial one. And it's sad that the man leading the way has been persuaded by his industrialist friends to change our city's complexion.

'Tell me, do yaatris come here because of the pull of Shiva, to see our devotion and heritage or some sound and light show? It is the arrogance of this government that they never asked us Banarsis what we think about all this. And yes, you outsiders are being misled. No old temples were unearthed. In fact, many temples were broken. What pains me is that there were gods and goddesses in the gullies all around [the temple], and we would pray to each one. There was the Panchakroshi Yaatra'—a thirteenth-century yaatra which circumnavigates Kashi—'for instance. And there is also the Antargriha route. How do you break a temple once God has been seated there?'

When I asked Mahant Rajendra Tiwari if he had any proof of older shrines being demolished, he forwarded me images of the Annapurna shrine, once seated in the north face of the Vishwanath complex, being taken down by workers. 'These labourers broke it with a stone cutter. With no respect,' he said, his voice quivering.

This same Annapurna idol has now been re-seated in the enlarged temple complex. But beside her, there now also sits a miniature idol of the goddess. 'This eighteenth-century miniature Annapurna idol was once stolen from Varanasi and taken to Canada from where it has now been retrieved after more than a century,' a pandit Hiralal Pandey told me on my visit to Varanasi in March 2022. 'After 108 years, Ma Annapurna's idol has returned to Kashi once again. And the credit goes to the MP from Kashi and Prime Minister, Narendra Modi. I express heartfelt gratitude to him on behalf of everyone in Kashi and the state,' the UP Chief Minister, Yogi Adityanath, said (as reported in *The Economic Times*, on November 15, 2021).

Having skirted around the recently broadened path, we, Pandit Vimal, Samar, Palakh and I, got to the lane leading to the Vishwanath Temple. As before, the place was lined with the familiar old row of shops selling the pooja samagri (Gangajal, bel patra, flowers, milk and prasad) needed for Shiva abhishek. During my previous visits, this would be where I'd deposit into a locker my shoes, leather wallet and mobile phone, keeping on my person only tens and twenties for handing out to the pandits.

It was here, deep inside Kashi's serpentine lanes that the diverse streams of the Great-Indian-Free-For-All engorged into a monsoon-swollen Ganga. It was here that the disparate Hindu tongues thickened into a unified voice intoning: '*Om Namah Shivaaya!*' '*Bam Bam Bhole!*' and '*Kashi Vishwanath ki Jai!*' It was here that my rational mind melted away, my soul moving in flow with the others.

Taking in the faces around me, I thought, if Sri Lanka was *India-Lite*, as I'd heard some backpackers call it, then Varanasi was definitely *India-Multiplied.* But what was it about this city that made it a microcosm of pilgrimage centres? For one, it was the sheer number of yaatris you saw here. Indeed, you see people from all corners of India at every major temple town, but nowhere did you see as many as you did in Kashi. The level of devotional intensity here was different by an order of magnitude. As palpable as money in Monaco or sleaze in Bangkok, faith in Kashi was visceral.

Kashi ke kankar kankar mein Shankar, locals said. And it was true: Shiva did live in every Kashi stone and grain of sand. Shiva was built into the city's houses and sprouted at its tree roots as Shivalingams. Was it Varanasi's location, then, that made it this focal point of religious convergence? Situated by the Ganga, at the eastern edge of 'Northern India' and near both Nepal and Bengal, Kashi was far enough for residents of these areas to find it 'exotic' but not so far as to be unapproachable. But as I glanced around I saw that this wasn't a good explanation either. How could it be given the enormous numbers of yaatris from distant quarters of southern and western India, and who were only increasing every year? Not to mention the wide-ranging seekers of wisdom or power Varanasi had attracted for hundreds of years, from the Chinese traveller Hiuen Tsang in the seventh century to Qutub-ud-din Aibak in the twelfth. Right down to the Modi and Kejriwal in the present day!

The explanation had to go deeper. But deep doesn't necessarily mean complex. The answer I think is rather simple: it is the mighty pull of the Ganga. It is the prehistoric call of Shiva. It is the concentrated surge of faith. And let's not forget that faith can supersede fact. According to lore, Kashi was Kashi before it became Varanasi. Which is to say Shiva was here long before the Ganga even arrived.

Hindus know of the significance of Kashi through its legend and stories contained in the Puranas, the most extensive being the *Kashi Khanda* in the *Skanda Purana* and the *Kashi Rahasya* in the *Brahma Vaivarta Purana*. Paralleling the story set in Badrinath, as per the *Shiva Purana*, once, Lords Brahma and Vishnu had an argument about who among them was supreme and Lord Shiva stepped in as the arbiter. To test them, He pierced the three Worlds—the *Swarg Lok* (the realm of the gods), *Paataal Lok* (the realm of the demons) and *Prithvi Lok* (our world of mortals)—as a Column of Infinite Light: a jyotirlingam where God's light transects the Earth just as it does in Kedarnath and in eleven other sites across the country.

Vishnu then took the form of *varaha*, a boar, and sought out the bottom while Lord Brahma became a *hans*, a swan, and flew to the pillar's top. On his way up Brahma found a ketaki flower drifting downward and he inquired, 'Where have you come from, O flower?' 'I was placed at the top of the light,' Ketaki lied. Brahma then sustained this lie and told Shiva that he had got to the column's top and offered the flower as his witness. But Vishnu confessed forthwith to being unable to find the bottom. Lord Shiva then took the form of the wrathful Bhairava and cut off Brahma's lying fifth head. He cursed him that he would not be worshipped from here on, whereas Vishnu would be seen as his equal for all eternity. For her part, Ketaki was cursed she'd no longer be offered to Shiva during pooja.

As Pandit Vimal said, 'Ganeshji can't be offered tulsi leaves, but adores grass. Vishnuji adores tulsi, but can't be offered rice. Shivji loves bel leaves, but they can't be offered to Surya. *Sab cheez ki kahani hai. Har cheez ka funda hai...*everything has a story, everything has a logic behind it.'

While devout Hindus will tell you Kashi exists from the Satyug, others go further. Kashi, they say, sits on Lord Shiva's trident. And since Shiva is the Great Controller of Time and Death, it follows that his city stands *outside Time*. Kashi, therefore, is not subject to the incessant periods of creation and destruction of the Hindu cosmic cycle. As Diana Eck writes, Kashi 'is the still centre which anchors the perpetual movement of time and space, without participating in the ever-turning world of samsara'.

As an outcome of this belief, Kashi is where Lord Shiva takes the form of *Tarak*, or *Tarakeshwar*, the Transporter of the Soul from this world to a Realm Free of the Cycle of Rebirths. Where a person, at complete bliss, can finally join with Brahman and attain moksha. A couplet by Tulsidas from the *Ramcharitmanas* recited by Mahant Rajendra Tiwari captured the Kashi-Shiva relationship perfectly:

mukti janm mahi jaani gyaan khaan agha haani kara
jahan bas sambhu bhavaani so kaasi seiya kasa na

Kashi is where, if anybody dies, they get moksha. It is where knowledge and wisdom overflow. Where only, ever and always, Shiva lives. This is our Kashi.

Even the city's geography bore Shiva's imprint, divided as it was into three distinct quarters, each representing a prong of Shiva's trident. While the Omkar Khand (home to Omkareshwar Temple) and the Kedar Khand (home to Kedareshwar Temple) took up the city's north-eastern and south-western parts, it was the Vishweshwar Khand, the home of Lord Vishweshwar, situated at the centre, that represented the trident's tallest prong. You could say then that while in Kashi Shiva was everywhere, it was in the Vishweshwar Khand that His light cut through the Earth most powerfully. As Pandit Vimal said, 'It is here that the *purdah* separating our world and God gets lifted.'

This faith was why you had Kashi's copycat towns, from Uttarkashi, Kashi of the North, in the Himalayas, to a Dakshin Kashi Shiv temple in Maharashtra. The Ganga's pull was why the Kaveri River, which flows through Karnataka and Tamil Nadu, was also called the Dakshin (southern) Ganga. And Shiva's pull was why, of all the temple towns in our land, Kashi was the one which the devout made it a point to visit at least once. Even if it was at death.

Pandit Vimal thrust the basket of pooja samagri into my idle hands. 'People's job is only to talk and create problems,' he said. 'Everybody here has got *mooh maangi keemat*...whatever they wished for, double the circle rate. So, why are people so greedy? When it is complete, this place will be first class. *Dekhna, Modiji char chand laga denge.*' Modiji, he was saying, will light up four moons here! The young priest gave me an uncertain look. 'Have you been here before?'

'Many times.'

'So, you know the *dhakka mukki*, the struggle, you have to go through just to see God. But now you see how things will change.'

Samar tapped on my shoulder. His eyes shone. 'Sid, I am getting such a good feeling here. Seeing so many bhakts from everywhere. It's amazing. The vibrations are so good!'

Though it was November, the tika Samar had gotten that morning from a pandit at the ghats was starting to melt down his forehead, while Palakh had wrapped her dupatta tightly around her face, as do so many Banarsi girls. But she did so not to shield herself from the dust but, I thought, to guard from the rising clamour around us.

'*Har Har Mahadev Shambho, Kashi Vishwanath Gange! Har Har Mahadev Shambho, Kashi Vishwanath Gange! Har Har Mahadev Shambho, Kashi Vishwanath Gange!*'

A twenty-something man in the line came up to Samar. 'Bhaiyya,' he said, popping out his phone. 'What a *lajawab* moustache you have. Can I take a selfie with you?' And a blushing Samar posed for a shot. In his white dhoti and red shawl, with his moustache twirls waxed firm, my friend did look somewhat like a thin Bhim from the TV version of the Mahabharata, I thought.

When a few minutes later, a family cut through the line overtaking us with a briskness that only wealth and caste privilege could buy, the elderly pandit leading them hollered, 'VIPs! Let us pass! VIPs, move aside! VIPs!' and Pandit Vimal wordlessly complied. But Samar's face now distorted from Bhim's into Ravan's as he yelled, 'Do we look like chu—yas to you waiting here for an hour?'

The VIPs had disappeared, though, swallowed up in Lord Vishwanath's hold. And the chants around were climbing to a vigorous timbre.

HAR HAR MAHADEV SHAMBHO! KASHI VISHWANATH GANGE!
HAR HAR MAHADEV SHAMBHO! KASHI VISHWANATH GANGE!
HAR HAR MAHADEV SHAMBHO! KASHI VISHWANATH GANGE!

'Whatever you say, Sid,' Palakh whispered in my ear, her face looked even more securely swaddled, 'you can't ignore all the development Modiji is doing. This city is so decrepit.'

And I thought her impression of Varanasi was valid, too. Even Mahatma Gandhi, speaking at the Banaras Hindu University in 1916, once said, 'I visited the Vishwanath temple last evening, and as I was walking through those lanes, these were the thoughts that touched me. If a stranger dropped from above on to this great temple, and he had to consider what we as Hindus were, would he not be justified in condemning us? Is not this great temple a reflection of our own character? I speak feelingly, as a Hindu. Is it right that the lanes of our sacred temple should be as dirty as they are? The houses round about are built anyhow. The lanes are torturous and narrow. If even our temples are not models of roominess and cleanliness, what can our self-government be?'

Still, I thought it was uncanny. While Varanasi, like the rest of the country, was swept up in showy, over-the-top expressions of faith, I was moving in the opposite direction. If there was a point of unity, it was that both Banaras, this city I'd come to love, and I were well on new chapters in our lives. While I'd embarked on a spiritual quest that I felt had only begun and would continue long after the yaatras in this book ended, Varanasi and my country were neck deep in a new politico-religious chapter of life.

And it is a chapter, Dear Reader, for which the story of the Kashi Vishwanath Temple and the adjoining Gyanvapi Mosque is an apt parable.

A Trip Down Varanasi's Lanes of History and Politics

In this short dive I draw from various quarters (recollections of things people said—in person, in TV interviews and news articles). But my main factual fallbacks are two books: Diana L. Eck's *Banaras: City of Lights* and Madhuri Desai's *Banaras Reconstructed: Architecture and Sacred Space in a Hindu Holy City*.

Dear Reader, in previous chapters I've dwelled on how faith awoke in me the magic of God. How it introduced me to the strong, if irrational, logic of ritual, and how it pulled at strings of familial love. About how I also understood that religion gives order to many people's lives, imbuing in each of us a sense of identity. And if I've come this far in my contemplations I can't remain silent on Identity's big brother, Politics, can I?

Politics and religion in many parts of the world are closely linked, but in ours they are indissolubly enmeshed. And just as with Indian politics you can't disconnect Hinduism from Islam, so in Varanasi you can't separate the symbolism of the Kashi Vishwanath Temple from the adjoining Gyanvapi Mosque. For before it was recently infused with grandeur, the first thing a first-timer to Kashi Vishwanath might have noticed was not the modest Hindu temple, but that it shared a wall with the more imposing Gyanvapi Mosque. And this was not just any mosque. Oh, no! You would soon learn this was *the* mosque Aurangzeb built in 1669 on the site of the older, much grander Kashi Vishwanath Temple.

Writing in *The New Cambridge History of India: Architecture of Mughal India*, Catherine B. Asher notes: 'Today known as Jami or

Aurangzeb's mosque, it dominates the famous Benares riverfront. Located at the top of the very steep steps leading to Panchganga Ghat, the mosque was even more visible and clearly symbolized a powerful Muslim presence in this holiest of all Hindu cities when its tall minarets still stood.' And it is precisely these minarets, towering over Kashi's presiding temple that are the cause of bitterness among some Hindus. For them, the mosque's mere presence is like a wound one can scratch with the telling of an old story and inflict pain.

In the old days, before you even entered the temple, just by the presence of the paramilitary Rapid Action Force (RAF) standing guard along the narrow lane at the entrance, you got the impression of a Hindu–Muslim fight on the brink. Then, when you were inside it, a pandit would tell you about how when Aurangzeb's men were destroying the older shrine, the head priest ran to save the Shivalingam and jumped with it into the Gyanvapi well. And when you stood by the well, which remains within the newly constructed temple's premises, he would point to '*that mosque*' over the fence, enclosed by high barbed wires, and say that if you looked carefully, you could make out the base of the older shrine. And how the statue of Nandi, also within the present temple's premises, faces the mosque. 'And as you know, Nandi can only face Shiva. *Hai na?*'

I've never managed to enter the Gyanvapi Mosque, it being barred to non-Muslims. But I did manage to bring it up casually in conversation with Banarsis, Hindu and Muslim. And while a handful did say that the mosque and temple, side by side, are an example of our mixed Ganga-Jamuni tehzeeb, most tended to be muted, describing it simply as 'an old mosque'. (Or sometimes animated if they perceived me being on their side.) One thing most Banarsis would likely agree on, however, is that Aurangzeb's legacy in the city is complicated. And from a strictly Hindu perspective, I would argue, complicated also therefore is Kashi's relationship with Islam.

As per Hindu memory, a Hari Chandra constructed the earliest Vishweshwar temple in the eleventh century. But as far as I've read, this assertion is based on hearsay rather than historical fact. Still, 'despite the obscurity of its early history,' writes Diana Eck, 'we know that by the twelfth century, Vishveshvara attracted the worship of a King Govardhachandra, for he left an inscription to say so. In the same century, an inscription from South India records that a certain king of Karnataka set up a fund to help the pilgrims of his area pay the Muslim-imposed tax so that they could visit Vishveshvara in Varanasi.' But this Vishweshwar temple was destroyed by Qutub-ud-din Aibak during Mohammad Ghori's rule in 1194 and a mosque was built on that site by 'the famous ruling princess of the Delhi Sultanate, Raziyyat-ud-din (Razia) during her short reign (1236–40)'.

For over five hundred years after the establishment of the Delhi Sultanate in 1206, Eck writes, the entire Ganges valley came under Muslim domination. And while 'the history of this period is complicated, and the various Muslim dynasties which came to power through the centuries were far from monolithic in their policies toward the sacred sites of the Hindus' and 'there were certainly high moments in these centuries, when Kashi recaptured something of its lost glory, with ambitious temple construction and stimulating scholarly activity, for the most part these were hard times. The religious life of the city was under almost constant threat. At least six times during these years the temples of Kashi were destroyed'.

Things changed in the 1500s 'during the liberal reign of the Mughal Emperor Akbar, who not only permitted, but in some cases sponsored the rebuilding of temples'. Pertinently, it was during Akbar's reign 'that the reconstruction of the Vishveshvara Temple, *perhaps on the most magnificent scale ever*, was undertaken by Narayana Bhatta in 1585…' (Emphasis mine.)

'Indeed it was with the patronage of one of Akbar's courtiers, Todar Mal, whose son ruled the Jaunpur area for the Emperor, that the construction proceeded. The temple was grand in scale and execution, consisting of a central sanctum, the *garbha griha*, surrounded by eight pavilions, or *mandapas*.' But '[t]he glorious day of this new Vishvanatha Temple…was very brief indeed. In less than a century, in 1669, it was torn down at the command of the Mughal Emperor Aurangzeb. Half-dismantled, it became the foundation for the present Jnana Vapi Mosque'. During the reign of Aurangzeb 'some of the city's greatest temples including Vishveshvara, Krittivasa, and Bindu Madhava, were razed…and their sites forever sealed from Hindu access by the construction of mosques'. Moreover, 'in his zeal for crushing Hindu idolatry, Aurangzeb even tried to rename the city "Muhammadabad", but the name did not stick'.

The net result of these tectonic events, however, was that not only is 'there is no major religious sanctuary in all of Banaras that predates the time of Aurangzeb in the seventeenth century' (as Madhuri Desai writes in *Banaras Reconstructed*), but that the memory of Aurangzeb's demolition was seared into the Hindu consciousness for generations to come.

Change came a century later when, in 1777, Ahilyabai Holkar, the Queen of Indore, sponsored the reconstruction of the Vishwanath Temple beside the Gyanvapi Mosque, and it is her temple where yaatris pay homage to Lord Shiva even today.

Not that Ahilyabai Holkar made the first attempt at reconstruction. Her father-in-law, Malhar Rao Holkar, a Maratha chief, had initially intended to rebuild a Shiva temple on the same spot as the older one after tearing down the mosque but his attempts never amounted to anything concrete. Nevertheless, the construction of Ahilyabai's temple marked a critical turning point, because from here on it is the Hindus who added accretions to the Vishwanath Temple extending well into our own times.

In 1828, Baiza Bai, a Scindhia maharani, is said to have constructed the low-roofed colonnade for the Gyanvapi well, and in 1835, Maharaja Ranjit Singh of the Sikh Empire donated one tonne of gold for plating the temple's dome.

'In a continued effort to assign "Hindus" and "Muslims" to their respective spaces,' writes Madhuri Desai, 'the colonial government handed the Gyan Vapi mosque to a local community of weavers in Banaras… But notwithstanding these efforts, the weekly Friday congregation in the mosque remained skeletal. Although the mosque was sparsely used, its plinth remained at the heart of rival claims well into the twentieth century. A peepul tree within the mosque precinct was an object of veneration as well as contention. As [M.A.] Sherring observed, "*the Hindus will not allow the Mohammedans to pluck a single leaf from it*".' (Emphasis mine.)

Then, moving into our own age, three significant events occurred: in 1992, the Supreme Court mandated the protection of the mosque, fearing that it could become a flashpoint after Hindutva activists demolished the Babri Masjid in Ayodhya. And in March 2019, Prime

Minister Modi laid the foundation stone of the Kashi Vishwanath Corridor, following which, in November that year, the Supreme Court ordered that the disputed land in Ayodhya be handed over to a trust to be set up by the government to build the Ram Janmabhoomi temple there.

Among the many reasons the Court gave for its verdict, two I thought were noteworthy. First, the Court said that as per the Archaeological Survey of India (ASI) there was evidence of a temple-like structure having existed on the land before the mosque was built. And second, the Muslim parties had failed to establish exclusive possession of the disputed land, while the Hindu parties furnished better evidence to prove that Hindus had worshipped continuously inside the mosque, believing it to be the birthplace of Lord Ram.

Could something like what happened in Ayodhya in 1992 be repeated in Varanasi? Was it conceivable for the Hindus of the city to make similar claims on the site of the Gyanvapi Mosque? Considering the meteoric rise of Hindutva in the last decade, can't one now reasonably say that it is the Indian Muslim rather than the Hindu who has reason to fear that her historical sites might come under the pall of destruction?

Unsurprisingly, I was one of many asking myself these questions. Michael Dumper, in his book, *Power, Piety, and People: The Politics of Holy Cities in the Twenty-First Century*, has voiced similar concerns, and he's not the only one to do so:

'To most Hindus, the demolition of the original temple housing the *linga* and its replacement with a mosque are a tragedy to be regretted and mourned. To contemporary Hindu nationalists, they are a desecration and an outrage that must be reversed. For centuries after the construction of the Gyan Vapi Mosque, the power of Islamic state authorities and subsequently the British colonial administration prevented any such reversions, and Hindus made do with a number of replacement sites close by… However, since independence and particularly since the rise of Hindutva parties in state and national legislatures and their success in the demolition of the Babri Masjid in 1992, the Gyan Vapi Mosque is now in the nationalists' crosshairs—its time possibly numbered and contingent upon the balance of demographic trends and political force in the city, in the region and across India.'

He adds, however, that several practical factors militate against such a scenario from arising. One, unlike Ayodhya, the Muslims of Banaras are a sizeable chunk, about a third, carrying considerable political weight. The Samajwadi Party, which represents the lower castes and Muslims, plays a significant role in the city's politics and has secured a majority in the state legislature in recent times. Moreover, Muslims provide the workforce for weaving, a key Banaras industry tied to the livelihood of many Hindu businessmen.

But more crucial than any economic and political imperatives, it is the other thing that Dumper dwells on that will, I believe, keep Varanasi in equal portions Kashi and Banaras, which is to say, a thriving city where Hindu orthodoxy sits securely alongside its Islamic heritage. Call me a romantic, but I believe the centuries-old mixed heritage of the Indo-Gangetic plains will keep Banarsi society, like its *lassi*, always luxurious and churning. Our Ganga-Jamuni tehzeeb, or sanskriti if you prefer, will always find ways to skim away our frothing hostilities.

It is not for nothing that Varanasi has been at the heart of that famed Hindu–Muslim mixed heritage of Uttar Pradesh, moving singers and poets to compose verses for hundreds of years. The poet Akhtar Sheerani, who was born in British India and died in Pakistan, wrote, (according to Ali Fraz Rezvi writing in *The Hindu*):

tamaam hind mein mashoor hai yahaan ki subah
kuch is qadar hai seher khushnuma banaras ki
(The mornings of Banaras are famous in all of Hindustan, such is their beauty.)

Rezvi further notes how, sitting at Dashashwamedh Ghat, Allama Syed Ijteba Hussain Rizvi described the sunrise in a *nazm* titled *Subh-e-Banaras* in 1933:

tamaasha ki wo arzaani wo ganga wo sanamkhaana
banaras ki seher asnaan ki taqreeb-e-rozaana
(It is a theatre of excess, the Ganga here, the temple there, people bathing in the ghats; these mornings of Banaras.)
haram waale zara kashi ka manzar dekhte jaayein
kabhi dekhenge jannat par abhi dekhein sanamkhaana
(Dwellers of the holy Kaaba must see the city of Kashi; they will see the heavens one day, but let them see the temples today.)

As Dumper also notes, if there is one place in Banaras which accepts all people, it is the Sankat Mochan Mandir dedicated to Lord Hanuman. It is a testament to its pluralistic nature that when it was bombed in March 2006, killing twenty people and injuring over a hundred, within a day, the city got back on its feet, with both temple bells and the azan filling the air. But more telling was that no sooner than the terrorist attack had been attributed to Islamic terrorists and the leader of the Hindu right-wing outfit Bajrang Dal organized a sit-in demonstration inside the temple courtyard with cries of '*Jai Shri Ram!*' than leaders of both religious communities worked together to diffuse tensions.

An attack on the Sankat Mochan was seen as an attack on Hindus and the wider Banaras community. As the shehnai maestro Ustad Bismillah Khan, who had played innumerable times here, said, 'The heavens have wept for what was done to vitiate the serenity of this city of Ganga… I am proud of this city, which is anointed by the holy Ganga waters, where there is no distinction between Hindus and Muslims. For us here, there has always been one God—call Him Allah or Ishwar or Ram.'

It is common knowledge that food, the arts and music have no social boundaries. Even so, it is to Sankat Mochan Temple's credit that in 2015 it even hosted Ustad Ghulam Ali, a ghazal singer, who became the first Pakistani artiste to perform there.

When I first read about this, I asked my mother whether it was because prominent Banarsi Muslims proudly called their city *Shivanagari* that artists such as Bismillah Khan and Nazeer Banarsi were so widely accepted by the city's Hindu piety. Ustad Sayeeduddin Dagar's Dhrupad delivery of '*Shiva Shiva Shiva Shankara Adideva*' did always move her to tears.

'Did you know that Ustad Bismillah Khan's uncle'—the late Ali Baksh 'Vilayatu'—'was the shehnai player in the Kashi Vishwanath Temple? Could such a thing happen today?' I asked.

'Of course!' she said. 'We Hindus are the most liberal!' But I felt her eyes were unconvinced of her own words.

In truth, though, I should admit that I've also for a long time supposed it is only Hindus who pray at the shrines of other faiths, even if my experiences have disproven this claim. And here I can share a personal experience with Samar itself:

Years ago, at a time I was depressed, I accompanied my friend for a weekend to his home, Jaipur. Hiding my unhappiness with forced humour, I said, 'I'm on a *See-Food Diet*, so I'll eat everything.' And for three days, I did just that. I gorged on *laal maas*, *junglee maas* and *pyaz ki kachoris*, until my tummy gave out. That was when Samar decided I needed a detox. And so, like the good Hindu boy he is, in addition to a regime of no meat and chilli, he also added to my itinerary a visit to the famous Jaipur Krishna temple, the Govind Devji.

'My friend will also join us,' he said. 'So, be nice. You Delhi people can be snooty.'

Dressed in a faded shirt and worn trousers, Vasudev was a thirty-year-old chap who spoke the lilting Hindi of the region. But more than his rustic language, it was the look of bliss I saw on his face as he prayed to Lord Krishna that led me to mentally slot him as a village bumpkin. Guileless and searching, Vasudev was just like the believers I'd seen at Shivsagar Ashram as a boy.

Back at Samar's house, as the three of us had daal-rice for lunch, I kept whining like a child about how insipid the food was, and an amused Vasudev smiled and said, 'Bhaiyya, when you feel fine please come to my place. My mother makes delicious *nihari*.'

I glanced at Samar. He cracked a grin. If you don't know, nihari is a slow-cooked mutton dish originally eaten by Nawabs during the Mughal Empire as a breakfast item after their Islamic morning prayer. Of course, it's not like South Asian Muslims have a monopoly over it, but the manner in which Vasudev invited me suggested he felt a sense of cultural ownership.

After he left, Samar told me about his friend. Samar had first met him at a musical performance in Jaipur of the Pakistani Sufi singer Abida Parveen. As Samar hummed and clapped, sitting in the audience, he said aloud, 'Is she singing in Punjabi or what?' 'It is Farsi,' Vasudev said. And the two men got chatting.

Vasudev worked in a hospital as an interpreter. His job was to translate the local dialects of patients for the doctors. His hobby was learning languages and his faith was in Govind Devji.

'Actually, my name is Abdul,' he then said. 'I belong to a Muslim family. We are Rajput Muslims... My father, he once called me a *kaffir*, so now I don't tell him that I like to go there.' He gave a shy look. 'But my wife knows, and she doesn't mind.' Samar asked Abdul if he had first visited Govind Devji out of curiosity and Abdul just said, '*Govind Devji se mujhe bulaawa aya tha*...I had a divine calling from Govind Devji.' With a shy grin, he added, 'My friends call me *Kanhaiyya*.'

'I tell you, Sid,' Samar went on. 'In those days, it was like Krishna was coming to me in different ways.'

As in the rest of north India, in Banaras, too, the one place where the fluidity between Hindus and Muslims is most apparent is at Sufi shrines. As Dumper writes: 'These shrines are devoted to saints, healers, and Sufis dating back to the eleventh century and have continued to be a platform for celebration and public displays of faith to this day.'

At the Banaras tomb of Hazrat Syed Baba Bahadur Shahid you see Hindu women and men seeking cures for various complaints, from cancer and impotence to drunken husbands and wayward children. Here a man prays that his *bawaseer*, piles, be cured, and a woman ties a red thread at the *mazar* so that her son may find a dutiful wife. '*Bhoot paret jin jinnat sab ho jaate hain yahaan ke gulaam*...all ghosts and demons are slaves to this shrine,' a sombre man with a skullcap bellowed into the air here once. And what he said, and how he said it, reminded me so much of how Dadima used to talk.

'*Kitni dargahon mein mannat mangi thi tere liye, ki buri nazar hat jaye*...in how many dargahs I prayed that the evil eye be lifted from you,' my paternal grandmother once said to me when I was a teenager.

'Really?' I said. 'I've never seen you pray once.'

My Dadi, who died in 2005, aged eighty-nine, was a staunch ungodly woman, and she and I had a fun relationship revolving principally around food and gossip. I could get away with making cheeky remarks with her.

'I sent a red string through somebody to be tied at Ajmer for you, you fool. When you were born premature,' she said. 'When they were little, I sent a string each for Madhu, Binoo, Sharat and Bardev'—she tapped the side of her sofa four times, once for each of her children—'to Ajmer or Fatehpur Sikri. And my *mannat* always came true. And so what if my legs won't carry me now. At least I can see my wishes get there.'

Quite the feminist for her times, Dadima frequently said things that could get you in trouble if you said them publicly today. Things like: 'Why should I worship your Ram? I can't worship a God who didn't respect his own wife! Who left her when she was pregnant.' As I stared at her, wondering if she'd got some part of the Ramayana wrong, she hit my leg. 'Now, don't you come up with excuses like other men. I've heard them all before.'

Yet Dadima, despite her brazen ways, was a believer, too. Though not religious in the traditional sense, she found tremendous comfort at Sufi dargahs. Never one to entertain a passing sadhu, she didn't hold back from seeking out the mullah in the mosque behind our house from whom she'd sometimes get a tabeez. She'd then proudly display this black amulet on her neck, though she never divulged what it was for. *Were my grandmother's unconventional leanings a result of her upbringing?* Like my other grandparents, Dadima, had grown up in a mixed pre-Partition Punjab where Hindus, Muslims and Sikhs, despite their differences and occasional clashes, had managed to live alongside largely peaceably for centuries.

By the time Partition happened, my grandparents had been settled in Delhi for over a decade. But still, Dadima would go on about 'how good things were in those days'. 'Oh, there was no difference between us. My best friend was this girl Ayesha,' she once said, starry-eyed. But then, her memories were shot through with bitterness, too. 'In the riots, those bastard *musallas*...they cut off women's breasts,' she said another time, her voice seething. 'You kids can't imagine what we saw.'

And it's true. I don't know what she saw. But what *I* saw was that when my grandfather died, and we were performing a havan in our home, Dadima, by then frail and brain-fogged, yelled out to the pandit conducting the prayers from her room next door: '*Maulvi sahib!*' She hit the side of her bed twice. '*Oh, maulvi sahib!* Do chant louder. I can't hear you!' And the pandit, assuming nonchalance, upped his voice, as papa, mummy, Mala and I all suppressed the urge to laugh.

I once saw a YouTube interview of the historian Romila Thapar in which she says that, as recently as the 1800s, many people who identified as Hindu or Muslim freely partook in the festivals of the other. Religious divisions were more flexible then than they would become a century later.

'There are differences of religion at the elite level,' she says. 'Very distinct identities, where the Hindus are describing themselves as *Vaishnavs*, *Shaivas*, *Shaktas*, *Tantrics* or whatever their sect is. And, of course, the subsect... [But] at the lower level which is about 60 to 70 per cent of the population, below the elite, there is very much of mixture... Who goes to the temple [and] who goes to the mosque? ... You have lots of castes returning themselves [in the census of India] as Muslim and when they are asked how many times do you go to the mosque to pray they say, "Well, on festival days, occasionally I go there," [but] when they are asked, "Which festivals do you observe?" they list all the Hindu festivals... Because at that level there is a communication. A living together, as it were. Which is very important. And this is what gets left out in our reading of history.'

There *was* a time when many people could be described, in Thapar's words in her paper, 'Tyranny of Labels', 'as being at the intersection of Islam and Hindu[ism]'. 'Were Hindus picking up some aspects of Islam, or were they Muslims practising a Hinduized Islam?' Who can tell? Who *should* tell?

So, why was it that despite our history of commingling I was still prone to believing that my faith was the most broadminded of all? Why did I still believe Hinduism is the most inclusive religion?

Perhaps the answer lies again in politics. I think I found it hard to shake off my conviction that Islam and Christianity held exclusivist worldviews. Muslims believed there is no God but Allah, and Mohammed was his messenger, and Christians maintained that Jesus was the Son of God and He was anointed as the saviour of humanity. The Quran said that Mohammed (PBUH) was the last prophet sent by Allah (33:40), and the Bible said that Jesus is the way, the truth and the life, and that no man could cometh unto God but by Him (John 14:6).

Only our Bhagavad Gita warned against this sort of exclusivism! The Gita said: 'And that knowledge by which one is attached to one kind of work as the all in all, without knowledge of the truth, and which is very meagre, is said to be in the mode of darkness.' (18:22)

As Maharajji once said, 'It is only we Hindus who see God in every place of worship and every grain of sand.' Or as Shashi Tharoor puts it in his book *Why I Am a Hindu*, 'It's we Hindus alone who readily venerate the saints and the sacred objects of the other faiths without feeling like we are betraying our own.' And I had, since childhood, taken my ability to embrace all faiths as unique. I believed even that this free-wheeling nature of my religion made my outlook 'universal', as it were.

So you can imagine what a shock it was to my system when, as a young student in the UK, I met people who said things to the exact contrary! Beneath their veneer of political correctness, I sensed that Westerners saw Hindus as primitive idolaters. Beneath their polite words, I felt some saw Hinduism as an inferior Eastern cousin of paganism, which they were fortunate to climb out of to embrace the higher plane of Christianity. You might justifiably say, 'Pal, who are you to speak for me?' And you're right.

But as I saw it, Christianity and Islam considered themselves the only true religions—true in the sense that they espoused a truth applicable to everybody and for all times, and they made such claims to the souls of *all* human beings. And as I've said before, it was precisely this chauvinistic attitude that stopped me at the outset from learning more about Christianity in my twenties. It was this same arrogance I had another peek of in my journey down the Ganga.

In his book, *The Sacred City of the Hindus: An Account of Benares in Ancient and Modern Times*, published in 1868, the Christian missionary M.A. Sherring writes:

'In short idolatry is a charm, a fascination, to the Hindu. It is, so to speak, the air he breathes. It is the food of his soul. It is the foundation of his hopes, both of this world and for the other. He is subdued, enslaved and befooled by it. He is, however, a willing slave, a willing devotee; for he loves idolatory, together with its superstitions and ceremonies, with all the ardour of religious frenzy. Moreover, it is of great importance to bear in mind, that, as a man can hardly be better than his religion, the nature of the Hindu partakes of the supposed nature of the god whom he worships. And what is that nature? According to the traditions handed about amongst the natives, and constantly dwelt upon in their conversation, and referred to in their popular songs, which, perhaps, would be sufficient proof for our purpose, yet, more especially, according to the numberless statements and narratives found in their sacred writings, on which these traditions are based, it is, in many instances, vile and abominable to the last degree; so that the poor idolator, when brought completely under its influence, is deplorably debased. Virtue, truth, holiness, civilization, enlightenment, human progress, all that contributes to human happiness and to a nation's prosperity, cannot be properly appreciated by him. His soul's best affections are blighted, and his conscience deeply perverted. Idolatry is a word denoting all that is wicked in imagination and impure in practice. *These remarks are especially true of rigid and thorough Hindus, like the Gangaputras, or the "sons of the Ganges", who may be regarded as representing, in their own persons, the complete results of their strange religion.*'

Granted, these are the words of a man keen to establish the moral superiority of Christianity. But it's remarkable how they can get my back up even today, as should be apparent by my emphasis in the quotation above!

And now that we're talking about religious chauvinism, let me take you down another tributary, Dear Reader:

If it takes me about a day to overcome Western misconceptions about my faith, then I should tell you it's taken me some thirty-five years to see that just viewing my faith as unique is, well, just another kind of hubris. Because when I sit down and think about it, I see that even if Hindu views on God may be 'universal', down here in our world of mortals, we've been the most exclusivist people of all!

Seriously. For all our spiritual quests and yogic stretches, we've *excluded* people on home soil like few others. And while it's true the Semitic faiths draw a line between themselves and the Others, we Hindus, well, we do the same thing! Even if not so much abroad, then certainly all the time at home. We continue to exclude people from *within*, and like the adherents of Semitic faiths, we also do it with the support of scripture.

According to our Shaastras, the Brahmins are believed to have come from Lord Brahma's head. The *Kshatriyas*, or the warriors and rulers, emanated from his arms. The *Vaishyas*, or the traders, were made from his thighs. And at the bottom of the heap lay the *Shudras* who did all the menial jobs, as they still do. They came from Brahma's feet.

I can literally see you—Yes, you, Hindu Reader!—shaking your head. I can hear you saying, 'Here, he goes again!' 'You should understand the "context", the time when these words were written.' And I say, 'Okay, we don't have terms like "heathen" or "kaffir" in our lexicon. But we once had "mlechchha", barbarian, didn't we?' We like to say '*Atithi Devo Bhava*'. We say, 'We treat our guests like gods.' But whom do we mean? And be honest, we don't mean our helpers and cleaners whose surnames we don't even know and who never sit with us at our dining table. We *never* mean the *Dalits*: people we still cruelly call *chooras*, *bhangis*, and *chamars*, terms highlighting their unclean and formerly 'untouchable' ancestral occupations, and of which we continue to know little.

So, let me tell you what these terms mean: Chamar, you probably know is the caste that historically worked in leather tanning, and bhangis are the sweepers and cleaners across northern India. But did you know that the term choora—another word for bhangi—is the Punjabi distortion of the Vedic term shudra? How much does my everyday vocabulary alone entrench caste divisions? I wondered when I learnt of this.

In my family house built in Delhi in the '60s, the bathrooms still have two doors. The one attached to the bedroom was initially meant for family use, but the one connecting to the hallway was to be used only by the bathroom cleaner. In the days before builder flats took over upscale urban neighbourhoods, many houses were built this way. So that the *jamadarni* could enter the bathroom, do her job and leave without you seeing her. So, that her eyes never fell on your space. As Dadima once said, 'So she remains outside only.'

Given our socially fragmented land, a land in which for a long time the only way to have a better life was to move up the caste ladder, is it a surprise that lower caste members asserted 'high lineages'? As my driver, Juggal, said, 'Actually, we are Rajputs. But if you live alongside *dhobis* you will also be called a dhobi. *Hai na?*

Juggal came from the caste of washermen, also regarded as low, but several notches above bhangis. While a growing economy and an enterprising spirit had made him wealthier than his neighbours, in the end, he still married a girl from his own community. 'Who else but a dhobi will give their daughter to go live in the dhobi ghat?' he said.

To be clear, Dear Reader, I'm not going all holier-than-thou on you. God knows I've benefitted from my privilege. All I'm saying is that it was on this journey that I began to become more self-aware. I began seeing that who I was came down not to merit, or karma, but to luck.

During one temple run to Uttarakhand, I took Juggal with me. As he drove on, I stared at the mountains, day-dreaming. When we stopped at a dhaba, I asked him to join me. I thought eating together would bridge the monstrous social chasm between us. Juggal declined my offer, but I insisted. And even though we ate in silence, I felt good about myself for a long while afterwards—until my driver asked for another chai break. As I spied on him furtively scoffing down an omelette, it dawned on me that the poor guy had been unable even to eat freely sitting across from me. When I think of this now, I feel embarrassed. How can our ingrained divides be bridged by a few free lunches?

When I dine at a fine restaurant in Europe, say, and I'm the lone brown man standing out in a very white setting, I sometimes consider, is this what it's like for Juggal daily? I realize that my comparison is silly. The fact that I can afford to dine at fancy places is in itself a luxury. But it's in these fine moments when I'm made to feel like I'm on the outside—like when the French baker looks through me to speak to the blonde woman right behind in the queue or when the English waiter seats me in a dim corner of a sparkling establishment—that I wonder if rather than *nouvelle* food what I'm actually being served is a mirror.

But then, I think looking at this mirror too is a choice. For it's up to me if I want to continue staring into it, if I look harder and deeper, or if I look away and just sit back and enjoy my cheese souffle. Then fly home and resume my position as a feudal prince in my country of so many paupers. Go hang clothes bought on Oxford Street but stitched in sweatshops in my backyard in my cupboard. Yell at Chhotu to set the house for the party tomorrow. Toss Juggal the car keys to run to Old Delhi where I ring Aslam Bhai, my kebabs-guy and one of three Muslim contacts on my phone. And say to my friends in the evening over clinking glasses of Merlot, 'Europe is lovely, but India is the best. Those guys are f—ing racist.' And tell the visiting Dutch tourist with a smug smile on my face, 'I'm telling you, caste barriers have broken down in our cities!' even if just a half hour earlier I'd said to Samar, 'Why've you come dressed like a chamar today?'

Caste is that voice in your head that's eternally there but never uttered aloud in polite company. When it does surface, it is crudely in the privacy of your home to remind the Chhotus and Juggals about their *aukaat*, their place in the order of things. Or to proclaim to your peers how democratic you are. Like this one time papa said to mummy: 'I'll give you ten thousand rupees if you take a *bhangan* with you to Rishikesh. Will Swamiji allow her to cook for him even after she washes herself a hundred times?'

I hate to admit it, but I'm the same. Even if I now call my 'servants' 'helpers', they eat separately as before. So what if I had that odd meal with Juggal up in the mountains. I know as he does that I wouldn't be caught eating with him at the Gymkhana Club.

Ambedkar once said, 'Democracy in India is only a top-dressing on an Indian soil which is essentially undemocratic...' He's right. No matter how you dress it, caste is Hinduism's Achilles' heel. Or rather, Duryodhana's groin.

In the Mahabharata, Queen Gandhari, wife of the blind king Dhritarashtra, was a great devotee of Lord Shiva from whom she had acquired spiritual powers. She summoned Duryodhana, the first-born of her hundred sons, before his final dual with Bhim, and asked him to meet her straight after a bath, in the nude. But on his way over, Duryodhana met Lord Krishna, who said, 'What? You're the Prince of Hastinapur, and you'll meet your mother like this? Have you no shame? At least cover up your private parts.' And embarrassed, Duryodhana did so. When Gandhari peeled away the blindfold around her eyes for the first time after marriage she released a terrific bolt of shakti, instantly filling Duryodhana with Shiva's energy.

Duryodhana was now invincible and as the fight with Bhim wore on he retained the upper hand. But just when Bhim was exhausted, just when Bhim realized it would be impossible to overpower Duryodhana,

Krishna gestured to him to strike his opponent in the groin. It was Duryodhana's weak spot.

This was God's shrewd act, but it was a necessary one. And it led to the Kauravas' ultimate defeat in the war.

Wasn't caste stratification just why so many of our lower orders sought Universality and Truth elsewhere? Wasn't the chauvinism of the *Gangaputras* one reason why Buddhism—anti-God and anti-Brahmin at its core—spread like electricity through the Ganga valley over two thousand years ago?

I know these big questions all have complex, nuanced answers. But since we're discussing politics and religion now, it's worth touching on another question mummy has asked rhetorically many times. 'Tell me,' she'd say, narrowing her eyes, 'how is it that even though the British ruled us for so long they never succeeded in changing our faith? It's because of our culture. Just look at what the white man did in America! They wiped the natives out!'

Call it a post-colonial complex or cultural pride, but I've found myself thinking along the same lines. How could we Hindus have been expected to give up our hundreds of gods and adopt an exclusive Christian one? If there was a Supreme Divinity, undoubtedly all His and Her manifestations led you to the One, no? You could get there by worshipping Krishna, the god of compassion and love, as much as by looking to Jesus, who also preached compassion and love. And like Banaras, Hinduism has also always been this Great-Free-For-All, right?

Undeniably, there are key historical reasons, too, as to why India was never Christianized, as were many former African colonies. But let me now put to you the rejoinder I'd served my mother: Unlike Christianity, Islam *did* leave an indelible mark on the Ganga valley, didn't it? Yes, Muslim rulers had been around centuries longer, and yes, Hindus and Muslims had had several generations to get acquainted. And yes, unlike the British, who kept themselves apart, many Islamic rulers came to stay. They mixed with the locals. They adopted local habits. They, in a sense, became Indian. 'So, if our culture is so open why did so many adopt Islam?'

Mummy answered coolly, like she'd figured out the lay of the land and her space in it. 'Everybody knows Islam spread by the sword,' she said.

But this is a comeback I've never been swayed by. Whatever the facts you rely on, it is a spontaneous reaction to shift the critical gaze away from yourself and lay all blame on the Other. It is so much harder to self-reflect. To ask: could this new faith have become attractive because people were discontent with the old way? Could what made many unhappy in our recent history be the same thing which drove some to challenge the practices of the Gangaputras at the time of the Buddha?

For some, things were never easy. And as the story of Nandanar, which a Tamil pandit once told me with perceptible vanity, illustrates, even your imagination can get you only so far.

Nandanar, a Dalit and Shiva devotee from Tamil Nadu in the eighth century, longed to get a darshan of the Lord. In the Sivalokanathar Temple in Tirupunkur, he praised Lord Shiva so much that God said to his Nandi statue, 'O child, move a little and let my bhakt see me!' and eventually Nandanar received Shiva's darshan. But there then comes a split in storylines: Nandanar is said to have purified himself by fire at the Thillai Nataraja Temple in Chidambaram. So, while upper-caste narratives portray him as a Brahmin trapped in an untouchable's body whose actual form was exposed by a trial of fire, Dalits underscore how Nandanar and other saints from his community were exploited by Brahmins.

Even if we Hindus understood that there were thousands of ways to see God, there was never a way to get around the Brahmin intermediaries to gain access, was there? Now, when into our mix came Islam, a faith which explicitly said, *There is only one God*, is it surprising many thousands found this message appealing? And Islam didn't say just this. Islam also said all its adherents are *brothers*. And this tenet was such a radical departure from the Hindu way. It was so path-breaking a route to God, to see yourself in His image. Why wouldn't those suffocating at the bottom of the Old Order race towards it?

I know, like all faiths, Islam too is divided into numerous sects, subsects, with certain surnames claiming high heredities. But my point is simple: Inside a mosque, you can *see* the idea of One Brotherhood taking a physical form. To pray alongside your brothers in one space with no marked divisions, with nobody separating you from your maker, with everybody under one sky, is a compelling message in a land riven by divisions. Sometimes, you need to look hard into the mirror to see your warts...

At any rate, history turned out as it did. Kings came. Kings went. People believed, and believed some more. The Banarsi lassi kept churning, sometimes frothing, but eventually simmering down. Our cultural crucible was stirred, which, in turn, stirred our customs, food, art, music and philosophy. And little by little, like mango juice in buttermilk, the attitudes of one faith seeped deep into the wells of the other.

During the Muslim period, much intellectual activity took place in Varanasi. The city experienced the Bhakti movement, 'a people's movement', writes Diana Eck, 'in which classical Sanskrit literature yielded to a vibrant new poetic literature composed in the languages of the people. And as before, great philosophies bloomed, especially Advaita (Non-Dualism)'. 'While some devotees expressed their love for a personal God, "with attributes" (saguna), such as Rama or Krishna, others praised a God who transcends every name and description, without the limit of any of the characteristics ascribed to God by the human imagination (nirguna). These latter devotees called God by many names, but spoke of a reality beyond all names, and indeed, beyond all the distortions of "religion", whether Muslim or Hindu.'

In architecture, Madhuri Desai notes, 'Masons modified Mughal fashion as well as transformed Hindu precedents, appropriated Mughal columns and arches, and experimented with archaic forms, particularly temple *shikharas*.'

And our shared manners went beyond what appearances conveyed.

Such were my ruminations in November 2019, as I stared out a taxi window one afternoon a couple of days before my darshan at the Vishwanath Temple with Samar and Palakh. After a round of shopping, the three of us were on our way to Deena Chat Bhandar, a famous chaat shop in the city, when a procession of what looked like hundreds of trucks held us up in traffic.

Each truck was packed with boys. There were boys waving green Islamic flags and boys waving the national tricolour. There were boys hooting and boys clapping. There were boys in white caps, boys in green caps, boys in blue caps, bearded boys and clean-shaven boys. It was so very amusing to watch. There were no orange shirts, but the ambience was just like the kanwar yaatra! In even our expressions, we're similar, I thought.

Of course, whether it was Shivratri, Muharram or the kanwar yaatra, only boys exhibited themselves in the open. Women were conspicuous by their absence.

'I think the one place where women dance openly is at Indian weddings,' I said aloud, and Samar nodded vaguely. Palakh, sitting between us, was absently scrolling through her phone. But she now looked up.

She took off her sunglasses. 'My God!' She stuck her tongue to her top front teeth. 'So many Muslims!'

And I thought, yes, we *are* the same people. But when our base emotions take over, we then see in ourselves the Other.

I got out of the car to buy paan.

'Where are you from?' the *paanwaala* asked.

'Delhi. What festival is this?'

'They are just doing their *shakti pradarshan*,' he said casually. 'They want to show their strength now that Modiji is rebuilding the city.'

So, I went up to a young motorcyclist who was a part of the parade of trucks. 'What is this festival?'

'Yes, it is our festival,' he said, unable to hear me through an announcement on a loudspeaker.

'Yes, what is it?'

The occasion was Prophet Mohammed's birthday, and the procession would take a while to clear. As Google Maps said that Deena Chat Bhandar was only six hundred metres away, we decided to walk over. The chaat shop was famous for its tamatar ki chaat, a sour and spicy tomatoey goodness topped with savoury, crispy bits.

Samar and I dug into our individual servings, and after only a bite, we ordered another plateful each. But Palakh plain refused to eat. 'I'll eat later.' She lowered her voice. 'It's filthy here.'

'*Arre*, try it,' Samar said. 'Stop being a firangi.' And Palakh diffidently leaned forward for a bite. 'Okay,' she said. 'It's good.' And she ordered a plate for herself, an extra spicy one, and after three bites, her eyes were smarting, and she was smacking her lips, fanning her face with her fingers. 'I love it.' She wiped the bowl clean, licking off the last residues, and sat back in her chair with a look of bliss.

And I now thought, Yes! If there was a food that best described Varanasi it was not lassi or biryani. It was chaat. Banaras is like this rich bowl of faith in which the Hindu base of yoghurt is dressed in the green of Islam. It is a place where the two distinct flavours are complementary. Where one element fires up only to simmer down and meld into the other—through its architecture, through its music, through its food. And it is only when you take in the entire lot in a hearty bite that the sweet-sour-spicy elements all come together to party in your mouth. And one thing I hope we can agree on, Dear Reader, is that just as chaat can't ever become sushi, Varanasi won't ever be Kyoto.

Banaras, this heaving melange of faiths. Varanasi, a powerhouse of culture, music and food. Kashi, which sits atop Shiva's trident.

But what was here before the ghats and buildings arose? Put this question to a Varanasi pandit and he might tell you that 'Varanasi' is so named for it is the stretch of land lying between the confluence of the Varun (in the north) and Assi (in the south) rivers with the Ganga, and that it has been sacred since the earliest days. He might even add that there was once a forest here, an *anandavan*, a Forest of Bliss, and many a yogi would seek it out to practise their meditations.

According to Diana Eck, from as far back as 1000 BCE this anandavan attracted all manner of seekers; from 'Upanishadic sages, who claimed that reality lay beyond the apprehension of the senses, to the materialism of the Lokayatas, who contended, rather, that Reality is precisely what can be apprehended by the senses... The most famous seeker of this age was Prince Siddharth Gautama, born a prince in a small kingdom that had been subsumed by Koshala... He came to be called the Buddha, the "Awakened One", and after his enlightenment or awakening, he struck out for Varanasi, to teach what he had seen to his companions, for he knew they would be there. He walked the two hundred miles from Gaya and crossed the Ganges by ferry to reach Varanasi. There in a park in the suburbs of the city he found his former companions and preached to them the teachings that have come to be called the Four Noble Truths and the Eightfold Noble

Path. In this first sermon of the Buddha he "turned the wheel of the *dharma*", which has been in motion ever since.'

This park is now called Sarnath. But at a distance of less than nine kilometres from the heart of Varanasi, 'even in those days, it fell within the Kashikshetra [Kashi zone],' Mahant Rajendra Tiwari had said.

So armed with my knowledge, I said to mummy over lunch one day, 'Did you know some of the earliest history associated with Varanasi is actually not Hindu, but Buddhist?'

'Hah, *Buddhist Kashi*,' mummy said, mimicking my voice. 'Kashi is a Hindu city! You liberals think you're so clever. Speak the truth!'

But the historical truth I was learning was far from straightforward. As Madhuri Desai writes, the city's Purana literature, specifically the *Kashi Khand* and the *Kashi Rahasya*, was more 'a collection of diverse and fragmented opinions' rather than a 'universal and timeless discourse on the city'. Moreover, 'the discovery of the Buddhist site of Sarnath to the north of the *Kashikshetra* (beyond the Panchkoshi circuit) in 1794 altered the city's history as well as its imagined geography'.

'That you view Hindus and Muslims as opposing factions,' my sister Mala said in her adult lawyer voice, 'is a British creation. You've said so yourself. So, why the hypocrisy, mom?'

On this point, too, Desai refers to H.R. Neville's official *Gazetteer of Benares* published in 1905. 'Neville framed this past within a historical timeline, beginning with a Buddhist Banaras, continuing into a Hindu age, followed by Islamic iconoclasm from which the city always seemed to bounce back,' she writes. 'The colonial administration tended to simplify events and gloss over nuances of opinion, viewing them as confrontations between monolithic groups of Hindus and Muslims. As a result...*the Gyan Vapi mosque was dissociated from the policies of a single emperor and placed within the grand narrative of inevitable Islamic destruction and iconoclasm.*' (Emphasis mine.)

And now papa jumped into the fray. 'You kids born yesterday, you think you know India, *haan*? Tell me, how much did Aurangzeb destroy in Banaras alone? Go on.'

And seeing papa on her side, mummy got more excited. 'Yes, the Mughals were goody-two-shoes, no?' she said, still in her mimicking voice. 'Oh, Aurangzeb was a saint!' When she saw me suppress my laughter her agitation crept to anger. 'Why do you like to bash your own culture?'

While the above family exchange is partly manufactured, it is essentially *true*. It accurately depicts dining table conversations in our home in recent years. And they were growing hilarious, weren't they? How ridiculous was it that despite their incalculable differences my atheist father and devout mother had found a loving bond in politics?

Knowing how things would go from here, I'd stay quiet. Or throw a wrench into the discussion and say: 'I think the greatest thing about Banaras is that it gave birth to Kabir. He was equally critical of the Brahmins and Mullahs.'

And papa would shake his head and say: 'Son, I think you don't know Islam.' And Mala would mutter under her breath: 'As if you know Hinduism.' And by the end of the meal, like those debaters on prime-time news, there would be four agitated lawyers having arrived at no conclusion.

So let me just put out the elephant in the room: While my parents were routinely sympathetic to Hindutva, my sister and I bemoaned its rise. Perhaps our divergent views had something to do with how our own lives unfolded. Despite our upbringing, my sister and I had transgressed in our romantic choices. Mala had married a Sikh man, and my partner, Armaan, as you know, is a Muslim-born atheist now flirting with Buddhism. But I'd argue that our choices were a product of our upbringing, too.

Yes, I'd inherited certain prejudices but I was still a product of a system that stressed all gods are One, no? My sister and I believed that everybody, of whatever faith, strove for the same Truth. And if the two of us born of this soil thought in this way, then didn't our parents also deep down believe the same thing? Didn't they have to?

In retrospect, I can say it was my search for *this* Oneness—one Humanity, one Truth—that led me to read more about three Greats, each of whom moved Banaras in his specific way:

(1) The Buddha, who spoke of selflessness at the heart of all existence. (2) Adi Shankaracharya, who spoke of Advaita or non-dualism between the Self and the Universe. (3) And Kabir, that

fifteenth-century irreverent mystic whose writings shaped both Hinduism's Bhakti movement and whose *dohas*, couplets, can be found in Sikhism's Guru Granth Sahib.

Some said that Kabir belonged to low-caste Banaras Muslim weavers. Others said he was a Hindu, and a pupil of the Ramananda. But everybody seems to agree that when he died, and followers of both faiths began bickering over how to dispose of his remains, when they lifted the cloth covering his body, they found a spread of flowers under it.

Always mocking religion, Kabir went nowhere on pilgrimage and was such a rebel that when death was nearing, he *left* his hometown Kashi and went to die in dusty Magahar, which, Diana Eck writes, was 'so impure and disreputable, according to Kashi Brahmins, that those who die there will be reborn as asses.'

I can hear somebody in my head. I can hear him say, 'Why do you keep going off on tangents? You think talking about caste and the Buddha and now Kabir is so cool!' I can hear him say, 'Why are you like this?'

Is this you, Dear Reader, or myself?

No matter. Let me answer. *Why am I like this?* It is because I'm fundamentally opposed to bigotry. And when I'm not, I'm realizing that I must be.

You see, like many kids who are different, I was bullied in school. I was mocked for my feminine voice and ways. One time, during music class, I recall the teacher making everybody sing a verse out loud and happy to finally show off my bathroom singing habits I sang my heart out. When I'd just finished and blushed with glee, a boy blurted out: 'I think you'll fit in better with the girls.' I remember everybody laughed. The boys, the girls, the teacher—they all laughed.

For those of us who are different, it's incidents like this that sink and accrue in our gut. Over years, they rake up old anxieties and birth newer ones. Indeed, as you get older your skin gets thicker. But you also learn how to disguise yourself. You learn how not to stand and how not to walk. You learn to make your voice deeper, stripped of its sing-song modulations; especially when speaking to boys and men, the patriarchs of today and the future. You learn to append 'motherfu—er' and 'bro' to your sentences. You learn to become mixable, malleable: 'normal'… And then there comes a day you start doing these things unconsciously. You put on one face for the world and keep *yourself* to yourself. You become a little less the dreamer in the pooja room and more the boy with a remarkable memory of the *Hanuman Chalisa*. And when a pandit congratulates you on your devotion, your bhakti, you want to say, *Really? Are you talking about me? Have I lost a part of who I was? Who I could have been in some alternate reality?*

One justification you give is, 'Look! Just look at the others!' And there have been times when I've been persuaded by this line of defence. I have felt your pull of tribal loyalty. I know it exists because being part of a team fills your chest with pride. It persists because when your team wins a match it sends blood rushing to the head. It perseveres down the line because being a team member gives you confidence and identity and structure. But as with all clubs your membership comes at a cost. In return for a strength in numbers, you're made to cede a part of yourself. In return for social approval you must shred all the *dishonourable* pieces which set you apart.

Your quirkiness. Your *crayzee*. They all must be tamped down: *This* is the contract of all religions.

Whenever I happened to conform against my wishes, I failed anyway in some critical expected way. Whenever I tried to blend into the standard mix, my jagged inner nature spiked somewhere, somehow.

It would take me decades—seriously, decades—to see that through my tries and fails I'd been seeing another thing and that this tiny abstract thing had stopped me from betraying my core. In the faces of religion's custodians, the patriarchs and matriarchs, the priests and politicians, I'd seen the very same thing. They all had the same prescribed manners: the same nods of the chin and the same wagging of fingers. They had the same easy certainties and the same things angered them. But they also had the same glint in their eyes… Oh, yes, they had the eyes of my class bully. And the boys and girls who laughed with him. Of course, the children had grown up. The adults had learnt to disguise their harassment as righteous speech and dress their punches as virtuous actions. But they remained the same people. They still picked on the different ones. The odd ones. The Others.

I saw that even if I was in their club today, they could otherize me tomorrow. So, you tell me, what choice did I have other than to be just as I was: irreverent and weird, dreamy and divergent?

Sometimes, I ask: Is it my inborn difference or my privilege that gives me an outsider's gaze? But on deeper self-examination, I've realized that such thinking also betrays hollow logic. Not only because such thoughts nudge me to go against my grain, my tendency to investigate what I'm told to take for granted, to be myself in little ways in the face of overarching conformity. But also because, if I am to go down the elusive corridors of my own faith—as I was now doing more than ever before—I could see similar calls to shed the ego and embrace humility. To move away from organized religion to a universe of silent inward reflection…

And so, Dear Reader, let's return to Kashi.

Just as an ethos of scientific truth-seeking in the eighteenth and nineteenth centuries spurred the Industrial Revolution in the West, the forests around Varanasi during the time of the Buddha and for centuries afterwards was *the place to be* for seekers from across the Ganga valley. Arguably, the two most well-known schools of Indian spiritual thought are Buddhism and Vedanta; so much that one might say that while the originator of Vedanta, Shankaracharya, has most informed the meditations of millions in India today, the Buddha has done the same for the introspections of millions abroad. However, as both philosophies were born in the same soil they share many ideas. Both, for instance, believe in *Samsara*, the cyclicality of life, the world, the Universe. Both believe in karma, one's actions and its consequences. And both stress on meditation to experience Truth.

Answers to many questions ancient seekers posed—often themselves couched as probing questions—could be found in the Upanishads, the lattermost part of the Vedas. What we call the Vedanta are in fact meditations upon this 'conclusion of the Vedas'—the Veda-*anta*. When it comes to Upanishadic thought and Buddhism, however, it remains a debate as to which influenced which. But scholars generally agree on the approximate order of events: the Early Period Upanishads (such as the *Brahadaranyaka* and the *Chandogya*, generally regarded as the oldest) came before the Buddha. Then came the Middle Period

Upanishads, such as the *Kathaka* (roughly 466–386 BCE), which came after the Buddha, and then came the Late Period Upanishads, such as the *Mandukya Upanishad* (0–200 CE).

The Upanishads contained a galaxy of ideas on the powers of introspection and provided a range of stars shedding light on what internal discoveries might result on exercising such powers. And so they naturally appealed to my old attraction to the otherworldly and my new one for interior growth. ('*That living soul [Brahman] is to be known as part of the hundredth part of the point of a hair, divided a hundred times; and yet it is to be known as infinite,*' says the *Shvetashvatara Upanishad.*) But what appealed to me most about these texts was that they retained a healthy scepticism throughout. That they gave no easy answers. Even the Vedanta school (which ultimately says that if you look deep within yourself, you will see that your soul equals to the Universal Soul) described the Brahman inconclusively. The Brahman is '*neti neti neti*'—not this, not this, not this.

I think the last four lines of the *Nasadiya Sukta*, a Rig Vedic creation hymn, summed everything up best:

Whence all creation had its origin, who knows?
The Creator, whether he fashioned it, or whether he did not,
The Creator, who surveys it all from the highest heaven,
Yes, he knows—or maybe even he does not know.

About God, doubt was and remains for me the *truest* Truth.

So, was it Banaras's oneness—namely that it was an ancient Hindu city with rich Buddhist and Muslim pasts—that made it alluring to me?

Was Varanasi's *chaatness* why when, in December 2021, against the backdrop of drum beats and feverish media celebration, Prime Minister Modi inaugurated the newly expanded Kashi Vishwanath Temple Corridor and news commentators hailed the temple opening as a 'civilizational makeover', nobody that I saw mentioned the presence of the Gyanvapi Mosque in a negative way?

At the time of the Vishwanath Temple Corridor's inauguration, I reached out to S.M. Yaseen, the general secretary of Anjuman Intizamiya Masjid (AIM), a body set up by the Sunni Waqf Board as the caretaker of the Gyanvapi Mosque, and asked for his views on his city's changing landscape.

'There was no pressure on us,' he said by phone. 'And there has been no blockage to our access. In fact, before there was only one way to the mosque and it was very narrow. Now because of the widened area we will have better access. I think the people who are more upset are from the other community…' He hesitated. 'I mean, the Hindu community.' I thanked him for his time and was about to hang up when he said, 'Yes, up until now I have felt no danger. But I cannot speak to the future.'

And, who knows, his concerns might one day turn out to be justified. For when I visited the Vishwanath Temple in March 2022, I sniffed rumours about the next phase of the Corridor Project, which, some said, would lead to the appropriation of more land from the Gyanvapi Mosque. Then, less than two months later, in May 2022, a news story broke about the apparent discovery of a Shivalingam inside the Gyanvapi Mosque, and I reached out to Mr Yaseen again. And again, he was his old measured self.

'As you know, they [the Hindu petitioners] are saying that a pole found in the *wazookhana* [place for ablution] is a Shivalingam,' he said. 'So, the area has been sealed, but the namaz is carrying on… Now the matter is with the Supreme Court.' As for the legitimacy of the petitioners' claim, his words this time were unequivocal: '*Jhoot jab logon ko sach lagne lage, iske bare mein hum kya kahein?* What can I say if people take falsehoods as truth?'

Mahant Rajendra Tiwari, too, was his old vigorous self: '*Patthar ka stambh mila hai fuvaare mein. Ki yeh Vishwanath hain yeh kisne pramanit kiya hai? Kashi Vishwanath koi samanya devta nahi hain. Pure brahmaand ke devta hain*,' he said. They did find a stone pole in the fountain. Who will decide if this is Lord Vishwanath? he said. Vishwanath is no ordinary God. He is the God of the Universe.

'If you walk from Gowdolia Chowk to Dashashwamedh Ghat, you'll see some two hundred stones just like this. Will people now start saying that these are also Lord Vishwanath? These people are making a joke out of the Lord's magnificence… And to all these people standing up for Dharma today, I want to ask again, where were you when our old temples were being broken?'

I asked Pandit Hiralal Pandey, the priest escorting me around the temple complex one hot afternoon in March 2022, to show me the wall bordering the mosque once again.

As before, the masjid stood behind high barbed wires, but it now looked rather derelict and sad, its dull minarets utterly subdued by the lofty Vishwanath complex. A lone elderly man with a white beard stood on a terrace, peering at the Hindu throngs with a look of awe.

'So what if this was the site of the original temple?' I said. 'Now, we have our grand temple. Everybody should just be happy.' And a young man turned to face me.

'Really?' he said, his eyebrows arching. 'The old temple was here?' As I backed away, I heard him say to his wife: 'The old temple was where this mosque is. They never tell us these things.'

In her book, published a few years before the corridor's construction, Madhuri Desai presciently wrote, 'Patronage for temples, monasteries, and other built elements was connected to contemporary cultural conditions. Consequently, the built environment of the city's sacred zones altered along with urbanization and politics.'

These words echoed in what she said to me by email in January 2022. 'The physical changes that are being envisaged and carried out for Banaras today are in keeping with the many-layered changes that have been made to its physical fabric through the centuries. As before, contemporary politics and visions continue to shape its built environment.'

But what struck me personally about Banaras's environment was rather something else. Something totally illogical and mythical: Wasn't it extraordinary that throughout the ages that saw some of Kashi's greatest temples—the Krittivasa, Omkara, Mahadeva, Madhyameshwara, Bindu Madhava and Kala Bhairava—lying in ruins, the one which kept rising up again and again, like Lord Shiva after every cosmic dance of destruction, was the Kashi Vishwanath?

As Madhuri Desai writes, '[F]ar from overturning religious sentiments and identities, the sheer act of dismantling it [by Aurangzeb] may have transmuted Vishveshvar into the undisputed centre and fulcrum of the city's ritual landscape.'

Three Temple Darshans and a Diwali for the Gods

As before, the Kashi Jyotirlingam, representing the (*nirguna*) Supreme Reality out of which emerges the (*saguna*) form of Lord Shiva, sits on a silver altar at the centre of the temple complex. As before, the jyotirlinga resides in the garbha griha, or sanctum sanctorum, which connects to the sabha griha or the congregation hall. And as before, the main temple building has three prominent structures: two buildings with conical spires, the one with the sanctum bearing a flag and trident and another with a golden dome. But in the olden days before the refurbishment of the temple complex, the innermost quadrangle of Ahilyabai Holkar's Vishwanath temple was tightly enclosed by Lord Shiva's *panchayat*. In the southeast stood the temple of Lord Avimukteshwar. In the northeast sat Ma Annapurna. In the northwest, Parvati. In the southwest, Lord Satyanarayan. And in the west, Hanuman. These old deities have now all been removed from their mool sthaan, their original seats, and in their place there now gleams a capacious marble courtyard cleared of the old mesh of wall-to-wall grizzled buildings.

Yes, the old deities are all very much there, along with some newer ones, like the idol of Ma Annapurna who was returned from Canada. But they now sit at some distance from the main Vishwanath Shivalingam.

The shrine was packed as always when Palakh, Samar, Pandit Vimal, and I entered the temple that afternoon in November 2019. So, Pandit Vimal suggested we first do a small pooja in the congregation hall before paying our respects to Lord Vishwanath. This struck me as odd but as Palakh had organized our darshan I followed her lead.

Pandit Vimal sat us down in a corner. 'Your mother has asked me to do a special pooja for you.'

'What pooja?' Palakh looked surprised.

As it turned out, Palakh's parents had matched her and Samar's horoscopes and found that twenty-two *gunas*, or merits, were in agreement. If this number exceeded eighteen, Pandit Vimal said, it meant the couple's marriage prospects were very good. It was also good that as per his birth chart, Samar belonged to the *Manav Yoni* (i.e. human birth) and Palakh belonged to the *Devta Yoni* (born from the gods). Which meant they would fit each other like lock and key.

'There are three types of Yonis ['source' or 'womb' as per Hindu astrology],' Pandit Vimal said. '*Manushya* [man], *Devta* [god] and *Rakshas* [demon]. There will be love between Devta and Devta and between Rakshas and Rakshas and between Devta and Manav. God protects Man and Man looks up to God, so a relationship between one born from Man and the other from God will work well. But if one is a Devta and the other a Rakshas, there'll be fights.'

Pandit Vimal's father had done a more thorough reading and found that while love between the couple was possible, there were some problems with Samar's birth chart. Deciding to play along with this charade or out of politeness, Samar nodded.

Pandit Vimal enlarged his eyes at Samar. 'You are experiencing a *Mahshani Dasha*. So, you may be feeling restlessness, health issues, sorrows, loss of near and dear ones, loss of income, delays in achieving results.'

The astrological house of horrors during which the planet Saturn casts a dark shadow over your life seemed so all-encompassing that I thought anyone could fit their troubles into it. And so Samar did. He squinted at the enthusiastic devotees around us. 'Panditji, you're correct,' he said. 'But what pooja do you want me to do *now*?'

Pandit Vimal began drawing a swastika pattern with red vermilion on the floor. 'This will help reduce your Saturn affliction.' He looked to Palakh. She turned to the ground.

'See. Both your horoscopes match. But you have a lot of mental confusion.'

Samar sighed. 'Can we do this quickly? I want to do my darshan.'

Palakh cleared her throat. 'Can we do this first?' she said and Samar wiggled his head.

Pandit Vimal half-grinned. 'Can I say something, bhaiyya?' he said. 'And you don't mind, okay? Please don't think so much. You think too much. *Shani dosh* can delay or cancel your marriage. A girl and a boy who come together bring their respective fortunes together and this impacts the other in a big way. If you marry a good girl, you can become a king because of her. And what do all men want? A girl who is *bhagyashaali*, full of good fortune. So, what do we do? We invoke our parents' blessings. We invoke God's blessings...

'You have confusion because [the demon] *Rahu* is sitting with the moon in your eighth house. Samarji, you must strengthen your moon. You can wear silver and feed a black dog on Saturdays, and I can give you more suggestions. But don't delay your marriage.'

Pandit Vimal beamed his grin more widely. Samar's cheeks reddened and I felt a bolt of deja vu.

'Thinking is good. But overthinking is bad.'

'Yes, panditji, I understood you the first time,' Samar said in a raised, out-of-character voice that made both Palakh and me look up. Palakh stared at Samar, then looked back to the ground.

'Please do your pooja in ten minutes,' he said. 'Then I'll do mine.'

Behind the Vishwanath Shivalingam, two pandits rode high crescendos in Sanskrit verse, their tones wavering with disapproval at the amount of time devotees were taking to pour on Lord Shiva Gangajal, ghee, bel leaves, milk, flowers. As my forehead made contact with the lingam, masses of Gangajal, yoghurt and ghee cascaded onto my face and neck. Then through this haze I felt on my back a *THUMP!* 'Move along,' the pandit said, his chanting and smacking continuing in rhythmic synchrony. And before I could verbalize a protest, a marigold garland was tossed around my neck, Gangajal splashed on my face, and a red tika drawn on my forehead just as both Samar and I were shoved out the exit to our right by the next batch of in-coming devotees.

As we stood out in the buzzing congregation hall with bewildered smiles, we said to each other at virtually the same time, 'Where's Palakh?'

Palakh was standing to the side of the sanctum sanctorum and

Pandit Vimal was holding her hand, persuading her to step inside. But the poor girl could barely put a foot forward before the hordes pushed her back out.

She saw me smirking, rearranged the dupatta around her head, and walked over. 'Don't you think God gets tired of so much pooja?' she said. 'Here.' She handed her container of Gangajal to Samar. 'You can put it on God for me. I'll pray from outside.'

Palakh and I went to a vacant corner of the courtyard and sat on the floor. 'This place is just crazy,' she said. 'I get no spiritual feeling at all!' She regarded me with an expression I put somewhere between disdain and awe. '... Seriously, the only time I've felt something spiritual was at the Golden Temple, sitting quietly by the lake.' She pointed to a man leaning over another to glimpse Lord Vishwanath and shook her head. 'I can't understand how you guys pray here.'

'You should enjoy the time for what it is,' I wanted to say. 'If you keep searching for sushi while eating chaat, you'll enjoy neither experience for what it is, now will you?' But I stayed silent.

'Darshan is a time to soak in God's energy,' mummy would've said. 'The clanging of bells and the showering of Gangajal bring your mind to the present. They take you outside yourself. Yes, meditating is essential, but it's for later, when you're alone.'

But Palakh was right in her way, too. In contrast to the muted murmurs you hear inside mosques and churches, Hindu temples are raucous places. To the ardent devotee accustomed to our fervour, the hubbub inside a temple is like the *masala* in chaat devoid of which your faith is bland. But to a novice, even a little bite can be overwhelming.

During a family trip to Siem Reap, Cambodia, in 2015, I was hypnotized by the raw beauty of the Angkor Wat and the Ta Prohm temples. The Angkor Wat was enchanting because apart from being the largest religious monument in the world, it was also originally a Hindu Vishnu temple built by the Khmer Empire before it was converted into a Buddhist one sometime in the twelfth century. And the Ta Prohm, or the Jungle Temple, built in 1186 CE, famous for its thick tree roots tearing through ancient stone walls, was as bewitching as haunting. But for Rashmi Masi, devoid of clanging bells, milling crowds and incensed air, the place was *only* haunting. 'Sid, please let's get out of here,' she said, leading me by the hand to the exit. 'I'm getting very bad vibrations.'

Hampi in Karnataka is another example of perceptory discord. While Israeli backpackers have found here a sanctuary away from 'Noisy India', a quaint town to get high as they look out at the expanse of rice fields peppered with temple ruins and mounds of boulders jutting out of the earth in fantastic formations, Hampi—a temple town after all—is not known to attract Hindu worshippers by the millions as do Madurai and Tirupati. Because despite its many charms, the place is considered by many to be despoiled. Hampi was once the wealthy capital of the Vijayanagara Empire in the fourteenth century. But after the city was plundered by Sultanate armies in 1565, it has essentially remained in ruins.

As Swamiji once said, 'We don't pray at temples that are *khandit*'—desecrated, emptied of their gods and energy. Or, as I'd say, have become chaat dried of its juices. And yet, after the Kedarnath flash floods of 2013, we did just this, didn't we? Hindus again prayed in a town that had been virtually obliterated. *Why?* 'Because in that case, though the floods destroyed the city, the temple stayed intact,' Swamiji said.

A short drive to Bodh Gaya

Like Palakh, my friend Sumeet also had a sceptical attitude towards faith. Except, unlike her, he didn't even step inside the Vishwanath Temple. On a road trip together from Delhi to Darjeeling in July 2016, Sumeet and I made two stops of religious significance. The first was Varanasi and the second was Bodh Gaya. And at the latter, he willingly came to pay respects to the Buddha at the Mahabodhi Temple.

'See, I'm not religious,' he said. 'But this I get. Buddha was a historical character. Not some made-up god.'

As Sumeet and I drove east from Varanasi, we passed a market of maize farmers squatting on the road, their orange produce laid out on the road tarmac, green fields spreading behind them under the sultry stare of the monsoon sun. We passed villagers shepherding livestock: buffaloes, goats, sheep, cows. In one small town, I saw a malnourished boy with a swollen belly sitting on a pile of refuse, wailing. In another, as the sky bloated grey, the road filled with happy children dancing to the tune of rain ropes lashing the earth. When I rolled down my window, I could taste the herbaceousness on my tongue. And then, in the middle of this wilderness that was as richly green as it was humanly poor, emerged Bodh Gaya: a small, underdeveloped town full of grand Buddhist temples and monasteries built by the Burmese, the Taiwanese, the Japanese, the Thai.

Buddhism, as practised in Buddhist countries, is not immune to opulent displays of architectural expression, by the way. From the Shwedagon Pagoda in Yangon to the Giant Buddha Statue in Kamakura, you see Buddhist temples as grand as the Akshardham in Delhi and the Sagrada Familia Cathedral in Barcelona. You see that Buddhists have made the Buddha a god. Or if not a god then definitely given him the stature of one.

Tired and hungry, Sumeet and I fortified ourselves with coffee and sandwiches at a run-down Barista Cafe. Then, we headed for the Mahabodhi Temple. In those twilight hours, when darkness is taking over but the day still holds out, yellow lights came on to illuminate scores and scores of stupas dotting the temple's expansive lawns. A soft breeze blew over, and I was overtaken by the rustling of leaves and the rioting of thousands of birds.

The Mahabodhi Temple Complex, with its pyramidal shape and rich detailed stone carvings, exhibited stylistic features I'd seen at the Meenakshi Temple in Madurai. And not just that. It also looked like the Ramanathswamy Temple in Rameswaram and the Sri Venkateswara Temple in Tirumala.

Principally associated with the Buddha's enlightenment under the Bodhi Tree, the Mahabodhi Temple Complex is one of the four holy sites related to his life and was first built by Emperor Ashoka in the third century BCE. Our guide said that the structure before us dated from the fifth or sixth century, and was one of the earliest Buddhist temples from the late Gupta period built entirely in brick still standing in India.

As I stepped inside the Mahabodhi Temple, my bare feet met a familiar stone-floored sanctum, the kind at Hindu temples. But what really touched me was the overwhelming quietude. In the outer chamber red-robed monks sat around the floor, quietly mouthing Pali verses, their fingers working through bead necklaces, their faces tranquil and still. A queue of devotees—mostly Southeast Asians and Indians—were inching forward to pay their respects to the golden, upright idol of the Buddha. Yes, a few pilgrims were prostrating themselves but there was no pushing and shoving, let alone ritualistic passion.

The place was a complete contrast to my experience at the Kashi Vishwanath temple earlier that day: the atmosphere here was like at the Todai-ji in Nara, Japan, or at the Wat Phra Kaew in Bangkok. It was reverential but sober. It was joyous but in a serene, inward way.

But as I was about to exit, a curious sight caught my eye: a middle-aged bespectacled Hindu pandit bantering with a younger, bald Buddhist monk. The two men, laughing at something, looked like friends.

I went up to the pandit. '*Namaskar, panditji*,' I said. 'Do you pray here also?'

The pandit enlarged his eyes and produced a big smile. 'Of course. The Buddha is an avatar of Vishnu, so we have to pray here, don't we?'

'But do you perform Hindu rituals here?'

'You didn't do a proper darshan,' he said, holding his pandit smile in place. 'Because if you'd go back, you'll see that opposite the Buddha statue there is a Shivalingam set into the ground.' And so I did go back, and sure enough, it was there: a Shivalingam set into the stone floor of the Mahabodhi Temple, under the gaze of the Buddha Himself.

'So, do you do abhishek of Shiva here?' I returned to asked him, my curiosity piqued. 'From where does the Gangajal and the milk flow out? Do you do Hindu prayers for the Buddha also?'

'We do a full pooja of Shiva here, with milk, flowers, Gangajal and ghee every day. And after we've done our rituals, we wipe the Shivalingam clean with a cloth. This is the Buddha's temple, after all. Shiva is here only in attendance.' He smiled again.

The ancient Bodhi peepal tree—said to be an offspring of the original tree under which the Buddha meditated without moving for seven weeks and attained enlightenment—stood at the temple's rear. And what a magnificent tree it was, deeply rooted, with intricate and far-reaching branches. *Like*, I imagined, *the nerves and connections in the human brain!* Here, too, monks and devotees were sitting around in meditation postures; unhurriedly rolling bead necklaces through their fingers, reciting prayers, prostrating themselves. But there weren't too many present, perhaps no more than twenty—as if their lack in number was also a silent nod to the Buddha's message of emptiness, godlessness and inner reflection.

Sumeet and I sat under the Bodhi Tree for a few minutes. I mean, we had to. After all, we were *here*. After complaining about no electricity in our hotel and mosquitos everywhere, we'd finally reached this place where the Buddha had attained enlightenment. Now neither one said a word. We simply sat and watched. We sat and took in the incense, the humid air perfumed with chants and a just-palpable magic.

Back in Kashi

As luck would have it, though, the practice of Hinduism at the Kashi Vishwanath Temple has now also been infused with a small degree of reticence. Or so was the case when I visited the renovated temple complex in March 2022. For during this darshan, ordinary devotees were not permitted to step inside the sanctum sanctorum. Unlike my previous visits, now I could no longer touch the Lord Vishwanath with my hands. I was made to hand to a pandit my pooja items, who then poured Gangajal over the Shivalingam for me. He presented to God my offerings, the bel leaves, rudraksh necklace, the flowers and prasad, hastily handed everything back to me, and moved to the next yaatri.

And could I blame him? The line of worshippers went on and on. As usual, there were yaatris from everywhere. Middle-class folk from Kolkata, Mumbai, Chennai and Delhi. But in these early days after the temple's inauguration, most pilgrims were from UP and Bihar's heartland, from places like Ausanpur, Baharipur and Mehdiganj. With Covid-19 lockdowns behind us, small town folk and villagers were thronging Kashi by the thousands. My guesthouse owner had told me that people who had no idea about the Vishwanath Temple were now coming to see what Modiji had built.

Police records showed that 14.22 lakh pilgrims visited the temple in January 2022, and the footfall remained above 45,000 per day. (As per *The Times of India*, March 5, 2022.)

'But are they even real devotees?' I asked Pandit Hiralal Pandey, irritated. 'Or tourists?' But even as I uttered these words, I wanted to reprove myself. *So what if they are tourists?* There indeed was a time when I was snooty about my sense of aesthetics and would say, 'I'm not interested in Akshardham. It was built in my lifetime.' But now I'm more inclined to say: 'Some tourists visit the Louvre. And some visit the Kashi Vishwanath Mandir. Get over it.'

Still, I felt short-changed and said, 'What kind of pooja is this? I want to do a proper abhishek. I saw Modiji do an abhishek here on TV.'

Pandit Hiralal Pandey was a thin, short man, so thin you could make out his spine through his stained kurta. But he had all the robust pandit's force in his voice. 'It is now like this only,' he said. 'Only ministers and all can go inside. Now you can only see God from here. Like in South India.'

After he showed me the new Ma Annapurna shrine and the old Gyanvapi well, Pandit Hiralal brought me back to the shop outside Gate No. 2 where I'd deposited my belongings into a locker. I paid him Rs 500 for saving me the bother of standing in the long queue.

A lot about Varanasi had changed. But so much was the same. The long line to the temple was still made up mainly of the devout poor, all slight in frame and swarthy in complexion. There was still an eager pandit to help me bypass them. *Me*: the well-fed, upper-caste urban man. Yes, the old jumble of buildings had gone and the freshly painted temple dazzled under the bright sun, but you could still sight paan stains lurking in hidden corners.

Pandit Hiralal Pandey had been an enthusiastic temple guide inside the complex, but outside he too changed his tune. 'What our Kashi used to be!' he said. 'Now people come here not to pray but for *phashion. Pehle jaisi bhaavna nahi hai ab*...the old feeling is missing.'

I nodded.

'Should I show you the Lovers' Garden?' he then said abruptly with a naughty look.

'The what?'

I was taken to the top of Meer Ghat. Holi was only two days away and the steps leading to the Ganga were dyed in blends of pink and blue. A balloon hit a sadhu walking along the river bank in the chest. He yelled at nobody and everybody he could see before moving on and teenage laughter from somewhere behind reverberated.

'What do you want to show me, panditji?'

'Just wait,' Pandit Hiralal Pandey said.

A young couple walking hand in hand ambled next into view and the teenagers now threw a balloon at the man's legs. The laughing couple hurried over to the next ghat. Pandit Hiralal Pandey was surveying the area as if he wanted to find something, and now he had. He pointed to another young couple licking ice lollies on the steps. The boy was pointing at a bunch of seagulls that had encircled a boat in the distance. The squawking birds were diving down and floating up and the boatman was failing at shooing them away. The boy whispered something in the girl's ear, and she giggled.

'What, panditji?' And Pandit Hiralal Pandey urged me to look again. He wanted me to see that the boy had his arm around the girl's shoulders. To see that the two were cuddling.

'These new tourists have made Kashi into a Lovers' Garden.'

As to whether the city's moral character has altered along with its architectural landscape, though, is moot. But when I revisited the Kashi Vishwanath Temple in June 2022, I was struck by just how immersive my darshan was this time.

It had been only three months since my previous visit. But in this short time metal slides had been placed at the mouth of every doorway opening into the sanctum sanctorum. Now, through these slides, devotees could themselves pour milk and Gangajal on Lord Shiva. There was a pandit stationed at every door whose sole job was to present your offerings to God.

We Hindus really do love our rituals, I thought. Hinduism and Buddhism were born in the same soil but we'd grown up in different worlds.

Back in November 2019. 8 pm

Samar, Palakh and I were standing on the balcony of my hotel room, admiring the goings-on below. Flickering and glimmering in motley designs—in Oms and swastikas, in circles and triangles—the Banaras ghats were ablaze with diyas and the Ganga was chock-full of vessels. I could see two large cruisers throbbing with LED lights, scores of motor boats and hundreds of wooden ones.

During a boat ride earlier on, I had an even more impressive view. The entire length of buildings along the riverfront was lit up in colours that changed every few seconds, from red to blue to pink to green, and Chinese sky lanterns were going up everywhere.

Celebrated on the last day of the Hindu month of Kartik on Poornima, the full-moon night, this was the night of Dev Diwali when the gods descended to Kashi. It was absolutely sublime. Having seen the Ganga aarti many times, I had been cynical watching it again just half an hour earlier. But these Dev Diwali celebrations, my second time witnessing them, were just as fairy-tale-like as the first.

Sitting beside me on the boat was a rustic woman. She said a prayer and set a leaf diya sailing into the murky waters. Then, looking ahead, she covered her head with the end of her saree and brought her palms together. A trio of boys from Trichy had their foreheads painted with tikas. They joined their palms joined together and fixed their eyes ahead. As the aarti wore on, one boy got tears in his eyes.

And then, one by one, everybody on the boat, some thirty of us, brought their phones out. Everybody but me.

To be fair, I saw the Ganga aarti's attraction. It was an arresting spectacle: seven young priests in shiny clothes, each raising a brass pyramid of diyas aloft and chanting ancient Sanskrit shlokas in unison to an even more ancient river.

The pandits did a clockwise twirl, resumed their base positions, raising the pyramid of lights to the Ganga, and then did the same thing again. But as I watched these performers prosaically going through their motions today, I blurted, 'They're not even well coordinated. Such a tourist trap!' Samar and Palakh were spellbound. But an elderly man sitting across smirked and shrugged his shoulders.

In a tweed jacket and beret hat, Mr Kapoor, in his sixties, was by far the most distinguished-looking man on this rickety boat. I thought he was an NRI, but it turned out he was a through-and-through Banarsi, but now lived in Gurgaon. This was his first time seeing the Dev Diwali celebrations in their present-day avatar.

'When I was a boy, there was no Ganga aarti like this,' he said. 'And definitely no Dev Diwali.'

Today, five pandits perform the Ganga aarti on Shitala Ghat and seven on the adjacent and more popular Dashashwamedh Ghat. In addition, an evening aarti is now also conducted on Assi Ghat, and one hears of more ghats coming up with their shows. But when I first visited Varanasi in 2007, the Ganga aarti was a small affair. In those days, only a few people gathered around to watch, for there was nothing much to see in the first place. There were no LED lights, no synchronized dance twirls and few smartphones. For years and years, Dashashwamedh Ghat had just one or two pot-bellied pandits chanting prayers and many more sadhus and beggars.

As a shop owner on Shitala Ghat said, 'Back in the '90s, there used to be only one pandit doing the aarti over here and one on Dashashwamedh Ghat. Then, somewhere around 2008 or 2009, it became like this, with five pandits here and seven there. Only after Modiji decided to run his election from here has it become more glamourous still.'

Mr Kapoor's face brightened when I asked him to tell me about the Banaras of his boyhood. 'Oh, ghat life was totally different then,' he said. 'Our house used to face the Ganga over there.' He pointed to the north. 'In the summer, we used to bathe in the river every morning and evening. Back then, the river was very clean. I myself swam across it many times. And on the other side'—across the Ganga where there is still nothing but an expanse of sand touching the horizon every morning—'you could find watermelon and many other fruits growing.

'In the '50s and '60s, our family owned a house boat and we would take it out on the river for a variety of celebrations. There was some festival every day: Ekaadashi, Nirjal Ekaadashi, Ganga Dussehra or something. And the city was empty. Not this crowded mess it is now.'

Mr Kapoor dwelled a little. 'Sometime in January, there used to be this festival for three days. In our local language, it's called *Budhwa Mangal*. It was a boat festival started by the Maharaja of Banaras. The Maharaja would come down on the Ganga in a special boat carved in the shape of a peacock; it was driven manually. He would drive it out from his fort in Ramnagar near BHU right up to Rajghat in the evening, and then everybody would come out in their houseboats. The *bajras* [boats] would go into the hundreds and under the roof there used to be a sitting place, and the top singers of that time—Badi Moti Bai, Chhoti Moti Bai—would sing our Banarsi songs.'

He hesitated. 'And yes, there were dancers also. They used to participate in *mujras*. Those dancers would come during those three nights, and in the moonlight they would dance on the boats with the tabla and shehnai. And the Maharaja would float through them all. Of course'—he laughed dreamily—'in those times there was no electricity, so we'd light a kerosene lamp. But it was magical.'

The pandits were doing another twirl and the cameras around were flashing away.

'Those traditions are gone. But now we have these new things, and this is also magical, *hai na*?'

'... Yes,' he went on, reminiscing about his childhood days, 'we used to have an *akaash deep* back then. On a big bamboo stick, people would place a lamp and raise it on ropes like a flag into the sky. Every Hindu family would light this lamp. The belief was that our ancestors watching from above could now see the lit path going down to Kashi. In the month of Kartik, for thirty days, there used to be thousands of akaash deeps along the Ganga. We would go down to the ghat in the evening to raise the lamp, and early the next morning, we'd take it down. Then we'd raise it again in the evening. I think they still do this on certain ghats. But there was no Ganga aarti like this. People did aarti if they wanted.'

Mr Kapoor brought out his phone and pointed it ahead. He laughed. 'Now they have commercialized it.'

Walking along the ghats that night, I crossed a group of chit-chatting village women with pots on their heads. Then, a skateboarder attempting a back flip on a slope. I crossed a group of Korean tourists with cameras around their necks and thousands of locals with their phones out. I followed Samar and Palakh down the ghat steps. Like a stairway to some dreamland, every step was lit with evenly spaced diyas. Old folk were releasing diyas into the water and the young set sky lanterns free by the hundreds into the sky.

Here in Varanasi you always found yaatri and tourist, gimmick and magic—the past, the present and the future, converging on Lord Shiva's trident. Was I witnessing the orthodox Kashi or the ever-changing Banaras? Is this Kashi's spell where God's light reveals Truth? Or is this just me again lost in Varanasi's lanes? *Me and my mind, always prising some sense out of the indecipherable. Me and my mind, always drawing patterns…*

'Where are you lost?' Samar said. 'Come here.'

Palakh and he had a sky lantern in their hands and a young man was waiting to take their photo.

'I can't believe you're doing this,' I said. 'Wait. I can also take your picture.' I brought out my phone. 'Smile!'

But Samar was putting as much effort into holding his grin in place as he was in keeping the lantern steady. 'Hang on,' I said. 'Let me take one more.'

Palakh's smile was solid, but Samar skewed his lips even more unnaturally, and then a wind came and the flame went out.

'Come, na,' she said, and Samar stepped out of the frame and dragged me into it. He reignited the fire under the lantern, put his arm around my shoulder and smiled.

'I don't know why I'm doing this,' I said even as I placed my hand on the lantern.

'Say cheeese,' the photographer said and we released our fire to join the thousands of others drifting up to join the gods in the heavens.

On the flight back home, we hit a pocket of turbulence and Palakh held Samar's arm. '*Om Namah Shivaaya!*' she murmured, with each bump. This was the first time I'd seen her pray aloud in the last three days and I stifled a chuckle. Samar grinned, too, but then he shot me a glare, put a finger to his lips.

The fear of death has a way of making a sceptic a believer and a believer a little sceptical, no?

I next met Palakh over a month later at a party at Samar's house on December 31, 2019. She was her usual fun self—'We need shots!' she hollered—but it was clear a certain distance had crept in between Samar and her. If before she naturally gravitated towards him, she now made it a point to sit some spaces away. Palakh's old possessiveness for Samar had, I felt, reverted to the sort of guarded pleasantness one reserves for 'family friends.'

Funnily enough, though, I saw a shade of her old purposeful self in conversation with a lanky guy I didn't recognize. A Rohit: Palakh's colleague.

I took Samar aside. 'So, you finally came out to her, then?'

Samar gave a funny look. 'Not exactly. I said I want to live a peaceful life. I don't want any change or stress.'

'*You* don't want stress?' I said. 'Let's hope Rohit is less stressful *for her*.'

Samar laughed.

'Anyway, listen. I might go back to Banaras for Mahashivratri. Wanna come?'

The bell rang and Samar walked to the door. A bunch of boisterous guys in their thirties appeared and he gave each one a warm embrace. Palakh narrowed her eyes in his direction, sipped her drink and turned back to Rohit.

I didn't know any of these guys well, but as with Palakh, I recognized them from previous gatherings at Samar's house. I just knew that this entire lot was as capable of getting drunk on faith as on whisky.

Samar led his friends to the bar. He opened a bottle of Black Label and began pouring out pegs. He looked back at me. 'I'll see at that time, na,' he said. 'How can I tell you right now?'

Loops of clarity

One morning, while sitting cross-legged on Assi Ghat, I imagined I was joined with the earth, spinning but still. I was a drop in the ocean—a part of it, apart from it—its waves my breathing. People around were bathing, lathering soap on themselves, brushing their teeth, washing clothes, doing yoga. But I was oblivious to all. I'd retreated so deep into myself that I didn't feel myself. And when I opened my eyes, I saw that oblivious to everything also was a dog.

A man pierced the air with a conch shell. A sadhu bellowed out, '*Ommm...*' And a chaiwaala shouted, '*Lemon chai! Lemon chai!*' But the dog, sleeping on the ghat's last dry step, napped through it all.

Then a boy jumped into the Ganga in a somersault—'*Ganga Maiyya ki Jai!*'—splashing water around, and now it awoke with a start.

In this instant, I saw such fear and confusion on the dog's face that I thought, *This Dog, he's not a dog. This dog is…a boy. A boy roused from deep sleep.* And then, as lucidly as a thought could come: *Man is Dog. Dog is Man.*

Of course, at an intellectual level, I know my insight was trite. What is life but little tweaks of DNA in the vast pool of bio-chemistry? But it's another thing when you realize mundane truths through your eyes.

And then I thought later that same day: if Man's soul equalled God's soul as our scriptures said then that dog's soul had to equal God's soul too, right? Suppose we're all products of the sun and the earth, children of carbon. Shouldn't it follow that every animal, bird, fish and tree also carries varying seeds of the same consciousness inside of it? And as all life has evolved from the same ingredients, shouldn't it follow that this spark flaming inside me resides in every being in some way?

Wasn't it *this* that the Upanishads were getting at? Everybody can be scared, angry, confused and sad as much as happy, peaceful, content and calm. And if every *being* possesses this aatma, is it a long shot to say that *everything* has some consciousness instilled in it?

Don't laugh at me. Actually, go ahead, laugh. But this was my logic: If everything is a product of the universe, then it should follow that *everything* has a seed of the universe inside it. If you boil me down to the basics, then what am I but particles, matter, energy? Whether stardust or star-fire comes down to your perspective.

So there you have it. My grand *Eureka!* moment. *Dog is God! God is Dog!* Even when I think about it now I'm tempted to laugh. *Was this the pithy Truth I'd been looking for?* The adage sounded like something stuck on the back of a twenty-year-old's car. And yet I couldn't stop myself from building more on this kernel of thought. Confined though I knew I was by my biology, chemistry and physics, I couldn't stop myself from drawing more patterns in the sky.

I'd soon learn that my new 'realization' was hardly novel even in the philosophical sense. The designs I was sketching today had been drawn by great philosophers before. And more sharply.

In India, Shankaracharya in the eighth century said, 'There is only one thing that never leaves us, and it is pure consciousness. This is the real, absolute Self, and it is the constant feature of all experience.'

In the West, Spinoza in the seventeenth century, defined God as 'the sum of the natural and physical laws of the universe and certainly not an individual entity or creator'.

Contemporary Western philosophers even had a precise name for my newfound way of seeing things in which consciousness was omnipresent and it was called 'panpsychism'. Encyclopaedia Britannica defined panpsychism as 'a philosophical theory asserting that a plurality of separate and distinct psychic beings or minds constitute reality'. And this worldview traced its origins all the way back to pre-Socratic Greece!

I could see why Shankaracharya said Everything was One. But I also found I agreed with the Buddha, who said the opposite.

The Buddha favoured dividing mental states into parts and degrees and he concluded that there is no Universal Self. Nagarjuna, widely regarded as one of the greatest Mahayana Buddhist thinkers, said that at the heart of everything there is *shunyata*, emptiness.

While Shankaracharya said the Brahman was supreme, Brahman was the Ultimate Reality, Brahman was Pure Consciousness, Brahman was eternal, immutable, infinite and absolute, Nagarjuna refuted any view of eternalism or absolutism in his philosophy of emptiness. 'The nature of [phenomenon] lies between absolute non-existence, and substantial existence,' he said. This was the Middle Way. Nagarjuna argued that all phenomena lack the quality of inherent existence, and so anything that appears to exist inherently or independently is an edifice of one's ignorance.

The *Prajñāpāramitāhṛdaya*, literally meaning 'The Heart of the Perfection of Wisdom', the most well-known *sutra* of Mahayana Buddhism, says, 'Body is emptiness [shunyata], emptiness is nothing more than body.'

In reading Buddhist philosophy, however, it was important to recall the context of the time, too, right? The Buddha (and Buddhism) arose as a movement to challenge the Brahminical orthodoxy. The Buddha formed the *gana-sanghas* (monastic orders), and these sanghas, unlike Brahmin schools of learning, admitted women. Buddhism used the language of the people, Pali, and not Sanskrit, the language of the

Brahmins. And as the Buddha rejected the notion of the Brahman, he also questioned the Brahmanical basis of the 'karma-moksha' (rebirth-salvation) cycle.

(As to how Buddhists reconcile the belief of karma and rebirth with an *anaatman* [not-self, no-soul] basis has been the subject of studies within Buddhism since its early days. Buddhists answer this question by referring to their doctrine of causality, or 'Dependent Origination', which maintains that everything has been caused into existence and that all causal links connect to other causal links. Nothing exists *ex nihilo*.)

Buddhism, therefore, was a protestant faith, for the Buddha's teachings questioned the authority of the Brahmins. And while the Buddha had respect for the Vedas as a body of knowledge, he did not consider them to be divinely revealed. Instead, he famously advocated self-containment: 'Be your own lamp, seek no other refuge but yourself, let truth be your light.'

When Shankara preached his philosophy, Buddhism was already a deeply entrenched religion in the country. Like the Hindu sages who came before him, he maintained that the Vedas were the true fount of knowledge. But he now added to this old belief an important spin, which has been in motion until today. Shankaracharya said that all the schools except Advaita Vedanta had misinterpreted the Upanishads, and this is why, it is said, he debated thinkers from within and outside the orthodox Hindu fold converting believers back to the Vedic way.

Yet the more I read, the more I found the two philosophies similar, so much so that some scholars had even called Shankaracharya a 'crypto-Buddhist'. Some researchers contended that Shankara appropriated Buddhist ideas in his teachings, but in a camouflaged way. 'It was to attract to the *Sanatana* fold, the convinced Buddhist, those susceptible to Buddhism and the fellow travellers,' writes S.G. Mudgal in his book *Advaita of Shankara: A Reappraisal.* Mudgal suggests that Shankara included Buddha as the ninth avatar of Lord Vishnu and that Buddhist practices such as *ahimsa* (non-violence) and monasticism were also introduced into Shankara's system to lure disciples. And while I was hardly competent to comment on the veracity of these claims, it certainly appeared to me that the Char Dhams (and their corresponding mathas) in the four corners of the country—Badrinath in the North, Rameswaram in the South, Puri in the East and Dwarka in the West—could be viewed as such: Hinduism assimilating Buddhism's monastic ways.

It also seemed that the politics of this ancient era had seeped not only into our history, but our philosophy too. The Human Ego could pierce the deepest layers of our consciousness and shape what we took to be *Eternally True*!

Could it not be said that the Buddha and Shankaracharya were saying the same essential thing but looking at Truth from different angles?

Both the Buddha and Shankaracharya believed the world was illusory. Both advocated non-duality. And both said, *Look within.* But while Shankaracharya stressed on the existence of an Unchanging Permanent Consciousness, the Buddha emphasized that at the heart of everything there was nothing. Everything depended on 'Causal factors, and nothing existed permanently and independently'. This appeared to be their main point of divergence; one might even argue, this was their only point of difference.

So, why did we view Shankaracharya's Non-Dualism and Buddha's Nothingness as diametrically opposed? Why couldn't we see the two schools of thought as different points along a philosophical continuum of Truth-seeking? And crucially, why did the fight between these two philosophies become so bitter that one faith had to leave the land of its birth? Seriously, for all our talk of oneness, why couldn't Sanatan Dharma find a way to coexist with a philosophy with which it shared foundations but diverged only in its conclusion?

As you might expect, again I was hardly the first person to be posing these questions. And so, my loops came crashing back.

Was I one with the One? Or like a grain of sand on this vast beach of existence, was I nothing? Was there an innate quality, a kind of stardustness, if you prefer, inherent in everything? Or was even such thinking the result of my conditioning?

The Buddha would probably say I was forcing links between disparate feelings to build some grand truth that was as comforting as it was false. But was it false? I wasn't quite so sure. And yet, since believing that you're one with the Ultimate Reality can plant in your ego a God built in your own image—the image of man—I certainly saw his point.

The more clearly I saw, the more tangled I saw. The more tangled I saw, the more clearly I saw. And my loops looped on:

Is God nothing more than the product of illusory configurations? Is God a deficient construction of my fallible senses? Is God a satisfying confectionery, arising from multiple perceptory functions beneath which there lies nothing? Nothing but myriad causal factors: a bottomless river of 'Dependant Origination' flowing back, back, back, into the depths of space-time to the Big Bang, and, perhaps, to a Supreme Nothing—a nothing made up of nothing—which (non)existed before!

But if everything is the result of causal events and there is no Real Me anywhere, how could 'I' arrive at any of these conclusions? Surely, the '*I*' who had arrived at this stage of introspection was 'I, the observer', the inner self, no? And *I had*, with my own senses, observed this same inner-self in another being, a dog, hadn't I?

Buddhism answers these questions by probing deeper into the 'Mental Formations': of feeling, perception, volition, contact, desire, wisdom, mindfulness, attention, decision, and finally, samadhi, or mental concentration. And a lot else. But all which reinforce its central premise that there is no real 'I' in *anything*. Even I, the observer, is the product of causal formations which can be broken down, parsed.

The Buddha thought that believing your soul is the same as an Eternal Soul was a rash leap of logic, and I could see one reason why he might have thought so. If you start believing your soul is the same as God's it can feed into a kind of ego-centrism. Not only can it give rise to a God built in man's image, it can nurture a lack of investigation. It can make you certain your way is the *only* way. And for these reasons, I knew I'd remain drawn to the humble and practical nature of Buddhism. To its Four Noble Truths that explored human suffering. To its Middle Way which sits somewhere between existentialism and nihilism, and its mind-blowing philosophy of godlessness and emptiness at the heart of Everything.

(Didn't I say that a faith which regards itself superior to another is deficient for this very reason?)

Despite my lingering doubts, though, one thing was becoming clear. Both Shankara and the Buddha urged you to *feel*. Both said, *Let go*. Shed all conditioning and just *be*. Both Buddhism and Vedanta say that the descriptive knowledge of the material world can take you only so far. Ultimately, you must fall back on non-verbal insight and find what you find.

And I accepted that my perceptions, refined by Western education and dulled by my smartphone, were limited. I could never see reality like the Andaman tribal who'd lived his whole life with nature did. Who had worked out *different truths*, truths from *his* lived experience that allowed him to predict a tsunami and climb to higher land before the waves hit. My mind was primed differently. I was trained to rely on evidence, on data, on science, admittedly spiked with a shot of faith. And my faith hung on because somewhere, I still felt that believing made me…*more human*. Because I thought relying *solely* on science to the negation of other shades of human experience brought conceit. And what is conceit if not a lack of empathy and understanding?

But my rational mind fought back. He said, 'Fine. Have "beliefs". But at least fit them logically.' To which my believing side said: 'That is a contradiction in terms!'

Yet I did try just this. I attempted to draw more patterns in the sky. Over several months, I tried, and I failed… Until one night, while driving behind a truck spilling sand onto the road—*the sandfall forming waves and crests and snakes on the tarmac!*—a fresh spark flew into my mind.

Like my hand, my brain was a human organ, too, right? And just as all hands are designed to do similar things—to hold, throw, build, write, text—so too couldn't my mind, which is, after all the brain in action, with practice, grow deeper and sharper like of monks and sadhus?

With repetitious concentration, could I not also receive sharper insights such that if I went far enough, I could one day become like that African seer who said to his tribe, 'You are just a *medium*?' Could I become like that Bhootha Kola spirit dancer (about whom, more later) who once told me that when God enters his body, he becomes music, he becomes dance? He who said he turns to *nothing*. Nothing but water in flow. Or perhaps he meant he becomes *flow* alone.

I've never reached such a profound state of immersion. But I think I glimpsed it one morning. Sitting on my bedroom floor with my eyes closed, I approached a stillness so deep that I felt my body going numb. There was no shifting of my bottom. No fidgeting of hands. No twitching of (crossed) legs. *Was I becoming a medium or some kind of nothing?* Who knows? But after a long silence, my mind turned into something like an empty cup catching a waterfall. *A Brahman-stream? Eternally flowing? Nothing happening?* Who knows? But I felt myself drifting. I was dreaming, but not asleep. I was alert, but not awake. Was I approaching *Turiya*, the background pervading the three states of consciousness—waking, dreaming, and dreamless deep sleep? Perhaps not, but who knows?

What I know is that I felt I was seeing a Truth that had been seen by only a chosen few before and would be seen only by a handful in the future. *Was this the edge of infinity or an old trick of a suggestible mind?* Who the hell knows? But I do *know* that one morning, I let go.

And yet… *And yet*, I thought the next day: Would I have drawn these patterns if I weren't raised in this culture in which Hinduism and Buddhism were born? How much of me was nature, and how much was nurture? Was I the Universe? The Brahman? Or was I stardust? A mere speck in the cosmos. An emptiness. A tadpole in the pond. *Just nothing at all.*

PART VI

A Whirlpool of Encounters in the City of Death

January 2020, July 2022 & November 2007

A Whirlpool of Encounters in Varanasi: Babas, Aghoris, Backpackers

Delhi. January 2020

Perhaps my father was right. Maybe faith does come down to the question, *What are we doing here?* I mean, what happens after I go? What continues? Will my soul ever reconfigure to my present approximation? Or will I be gone forever, like an old tune lost in the wind?

Armaan and I would often have conversations in this vein. I recall one at Starbucks in Connaught Place in particular.

'Why should we set limits on rationality?' I said, playing devil's advocate. 'Maybe a superstitious mind is natural to human evolution? Maybe having beliefs is an admission of our limitations, and so to *reject* faith goes against our nature? Maybe it's actually *logical* to believe because if we don't, we become robots. We reject the wonder that makes us, us.'

Ultimately, I reasoned, no matter how far science takes us we're still cavemen drawing patterns in the sky. 'Surely, I'm more than just random breaths and thoughts. And really, scientists can measure the neurons and all that stuff in your brain, but they can't tell you what you actually *feel.* Feelings are yours and there's no measurement for them. Science can't properly measure happiness or sadness. Or…'—I pointed to my drink—'just how disgusting this turmeric chai latte tastes.'

Indeed, like the panpsychists who said there was a universal consciousness, I too was making a leap of logic. But only because a purely materialistic worldview left me wanting more. Because science was always hung up on quantifying things. And because at some level, I'd come to feel that my sense of aliveness, my consciousness, was not bunk. It was *something*.

'And…like a dog or bat, our senses are also limited by our biology and chemistry, no? No matter how powerful a telescope gets, a human eye is a human eye. No matter what discoveries we make, our brain is still human!'

I don't remember how long I prattled on, but at one point, Armaan held my hand and said, 'Sid, all this that you call "wonder"'—he drew inverted commas in the air—'is actually us not fully understanding things.' He sucked on his straw. 'Not knowing the unknown becomes a fear of the unknown. Not knowing what happens after death becomes fear of death. And fear is faith. I'm convinced faith is just fear, actually.' Armaan said this dismissively, but I knew him. I knew that a lot of thought went into his words.

Beyond the cafe's glass doors, the traffic signal turned green, and the cars and autos started up their engines. They began inching forward, then gliding. Everybody moving to the predictable design.

I met Armaan in the eyes and leaned back in my chair. Maybe it really *did* come down to fear.

(One advantage of telling people I was writing about my experiences with faith was that everybody wanted *in*. Everybody wanted to share their expertise. A man at a dinner party had recently told me he visited Tirupati once every month and shaved off his head on every pilgrimage—offered his hair to God. His wife was fed up, he said with a touch of glee. When I asked him why he went so often, he said, 'No, man. Nothing is wrong! Everything is good. But I'm scared. I *don't want* anything to go wrong.')

'Basically, what you're saying is a grand way of saying that science can't answer everything,' Armaan said. 'It measures things that are testifiable and verifiable. So what?'

'Yes!' I said. 'Science doesn't explain all facets of reality.'

He took another lazy sip. 'So, this is all actually fear. Fear of what will happen in the future. Fear of disease, death. Blah! Blah!'

Death. The finality of it. The *life-alteringness* of it. The certainty of it. It was true, it did tie up with faith in the profoundest of ways, didn't it?

Everybody fears death. Even those who said they didn't themselves fear it, I could see feared it for their loved ones. And it was something I hadn't looked into seriously at all. *Why had I completely left this vital fact out?* Was it because it hadn't yet touched me personally? And who could I talk to about it? Swamiji? No. I wanted something fresh. Something original. And as it was from Varanasi I'd most recently returned, my mind returned to it: it was, after all, the *City of Death*.

The image of the burning pyres at Manikarnika Ghat popped into my mind and I felt a smirk spreading across my lips.

'What silly argument are you thinking of now?' Armaan finished his drink.

I shook my head. The answer was staring me in the face all along! Kashi wasn't just where Hindus went to die. It was home to the Aghori babas, those black-robed, wild-eyed sadhus who meditated on charnel grounds. I'd seen them, their face smeared with ash, a skull bowl in hand, wandering the ghats. These men really were the picture of death. They defied norms even for rule-breakers as myself. Why hadn't I spoken with them before? The fact that they creeped me out could partly explain it. But still.

I would go back and speak with them. Plus—I felt my smirk widening into a crooked smile—they'd be another solid hook for my book!

'Seriously, what are you thinking?'

'Nothing.' Despite my instincts pulling me away, I drained the last dregs of the latte into my mouth. 'Let's go.'

As with the Naga babas, there was great mystery surrounding the Aghoris. Both sadhu sects dressed in black and applied ash on themselves. Both shunned people as much as we shunned them. And both roamed the ghats declaiming '*Alakh Niranjan*'—*alakh* meaning 'the one who can't be seen', and *niranjan* meaning 'the one who is pure'—for their ultimate aim was merger with Shiva. But the two sects were somewhat different. Unlike the Nagas, the Aghoris were not warriors, but occult practitioners.

I knew that *ghor* meant fear, and *a-ghor* was the one who doesn't fear. And I knew that the Aghoris meditated in cremation grounds to overcome the fear of death, to remind them of life's transience. But I was now reading that they were *so much more*. The Aghoris had taken the philosophy of non-dualism to an extreme like no other Hindu sect. They rejected worldly pleasures like other sadhus, yes. But in their pursuit of an Undifferentiated Oneness they also categorically broke down all notions of order.

Although modern Aghoris traced their origins to a Baba Keenaram who lived at the time of Shah Jahan, it was difficult to construct their true historical roots. Some believed they were a relic of lost Buddhist orders that merged into Hinduism. Other accounts put them down as the forerunners to an archaic sect in the ancient kingdom of Magadha. But the most famous origin theory was that the Aghoris grew out of a presumed extinct school of sadhus called the Kapalikas.

In his book, *Two Lost Śaivite Sects: The Kāpālikas and Kālāmukhas*, David N. Lorenzen writes, 'Sanskrit sources usually portray Kapalikas as charlatan ascetics who wander about with a skull begging bowl and drink liquor freely for mundane as well as ritual purposes.' Lorenzen refers to Ramanuja, who discusses the main features of Kapala (Kapalika worship) as follows:

'As the Kāpālas declare: He who knows the essence of the six insignia (*mudrikā-ṣaṭka*), who is proficient in the highest *mudrā*, and who meditates on the Self as seated in the vulva (*bhagāsana-stha*), attains nirvāṇa. They define the six insignia (*mudrā*) as the *kaṇṭhikā* (necklace), the *rucaka* (another neck ornament), the *kuṇḍala* (earring), the *śikhā-maṇi* (crest-jewel), ashes and the sacred thread. A person bearing these insignia is not born again in this world.'

All features bearing a striking resemblance to modern-day Aghoris, I thought.

'Rāmānuja's *Śri-bhāṣya* ii.2.35–37 concludes with a disparaging description of the Kāpāla vow (*vrata*): Likewise, they (?=*Śaivāgamas*, the four sects, the Kāpālas) state that even men belonging to lower castes can attain the status of Brāhmaṇa and the highest *āśrama* (=*samnyāsa*, mendicancy) by means of special rites. (For it is said:) "One instantly becomes a Brāhmaṇa merely by the process of initiation. A man becomes a great ascetic (*yati*) by undertaking the Kāpāla vow." Lorenzen continues, 'This may be compared with the following verse from the *Kulārṇava-tantra*: "Gone is the Śūdra-hood of the Śūdra and Brāhmaṇahood of the Brāhmaṇa (*vipra*); there is no division into castes for one who is consecrated by initiation." *Hostility to caste consciousness is a normal feature of tantric worship and is consistently espoused by Kāpālikas in Sanskrit literature. From a modern point of view this hostility may be commended, but for orthodox Hindu writers such as Rāmānuja an attack on caste was an attack on the whole divinely ordained social order (varṇāśrama-dharma).*

'... In most tantric works the denial of caste occurs only in ritual situations. In day-to-day affairs, caste distinctions are still maintained. Thus *Kulārṇava-tantra* viii.101 says: "In this *cakra* (circle of worship) there is no division into castes. *Everyone (in it) is declared to be equal to Śiva.*" Elsewhere, however, this text prescribes different lengths of studentship for members of different classes. The *Mahānirvāṇa tantra* seems to accept class divisions without qualification... *In the supramundane universe of the ritual, opposites coalesce and change places—the lowest is highest and the highest is lowest. In relation to caste, this mystical principle culminates with the apotheosis of the ḍombī (washerwoman) in Kāṇhapāda's tantric Buddhist songs.*' (Emphasis mine throughout.)

And now I literally clapped my hands. *Yes, I'd seen the same thing!*

In 2014, at a village temple by the beach near Suratkal, Mangalore, I'd witnessed the Bhootha Kola dance festival, where two men danced with abandon as the entire village watched spellbound. The men's faces were painted yellow, their heads were covered in ceremonial crowns, and their legs were draped in long skirts made from jute strings. When the drumming began, though, they turned into *supermen*. Their eyes grew big, then small, their lips quivered, and their heads whirled. As they leapt from spot to spot holding fire torches, their feet kicked up sand and when they spun around to deafening drum beats, the jute strings lifted around their legs like a whirring fan.

But I was told these were ordinary fishermen belonging to a low caste and were not normally permitted to enter the temple grounds. It was only on this one night that they took centre stage. Only tonight did the village's Brahmin elders bow to them in obeisance. For tonight they were not men, but demigods: transient avatars of Shakti, of Shiva.

And like these Bhootha Kola dancers, the Aghoris were also revered as incarnates of Bhairava at the Kumbh Mela. And like them, they were also sought out for their extraordinary powers but were ordinarily shunned.

People said the Aghoris had conquered all fears. People said they ate the flesh of corpses. People even said they were necrophiliacs. But what was fabricated? What was true? Books would provide all kinds of answers but the only way to get real ones was to go and speak with them myself. And so, I closed my reading list and brought up the Indian Railways website. I rang up Armaan and asked him to join me. But he said he 'will see'. So, I rang up Samar. And my friend too just hmm-ed.

I hung up the phone and booked my solo train ticket to Varanasi for February 20, 2020. February 21, 2020 was the night of Mahashivratri, the Grand Night of Shiva. The night the Aghoris emerged from the shadows and paraded in the city's streets.

A loop back to a dying baba. November 2007

But before I take you on this visit, since we are talking about death and Varanasi now, it occurs to me to mention that it was the matter of death that first took me there. More specifically, a dying sadhu. The sadhu's name was Swami Satyenderpuriji, and he'd been associated with my family since the 1970s—which was when my mother, then in her twenties, first met him.

My grandparents had been patrons of Shivsagar Ashram for about a decade and had become close enough to Maharajji so that whenever he visited Delhi, he'd stay at their house. Maharajji never asked them for anything, but this one time he made a specific request. 'There is a mahatma in Rishikesh,' he said to my grandfather. 'He's a very learned man and very dear to me. He's had a fall and needs medical treatment. Can you get him shown to a doctor in Delhi?'

When a sixty-something Swami Satyenderpuriji turned up at my grandparents' house, the first thing my mother noticed about him was his funny appearance. The sadhu had a shambling gait, bucked teeth and wore thick glasses through which he peered at you with froglike eyes. Satyenderpuriji, she decided, was a 'simpleton', and his manner of talking, the way he appended his sentences with a giggle, was very silly. So, she named him Mr Bonga.

However, after a few weeks, mummy's mocking of the man turned to admiration when she saw him bathing with cold water in winter, taking long walks in his *khadaun* (wooden sandals worn by some

Hindu ascetics even today), and eating no more than one roti for lunch, the only meal he had in a day. But what most impressed her was how Satyenderpuriji's outward simplicity was vastly outstripped by his knowledge of the Shaastras. For within a week he became my grandmother's personal tutor, teaching her verses from the Gita every afternoon, an exercise he persisted with for the three months he stayed in the house.

In the following years, Swami Satyenderpuriji grew so close to my family that when my great-grandfather was dying, he sat by his bedside reading out verses of the *Vishnu Sahasranaam* so that Lord Vishnu take his soul free of encumbrances to *Vaikunth*—the Eternal Heavenly Realm. It was something mummy herself repeated at Nanima's bedside when my grandmother was taking her final breaths.

I was twelve at the time. On a particularly hot afternoon, as I sat playing on my Nintendo after returning from school, Satyenderpuriji beckoned from his room. I ran over, ready to give him a glass of water and get back to Super Mario Brothers.

'Which class are you in?' With his large, bespectacled eyes, he did look like a Mr Bonga, I thought.

'Class VII.'

'Do you know *pahare*?'

Now, let me tell you, having spent my childhood in an English-medium school, my spoken Hindi was pitiful. I had no idea that pahare was Hindi for multiplication tables. 'No, Swamiji,' I said. 'But you can teach Mala this shloka.'

He stared at me from above the rim of his fat glasses. 'I'm talking to you right now,' he said, and ordered me to bring him a pen and writing pad.

And this was how, for one week every afternoon after school, Satyenderpuriji taught me multiplication tables. It was a week in which I grew rather fond of the man in the way a pupil does for an eccentric tutor. Satyenderpuriji would cackle like a wizard and I'd giggle at his voice and mannerisms. And sometimes, he'd laugh with me even though I'm sure he knew I was laughing *at* him.

In July 2007, when Nanima died, my mother and aunts wanted to do the traditional Hindu thing of giving charity to the poor in their mother's name. So the question arose: Was there somebody Nanima knew who desperately needed money? Swami Satyenderpuriji swam to the top of the list.

I learnt that Satyenderpuriji was now in his nineties. He had left Rishikesh some years before and now lived in Varanasi. He'd told everybody that it was time for him to go to Kashi to die. Swami Shraddhanandji, Swami Atmanand and others tried to dissuade him. They knew he was not a man of the world. But he left.

About two months later, in September, my mother and I reached Sadhna Bhavan, an old, dilapidated ashram by the river bank in Varanasi, to see him. From Lalita Ghat, we walked up a steep stone stairway that led us to a dark alcove. From here we climbed up an even more unlit, prehistoric stairwell in which I could hear bats screeching overhead, and arrived in an open-air courtyard that had a tulsi plant at the centre and five or six rooms along the sides, as in old havelis. A young boy in white robes pointed us to Swami Satyenderpuriji's room and we went over.

'Swamiji?' mummy said, standing in the doorway. A look of horror engulfed her face.

Swami Satyenderpuriji was a thin ghost of the man I remembered. His body had withered and he crawled on his fours with his hands supporting his haunches. His glasses had grown thicker and beneath them his eyes had gone milky as of blind beggars. He clearly couldn't see and going by his fat hearing aid, I doubted he could hear. Still, by touch and smell he was moving about.

He placed a jar on the shelf above the stove and I saw burn marks on his hand. His food, boiled *lauki* with turmeric and cumin, sat uncovered on the stovetop. A fly hovered over it. *A buzzing life in this dying world...*

Satyenderpuriji turned around and crawled towards us. 'Who is it?' He adjusted his hearing aid.

Mummy squatted down to his level. 'It's me, Shashi!'

'Shashi?' He crawled closer. 'Has Shashi come?'

Mummy held his hands in hers. 'Yes, Swamiji.' Her eyes were moist but she kept her voice steady.

'Is it you?' He adjusted his glasses. '*Hai Prabhu!* It really is you!' And in a matter of seconds, the sadhu began to cry.

Satyenderpuriji cried as he said that he was now blind and deaf. He cried as he said he was incontinent. And he cried as he said that some sadhus were waiting to kick him out so his room would be free for men who could contribute to the ashram. 'So I've been praying to Mahadev that if some miracle doesn't happen within two days, I will go to some place near the Ganga and leave my body there. I will go on a hunger strike and I'll go. And look, Shashi, you have come at this exact time.' And he wept again.

After this day, mummy visited him several times a year, bringing with her blankets, clothes and cash. She even arranged for an attendant to cook and clean for him, a twenty-two-year-old boy named Yuvraj, but Swami Satyenderpuriji resisted the imposition.

One day he rang her up and yelled: 'Stop giving me comforts. Stop spoiling my tapasya.' But could mummy stop *her* tapasya? Every week, Yuvraj would ring her and say he wanted to leave, and every week, mummy would say, 'Just a few more days. Please.'

Then, one December day in 2012, Swami Satyenderpuriji passed away in Kashi by the banks of the Ganga, like he wanted, and mummy's visits to Kashi lessened considerably. Even though I kept going.

One afternoon, a couple of years before he died, I recall sitting with him in his room together with mummy. In my slightly curious way, I asked if he'd ever seen Shivji here. After all, Varanasi was where Lord Shiva lived.

'Why did I come here?' Satyenderpuriji began rhetorically. 'Because this is the land of Shiva. And Shivji is also called Tarak. He takes you from this world to the next. Kashi sits on Shiva's trident so no floods, nothing can affect it. Whoever leaves their body here does not have a next birth. So, it is also a place where, if you commit a crime and then die, you won't get another birth to redeem your sins. You will be stuck in eternal *dukh* [discontentment]...'

'Yes, Swamiji,' I said. 'But have *you* seen Shivji here?'

And the old man cackled, exposing his bucked teeth in the way certain people of his generation felt no qualms about doing. He fell silent. 'Yes,' he said. 'One time, something strange happened. I've told your mother.' He glanced at her.

'When I left Rishikesh, I first went to Hapur,' he said. 'I had no money, but I knew one mahatma there, so I stayed with him for some time… At the time, I had saved just enough money to buy a train ticket to Varanasi, so one day I decided to come here. But when I got off, I realized I was at the wrong station. I didn't know where I was, but I knew I was someplace far away. I had no money or anything, so I decided to walk. I kept walking and walking till it got dark. My mouth was dry and I was thirsty. But I kept going.

'It was the middle of the night, and I was on this big road, and a *rickshawaala* came and stopped beside me. He said, "Swamiji, you look tired. Come, let me take you." I told him I wanted to go straight to the Kashi Vishwanath Temple but had no money. But that man insisted. He said, "You sit." I said, "Bhai, I have no money." But he wouldn't listen. He said, "I know, Swamiji. You just sit."

'I kept saying, bhai, I don't have money, and then'—he laughed—'he just lifted me up and put me in his rickshaw! Like I was a child.

'When morning broke, he stopped at one shop and gave me hot milk and *barfi*. I kept saying, "Arre bhaiyya, leave me alone. I don't have anything to give you." But he said, "Swamiji, don't worry." But I was starving too. So I put the barfi in my mouth in one go and that man laughed happily.

'He dropped me off outside the temple and I told him to wait. I said I would find somebody. So, I first came here'—to Sadhna Bhavan Ashram—'and got some money.' He glanced again at mummy. 'But when I got back, he'd gone. Vanished like a ghost…

'And this is not even the whole story. The temple pandits didn't ask me for money because I'm a sadhu. But I was still worried about how I'd go back.' He stared at me with his foggy eyes. '*Aur aap vishwaas nahin karoge…*you won't believe it, but I found a bunch of people from Hapur inside the temple itself! Those yaatris had come in a big bus and they said, "You don't worry, swamiji. You will come with us. We have lots of space." And they looked after me so well.' Satyenderpuriji cackled again. 'It was like Mahadev had arranged everything for me. I came here with no money and went back with no money. That was when I realized, Siddharth, that the rickshawaala was none other than Shiva himself.'

Varanasi. February 21, 2020. 6:10 am

I got off the Shiv Ganga Express and stepped into Varanasi's smoggy streets and flagged down a Vikram autorickshaw. I joined three others, all women from Baroda, who had come to pay their respects at the Kashi Vishwanath Temple.

The woman facing me, a plump, effusive sort, asked if I was visiting alone or had brought my wife too, and I said that a friend might join me later. But this time, speeding past cycle rickshaws, sadhus, hippies and clouds of smoke and dust, I knew I was alone. Which wasn't such a bad thing after all. I had nobody to distract me on my mission.

'What about your family?' I said.

'We left our men at home,' she said, and her friend laughed.

I checked into my hotel by the ghat, took a shower and still high on that adrenaline that being active on cold mornings lends you, I ran down to Meer Ghat. By 7:30 am, I was drinking chai and taking in the spectacle of the Ganga and the hundreds of men, women and children bathing in it.

A few steps on came a young, slender man bashing his clothes on the ghat's steps. The soap lathering in the water gave a vivid backdrop for a picture of a woman doing namaskar to the sun behind, so I spontaneously brought out my phone. I took a furtive photo of her, then of the man, and a few more.

I was crouching down on the steps, trying to get another wide-angle shot, when he looked straight at me with hurt eyes. I'd already put my phone back in my pocket when a middle-aged wiry sadhu strode up. He had been praying in a little alcove set into a wall nearby. He had a swarthy complexion and thick grey eyebrows.

'What're you doing?' he said gruffly. His Hindi bore a South Indian accent.

'Nothing. Where are you from, swamiji?'

'Where are *you* from, bhai?' he said. 'Your photo will get this poor man in trouble. You people all talk about "Swachh Bharat" [literally, clean India, but a reference to the government-sponsored sanitation campaign] and only make our life hard. This poor man is washing his clothes in the river. Where is he supposed to go? Will you give him a bathroom with running water? Where should he go?' I said I was sorry, but the man carried on. 'Then why do you judge him? Please delete *karo. Abhi!*'

He took a step closer and I brought out my phone and deleted the photo. 'Okay, babaji. I've done it,' I said.

I asked if he could spare a few minutes to talk, and he continued talking rapidly and irritably, but also excitedly, like he enjoyed getting things off his chest. Speaking in Hinglish he said his 'native place' was Nellore, and that he'd been to temples in the whole of Hindustan. Nothing was left. 'And not just in Hindustan. I have also been in *Tibbat*... Tibbat. You know, in China?'

I nodded.

'I went with a *fauji* many years ago. He had come to Kashi. And like you are sitting and talking to me, he was doing the same. He became my bhakt and after some days he started staying with me and he later took me there.'

'Do you mean Ladakh?'

'No, no, Tibbat. The fauji had his duty there, so he took me with him. His brother was also posted there and they made my papers and everything.' His eyebrows knotted up. 'You are not believing me? So, let me tell you, there was a big wooden house and for food they gave us simple *makkhan*, *sag* and *bajre ki roti*. I can also tell you that there is a river which comes out of the white mountains and it goes in all four directions. I think one river goes to China, one to India, one to Pakistan and one somewhere else.'

'The Indus?'

'Yes! And the mountains are so white.'

'I've been to Ladakh and the view there is also like this,' I said. 'Very beautiful.'

'But I went to Tibbat! Do you take me for a fool? Because I know that I saw the *Shiv Parbat*, the Kailash Mansarovar. And I can tell you that nobody is allowed to climb it. The *lama log*...their Gurudev is also there. I spoke to those *lama babas*. They also believe in the Shiv Parbat.'

The sadhu said that he was sixty-eight, 'now maybe sixty-nine,' and that people called him Shivmani Baba. He said it had been twenty-five years since he had left his old life and that he had never married.

'Never?'

'No, I married, but my wife died early. I had kids, but when my wife died, *mere bachche apne man ka ho gaya*...my kids went their separate ways. So, I came here to Baba's nagari [Shiva's city], and now live here permanently. In the evening there is the Ganga aarti, I go for that. Then in the morning I attend the temple Mangal aarti. Then I sit with my friend near his shop. At around twelve there is a bhandaara in the Annapurna Mata Mandir. Many people come there from South India so you get to eat: *bhat, sambar, sabzi, bhujia, dahi, meetha papad*. Everything. Then at Lalita Ghat they distribute food to labourers so I go there sometimes. I keep moving from place to place. But I never leave Varanasi. I am a Shiva bhakt.

'I have been everywhere in the Himalayas. To Gaumukh, Kedarnath, Badri—and everywhere I went walking. And in 2010, I went to Amarnath also so now nothing is left.'

About his living arrangements in the Himalayas he said, '*Bahut achchha tha. Chhota chhota gaon log bahut seva kiya*...It was very good. The small village people looked after me well. These mountain people do good seva. Much better than the plains people.' He gave a little laugh. '*Waise*, where are you from?'

I answered. Then asked, perhaps offhandedly: 'So you're at *shanti* [peace] here, babaji?'

Shivmani Baba laughed again. 'Will you get shanti by going to some place? Will you buy shanti in some palace? You have to still your mind first. The world is so big, and the mind is *chanchal*, restless,' he said. 'Don't your thoughts run from you like electricity?'

I nodded and he gave another big laugh.

What did he think of Aghoris? Did he know any?

'These Aghors eat fish and meat,' he said. 'You see them walking around with a *khopdi* [skull]. They have totally separate customs to us,' he said. 'You will find them in the cremation grounds, in Harishchandra Ghat and at Manikarnika Ghat.' He thought a moment. 'See, nobody has a shortage of anything here. They can eat what they want, but they also do *nasha*. They take intoxicants. This I don't like. It's fine to have your own path to God. They have theirs, but why do nasha?' He glanced at the young man washing clothes and made his voice deeper. '*Dekho*, for a sadhu, ganja may be okay.'

'It is okay?'

'It *may* be okay. *Lekin nasha naash ki jad hai*...drugs lead to destruction. Let me tell you what happened the other day. After the aarti, I asked one man for *dakshina* [donation], and he said he won't give anything because he had seen one sadhu drinking his money away. This man saw one bad sadhu, but his actions make us all look bad, na?'

'Oh yes, some sadhus in the Himalayas don't even touch money,' I said, this time actually wanting to take the conversation forward. But Shivmani Baba again raised his voice.

'It's easy for you to say. But if I have to do latrine, I have to pay five rupees. If I ask for tea from the chaiwaala, he will give me free one time. But will he give it to me every day? A little money even we sadhus need. But is there an end to greed? Is there an end to desire for wealth? ... We need very little.'

8 am

Because Manikarnika Ghat is the most obvious place to find the Aghoris, I began walking to it. And would you believe it, no sooner had I ambled two hundred metres than I came upon an Aghori baba!

The man in his early fifties looked formidable with the hallmark long flowing beard, black robes and a face smeared with ash. There was a large Shiva's Third Eye painted on his forehead, too, and most outstandingly, he even had a *kapal*, a human skull, in his hand along with a wooden staff lusciously curved at the top. I had seen him roaming the ghats on previous visits.

I did a namaste and asked to take his picture, and he posed grandly for the camera like he'd dressed up just for this very occasion. Then he held out his skull for money and I fed it Rs 50. But when I asked him if he could talk for a few minutes, he grunted a 'No!' picked up his robes and strode away tapping his stick on the steps like an irascible warlock.

A young man came jumping over the boats parked in the shallows at Scindia Ghat. He scampered up the steps. 'You want boat ride?' he said in English. He had dopey eyes, a cheerful smile and a put-on American accent, which I supposed he'd learnt through YouTube.

'No.' I grinned. 'But can you make me meet Aghori babas?' I replied in Hindi.

He continued in English: 'Oh, you do talkings to sadhus like a firangi, man?'

'Yes, like this.' And I showed him a picture of the baba I'd just met.

'Oh, I know him. His name is Kalu Baba, no?'

I shrugged.

Om Prakash, the boatman, said he was twenty-three, and that he was not just a boatman but a tour guide, too. When I chuckled he said he was born and raised on these ghats and knew them better than most. Why, didn't I believe him?

'I can make you do talkings with *doms* [corpse burners] and sadhus. I know one Aghori but he is coming in nights only.'

This guy was too entertaining to let go of so I asked him to accompany me.

'See, I showing you babas. But I don't say anything about them. Because all tourists doing their own thinkings. I just showing to people. Not doing thinking. Okay?'

'And what is your thinking?' I said, and Om Prakash's eyes lit up.

'I think your photo is not of real Aghori,' he said. 'I think even the one coming in the evening is not real.'

When I asked him where I'd find real Aghoris, he told me what I expected. To head to the Baba Keenaram Ashram, the Aghori ashram in Banaras. But knowing how straitlaced Hindu ashrams tend to be, I was putting off my visit for later.

8:30 am

You might have heard, Dear Reader, that Manikarnika Ghat is where Varanasi's dead have been cremated for hundreds of years. But if you didn't have this knowledge, you probably couldn't tell just by looking at the place from afar. From a boat, the burning funeral pyres look like a carnival of fire, a collection of yagnyas. And the men coming in at irregular intervals hollering '*Ram Naam Satya Hai!*' appear like ancient ritual conductors. It is only when you're actually standing here in the thick of it, with ash raining down on you and the smell of burning flesh seeping into your nostrils, that the deathliness of the places assails you.

It's ironic, though, isn't it, how in these modern times, this place of death has become this hive of activity? All the more so since *quietude* was the original reason Aghori babas sought cremation grounds out in the first place. (As one Aghori, Badri, would later say: 'It's only in the world of the dead we can shut out the noise of the living.')

Even so, amid all the noise and crackling, in inconspicuous corners you'll find at all times a handful of sadhus immersed in silent introspection. Om Prakash pointed me to one such orange-robed man sitting in one spot and one wearing black in another.

'See, you seeing two-three right now,' he said. 'But at night more Aghori is coming.'

He gave me his number. 'If anything else you want, like ganja or anything, you call me. Okay?' he said with a grin. I laughed and tipped him, and he put the earphones hanging around his neck back into his ears and walked off humming a song.

I went up to the orange-robed sadhu who was just getting up from his meditations and did a namaste. The man had a salt-and-pepper beard and large, demure brown eyes, and as he nodded, I detected in him something bashful, something diffident.

I've come to see in holy men an expectation of reverence, if not a display of outright arrogance. But in this man, I sensed servility, an obsequiousness of the sort the poor have had to cultivate in their dealings with the better-off. And I was right.

Sixty-four-year old Mr Dubey was not a sadhu but a former Mumbai taxi driver. He wore orange because he wanted to. Because he was a Shiva bhakt and Varanasi had been his home for four years. Yes, he had a wife, but she was also a bhakt and led a spiritual life back in his village. Rather, he said, it was she who'd brought him on this path of devotion. He had a son who drove a truck in Jaunpur and was happily married.

'It's me who is still wandering around,' he said, laughing.

I told Mr Dubey I was speaking with all manner of babas, and even wanderers like himself. So he asked: 'But what kind of men are you looking for exactly?' and I said, not misleadingly, 'Men who are seeking truth.'

He chuckled. 'I have been coming to Banaras since '95. And I can tell you I've not found one true man.'

'Who is a true man?' I asked, and he answered without prevarication: '*Jo matlabi na ho*...he who is not selfish.'

About the Aghoris, though, he offered more hearsay: 'I don't know much about them. Who knows what they do? They do everything in secret.' But then he remembered an incident:

'*Ji, ji*, one time, years back I was sitting right here, and I overheard one Aghori talking to another man,' he said. 'That Aghori said that yes, they drink, but they don't drink for nasha. He said they do it so that they can tolerate their hard life.' He looked up, as if still recalling. 'I think nothing is taboo for them. No food or anything. Some people also say that they have special *siddhis*, but I don't know.'

Throughout my interaction with Mr Dubey, I'd been eyeing a young sadhu in black robes on the other end of the ghat. He was sitting in the padmaasana posture with his back upright and neck stiff as if he were peering into another dimension. His face, arms and chest were evenly coated in ash. Was he putting on a show? And if so, who was he impressing when nobody noticed him?

As it happened, while I'd been observing him another man had been watching me and he now stepped forward: 'Do you want a tour?' he said.

The man had a round face hatted by a flop of well-oiled hair and wore a worn grey shirt and trousers. He said he'd show me the half-submerged temple at the back, the Ratneshwar Mahadev, and the Blue Lassi shop, also not far away. I asked if he'd just talk instead and he agreed.

Ashok, forty-three, lived on Lalita Ghat and said he was a volunteer at a local hospital. He looked after ailing men who had come to Kashi to die. He gave them wet sponges and wiped their shit and piss, and never took money for all this. 'These people don't have money anyway,' he said. 'They are poor.'

I turned to Mr Dubey. 'Now, here is a selfless man, no?' I said, and Mr Dubey smiled weakly.

'See what God has given me,' Ashok said, 'My knowledge and ability. I like to put it to good use. In this time of Kalyug when everybody is selfish, I get a lot happiness from my work. Whoever does good karma always gets good results.' He turned to Mr Dubey. 'Even if we have to wait some time. *Hai na?*'

Mr Dubey nodded.

About the Aghoris, Ashok agreed that although they had some powers, he'd never seen them perform a miracle.

'My guru is from the south, and he practices *Tantra* in the open,' he said. 'Not secretively like these men. He has such a jadi booti [herb] that you cannot believe. It can guarantee you'll live for hundred years. In the hospital, they will give hundred medicines to save a man but my guruji has just one jadi booti which can do this.'

Like the Aghoris, Ashok's guru was an occult practitioner. He was a *Tantric Samrat*, a King of Tantrics, as Ma Kaali had bestowed him with shakti. 'I've seen him give jadi booti to a man who had mental problems for many years and in one second he became all right. *Jab shaitaan kisi ke andar aata hai to woh apni shakti se nikalte hain*...when the devil comes to possess somebody he can remove it with his power. But I've not seen any miracle from Aghoris. They show us something but do something else.' He laughed. 'Why do things secretly unless you have something to hide, *hai na*?'

He turned to Mr Dubey who was still holding on to his expression of placidity. Ashok sighed, turned back to me. 'If you wait, one Aghori will come in the evening,' he said, and went on his way without asking for a paisa.

These half-sadhus, like Mr Dubey and Ashok, are all men drawn to the mystical. But they're also oddballs. Does one have to live at society's margins to become interested in spiritual pursuits? *Or do you just have to be a little unhinged and totally impractical?* I chuckled.

I would return to these questions later. But for now, I gave Mr Dubey Rs 200 and got up. After breakfast, I'll head to Baba Keenaram Ashram, I thought.

No more than twenty minutes had passed when at Dashashwamedh Ghat, yes, the main ghat, I saw something in full view that you can only see in Varanasi: *a dog chewing on a human skull and nobody caring to look.* Now this I had to take a picture of. I took many in fact.

I'd walked only a few steps ahead, though, when I heard frenzied barking, and turned around. A man—an Aghori!—was swearing. He was attempting to yank the skull away from the dog and the dog was growling, pulling back hard. The dog then lost its grip and leapt forward, but the Aghori was quick. He hit it with his stick and it gave a yelp and scurried away.

The Aghori was making incoherent noises, spitting into the air, but I went up to him undeterred and trotted out my well-rehearsed introduction.

The man, probably in his late forties, had a thick, unkempt black mane scattered with fine threads of white amid which nested a set of mud-brown teeth, several of which were missing. Six or seven colourful bead necklaces hung down to his bare chest—black, brown, white and red—all which made him look vaguely menacing. But it was his eyes that most unsettled me. His veins cut into the whites—whites which had gone a deep yellow—in violent red gashes.

... *But I had found what I was looking for!* So, I went up to a chaiwaala nearby and bought him a cup.

'Can you tell me about your Aghor philosophy, babaji?' I said, foolishly jumping in with the big question, clearly the wrong approach to strike up a conversation with anybody, let alone an Aghori.

'Look, it's nothing,' he said, his words slurring. 'It is Brahma, Vishnu, Mahesh.' He pointed to the three prongs on his trident. 'Nothing beyond this.'

The man regarded me with his unstable eyes, then roared into the air: 'I am an Aghori. That means *audhoot... Main hoon audhoot maharaj. Audhoot se bhaaga bhoot. Mere guru ke saamne koi nahi hai, bachcha. Main Aghori hoon aur main Naga bhi hoon...* I am an audhoot. From audhoots, ghosts run away. In front of my guru, all are nothing, child. I am an Aghori, but I am also a Naga.'

While the designation *avdhoot* is applied principally to men who've shed all social norms, along with their clothes, men who have come to be associated with the crazy modes of sadhu behaviour, it's a term that also connotes a type of ascetic who's gone beyond the senses. Gone beyond the ego.

Is this man an Aghori or a Naga? I wondered. Or both? He's definitely high. But is he trying to confuse me, or is confusion his general state of being? His manner betrays a mix of craziness and undirected anger. But is he a rebel with or without a cause? Definitely with a cause. Outcasts always have reasons to be rageful.

He enlarged his yellow ponds. 'I am Shiva,' he thundered. 'If you come to my akhara near Assi Ghat, you'll get scared, child. It is so crowded that there is no space even to place your foot. And today'—he grabbed my hand, I pulled it away—'you will get *machchhi waad* prasad. Fish prasad.'

I fixed my gaze on him but he tore his pupils away. 'Why do you carry this in your hands, babaji?'

'This?' He smiled at the skull by his side like it was his pet. 'See, there is nothing in this.' He made his voice deeper: 'Now listen to me. *Om Ma Kreem. Om Namah Shivaaya.* Repeat after me.' I did. Then he opened his arms towards the Ganga. 'What does this mean? This is Kashi.' He pointed to his trident. 'This is my Trishul. And this is what my guru has taught me.'

Hmm. 'What do you eat, babaji?'

'Oh, you think I care?' His spit flecked his beard. 'If I find something, or if somebody feeds me, only then I'll eat. If I don't find anything, I don't eat. And I'll take anything. Alcohol, meat, anything... BUT'—he enlarged his eyes, looked fondly at his skull—'I always feed him first. And if I go hungry, he also goes hungry.

'Oh, what I eat, you won't be able to eat, child. And I make my food with my own hands, and once I've eaten'—he massaged his belly—'I feel I have become *amar* [immortal]. Other sadhus have to keep running for prasad. But I don't care. I eat anything.'

The Aghori looked ahead blankly and I felt a slight warmth of appreciation wash over me. The sort of warmth I'd felt speaking to Naga babas the year before. Now, here's a man, I thought, who has no regard even for the most basic of basics—food and drink. Even the simplest of sadhus insisted that their food be saatvic, free of onion and garlic. But this man here has shed attachment to such a degree that he doesn't even care what he puts in his mouth.

'*Yeh police waale chu—ye hain...* these policemen are assholes,' he yelled, and the brief spell broke. He stood up and bared his teeth at a passerby, and the young man, a local, responded with a similar mock scary face.

That's it! This is getting absurd. If he can be tenacious, so can I. 'Babaji, have you acquired any siddhis?'

The Aghori baulked. His yellow ponds an ocean of pus. 'Give me your hand.'

I blinked a moment, but then complied. He held my right hand in his left one and held up a rudraksh bead between his right thumb and forefinger.

Rudrakshas, the dried stones of the fruit of the *Elaeocarpus ganitrus* tree, have been used as prayer beads by Hindus likely for well over a thousand years. The jagged brown one in the Aghori's hand looked like it had been pulled from the third necklace around his neck. He appraised it like it was a pearl. Then he pressed it into my forefinger.

I flinched: a pinprick of blood. I yanked my hand away. 'Are you mad?' His pupils slid around those yellow puddles like insects in scum.

'Are you crazy?' I got up, and he mumbled something to his skull. 'What the…!'

He kept muttering like it was he, not me, who'd been assaulted.

Now look, Dear Reader, I never fall for such tricks. Really, *never!* Not after this one time when I was fifteen and a so-called holy man came knocking on our door one hot afternoon. The clean-shaven man, in his forties, was dressed in a white dhoti and white shirt. He looked rather proper with neatly combed hair and a tika on his forehead. Relatively well-off, even. Neither mummy nor papa were at home, and the man was only asking for a few minutes of my time. So, I let him in.

I remember that he took a seat in our living room and I offered him tea, and for a few minutes, he didn't say much. He watched me watching him, took delicate sips from his cup, making sounds of satisfaction. Then he said, 'Can you bring me a pen and paper?' He asked me to write down the answers to three questions on the square sheet ('*What is your favourite colour?*' '*What is your biggest fear?*' '*Whom do you confide in?*'), to then fold it and hand it over. He folded the paper further still and told me to go hide it in a safe place. A place only I knew.

When I returned, he looked up from his teacup. 'Only you know what you have written. Yes?' he said.

I nodded.

'I have no idea what you've written. Yes?'

I nodded again.

And now he proceeded to tell me all of my answers, *answers only I knew*, careful though he was to not state them verbatim, to disguise them just a little. He drained the last of the tea into this mouth and watched with glee as surprise filled into my face.

A few years later, I saw the British mentalist Derren Brown debunking a similar magic trick on television. The type of trick the holy man had performed was known as the 'centre tear' or 'peek' trick and it was a common one used by magicians worldwide whereby they created the illusion of mind-reading.

So, why did you go along with this Aghori, then? you ask. Because I thought doing so would make him yield *something*. Or perhaps because something about holy men *still* makes me subconsciously compliant.

Later that evening, standing on the balcony of my hotel room, I thought about the Aghoris. For sure they relished offending you. They revelled in it. It was almost as if their offensive nature was their point. But why were they like this? *Had we made them so?* Like the squalor in our midst, were they a reflection of an ugliness we choose to keep at bay? Were they a personification of a hideousness we never wanted to see but was present in each of us? Were they an illustration of some errant anger we had in us? Or *I had in me*? Anger at having to conform. Anger at being told what was pure and impure, clean and unclean, right and wrong. Anger that on some days made me want to shout:

F— YOU! F— you, world! This is me. Deal with it.

Far below, the thousands of spectators had taken their seats, and the seven pandit performers had taken their positions. The Ganga aarti was about to begin and a drone hovered above the scores of boats lined up at the riverfront. I lit up a cigarette. So, if that man's message was a *F— you!*, I saw his point.

But were there points I could not see? Was it possible that this man who'd shed even the last vestiges of comfort had grown so impervious to the innate impulses of what I took to be clean and unclean that he had, through his bizarre form of renouncement, become sensitized to truths I couldn't see? Like Wassily Kandinsky, the pioneer of abstract painting, who some said could even *hear* colours, could the Aghoris see things I was blind to? *Was this possible?*

I chucked my cigarette stub to the wind. *What rubbish you think!*

I thought. But I also thought: *Who are you to speak for another man's Truth?*

Of course, I was coasting along these contours of intuition only eight hours later as I gazed out at the world from the comfort of my room. At 10:45 in the morning, though, I was running fast—away from that total raving lunatic!

As you might have guessed, I didn't visit Baba Keenaram's ashram that afternoon. I'd had had enough for the day. Enough of the Aghori's theatrics, my search for 'Cosmic Unity', and frankly, this nonsense! What I badly needed was to calm my nerves with something sensorily pleasing: I needed a hot cappuccino and a big eggy breakfast, and I knew just where to go.

It was so stupid of me. Why did I give in to him? I thought. Why do I always give in to them? I texted Armaan: *I should know where to draw the line with religion sometimes*, and hopped into the shower. I scrubbed myself vigorously and washed everything away. The smell, the grime, the crap. I washed it all away. I enjoyed watching the foam collect at the drain. Then, go *down, down, down* into the gutter.

I scrubbed myself again. My pricked finger, I scrubbed five times. *Did I need a tetanus shot?*

I came out of the bathroom, all sweating, still fuming, and picked up my phone.

Armaan had texted back: ':)'

A spin back into Varanasi's meditative gullies

As it is close to Sarnath, Buddha's Forest of Bliss, Banaras is home to a fair few Japanese and Korean cafes. I tucked into an egg bibimbap at one such place. And now with my anger somewhat abating, I was enjoying a chocolate cake and taking in the world go by.

Dear Reader, I know I've said so before, but I will again: you really take in incredible sights, sounds and smells here!

Just on my way over, I'd passed a sadhu sleeping in an alcove with his dog; a woman stopping to take the blessings of a cow blocking her path; the beat of tabla and the song of harmonium from a classical music school; the sizzle of dosas frying on a pan; the waft of *kachori* and *chhole* from a food stall under a peepal tree; and cow shit splattered in the gulley!

Two tables away from me a white guy of roughly my age was speaking in strained Hindi to the waiter. Everybody had on a jacket, but he was wearing a T-shirt and ripped jeans. I smiled at him and he smiled back. He had a three-day-old stubble and blue eyes and was languidly rolling tobacco into Rizla. 'I try,' he said.

'Your Hindi is not bad,' I said. And a mere ten minutes after we'd made our introductions—Would you believe it?—we were debating on deep spiritual questions: *How do you define God? Do you see Advaita and Buddhist Philosophy as two sides of the same coin?*

At one point he even said, 'I was just trying to figure out, you know, why am I here?' and I momentarily considered, *Was it God's design that I'd run into him?* But then, I later thought, *No.* Our meeting was no coincidence at all. For who else will you meet at university but other students? Who else will you come by in Varanasi but other seekers?

Martin was from Bern, Switzerland, but had spent the last two years in Vashisht, Himachal Pradesh where he'd studied Hindu scriptures from a Canadian Guru, who, in his words, had 'become Hindi.'

'My journey began when I was twenty-eight and I had depression,' he said. 'I had a perfect Swiss job and a nice girlfriend. But I was close to suicide, you know. I came to that point where nothing made any sense. I didn't enjoy my life. And I felt that nothing I was doing was actually *me*. My apartment, my gaming—I used to play video games and smoke weed all the time—none of it was me. It was like I was losing ground, *hai na*? And I was trying to figure out my purpose. I thought, I am a logical person. Why is this happening to me? So, I was figuring this out.'

As you can see, Martin, aged thirty-eight, my age at the time, spoke freely. So much so that I can't recall if our conversation turned into a formal interview. What's more, his English sounded more Indian than European to my ears, not least because he sprinkled it with words like *achchha* and *hai na*.

He put a cigarette to his lips. 'One day I was sitting at my home alone and I thought if I switch on the gas in my kitchen and close all the doors and windows I could just go and nobody would notice.' His eyes were effusive, too. They had a fire.

'Then I met a guy who told me to see a Shiatsu. In Hindu, you would say "working with your *nadis*"—your energy channels. And I was scared about this because some people who tried it are like zombies now. But at that point I was ready to try anything. And this was my first contact with something I could not explain. This guy… with his fingers he would touch different parts of my head and neck, with slight presses. It was like he was reconnecting me to the earth. Because I was up in the clouds, thinking too much. That man worked on my nadis and after this session I felt more human. Like…I actually started feeling again. I felt hungry and tired and sleepy again. Before I was so lost, I was so disconnected, but now I felt grounded again.'

A part of me wanted to dismiss this man's account as yet-another-Westerner-coming-under-the-thrall-of-Eastern-mysticism. But the more Martin talked the more I found him to be an intelligent and thoughtful individual. He spoke deliberately, taking time to gather his thoughts. I felt, actually, that he was a *bit like me*: another guy who found a nine-to-five routine impossible and had invested much time reflecting on various things tangential to modern life.

He took a long pull on his cigarette. 'So, slowly I got better, *hai na*? But then I also got curious. And so I started reading about these stuffs. My first book was given to me by a friend. It was called *Oneness with All Life* by Eckhart Tolle. And this friend later took his life. It was around this time that I started meditating. First, I did some basic breath-work and then slowly I started to see changes in my outlook.'

In 2016, Martin went backpacking to Southeast Asia for five months, and during his travels, he met a 'beautiful Indian lady' who taught him yoga. 'She did a yoga course,' he said, his eyes lighting up. 'And I thought, I would *love* to do yoga instead of my boring finance job… If I won the lottery, the first thing I'd do is quit my job.' He laughed. 'And when I went home I did quit my job and I gave up my apartment and almost everything I had.'

Then, in 2017, Martin got a one-way ticket to India. He headed first to the Shivananda Ashram in Trivandrum where he practised *panchkarma*—an Ayurvedic method used to clean the body of excess doshas, faults, and correct imbalances created in the system by toxins and disease. 'And so, little by little, I got more into yogas and energies.'

He smiled. 'I also met a girl there and we were together for three years and through her I learnt about Advaita Vedanta. She brought me into the whole Vedic way. And then, two years back, in Himachal, in a cafe in Vashisht, I met my Canadian Guru. He's been studying philosophy since he was sixteen but is now sixty. He told me about the connections between religions.'

Martin's guru said that all religions spoke of non-duality. They may have different manifestations but in the end they say All is One. Martin said that 'the Sufis said this and even the Buddha in his own way said this', and for some reason the lawyer in me now awoke.

'Is this accurate, though?' I said. 'From what I understand, Christianity and Islam don't speak of non-duality. And Buddhists speak of non-duality, but they're against the belief in God.'

Martin shook his head. 'In Christianity and Islam it is in the metaphorical books. Sufis in Islam and mystics in Christianity both wanted to figure out God and they both wrote things like, *God is everywhere. God is everything...* You will find these basic statements in both faiths. And'—he gave a wry smile—'even in Hindu, you have books like the Gita and Mahabharata which are more accessible whereas the Upanishads go up into philosophy, *hai na?*'

He put out his cigarette, met my eyes. 'Even non-duality is consciousness, no? And I think non-dual consciousness itself is God. In Hindu, Shankaracharya's Advaita Vedanta is like a radical non-dualism, and in my view it is very close to Buddhism. But you also have other lineages like Chaitanya who have a more inclusive dualism. Chaitanya said, "You are one with and different from His creation."'

Shri Chaitanya was a Bengali philosopher of the early sixteenth century who preached the concept of *achintya-bheda-abheda-tattva*, or the Truth of Simultaneous Oneness and Separateness. While Shankaracharya maintained that the Brahman and the aatman are One, Chaitanya was of the view that though the two are interlinked, they're separate. In the way sunbeams are different from the sun, the aatma and the Brahman are similar qualitatively, but not quantitatively.

'So, from my point of view, Shankaracharya and Buddha are similar. I mean, Krishna once even said, "*Every path leads to God.*" So, when you think of non-dual consciousness, you see it can be seen in many ways.'

Martin crossed his arms at his chest. 'I can say God is love. But

I think it's more. Because God is also an ecstatic feeling, but'—he touched his hand to his forehead—'it is also a calm feeling. Feeling compassionate like the Buddha is God. But so is feeling Krishna's ecstasy.'

Martin stared out at the gulley where pedestrians were sidestepping the cow dung in their path. Flies circled the shit. *Their own little cosmos…*

'It depends on what you look for. Even if you split the atom and keep splitting it, you will find some lowest indivisible particle. A void, *hai na*? So, you can also say that this void is God. Or you can just call this'—he enlarged his eyes, raised his hands—'Is, or Being.'

He relaxed in his chair. 'So yeah, the Buddha said that at the root of everything there is nothing. But what did he mean? Because the Buddha was there and he talked. And his talking means something, *hai na*?'

'Yes!' I said, letting loose some inexplicable well of exhilaration that had been rising within me. 'Yes. This is why the Upanishads say you are not created by God. You *are* God. This is why the Upanishads say that cosmic consciousness is the same as your soul.'

And Martin looked at me and smiled as though he agreed with me. But also as if he didn't fully agree.

I rang up Armaan right afterwards. 'You know, I met somebody just like us,' I said. 'And he's so deep.' And I repeated some of what Martin had just said, infusing it with some of my own evolving views. I told him how Martin said that all faiths are trying to reach the same thing. A sort of Ultimate Numinousness, a Universal Consciousness, or Non-Consciousness, if you prefer. A Singularity, which every faith in its own way calls God. 'I think everyone is aiming for an integration, a connection, a union.'

Armaan heard me out, but after I'd run out of air and big words, he coolly said: 'If you want to look for it, you will find it anywhere, Sid. But I think this guy has got his basics wrong. Non-duality in your Hindu sense does not exist in Islam and Christianity. He's just giving you snippets from here and there.'

I exclaimed. But he overrode me: 'Of course, you will find these thoughts, but this is not the main narrative. In our holy books there is a clear separation between God and his creations.'

When I reminded him that Rumi had written verses that sounded like something straight from the Upanishads—'*You are not a drop in the ocean, you are the ocean in a drop*' and '*The universe is not outside you. Look inside yourself; everything that you want, you already are*'—Armaan insisted that such men were exceptions to the Judeo-Christian norm. Rumi spoke of non-duality. And so did Mansoor Hallaj, a Persian mystic who lived in the ninth and tenth century, who even said, 'I am the Truth,' but he was executed for blasphemy.

As for the concept of *tawhid* in Islam, which refers to the Oneness of God, and the Holy Trinity in Christianity, which refers to One God in three persons—the Father, the Son and the Holy Spirit—he said that these tenets stressed on the oneness and indivisibility *of* God. They did not say that you were one *with* God.

'You should tell this Martin person to look up the difference between monism and monotheism.' He sighed heavily. 'I don't think you get the Semitic faiths, Sid. So, stop making your comparisons.'

Maybe I don't, I wanted to say. But that's not the point.

Martin stepped into the lane with his backpack tight on his back and put another cigarette to his lips. With chappals on his feet, he looked like he was ready to head off to another session of chai and theological discussion. 'Where will you go next?' I said.

'Wherever I feel like.' He had a glint of light and play in his eyes. 'I don't like to plan things.' He touched his hand to his chest. 'I like to go with my spirit. So maybe, Indonesia? Sounds nice.'

I'd expected him to say he would head to an ashram in Rishikesh and couldn't help ask, 'And what about all the Hindu spirituality?'

'I have learnt a lot in your country,' he said. 'And I'll continue my studies. But I don't need to be here to read, *hai na*?'

The next time I spoke to Martin was over the phone in the summer of 2022. He was back in Switzerland now and sounded just as garrulous as before. The difference this time being there was no Hindi in his speech. He was now gearing up for a trip to Mexico. As for his views, they were the same, but were now sharper.

My past year had been stressful with dear ones falling sick. I asked if he'd been all right through the pandemic and he told me he'd been travelling in Africa the previous year but had somehow managed to get back to Switzerland.

'And don't even ask me how I re-entered Europe without a vaccine certificate,' he said. 'No way am I going to inject myself with this shit,' he responded when I expressed surprise.

'Ayurveda believes in the intelligence of everything,' he went on. 'In your system, the human body has intelligence and organs have intelligence. We get sick in certain conditions and we heal in other conditions. And now, even Western science is catching up with this. Now, even they are saying that our organs talk to each other!'

I chuckled. A part of me agreed with Martin. The same part which secretly gloats when I read scientific articles about the benefits of turmeric, or of deep meditation's ability to enhance your immunity. (Things we've known for hundreds of years!) But a good part had tuned out.

Don't blame me, Dear Reader, for again reverting to my mother, but here I must. What can I say? She's my main reference point!

Like Martin, mummy too had refused to take the Covid-19 vaccine and it was only when people dear to her started getting sick in the summer of 2021 that reality hit her in the gut and she gave in. 'My yoga and healing will protect me better than your injection,' she'd earlier said with her determined face, making my veins throb in fury. But that I'd won one battle never guaranteed I wouldn't have to contest her again. Most recently she had had a bad stomach ache and had decided to cure herself with homeopathy and her newest thing: *bell healing*.

I'd agreed to sit with her for a session if she'd go see a proper doctor.

After a senior Delhi gastroenterologist examined her she said to the elderly man in her cogent way, eyes rapidly blinking, 'Doctor, I won't say much. I'll just tell you what I did and you can make up your mind.'

'Okay.' He leaned back in his chair.

'I had a sharp pain in my stomach for a few days so I decided to try some bell healing. It's a system that heals the body through sound frequencies.'

The doctor blinked slowly and picked up his pen.

'And after about twenty minutes I noticed that my pain went away.

So, I continued with this for three days and every time my pain went away. But then this morning it returned, just a little. So, I thought, why not get it checked out?' She giggled.

'I see.' The doctor was composedly scribbling on his notepad. I peered forward, saw scribbled: *Diabetic. Radiculopathy? Kidney stone? Infection?*

He looked up, his expression inscrutable. 'See, I will never dismiss these things,' he said. 'After all, how does an ultrasound work? In an ultrasound also sound waves are used to look inside the body.' Mummy smiled broadly. He handed me her prescription. 'But here are some tests. Just to be sure.'

In the end my mother's blood work revealed that she had an infection. In the end it wasn't bell healing, but a round of antibiotics that cured her.

As before, I carried forward with Armaan the discussion about religion and science, faith and reason that I had had with Martin. As before, he said something like, 'This is why, Sid...this is why religious stuff is nonsense.' And as before, I felt some compulsive need to take the defensive line:

'But don't you think science and spirituality are looking at things from different angles? Everybody is making their own connections, right?' I felt a flicker in mind: 'Don't you think God is the name we give to that entity who knows all the variables? Things we can measure and things we can't. Because there is a lot we don't understand.'

Armaan sighed. 'This is the classic God of the Gaps fallacy, Sid,' he said.

But my thoughts were assembling, a force was building. 'Wait. Maybe faith has its own logic. But it's a logic in the realm of intuitions, and it can't be quantified! It has a different language... Because, think about it, just the fact that millions believe means something, right? That millions have always had faith, it must mean something, damn it!'

I was relieved that Armaan didn't interrupt me. 'Okay, I'm listening.'

'Maybe God is simply a name for the sum of *all infinities*... The variables which make up our material reality and the ones that make up our emotions and consciousness.'

I felt like I was on the road to an epiphany and was thus caught off guard when Armaan stood up and began clapping his hands. '*Wah*, Sid! You're a genius!'

'What?'

'What you're saying is what all religions say! That God is all knowing and all encompassing. This is what Muslims say and this is what Christians say and this is also what Hindus say. *Upparwaala sab jaanta hai...*the One above knows all.' He fell back in his chair with a huff. 'This is a fallacy.'

'No, no, hang on.' I was nearing the summit and I wasn't going to give up. I had to ejaculate my point, even if I didn't fully understand what the point was. 'Look, science is important. But you agree that it can't answer everything, right?'

'You keep saying this. So what?'

'And you agree that the belief in a higher power encumbers the lives of billions. And that many highly intelligent people believe, yes?'

He shrugged. *So?*

'So, don't you think that this reveals something about human nature? About reality even? How can you eliminate all doubt? How can you be so arrogant even to deny the possibility that there may be *something*?'

Armaan shrugged again, but seemed a quarter amenable. 'But intuitions are not enough, Sid,' he said. 'Intuitions are flawed. The mind is always looking for causality... And this way of thinking creeps into every aspect of faith.'

'I agree. But maybe the problem is with *too much faith* then. The problem is that if there's a clash between faith and science, believers go with their gut. The problem is we can't accept what's true because science is leaping ahead at this crazy rate and our minds just can't keep up!'

I felt Armaan was on my page now and I was on my final line: 'We have our gut saying one thing and the experts saying another. So, maybe the problem really is knowing where to draw the line.'

As you can probably see, Dear Reader, I was making a zealous case to justify my own contradictions. But when Armaan gave in, when he finally grinned and said, 'This I can sort of go with, Mr Lawyer,' I felt I'd made a solid point.

Leeds, Yorkshire, England. March 2023

'How do you see things now?' Armaan said one Sunday morning in a cafe in another part of the world. He'd relocated to the UK now and I was on a long visit.

We were in Leeds City Centre and had just finished eating. I had the full English breakfast consisting of bacon and eggs while Armaan the vegetarian had the vegan kind. And now, as we sipped our coffees, we were doing our old thing: cogitating on faith, life and the universe.

Soon he'd return to his book, *Practical Ethics* by Peter Singer, and I'd begin penning down notes on this conversation we were about to have:

'Has the needle moved for you in this time?' he said. 'About faith, I mean.'

After thinking a moment, I said, yes, in many ways things had changed, and also not. I'd become more self-aware, less judgemental. And although I was now less certain there was one universal way I was more certain of the right way for me. 'I'm not as religious as I was before,' I said. 'And I'm definitely not ritualistic.'

Armaan raised his eyebrows.

'Sure, I do pooja sometimes and I'll ask a pandit to look at my kundli,' I said. 'But I don't follow any proper way.'

Armaan's eyebrows were still up.

'C'mon. When have you seen me pray?'

Armaan still never took God's name. Not of any god of any faith. If he'd been finding himself these past few years, what he'd found was not an affinity for any belief but for feelings, for intuitions. Particularly meditation, the one thing we now bonded more and more on.

He smirked. 'I've seen you pray with your eyes closed before sleeping, Sid,' he said and I felt a prick of the atheist's scorn for believers in his voice.

I smirked back. 'Okay. I do. So what?' How could I explain myself? *Why should I explain myself?* But I wanted to.

Later in my notes I'd write:

Yes, faith still has a strong pull but my rational mind intrudes more powerfully than before. Yes, I pray. But I do it out of comfort and habit, curiosity and marvel. Yes, I realize the irrationality of what

I do. But I do it because I still *feel.* And when I'm absorbed in the act of prayer I don't feel what I'm doing is illogical at all. Rather, I feel the opposite. I feel I'm letting go. I'm relinquishing control to the universe, *like a leaf falling from a tree surrendering to the wind…*

I believe because my faith pierces through our modern world when I least expect. Like it happened just last week when a pandit said that my *Shani Dasha*, or Saturn Period, was ending—a difficult period as per Vedic astrology—and that since my *Buddha*, Mercury, was ascendant, there'd be a growth 'in my education, in business, and I'd see results.' I remember thinking, *Yes, this actually was happening!* After years of ruminating, I was now waking up to a new world. Things were finally coming together. I had you, a partner, a book deal and bubbling ideas for another one. (A food business, too.) I felt in control.

I believe because even though astrology has no basis in science, I'm drawn to it because this *Jyotish* system was also devised by ancient humans drawing patterns in the night sky.

I believe because even though you'll say my views are messy I'm at peace with them. I like that I carry in myself a world of delusions alongside this unfeeling cold reality. *Okay?*

It was a sunny English day and we were sitting out in the open where three steps away from us two pigeons were hopping around looking for tidbits to eat. 'Have you noticed anything about the pigeons here?' I said.

Armaan's eyes sparkled. 'Ya! They don't get scared. They don't fly off when you go near them.'

'Exactly!'

'But tell me, Sid…' he said, not letting me change the subject.

'Hmm,' I said. 'I think we're all on a journey and it keeps changing like a painting the more you draw on it.' Or to refine this metaphor: Like an artist changes the canvas with each brushstroke building on and erasing the world that existed before. 'What's funny is that even though mom's still very religious we agree on many things. Like Buddhism's draw.'

As I've told you, mummy is a lawyer. But did I mention she was also student of philosophy? While mummy's faith remains ritualistic, age has made her deeply meditative too. Yes, she still does pooja every day. But she now also immerses herself in long sessions of silent healing in the afternoons. Sure, even today she tells me not to eat meat but she's now much less insistent. Because she gets that as she adheres to her inner rhythms, I follow mine.

'Anyway, what about you?' I popped out my phone recorder. Of course, I'd seen closely how Armaan had changed but I wanted him to answer himself.

'I've told you, Sid,' he said. 'I was very religious as a kid, and it was books that changed me. How do you expect me to condense ten years of my life?' He brushed my hand aside. 'You know it. Put your phone away.'

But then: 'Okay. Let me try. The first blow was Aristotle's *On Generation and Corruption*. He challenged my belief in a personal God. Aristotle taught me to resolve my inconsistencies.' He produced a mischievous glance.

I rolled my eyes.

'Then, after reading Spinoza's *Ethics* I gave up on this idea of the separation of God from Nature. And after reading about Buddhism and your Hindu philosophy I found connections between the two concepts. But I think it's the Buddha who most affected me. If you ask me, he's one of the best thinkers the world has ever known!'

He glanced at the pigeons. 'But now I'm thinking more about ethics.' The book on the table, *Practical Ethics*, argued that the principle of equality should extend beyond human beings and include all species who have a capacity for pain or pleasure. 'And I'm trying to tie this to my Buddhist beliefs. This is why I think I can't eat meat ever again.' He laughed. 'But this vegan business I can't do. It's too hard… Anyway, I think that it's important to connect my philosophy to my life and politics. Otherwise, what's the point?'

'But about God…' I pressed. 'Don't you think it's silly to put people into tight slots? Atheist and believer. Scientific and gullible. If we just change our vocabulary maybe more people would agree. Because faith is sometimes just another name for feeling and intuition. No?'

'No,' Armaan said. 'You're mixing up two separate things.'

But like Armaan, I too was thinking of the books I'd recently read: *The Awakened Brain* by clinical psychologist Lisa Miller, *Why God Won't Go Away* by neuroscientist Andrew Newberg and psychologist

Eugene d'Aquili, and *Buddha's Brain* by neuropsychologist Rick Hanson.

'Look, even scientists act on their hunches,' I said. Here I was thinking specifically of one book, *The Intuitive Edge*, which made the case that numerous thinkers used their intuition to achieve great things; how even Einstein and Newton relied on their intuition to advance their research. Meditators did the same thing. They built on their insights. They went deep into the mind, and sometimes they approached something big.

Admiring the two pigeons, Armaan gave a yawning yes. 'Ya, ya, this is your old point. But there's a difference, Sid. Science is humble. Science moves forward. But religious people never admit they're wrong. And they're always looking back to some glorious past.' One pigeon flew away. 'Yes… It's like we're stuck. Science moves forward but faith is stuck where it always was. Ya, that's it.' He sounded tired, but also like he'd made a good point.

'That's also true,' I said. 'Quite true.' The second pigeon flew away too.

Later

'Hey! … You asleep?'

'…'

'I think I got a way to reduce one inconsistency. You awake?'

'Let me sleep.'

'Can't we say that just like the flat earth exists beneath my feet… like it feels totally real…and just like Newtonian physics is true on one plane, even though Einstein modified old principles, in this same way faith is true on the spiritual plane but science is true on the material plane? That they are not mutually exclusive, but separate aspects of reality?'

'…'

'And everybody believes, right? Atheist or believer, everyone is looking for sense inside themselves regardless of what others say. We each have our gut pulling in one direction and our mind saying, *No. You're wrong!* yanking the other way. In the end everybody believes *something*!'

'Interesting,' Armaan said. 'Now, can I sleep?'

The Grand Night of Shiva: Mahashivratri, in Varanasi

February 21, 2020

I returned from the balcony to my room and lay on the bed. My phone rang: *Samar calling.*

'Ya, hey.' I was terse. I hate it when friends make travel plans and back out.

'Where are you?'

'I'm in Banaras. You know that.'

'No, I mean, over *here*? I'm at the main ghat. Dashash—'

'What?'

I threw on my slippers. Was he kidding? No, he wasn't. I could hear the same loudspeaker announcement over the phone as I could coming through the balcony. I ran down my hotel's steps to Meer Ghat and seven minutes later I found Samar at Dashashwamedh Ghat. He was back in a dhoti and white kurta, the same pair he'd bought on our earlier trip, a broad smile etched on his face.

'I can't believe you!' I embraced my friend.

'*Mera bulaawa aaya tha*...I had a calling, Sid,' Samar said. 'I had to come.'

Samar had been talking with a holy man in black and orange clothes. The baba, about fifty, had the archetypal white beard. But the way he regarded me, curiously but shiftily, made me instantly suspicious of him.

'This is my friend, babaji,' Samar said, and the man raised his palm to me.

I found his manner rehearsed and gestured to Samar that we get going, but he wanted to finish what he'd begun.

He turned to the baba. 'And what do you say about him, babaji?' he said, and the baba produced an ingratiating smile.

'He also may not be,' he said. 'He doesn't look so.'

'Doesn't look what?' I said.

'Married.' Samar grinned. He then proceeded to tell me how the man was a palmist, and from just a glance at his hand had guessed that he was single. '*Aap jeevan mein bhatak rahe ho*,' he'd accurately said. 'You're going through life without purpose.' And he could even tell that he was one of three siblings.

'If your friend shows me his hand,' the baba said, 'I can tell him things too. But for that, it'll be two hundred rupees more.'

I took Samar aside. 'How much did you pay him?'

He didn't answer.

Thoroughly disappointed with the ways of Varanasi babas from my experience with the Aghori that morning, I told my friend that the holy man was a classic fake because (1) he openly charged money when a real sadhu would never do this and (2) he claimed that he had siddhis, powers, when a real sadhu would not say such a thing either. I said that the baba was employing cold reading and Samar furrowed his brow.

'Have you heard of the Barnum Effect?' I continued, ready to talk about the psychological phenomenon whereby general statements are perceived as accurate and applicable to the person being 'read'. But my words were falling on deaf ears. Before the baba could go on, though, I stepped in. 'Babaji, can you recite the *Hanuman Chalisa* for us?' I said, and the man enlarged his eyes.

'You doubt me?' he said, operatically. 'You doubt me?'

I didn't flinch. 'Just recite the *Gayatri Mantra*, then.' I ensured my voice had steel in it. And now the man caved in.

'See, I never said I was a sadhu,' he said. '*Arre hum to anpadh hain...*I am illiterate. But I have siddhis. Do you want to know about yourself? If you show me your hand, I can tell you.'

I gave my friend a look of vindication and he turned his eyes upward.

'You can give him money. But I'm not,' I said.

The baba went on in his solicitous way dishing out generalities—'Yes, you will find love but you'll have to work at it,' and 'Money doesn't stay in your hands'—and Samar nodded along. But at one point the baba shed his theatrical style and became humble, even mentor-like, and now I listened in.

'Everybody has two spirits living inside them,' he said. 'One part is small, and he is spurred by small emotions, by pride and envy and anger. But there's another part, and this part is linked to God. This person thrives on feelings like compassion and openness and sharing in the happiness of others. And the secret that nobody tells you is that each of us has these two shaktis inside of us. Everybody. *Bada aadmi aur chhota aadmi*...rich man and poor man, everybody has these forces fighting inside them but we are totally unaware of it.' He gave a hearty laugh.

'But how do I stop my mind from wandering, babaji?' Samar said. And the baba gave my friend some practical advice. He told Samar to wear a silver ring on his little finger, to pour milk over a Shivalingam on Mondays, and to soak in the moonlight on Poornima. All this was to calm the mind.

But he also said: '*Aap jis aag mein tel daloge us hi aag ki shakti badhegi*...you become the kind of fire you add fuel to.'

Samar and I walked along the ghat not saying a word. Speckled with water and light, a gentle evening wind blew over us from the Ganga.

Yes, faith was for the persuadable, I thought. But it was also therapy.

Under a rampart alongside the Dashashwamedh Ghat, a place usually filled with drifters, we passed a tall white tourist in a heated exchange with a wiry local man.

'I paid you the full amount! You take. No more. No more!' the American yelled.

'No, *saar*. No, *saar*. I giving head massage and body massage,' the local said calmly. 'You paying both.'

'But my head is a part of my body, isn't it?' the American yelled again.

I laughed. *Yes, there's definitely something in the air here!* There is fakery and filth. But there's also much ingenuity and beauty. There really is a thing called the vibrations of Kashi.

9:30 pm

If there's one time when the Great-Indian-Free-For-All comes most alive, it's on Mahashivratri. For tonight, Lord Shiva marries Parvati and performs his *tandava*, his Dance of Destruction and Creation.

Throughout the day preceding Mahashivratri, you see *jhankis*, or tableaus of the faithful revelling in the city's decorated streets. You see parading bands of snake charmers and monkey charmers; all grades of sadhus and babas; Nagas and Aghoris; bands of drummers and trumpeters and child performers dressed up as Hindu gods, and even poets, professors and Bhojpuri actors. And not just people, you see quite the collection of animals, too. You see draped horses and camels and bulls and elephants. But perhaps what most charges the air is the *Holiyana mahaul*, or the Holi-esque atmosphere. For between the tableaus, all day and night long, boys burst into spontaneous dance in the city's streets. On Mahashivratri, Kashi turns into an open-air rave party and devotional Shiva music gets charged with techno beats.

Samar and I were standing at the side of Gowdolia Chowk, and one such group was dancing before us. There was the old church to one side, a bhang stall on the other, and the old shops running down DG Road a third end. A boy wearing sunglasses was gyrating like a jellyfish, his body flopping and bouncing to the rhythm of the Shiva tandava infused with progressive house music. Another boy was dancing like Salman Khan from *Dabangg*, and another like Prabhudeva in 'Muqabala Muqabala'. A cycle rickshaw, attached with spinning disco lights, acted like a moving stage, lighting up euphoric faces in a dazzling fireworks display.

Mahashivratri was an evening when the prescribed manners of the devout fell away and masti fully took over. Kashi went into Banaras mode and everybody who could dance danced. Sure, you saw mainly boys, but there were a few groups of school-going girls, too. And it wasn't just the gender divide which partially fell away, social barriers did as well. Although nearly everybody out was Hindu, as on Holi, a few Muslims were accompanying their friends, too.

In fact, I was to later learn from local news that while the part of Lord Shiva in the *Shiva Baraat* was played by a well-known poet, Saand Banarsi, the role of Goddess Parvati was enacted by a Badruddin Ahmed.

One boy in the group took his shirt off, spun it above his shoulders and chucked it aside. It landed by Samar's feet. 'Why don't you join in?' I said, laughing, and Samar smiled coyly. But I could see his eagerness. Everybody around us was drunk and the drink on open offer was bhang, lassi spiked with cannabis, and it was something neither Samar nor I had tried before.

The boys moved on and there came a float of a massive Shivalingam with Shiva's third eye in the centre flickering as a blue light.

Then: a band of drummers. The boys had three horizontal white lines—Shiva tilaks—on their foreheads but they wore yellow T-shirts and jeans. At first they drummed slowly: *dhadak…dhadak…dhadak…* Then faster and faster and louder and louder: DHADAK, DHADAK, DHADAK. They topped off the act with a full-throated *Har Har Mahadev!* before moving on.

The bhang stall on one side of Gowdolia Chowk was sending a pair of boys bearing trays of bhang glasses onto the road. They were stopping cars, scooters and pedestrians, offering everyone a drink. And on the other side of the chowk, the side leading to DG Road, there stood behind a wooden railing a long line of worshippers waiting to do abhishek pooja at the Kashi Vishwanath Temple. A group of men had large brass jars filled with Gangajal on their heads. They looked South Indian. I went up to them. One man said their group numbered 532 and that they were all from Kochi. I couldn't believe my eyes. *The queue to the temple had reached all the way to Gowdolia!*

I rang up my mother. Even though mummy stayed up all night on Shivratri, she had never seen the celebrations here in Kashi. I gave her a glimpse. 'Look!' She smiled, but preoccupied chanting the *Shiva Mahiman Stotra*, she hung up.

Tonight the devout stayed up to pray and the revellers danced. And I was in the mood to party.

A boy with a tray of bhang glasses came up. 'How much?'

'*Bas pee lo. Bhole Baba ka naam lo aur pee lo…*just take Shiva's name and drink it,' he said with a grin. But I was suspicious, not of his warmth but of the level of hygiene.

'I'm getting a glass each for us,' I said to Samar. 'I'll buy it from there.' I pointed to a stall with many customers. 'It looks safe.'

'Na. You have it.' Samar shook his head. 'I won't.'

'Stop your drama.' Of course he was going to! And I bought us two glasses of cardamom rose bhang lassi.

Samar was furiously texting somebody, deliberately not looking at me. 'Is there 3G here?' he said aloud. 'I'm not getting a signal.' And a man passing by said, '*3G chhodo, japo Shivji...*leave 3G, chant Shivji.' I laughed.

Samar produced a mock glare. 'You're just too pushy, Sid.' He laughed, but then took one glass from me. 'If something happens to me, you tell my mother.'

I rolled my eyes and took a sip. And so did he. 'It's not bad,' he said. And a round of fireworks went up in the sky.

The Varanasi Shiva Baraat procession begins around 7:30 am and continues for eighteen hours until around midnight when, at the *Jaimala* ceremony, Lord Shiva and Parvati exchange garlands. The morning baraat had started from Tibhandeshwar Temple and ended at Gauri Kedareshwar Temple, while the evening one began at the Mahamrityunjaya Temple at Daranagar, and going via Gowdolia, it would end further down DG Road after paying its last respects at Gate No. 1 of the Kashi Vishwanath Temple.

Samar and I were swinging with the crowds. I'd chucked my drink after having only a fourth of it, but he had nearly finished his and was now sashaying around with his dhoti like it was a skirt. He didn't look like he'd get sick, but I was getting a bit worried.

When a wooden Ganesha came riding on wheels, he bowed his head and yelled, '*Ganapati Bappa Moriya!*' When a girl dressed as Mother India went past, he bowed his head again and again. And now, as one foreign sadhu woman came down on a chariot with her three *chelas*, he and some of the boys blew kisses at her. (*Chela*, the old Hindi term for 'disciple', in casual conversation nowadays often simply refers to 'flunkey'.) Then came Hanuman, with Ram and Sita. And then a young boy dressed as Shiva, and a girl made up like Parvati, sitting on a stage mounted on a chariot. *Were they the main Shiva-Parvati act, or would there be more?* Who could tell? Who cared? Nobody, I guess, for soon another wedding band appeared and the road filled with dancing boys. If Rio had its Carnival, then Varanasi had Shivratri, I thought.

I was pushed back by this particularly raucous bunch among whom I saw at least three boys doing pelvic thrusts to a Bhojpuri number. They were wildly gesticulating, almost grinding. Samar was swaying his head to the tune too, *dhik dhik dhik dhina, dhik dhik dhik dhina.* I said in his ear, 'It's like they're sexually frustrated.'

'Oho, can you stop your firangi analysis?' he said, half-dancing.

A six-year-old boy astride his brother's shoulders was waving a plastic trident at the crowds. His face was painted blue and he had a plastic snake around his neck.

A hawker with pakoras stacked on his head stopped mid-walk, did a little twirl and a hip roll, and moved on.

And now somebody pulled Samar into the lot. He half resisted, but then let go. The song changed and the volume increased. *Har Har Mahadev Gange, Kashi Vishwanath Gange! BOOM, BOOM, BOOM.* Holi colour was thrown into the air, more shirts came off, and the dancing went up to the next level.

'This is incredible,' I said, also joining in.

Samar didn't say anything. He couldn't even hear me. He was dancing madly now. He and I and the entire world were dancing to *Har Har Mahadev Gange, Kashi Vishwanath Gange!*

At about 11:30 came the final procession of the Nagas and Aghoris. The City of Shiva gave the two sadhu sects pride of place for being the extreme devotees of Shiva they are. But it was also the night when the Aghoris and Nagas married Lord Shiva, spiritually speaking.

First came marching a slew of ash-faced babas in orange, raising their eyebrows and beating their damroos. And then came the Nagas. Hundreds and hundreds of them. *Thousands?* Nearly all the men were nude and coated from head to toe in ash, and all were declaiming, *Har Har Mahadev!* Their hands going up in the air, then falling, and their one chant rising and rising.

The Nagas were a sea of ebony, powerful and intense, and they closed in on us with such unstoppable energy that I was sure even the most doubting heart would stir awake with something more tangible than awe. And then, they were dancing. Not dancing with abandon like the boys before, but moving in their own way, waving their damroos and tridents and sticks. When they tossed ash in the air, spectators leaned in to drink the powdery rain.

A passing Naga smeared ash across my forehead and vanished into the grey sea like a ghost. *What the hell!* Was this an act of baptism? Was I a cypher being marked? I was tempted to get angry, but all I could expel was laughter. As if it mattered what had happened! What mattered was that tonight was wild and I was one with the wildness.

Now, finally, came the Aghoris: only some fifty men. Their bodies were covered in ash too, though they had a cloth tied around their waists and yellow wraps around their heads. They too were intoning *Har Har Mahadev!* But their demeanour was different to the Nagas. These men were calmer. Stonier. With skulls in their hands they exuded an aura of fear, and they knew they didn't require any additional histrionics.

The Aghor leading the group wore a necklace of skulls. I counted nine. These were human skulls. *Real* skulls.

By this time the crowd had dwindled to only about a hundred onlookers and everybody was following the Aghoris as they marched along. We halted at a tent stall run by the conventional orange-robed sadhus, the banner above which read: *Shiva Baraat Swagat Samiti*—the Shiva Wedding Procession Welcome Committee.

The drumming and the *Har Har Mahadev!* continued steadily until an elderly sadhu came on the microphone. He gave a laudatory speech about how his akhara welcomed the Aghoris because they were '*Bhagwan Shankar ka roop*', a version of Shiva, and it was only through their participation that the auspiciousness and greatness of Mahashivratri could be taken to the height of spirit it was at today.

'*Har Har Mahadev!*' the Aghoris roared collectively in thanks.

I don't recall the specifics of what happened afterwards. But I remember a couple dozen of us continued following the Aghoris down DG Road. I remember an incessant drumming and people making videos on their phones. And I remember that from somewhere there then appeared a bull.

The bull was jogging at first, but then it was charging, and everybody was running. Samar and I were too. We were running and laughing. And then I remember that Samar fell to the ground and his dhoti came undone. He stood up, his eyes lanced with bewilderment.

He turned his face away from the road and quickly put himself back together.

I remember laughing and laughing. Samar was too.

Later that night, at around 1 am, we sat under a yellow street light on the steps of Dashashwamedh Ghat. There was an extempore skit going on there and a boy with a dupatta around his head was making womanly sounds as his friends hooted and clapped. Beyond the Ganga, grey and discreet, the sandy plains were black and invisible.

The effect of the bhang had worn off, and I was thinking just how amazing tonight was. Just how full of both masti and bhakti. Only in this city, and on this night, could everything traditional turn on its head: orthodox sadhus bowing in submission to men who drank from skull cups; men dressed up as Shiva openly drinking bhang; men dancing as women. It was a night of complete clarity and obfuscation. A night that at once maintained and blurred the Old Order.

'So,' I said to Samar, savouring the cool air with my fingertips. 'What that baba said… And your experience. What do you think? Like…do you have a takeaway?'

Samar was admiring the performance with a look of glee. He turned to face me. 'I am happy right now, Sid,' he said. 'I get a good feeling here. What more should I say?'

A Last Swim Back to the City of Death

July 2022

What about the Aghoris though? you ask. No, I hadn't forgotten about them. Over the next few days I did wonder: Had I been asking these men the wrong questions? Rather than talking to them had I been talking *at* them, like they were some strange species? I mean, they *were* odd. They challenged you because they upended what you found disgusting. Because in embracing the disgusting they reached a place *beyond*. But did they?

Many men must certainly have adopted this life of indignation and intoxication to get away from reality. They coped with the real by showing us their middle finger. But so many of them were not offensive. Isolated and self-absorbed, they appeared to have taken to their strange path out of choice, not poverty. Or at the very least, not *just* poverty. The Aghoris believed that by not seeing a distinction between the pure and impure they had merged with Shiva. They had become 'a dried seed, unable to produce karma'. But other than my observations and much hearsay, by February 2020, I had only one proper interview, with that crazed drug-addled baba.

I had to go back. But then Covid-19 arrived, and the world stopped. Reality was upended, and through the high pandemic years of 2020 and 2021, like you, I was upended with it.

At first, not much happened. Time moved slowly and freshly. The mornings showed new birds and the afternoon revealed old shadows; and without cars on the roads and smoke in our skies my sense of space widened. There was even a nervous excitement in the air at what good things our new world might bring. But then came the storm. People were dying, and between looking after my parents' health and preserving my own sanity, I struggled. I felt again the faint presence of that old awful companion, depression, slithering its way back up. After a long time, I felt alone. I felt anxious.

Covid-19 was making us collectively confront death more than at any time in living memory. And seeing as our reality was so brutally fact-based, shouldn't I live in it instead of in my head? I found myself asking. Shouldn't I put God aside for some time? Especially as I was constantly yelling at my parents to 'Get real.' Both were now in their seventies and as far as I could tell seemed not to have understood the gravity of the situation at all.

'If the experts tell you isolate, you do it,' I said to papa. To mummy I said, 'Did even one holy man predict *this*? No!' I think even papa was irked.

But as time wore on and I returned to this book and interviewing and re-interviewing the people in it, I found myself falling back to old comforts. To becoming interested again in faith, even if not altogether believing in God. It was as though the very thing testing my faith—disease and death—was simultaneously intensifying my curiosity about it. I would have thought that the stark truth of having to fight an unfeeling, unalive virus—SARS-CoV-2—with masks, hand sanitizers and vaccines would lessen the hold of belief. *But the reverse was happening.*

At the start of the pandemic, religious gatherings had been blamed as super-spreader hotspots. But when some months later temples and mosques began to reopen, nowhere did the numbers fall. Despite worshippers testing positive at Tirupati and priests themselves contracting Covid-19, the devotees to the shrine only increased. In fact, in December 2020, devotees even protested curbs imposed by the Tirumala Tirupati Devasthanams on pilgrim footfall at the shrine, which at the time was already was letting in 30–35,000 devotees a day. By March 2022, the new Kashi Vishwanath Temple complex had an average footfall of over three times what it had been in the days before the pandemic.

And not just in India. Covid-19 appeared to have strengthened the faith of millions the world over! In the early days the Roman Catholic Church livestreamed the Pope's daily mass; and some parishes in the

US offered drive-through confessions; and the renowned wellness guru Deepak Chopra even offered 'a moment of Zen for people in a time of uncertainty', a meditation stream which crashed due to too much traffic.

Maybe the question at the back of everybody's mind was: *Why is God doing this?* It was an old inner disquiet among believers the Greek philosopher Epicurius had encapsulated best in these lines:

'Is God willing to prevent evil, but not able? Then he is not omnipotent. Is he able, but not willing? Then he is malevolent. Is he both able and willing? Then whence cometh evil? Is he neither able nor willing? Then why call him God?'

And yet, God had proven Himself wholly capable of adapting to our changed world. God was in no need of saving.

Varanasi. A day in July 2022. 12 pm

Outside, on either side of the gates sat statues of two human skulls. Inside, under an old banyan tree, stood a bunch of incense sticks delicately perfuming the monsoon air. Straight ahead was a large water tank, beckoning. At its centre stood the white statue of a bearded man wearing several bead necklaces, pearls and flowers. He was Baba Keenaram, the founder of the Aghoris; and away from the old streets and ghats of Kashi, in a more modern, spacious part of town, I was in Baba Keenaram's ashram.

The priest sitting on the floor at the entrance to the Aghori temple was speaking to another man. So, I went to the edge of the tank. The Kreen Kund, it was called, and I walked down the steps leading to the water. Large blue and yellow fish swam around my ankles inviting me deeper. A turtle, too! But I turned around and stepped out. I had to complete what I came here for.

The baba was alone now so I sat on the floor beside him. I bowed my head forward and he smeared my forehead with ash and handed me prasad: wrapped in paper, more ash.

After a few silent moments I said, 'Babaji, are you an Aghori'?

He nodded.

Of course he was. Stupid question. But then this man was wearing white robes, not black. And unlike the hirsute Aghoris I'd previously encountered, he was bald, clean shaven and overweight. In his fifties, he looked rather like a Jain monk.

'Some Aghoris wear black,' he said softly. 'Some grey. *Lekin yeh sab dikhaawa hai*...all this is for show. *Sachcha sadhu aapke saath saade vastra mein bhaitha hoga aur aapko pata nahin chalega*...a real sadhu maybe sitting beside you in ordinary clothes and you would never know he's a saint.'

I asked if he could tell me a little about Aghor philosophy and he said that all the information was contained in a booklet sold at the gates. There was a touch of weariness in his voice, too. But then he continued anyway: '*Shiva ke paanch mukhon mein se ek mukh aghor hai*,' he said. Aghor, or the Destroyer, is one of the five faces of Lord Shiva. The other faces are *Sadyojata* (the Revealer), *Vamadeva* (the Concealer), *Tatpurusha* (the Cosmic Being) and *Ishana* (the Lord).

'*Aghor saadhana Isa ke kaal se pracheen hai. Pracheen kal mein bahut sadhu aghor the, jaise Vasisht aur Dattatreya*...the aghor way precedes the Christian era; in the ancient days many sadhus were aghors, like Vasisht and Dattatreya. But the present aghor incarnation traces back to the 1600s. At this time, chaos reigned the earth, a king inflicted hardships on his people. And so Lord Shiva birthed Baba Keenaram.'

The baba's narration was a little tired and I wanted to break the ice but felt like I'd lost the skill on how. 'May I know your name, babaji?' I said. 'I've been talking to Aghoris along the ghats for some time and I haven't got a proper answer to my questions.'

'Badri,' the man said inaudibly.

'*Ji?*'

'I am Badri.' Badri—Lord Vishnu's name.

'*Ji*, Badriji. So, I'm looking for an answer... Who's a proper Aghori?' I took out my phone one last time and the man fell silent, staring at something behind me. I turned around but there was nobody there.

Then he met my eyes and sighed deeply.

Badri said that Aghoracharya Baba Keenaram was born on Chaturdashi in the (Hindu calendar) month of Bhadrapad in 1601 CE in Ramgarh village of Varanasi district (now Chandauli). When a childless couple—Shri Akbar Singh Raghuvanshi and Mansa Devi—finally had a boy, they were overjoyed. But for three days the boy neither cried nor suckled at his mother's breast. It was then that three monks (who were believed to be manifestations of Lord Sadashiva—Brahma, Vishnu and Mahesh) came to the house. When the trio whispered some mantras in the boy's ear he finally let loose a cry.

The boy was wed at an early age but his wife soon died and that was when his journey began. He walked in his khadaun from Junagadh through Kutch and the desert of Rajasthan and reached Ma Hinglaj Mata temple (in present-day Balochistan, Pakistan) where he did tapasya for many, many days.

Every day, a woman would come to feed him. So, one day he asked her who she was and she revealed herself to be Ma Hinglaj. She said that she would go to Kashi with him. She came here and immersed herself in the Kreen Kund.

Then, at Girnar Parvat in Junagadh, Baba Keenaram received the darshan of Guru Dattatreya, and thereafter he went to Kashmir, and to Delhi, before eventually returning to Kashi.

In those days, there was a Baba Kaluram who presided over the city. Baba Kaluram lived in a cottage beside the Assi River and he was waiting for Baba Keenaram at Harishchandra Ghat. But when Baba Keenaram arrived he was astonished by what he saw! Baba Kaluram was summoning skulls of burnt corpses at the cremation ground with his siddhis and feeding them *chana* (chickpeas). So, Baba Keenaram decided to show his own powers, too. He stopped the skulls from going towards Baba Kaluram, and right away, Baba Kaluram recognized him.

Baba Keenaram asked Baba Kaluram, 'Maharaj, what game are you playing? Come to your seat.'

And Baba Kaluram said, 'I'm very hungry, please arrange some food for me.'

So, Baba Keenaram said to the Ganga, '*Ganga Maiyya, la machhli to de ja...*Ganga Ma, give me some fish.' And three large fish sprang out of the river and fell into the smouldering fires of the cremation grounds.

The two mahatmas then ate the Ganga's offering as prasad.

'So, it was Baba Kaluram who awakened the consciousness of "Aghor" in Baba Keenaram,' Badri said.

He glanced over my shoulder again. But this I now saw was the man's habit. The Aghori was relishing recalling his old spirits. And I too was returning to my spirit of inquiry.

Another interesting story Badri told me was about an interaction between Shah Jahan and Baba Keenaram.

Having learnt all that Baba Keenaram was doing for the welfare of Kashi's residents, the Mughal emperor gifted him precious stones and gold. But the Aghori returned everything saying none of this was of use to him. Instead, he asked the emperor if the semi-burnt wood from the nearby cremation grounds could be sent to his ashram; it was of no use to anybody. Shah Jahan agreed. He decreed that wood amounting to one-*kaffan pratishat*—approximately one coffin—from all nearby villages and towns be sent to Baba Keenaram's ashram.

It was at this time that the custom of handing out ash from cremation grounds as prasad began. 'The *bhasm* [ash] that comes out of the *dhooni* [sacred fire] is the main prasad here,' Badri said. 'And it is for everyone, rich or poor. The dhooni which burns here is lit from the wood at Manikarnika Ghat, and Baba Keenaram had started the sacred fire himself.'

He gestured for me to lean closer, and he again smeared my forehead with ash.

3 pm

Badri has enough to eat but he lives without any comforts, I typed, *without a family. Yet he's so calm, like he has no desire to better his life. Like desire is never on his mind.*

I was sitting on the steps of Tulsi Ghat admiring the seagulls and intermittently recording my thoughts while a baba sitting on a ledge across was stealing glances at me. I looked up. The baba met my eyes and grinned. Like many sadhus, he was dark skinned and bearded and wore orange. But unlike the rest he had a red backpack beside him. Like Mr Dubey, the taxi driver, I put him down as a wanderer. Not a real sadhu.

What is it about these men that makes them this way? I wrote. Perhaps one thing is their sense of fatalism. Maybe it is their deterministic perspective that helps them carry on. Indeed, karma says that your present actions affect your future lives. But in practice, karma much more emphatically emphasizes how your present circumstances are the result of past lives beyond your control. It is as though our fatalistic attitude, out belief in kismet, this old stream running through Indian thought, prevents the poor from bettering their material conditions…

'It's so hot here,' the baba broke his silence. 'I was in Badrinath for two weeks and it was so nice there. I wish I could go back.' He gave a stoic laugh and rubbed his hands together. '*Lekin sadhu ke liye barsaat kya, garmi kya*…what does it matter to a sadhu if it's hot or it rains?'

I was in no mood to engage and I gave a thin smile. On previous visits I'd actively seek out such men but this time I was tired. I told myself I didn't want to detract from my sole assignment of speaking to real Aghoris, but for the first time in a long time I also had faith-fatigue. Maybe this was because of the pandemic. The harsh reality of the virus had brought home the many futilities of faith. But I think it was also age. I was now forty, and with adulting fast creeping up on me, I felt plainer and saner. I felt more surefooted of where I lay on the faith-spectrum and also more certain of what others might say. A good part of that youthful excitement from six years ago had evaporated and it was now being slowly substituted by what I can only call a dull pragmatism to get on with real life.

It was rather sad, I thought. Talking to babas was like visiting a new mall. The layout was slightly different but you got the same brands.

The man's name was Chandrama Saraswati. He was sixty, from Bengal, but kept moving.

'Where were you before Badrinath?' I said.

'Kamakhya.'

'Assam?'

Wow. 'You went by train?'

'Yes, train and bus,' he said. 'A man like you gave me money to go there. *Nar mein bhi Narayan aate hain kabhi kabhi*…God comes as man, sometimes.' He wiggled his chin. '*Kyunki bhagwaan chariya hai, woh pehchaan mein nahi aata*…because God is a trickster, He is not easily recognized.'

The man chuckled and I smiled. Maybe you got the same brands, but I was still buying.

I looked down at my phone. Ah! *Found him.*

6:30 pm

Om Prakash, the boatman-guide was waiting for me at Scindia Ghat. With his earphones in and his smirk in place, the young man appeared to have retained his youthful face and I-don't-give-a-toss expression. But his hair, which I hadn't noticed before, now fell in a big swish over his forehead.

'How are you?' I used English.

He pushed his hair back. 'Very good.' His eyes were dopey, but in the present. He drew a joint from his pocket and offered it to me. I declined and he put it back safely.

'Okay, so now we going to Manikarnika Ghat. You giving me what you like later. I am not asking for price now. You see yourself how much you giving? Okay, cool?'

'Cool.' I laughed. I was definitely a buyer.

Manikarnika Ghat was hot and eventful even from a hundred metres away. But as I stepped into this open air cremation ground I was again assaulted by the *aliveness* of death. It does hit you. Every single time. The doms, the corpse burners, busy in their jobs. The stray dogs (three) loitering about. The gloomy drifters. The smoke. The ash raining down from the skies. The sting in my eyes. And the dead, just burning.

And right in the centre of the fires there was—unmistakably—an Aghori. Sitting cross-legged with his back upright, he was petting a stray and talking to another man.

The Aghori looked about fifty. He had very dark skin, long, unkempt hair, a part of which he'd tied up into a bun on top, a greying beard and several rudraksh necklaces around his neck. The younger man also had on a black dhoti, but he wore smart-looking glasses. He was obviously not an Aghori. Unlike the baba who, with his shrivelled skin and skeletal frame, was evidently poor, the young man, though thin, appeared healthy.

I went closer. The two men were speaking in Tamil and I turned to Om Prakash: *Know them?* He shook his head. So, I stood nearby, waiting, and in a few minutes the younger man noticed me, and after I'd introduced myself—a routine I shan't bore you with again—I was interviewing the Aghori, Baba Lingaraja, through Prithviraj, who had agreed to be my interpreter.

Prithviraj, thirty-two, was from Salem, Tamil Nadu and had come to Kashi to meditate. He had met Baba Lingaraja Aghori on the ghats only two weeks before. Baba Lingaraja was forty-eight and came from Peraiyur, a town near Madurai and spoke only Tamil.

'He basically came here to pray for his family because they are facing financial problems,' Prithviraj said. 'Because they have no money... And not only he, but his father and grandfather were all like that. No money. So, he came here.'

This man was not a proper renunciant then? 'Has babaji been inducted as an Aghori at an ashram?' I asked.

There was a long exchange between the two but which in the end only confirmed my suspicion. Baba Lingaraja had had no formal induction as an Aghori sadhu. He was a mason, a daily wage labourer, and had come to Kashi to pray because Lord Shiva had appeared to him.

'Shiva appeared to him in his village and instructed him to meditate for three years. He says that Shiva said he would take care of him. He feels like the Lord gives him direct instructions. He says Shiva has told him that after he completes his tapasya here he will himself give him an initiation.'

Baba Lingaraja was inspecting me from behind. *Why did all Aghoris have such red eyes?*

He said something to Prithviraj who translated. 'Five years back he prayed to God in Rameswaram to remove the curse on his family. He used to have a wife and children at the time. But his intuition then led him to Kashi and he's now living here alone. So, he says he is a baba only. He has no family.'

Baba Lingaraja meditated at five ghats: Panchganga Ghat, Manikarnika Ghat, Dashashwamedh Ghat, Kedar Ghat and Harishchandra Ghat and he'd been following this routine for the last three years, before which he lived in Prayagraj.

As Baba Lingaraja chattered on, his face tightened, then wrinkled, and while I couldn't understand him I felt his words stretched into the ether. He spoke like a homeless man who had a lot on his mind but had lost the art of communication. He clearly liked talking but Prithviraj was finding it hard to keep up.

'Can you ask him why he chose this path?' I said. 'Why not become a normal sadhu?'

Prithviraj answered after another discourse. 'If somebody wants money, they have to do it full time. He says that just like that, if someone wants meditative powers they have to give everything to tapasya.' He furrowed his brow; his forehead exposed a deep line. 'But these saatvic [ritually pure] people...they are mostly doing it for money. They want to live a comfortable life. They want their devotees to give them money. But he'—that is, Lingaraja—'doesn't care about comforts... These babas do not care about anything. They are not bothered about dead bodies, not even their dress. They sit naked and meditate till they get some siddhis, some enlightenment. He says that is the difference.'

Baba Lingaraja made an assenting sound.

There was a grain of truth in what he said, I felt. Like Badri, Baba Lingaraja had no desire for material comforts. But then wasn't it his dire material condition which brought him on this path? And so what if he wasn't a 'proper Aghori'. Aghoris were hardly proper anyway. Who was I to decide these things? But I wanted something concrete. Something which tied into my comprehension of these men. There was no easy way to put this, so I just did.

'Do you eat human flesh?'

'There are some aatmas, spirits, and they don't liberate due to past karmas,' Baba Lingaraja said through Prithviraj. 'They roam around like ghosts. They are not at peace. So, I control them and guide them to peace. To remove their bad karma, I sometimes eat flesh. But rarely.'

Didn't the Aghoris eat human flesh to break the illusory barrier between what was pure and impure? I told Prithviraj what I understood about Aghor philosophy and he turned back to Baba Lingaraja.

Yes, I know, Dear Reader, I was leading my subject now, but I couldn't help it. The man was yielding nothing new. And maybe I didn't want to see it, but of course I did. *He was right there*: this miserable, poor man, drunk on some substance—or his dreams.

'Yes, there are many reasons,' Baba Lingaraja said. 'But *I* do it to bring peace to restless spirits.'

I paid Baba Lingaraja for his time and he touched the money to his forehead.

'Can I take your photo?' I then said.

'*Am. Am*,' he said, his facial muscles loosening, and right away adopted the padmaasana posture. As if in deep meditation, he closed his eyes and joined his thumb and index finger. Om Prakash sniggered. I wanted to say, *Be natural.* But I let it go. I took a bunch of photos and showed them to him and he wobbled his head, half-smiled.

Baba Lingaraja's eyes were red, but he didn't seem bitter or angry. Rather he looked defeated and sad. His stray dog scurried back to him and he fondled its neck, dug his face into its body. He looked up, smirked again. Yes, he was a kind man, too. The sort of man who'd learnt to find little joys in a miserable life: in petting a dog, in ganja, and in shutting his eyes to the world.

An equation floated up in my mind: Poverty→Fatalism→God. And sometimes, really, God = Dog.

'I have done electrical engineering,' Prithviraj said. 'I am thirty-two now, but still I am not married.' He sounded much too serious.

'That's okay. I am not married either.' I laughed and he bobbed his head, didn't smile.

But the young man wanted to talk to me. In these burning ghats we were most alike: two English-speaking urban men finding our way. 'See, in my life, I was in deep confusion,' he said. 'Like, what should I do? I felt like I was not realizing my purpose so I told my guruji about this and he led me to do meditation here. And the process is still ongoing.

'When I was sixteen I learnt meditation. I went to temples, I did pooja, but even then I couldn't realize my purpose. I read the Bhagavad Gita. In the Gita, Krishna says that everybody has their own responsibility. One must do their own duty without any expectation… But I felt like I could not find my responsibility. So, my guru told me to go to Manikarnika Ghat in Banaras. He said I would realize my purpose here. I would get some clarity. So, it has been two months and I think I'm getting it slowly, slowly.

'… I have got rid of some fears. I used to have a fear of heights. I would not even go to the terrace in my house. Now I sit there'—he pointed at a building—'and I don't mind.'

Prithviraj fidgeted with his hands, picked up a twig. His nails were bitten down, uneven. 'Two days back I saw a man drown in front of me at Scindia Ghat. Nobody could save him. He died. Had I seen something like this sometime back, I would be shaking for days. But with so many bodies burning here, I feel this is life. Life and death… Like, that man went into the water and then in fifteen minutes he died.' The stress line on his forehead resurfaced. 'But then I saw that this was not giving me a shock. Otherwise I would be fainting. Maybe even getting a fever. But I saw that this is what God has decided—to liberate him. And I felt a little relaxed.' His crease faded. 'Still, [some] fears are there and I hope to come out of these also.'

Prithviraj was articulate. But he was so scared that I had to restrain the urge to put my hand on his shoulder. An older equation floated up: Fear→God.

Was I like this six years back? *I hope not.*

'Your tapasya is making you stronger, I hope?' I said.

'Oh, yes. And my self-confidence is also boosting.'

'That's good.'

My eyes were stinging from the fires and I stood up. But I had to ask Prithviraj what his future plans were. Would he return to Bengaluru, where he now lived, and get a job?

'I have got some clarity,' he said. 'I'm getting visions, like that. Not thoughts, but visions. Teaching spirituality. Teaching mediation. Teaching is what I am seeing. I'm getting glimpses that I should share what I've learnt with the world. I'm feeling this is my purpose. But I have to get it more strongly.'

The twig in his hand snapped and he threw it away. 'So, you are leaving?'

'Yes. But I'll come back.' I looked around. 'My guide says that one Aghori will come at night.'

'Oh, yes. Kannan Baba. He is also from the South. From Kerala.' Kannan is Tamil for Krishna.

'Oh! Can you introduce me?' Prithviraj was proving way more helpful than Om Prakash.

'Yes. You come at nine. He will come at nine or ten, like that. If you want to talk with a proper Aghori, I think he is the most proper one.' His stress line returned, but it now lent him a sagacious aspect. 'Kannan baba has seen with his Third Eye.'

I enlarged my eyes.

'Yes, he has seen *it*,' he said.

'Hmm, so I'll see you in an hour.'

I dusted off my jeans, sanitized my hands and fiddled with the mask in my pocket. The Omicron-variant wave had begun. But as with faith, Covid-fatigue was setting in too. Besides, putting on a face mask is the best way to block open communication, right?

'Some of these babas,' Prithviraj said. 'They don't care about anything. I've realized this. They sleep anywhere, eat anything. And this why they get enlightenment. I think you only get it when you stop caring about your comforts.'

Through the smoke I saw Baba Lingaraja laughing and tickling his dog. I licked my lips and could taste the burning flesh in the back of my throat.

'And over here it is not just babas, even some foreigners are living like this. There is this boy from Peru. He is like you. He is also not following a guru but finding his own way. He is making a documentary about the babas here. His name is Suryadas. He doesn't wear sandals also. He eats at the Satuwa Baba Ashram. He's living like babas only.'

Om Prakash materialized along with his blasé expression. 'I know Suryadas. You want meeting?'

'Yes. Where were you?'

'I am here only.' Surrounded by the fires, Om Prakash's eyes appeared even redder but he was still his detached, frisky self. 'Right now he is sitting in Lalita Ghat, I think so.'

'Let's go then.'

8:12 pm

Prithviraj was right. If I found him to be a *little* like me then I thought Suryadas was a whole lot like me. The young Peruvian was a slim man with a fair complexion, but his eyes were dark, as was his hair, which he kept long and open. He wore a yellow dhoti and had a red tika on his forehead, but spoke a fluent American English. And as you'll see, his outlook, like his looks, was also a product of miscegenation, a pleasing blend of East and West.

The young man was sitting on a ledge at the ghat and belting out a *kirtan*—'*Aao baitho japo Hari ka naam Shivji ke mandir mein.*' Come sit and sing Vishnu's name in Shiva's temple. And from the moment I heard him I felt that curious recognizable something: *That uninhibitedness of a Sufi, that unfathomable cry out for God.*

Om Prakash introduced us. 'He is also doing talkings with sadhus,' he said in his offhand way and plonked down to one side of Suryadas. I took the seat on the other side and introduced myself a little better.

Om Prakash lit up a joint, took a drag and passed it to Suryadas. He tilted his head to one side and took a pull on it. At the start the young man spoke a tad formally. 'Suryadas is my spiritual name,' he said. 'But my birth name is Alvaro. I am from Peru, South America, and I came to India to find a deeper connection with myself. And with God. So, I have been in Rishikesh, Dharamshala and now I'm in Varanasi for the last two weeks.' But when I relaxed a little, asked Om Prakash for a Gold Flake, lit it up and said, 'Slow down, man. We have time,' he laughed.

He tilted his head back, took another long pull and released smoke through his nostrils in a way that suggested he'd been waiting a long time for a hit. Then he gathered up his dhoti and straightened his back. 'I think I have been looking for a connection since I was five or six,' he said. 'First I was looking for it in my faith, in Christianity, but as I grew older, the connection was lost because of the institutional part of it. There were many rituals and these exterior things did not tell me about how to develop a deeper connection within myself. They did not give me specific techniques to deepen that connection. And so in my search for finding something deeper I came to a yoga class and from there I came to know more about India.'

Like Martin from Switzerland, Alvaro also came to India through yoga and a Vipassana Meditation course 'from where it all slowly started to come together'.

A couple of years before, Alvaro had worked with 'master plants' in the jungles of Peru. 'You know like in India there is the *Soma*, there are master plants in the jungles of Peru which activate your consciousness,' he said.

Soma, of course, was the Vedic ritual drink, made from a plant of the same name. It was mentioned in the Rig Veda. There was no consensus on what the plant exactly was but there were candidates. The British historian Michael Wood had suggested that it was *ephedra*.

('When infused in boiling water ephedra produces quite a powerful sensation of euphoria'—as I can testify!—'But here it may have been mixed with other ingredients—poppy seed and cannabis—a fitting tipple for Indra!' he writes in his book *The Story of India.*) But an R. Gordon Wasson, an American author, ethnomycologist, and a former Vice President for Public Relations at JP Morgan & Co, said in his 1971 paper 'The Soma of the Rig Veda: What was it?', that Soma was a mushroom, the fly-agaric, called by mycologists *Amanita muscaria.*

The term 'master plants', on the other hand, referred to certain plants of the Amazon region which are believed to carry strong curative and spiritual powers. The most well-known one is Ayahuasca (a word which refers both to the plant and, as a quick Google search will reveal, 'a type of brew made from ingredients with hallucinogenic properties. Though some claim that it can benefit brain health and well-being, it is also associated with several potential risks').

'Each master plant has its own spirit,' Suryadas said. 'In the jungles of Peru we believe this. Like Ayahuasca is an incredible healing plant, but its spirit has to be experienced to be understood. In the jungles of Peru there is a different approach to spirituality. It is based more on a transcendental experience in which you get in touch with the gods or the spirits. Then you come back to the regular state of consciousness. It is based on actual experience rather than some dogma behind it. It is about the experience and out of that experience comes, let's say, the harmony in life… And I went to one centre in the jungle which is a pioneer for integrating yoga philosophies with the use of these psychedelic plants.'

A seriousness came to Suryadas's face as he explained these things to me. And I also noted that he'd said 'jungles of Peru' three times. If he saw a touch of surprise on my face, he wasn't wrong. Psychedelics were hallucinogens, I thought. They altered your mental state. They couldn't sharpen it, could they? So, he was quick to say that 'Ayahuasca is actually a mixture of different plants and it has been made for hundreds if not thousands of years by the shamans in the jungle.'

He gazed wordlessly into the distance and I heard the clanking of a metal skimmer on a griddle. I could smell potato frying.

'How shall I put it?' he said. 'You can say these plants can give you a darshan of a higher spiritual dimension. So, you really have to experience it. And I want to now integrate the shamanic path I have learnt in the jungles of Peru with the yogic path and the Bhakti path I have learnt here. My path is to integrate the Eastern traditions of yoga philosophy and Hinduism with my local wisdom of working with plant medicine. This is what I mean by integration.'

Like Martin from Switzerland, Suryadas spoke coherently. And like him, his manner was unguarded. Why, I thought, like Martin and Prithviraj and myself, Alvaro must have been a social misfit. I could see it in his trusting eyes, in his open smile, in the four pooja threads around his wrist. *I saw it*: his dissatisfaction with the staid path which had led him to seek something *beyond*. Can science ever obliterate such curiosities? I wonder.

All the weed smoke had made me rather hungry. I bought a plate of aloo tikki from the hawker nearby and offered it to my two companions as well. Each took a bite.

'My journeys are happening on their own,' Suryadas continued. 'I didn't come to India thinking, *Let me connect the two philosophies.* These things are just happening. I am working on intuition and this intuition is guiding me forward. My only intention is to surrender to this feeling. And what I have seen is that my goal is to integrate what I see here on the streets of Varanasi with what I saw in the jungles of Peru.'

As I chomped down on the hot potatoes I realized I'd forgotten to ask him his age. He sounded so perceptive, even a little precocious. But he looked only twenty-five.

'How old are you by the way?'

'Twenty-seven,' he said. 'But I have been interested in spirituality since I was eighteen.'

'Did you find something in common between Shamanic practices and Hindu and Buddhist ones, then?' This came out somewhat glibly but Suryadas answered without blinking.

'All is one, man. All is one,' he said. 'There is one summit but many ways to get there.' And I just knew he'd said these words before.

'From the minute I arrived here, I felt like I had an old memory of having lived here many times. Maybe previous lives, *haan*? So, it felt like a recognition of something I already knew. And I found I blend in so well with the locals.' He grinned at Om Prakash and Om Prakash smiled with his eyes. 'In India, in each place I had a different mission: in Rishikesh it was to spread more kirtans. In Dharamshala, it was Vipassana Meditation. And in Nainital, I was in Kainchi Dham connecting with my guru, Neem Karoli Baba. For me it is interesting to mix different elements and create my own way. Because this means you are being authentic to yourself.'

'Yes,' I said. 'Even when you speak to different sadhus you'll see they have different approaches.'

'Exactly. You've to be authentic to your self.'

'Exactly.'

I told the young man it was a pleasure speaking to him and got up. But then I looked back: 'Can I ask you one personal question, actually, if you don't mind?'

'Sure.'

'Was there something that happened in your life that brought you on this path?'

Suryadas smiled a boyish smile. 'Yes, I had a profound spiritual experience when I first smoked ganja when I was seventeen.'

I laughed. 'Seriously?'

'Yes, I smoked ganja with a girl I wanted to be with. She was smoking a little and I was smoking a lot. And I was chilled'—as he put it—'for the first fifteen minutes. And then I felt more chilled so I thought this is the effect of the ganja.' Om Prakash was gawking eagerly at Suryadas who had now reverted to being teenage Alvaro. 'But then all the ganja hit my head and in that moment I had an out-of-body experience and I thought that I was dead… My whole body was cold. But it was a new type of cold. I mean, I imagined that this was what being dead felt like. It was horrible. I had entered a deep state of paranoia and sadness. And that girl later told me that I was in this state for three hours, but for me it lasted a whole life!'

Alvaro was giving way to Suryadas now: 'This may sound like nothing but this experience was so tough that when I came out I made a commitment to myself to do everything that I could so that when I die, I will be ready. That day was the shift in me. It made me realize how afraid I was in life. I had so many fears that from the very next day I began to search for a way to let go of those fears. And the ultimate fear is death. So, that's why I'm here in Varanasi. Because I felt that over here I could make death my friend…'

He was going to be here for another week, he said. Then he would head to Mexico, to a Hanuman temple—the only Hanuman temple in Mexico! Eventually, he planned to return to his country and start a spiritual retreat in the mountains of Machu Picchu.

I looked at my phone: 9:13 pm. As I walked down the steps, Suryadas went back to singing: '*Bolo bolo, submil bolo Om Namah Shivaaya, Om Namah Shivaaya…*' His accent was Spanish, but his cadence was resonant and pitch-perfect.

I turned to Om Prakash. 'Would that Aghori have come now?'

It was 10:45 pm when Kannan Baba sauntered into Manikarnika Ghat. Baba Lingaraja was meditating unobtrusively in a new spot. Prithviraj and Om Prakash got to bantering about this and that. A worker at the ghat was striking a burning pyre with a wooden log, freeing sparks and embers and a shaft of smoke going up into the heavens.

Prithviraj's hair and mine was covered in ash. 'Yes, it is him,' Prithviraj whispered. He had told me about how well-connected Kannan Baba was. How he had been to thirty-two countries and had tremendous knowledge of the scriptures. But the man before me—the Aghori who strode up to a metal casket used for burning bodies and sat back in it like it was an easy chair and lit a joint—looked nothing like the picture I'd created in my mind.

Kannan Baba was about five-foot-ten, had muscular arms, a hairy chest and open, black curly hair. His face was unkemptly bearded, but striking, like that of a villain in an '80s Hindi movie. He had a certain swagger, too, the way he was strutting around in his bright purple dhoti.

Prithviraj said he was thirty-nine, a year younger than me. But he was intimidating. What was he flaunting though? *His virility? His position?* Whatever it was it worked because there were three chelas trailing him.

A man came up to him and said something in Hinglish. I caught only snippets: 'I am so angry… Next time, I will…' And Kannan Baba heard him out, then said, 'Don't worry. I will deal with it. But don't be angry. Does anger solve anything?' He touched his hand to his chest. 'Only give love. This is what I am saying. Only give love.'

He eyed me, looked away, then looked back again. The way he chaired over affairs here had conveyed everything he wanted to say: *I was on his turf and had to give him the due respect.*

I stepped forward. 'Om, babaji,' I said. 'I have been talking to babas and I'd like to interview you, if you don't mind. I have heard so much from—'

'What have you heard?' He blew out smoke rings.

'*Ji*, I have heard you've been meditating here for eight years. That, you've—'

'First you tell me, what do you understand by Aghor?'

He was intense, if unpredictable. Like a drunk man pretending to be sober. He could embrace you but he could just as well stab you.

'I understand that Aghor is a way of *saadhana*,' I said. Spiritual practice.

More smoke rings. 'It is not a way,' he said. 'It is a stage.'

Kannan Baba's English was the English of a man educated in the language. His demeanour was confident, too. Unlike Baba Lingaraja, he came from privilege.

But if Baba Lingaraja was driven by poverty and Alvaro by inquiry, what was this man driven by? Whatever it was, he was rather severe about it.

His joint went out and a chela ran up with a match. But before he could reach him, Kannan Baba went over to a burning pyre and lit it himself. He then walked over to a corner behind a pillar where wooden logs were stacked and took a piss. I turned to Om Prakash. He giggled.

Now I am not one to preach propriety, but this was all a bit much coming from a *holy man*. Could a man who claimed to have glimpsed God behave like this? I was suppressing the urge to walk away, but when Kannan Baba returned, I pressed on. I told him about my association with Shivsagar Ashram, and my yaatras to the Char Dham. I told him I was recording my experiences. Kannan Baba smoked along as if he didn't care, but he was gauging something about me. He knew about Shivsagar Ashram, he said. He knew that it followed Shankaracharya's teachings.

'Shankaracharya was a Namboodiri Brahmin, like me. I am from the same community,' he said. He narrowed his eyes. 'So, say. What do you understand by Aghor? What to you is Hinduism? What is God?' He flicked his joint into the fire. 'People are asking me why I am here. People are asking me this all the time. I am a Rawal. Men from my community are priests in Badrinath. Can you tell me what I'm doing here?'

He didn't break his gaze. 'I am here because after everything everybody lands up here only. You understand?' His eyes were penetrating. 'Some people are saying Aghoris are eating dead bodies. All things, people are saying. But you want to see what an Aghori does?'

I nodded and he motioned one chela, a thin young chap, to come over. His T-shirt had 'Being Human' written on the front. *Weirdly apt.* The chela pressed play on his phone and a video came on of Kannan Baba meditating on top a funeral pyre about to be set alight. He swiped right: Kannan Baba was standing on one leg and submersing his other one in and out of a cylindrical metallic cage propped up beside an open fire. Another swipe: Kannan Baba was beating his chest with a metal chain with a fireball attached on the end.

Kannan Baba wobbled his head. '*This* is Aghor,' he said.

What I'd just seen matched closely with many YouTube videos on these men. All were designed to shock the viewer. I wasn't shocked. I don't want an episode from *Fear Factor*, I wanted to say. I want you to tell me something original.

'I went to Baba Keenaram's ashram earlier,' I said. 'One baba told me a little about Aghor saadhana…'

Kannan Baba gave a long sigh. 'Before Baba Keenaram there was Baba Kaluram. But if you want to understand Aghor you have to go back to basics. To the original state.' He shook his head. 'I think you are not understanding it.'

He leaned back in the metal casket. 'What is Hinduism, you know? Hinduism is not idol worship. There is no idol worship in the Vedas. What is happening today is actually mixture of idol worship and Buddhism.'

'Buddhism?'

'Yes. What we are doing today is the Buddhist way, not the Vedic way. But we…we are at a different stage.' His unwavering glare was making me uneasy. 'Okay, tell me. If I take your hand and write "sugar" on it and you lick it, will you find it sweet?'

'Erm…no?'

'Of course, no! This is what. When a baby is born, he is also an Aghor. A baby is tasting his shit and piss and mother's milk and for him all are same. He is tasting everything. A baby does not know what is clean and dirty, everything is the same. Only later his mother and father are telling him the difference.'

I nodded and he lowered his voice.

'Aghor is about unlearning what you have learnt. And learning everything again, with your senses,' he said.

Now this was worth noting down. Aghor was about returning to an original state of awareness. A kind of primal sensory experience.

But I also thought: if it's about the damn senses then follow yours. *Leave!*

Mercifully, a few moments later a chela brought a woman forward. She was in a salwar-kameez, likely not from an affluent background and of about my age. She bowed in a namaste to Kannan Baba. She was also from Delhi.

'Oh, he is also from Delhi,' Kannan Baba said. 'What do you want to talk about? Tell me. I do everything in the open.' The chelas, Prithviraj, Om Prakash and a handful of others were watching expectantly.

The woman gave a sheepish smile, looked down to the ground and shifted on her feet. The chela then whispered something in Kannan Baba's ear and he rose.

'Come with me.' He then led the woman to a corner where the two sat down to discuss the occult solutions to certain real life problems. Presumably.

Kannan Baba hadn't let me record him. And so, sitting on the ghat steps, I was typing everything down.

'What are you doing here?' a man said and I looked up. He was middle-aged, scruffily dressed, and sounded very concerned for me.

He was Om Prakash's friend, another boatman. Om Prakash told him what I was doing and he laughed.

'Kannan Baba,' he said mockingly. '*Arre, woh toh chu—ya hai. Logon ko ullu banaata hai*...that man is an arsehole. He makes a fool out of people. If you want to speak to proper Aghoris you should go only to Baba Keenaram Ashram. Look nowhere else.'

Om Prakash looked at me. He said nothing but his look to his friend said it all: *Don't spoil this. He'll pay me.*

I had to smirk. 'And what have you done? You haven't shown me one new thing.'

Om Prakash giggled. 'See, I'm not saying anything. These babas, they not telling you something you don't know. They only saying some things you know from before.' He stood up and held out his hand. I took it and he pulled me up. 'But I'll take you to one new place.'

I was then led to a spot tucked away behind Manikarnika Ghat where, in a dark alcove invisible to all but those who know of its presence, stood a small dingy shrine. Inside soot-covered walls sat Baba Keenaram's picture in front of which burnt the dhooni, the sacred Aghori fire. Om Prakash bent down and lit another cigarette from its flames. Then he took a bit of ash and put it on my forehead and giggled again.

It was past midnight when I walked down the ghat steps. Kannan Baba was still talking to the woman from Delhi but he spotted me sneaking away. He called out, but I didn't turn around. My legs were taking me forward even though I was tempted to look back. I kept walking, going further along the ghats, and the fires and voices and ghosts receded further and further into the distance.

Back in my room, I bolted the door, undressed and went straight into the shower.

So, can I put down for you what I gleaned from these men?

That night, I tried. I wrote that even if the Aghoris were saying different things, they were saying the same sort of thing. They were saying: this is our way. In roundabout ways, they were saying that if we can remove fears and judgement we can dissolve our artificial human borders. We can feel God in all people, in all things. They were saying that their proximity to death had revealed that Everything was One.

'They were saying that just like the earth sees no difference between fallen flowers and shit, they make no distinction between kings and lepers.'

I put this to Badri at Baba Keenaram Ashram the following morning and he said, '*Bilkul yahi hai*...this is it. *Aap samajh gaye*... you have got it.'

I also got that each Aghori was human and so as different to the next person as one believer is to another. But I had to clarify some things: '*Kya Aghor tapasya sanatan dharm ke vipreet hai?* I said. 'Is Aghori philosophy "opposed to" traditional Hinduism?' What I really wanted to say was 'unorthodox', but characteristic of me, the wrong word came out.

'No, it's not,' he said. 'It just looks it. People say we eat the flesh of corpses, but I tell you this is wrong. People say Aghoris drink alcohol like it is water. You must have seen a TV show about Aghoris on Aaj Tak channel?'

I shook my head.

'In it they show a man drinking liquor out of a skull cup on Harishchandra Ghat. All this is wrong.'

Badri asked if I'd heard of Raja Chait Singh of Banaras. I half-nodded, thinking instead: Who was an Aghori, then? Were neither Kannan Baba nor Baba Lingaraja real Aghoris?

'During Baba Keenaram's time the king of the area was Raja Chait Singh. On his walks he would often see Baba Keenaram wandering the ghats and one day Baba Keenaram said to him, "Please give me something to eat." So, the Raja said to his minister, "See that corpse floating in the Ganga? Give it to him." Baba Keenaram then covered the Raja's offering with the cloth he had around himself, and when he uncovered it, the Raja, to his astonishment, saw there now lay spread before him the choicest dishes! *Ek se ek pakwaan, jo Raja ko bhi naseeb na ho.*

'Raja Chait Singh then asked Baba Keenaram for forgiveness, but the Baba didn't relent. Even today, Raja Chait Singh's fort is lying *banjar*. Barren, lifeless. You can go see it for yourself.'

Badri glanced over my shoulder. 'The ones who eat flesh, they like to show off. They are not real Aghoris. *Yeh fardi hain*...they are fakes,' he said. 'Yes, it is true,' he went on, '*kaiyon mein aise siddhiyan aati hain. Jo shakti yeh log prapt karte hain, uski wajah se yeh log sab karte hain, jaise aag mein haath daalna, aur yeh sab. Jab yeh logon ko dikhaate hain, uska parinaam hai ki yeh shakti hi bhugatti hai.*' Some of them do acquire special powers, he said. And this power allows them to do extraordinary things, like putting your hand in the fire, and so on. But the result is that the sacred power suffers because of their abuse of it.

Badri once again spoke gently, respectably, like a *proper* sadhu. But wasn't it curious how even these men who'd shed all barriers between the real and illusory drew lines among themselves?

'What about consuming shit?' I said. I didn't mean to offend the man. I just couldn't recall the Hindi equivalent of 'faeces' (*veshta*).

Fortunately, Badri didn't take offence. 'This is correct,' he said. '*Mutra ka aur veshta ka sevan kiya jaata hai. Lekin sab koi kar nahi paate. Bahut kam kar paate hain. Jo wahaan ja paate hain, woh bahut kam hain.*' Urine and faeces is ingested, he said. But not everyone is able to do this. Only a few can reach there.

Reach where?

He looked over my shoulder again in the direction of the skull gates. The past two days had considerably inured me to the Aghori way but Badri saw through my disgust. '*Yeh sevan ka khul ke prachaar thodi kiya jaata hai. Yeh gupt roop se hai*...such consumption is not openly propagated; it is kept a secret,' he said. 'It's only for those who reach there with their spirituality.'

Reach where?

He dwelled a moment. 'There is a reason for doing this. Have you observed dogs?'

I nodded.

'Have you paid attention to their behaviour? Have you noticed that they lick their genitals the whole day?'

I nodded again.

'It is because they do this that their senses become sharp. And this is why they see things that we can't.'

It was weird, I thought. But there was the weight of lived experience in the man's words, too. Like me, Badri was drawing patterns in nature.

Sitting in the Shiv Ganga Express back to Delhi, my smaller thought broke out of parentheses. What Badri said was no different than what

Kannan Baba said—about returning to the unconditioned state of your senses as a baby—was it? Nor was it more comprehensible than what poor Baba Lingaraja had said—about how consuming the flesh of the dead released the shackles of tormented souls. I was only paying him heed because he spoke free of affectation and wretchedness. Because he looked somewhat respectable. *Why couldn't these men get real?*

Then, just two days later, I did a U-turn. Lying in bed I asked myself if was I right to question these men who'd seen things I couldn't see. Things I had myself come to feel made their minds focused and bodies hard, such that they carried on wearing nothing, sleeping anywhere and eating anything, while here I was cursing my luck at having lost my sense of taste and smell after contracting Covid-19.

Who was I to question Badri who had arrived at the same truth I had of a Oneness in Everything? The same Badri who said: '*Aghor ka ek varna hai Ganga. Ganga mein jo kuch bhi dalo sab pavitra rehta hai. Brahmin ho ya jo bhi ho, Ganga mein sab ek samaan hai.*' One example of aghor is the Ganga. Whatever you put in the Ganga becomes pure. Be it a Brahmin or anybody. Everybody in the Ganga is one.

God, I really was my mother's son!

PART VII

Union with the Sea

March & April 2015

Merger in Ganga Sagar

The Sagar Island lies about one hundred kilometres south of Kolkata in the estuary of the Hooghly River, the eastern tributary of the Ganga, where it meets the Bay of Bengal. Every year on Makar Sankranti (mid-January) a large number of Hindus congregate at Ganga Sagar, an expansive grey beach on the southern tip of the island, for this is where the Ganga joins the sea.

On account of the sheer difficulty involved in getting here, in the olden days Hindi-speaking yaatris had a saying: '*Baaki tirath baar baar, Ganga Sagar ek baar!*' Literally, 'Other pilgrimages, many times; Ganga Sagar, one time!' And so, as if keeping to this guideline, it is only once that I've visited it.

March 2015

It was dinner time and my family—which tonight was my aunts Rashmi Masi and Minna Masi, my cousin Mayank, Rashmi Masi's son, and his wife Rachna, mummy and I—were discussing where to go for a break on the long Easter weekend of April 4th and 5th.

'Goa will be warm,' I said. 'But it's a good option.'

'Actually, even Phuket can work,' Rachna said. And Rashmi Masi, who was delicately dipping a section of her dosa into chutney, suggested Bengaluru, the city in which the Malhotra sisters had grown up, when my mother jumped in.

'Actually, Swamiji is taking us to Ganga Sagar for a dip during the full moon eclipse, and since we are going there, some of us are also going to Puri before that.' She swallowed her food at length. 'Sehdev is coming. And Sarla Behenji, Veeranwali Mataji. And Prahlad and Saroj and all will also be there. Over one hundred people.'

The names were familiar, all Swami Shraddhanandji's devotees.

But while Sarla Aunty and Veeranwali Mataji were old followers of mummy's guru, Maharajji, Prahlad and his wife Saroj were new entrants on the scene. They saw Swami Shraddhanandji as their guru.

Mummy turned to me. 'You can cancel. But I've booked your ticket. If you're interested.' She averted her gaze, turned to Mayank.

Mayank and his wife Rachna, then as now, are as prim and proper as couples go. So proper, Dear Reader, that Mayank has told me to not to describe him in too much detail. Still, here's a rough description: Mayank was a slender, clean-shaven man of average built and he only ever seemed to wear trousers and full-sleeved shirts, while Rachna, also of trim built and pleasant appearance, was much more experimental in her clothing, be it saree or Western dress.

Then in his forties, Mayank was an advocate at the Delhi High Court while Rachna was a homemaker. The couple had recently purchased a flat in Delhi's Panchsheel Park for which they had had a housewarming ceremony. After the pooja, the couple made the requisite donations to the pandits, distributed food to the poor who formed a long line outside the house, steel plates in their hands, and gave their guests a mithai box to take home. Each box was tied in a red and gold string and had a cursive Ganesha painted on it.

Mayank was the biggest believer among my cousins and it was a running family joke that mummy considered him her real son, not me. But I was now seeing that his influence had rubbed off on his wife, too. The couple had recently undertaken a yaatra to Amarnath the previous summer and after their darshan of Shiva in the form of an Ice Lingam up in the Himalayas at 12,756 feet, Rachna fell victim to high altitude sickness. As Mayank yelled at the tour organizers for convincing him it was safe to ascend from Pahalgam (at 8,990 feet) to Pachtarni (at 12,000 feet) by helicopter, Rachna, through laboured breaths, said to him, 'This is all destiny. Don't get worried. Whatever God has chosen will happen.' But Mayank yelled some more, procured an oxygen cylinder from somewhere and fortunately nothing untoward happened.

So, perhaps it's more reasonable to say that if Rachna was a believer beneath her visage of urbaneness, Mayank was more a practical believer than an emotional one. I mean, sure, he had long chats over tea and samosas with astrologers and *Vaastu Shaastra* experts; and yes, he wore three stone rings on his fingers; and he'd even fought a property dispute matter for the Vairagya Teerath Gyanpeeth Ashram Trust, something that had earned him Swamiji's respect. But unlike mummy, Mayank had that lawyerly instinct for knowing where to draw the line. He knew just when to zip his wallet and how much to pray in order to get on with things without getting bogged down with *every single thing*.

Mayank heard out mummy's proposal and turned to his wife. 'What do you think?' I felt my heart sinking in my chest. '*Challo*, for this I'm in,' he said.

'Bhai, I can't do your hectic train journeys any more,' Rashmi Masi said. 'I'll fly to Calcutta. Puri I can miss. I've been before.' She looked to Minna Masi who said, 'Same.'

Rachna leaned forward and gave me a wink. 'Calcutta has very good food.'

I snorted. 'Veg or non-veg?'

'Look.' She lowered her voice. 'If we go together at least you will get a nice hotel and good food.'

This was not an unimportant point. Apart from Mala and myself, Mayank and Rachna were the only other non-vegetarians on my mother's side of the family. Even if they were the I-eat-only-chicken-only-once-a-month sort.

Incidentally, Rachna's family, also Punjabi, were vegetarian like ours. Or at least Rachna and her mother were. The men I was told ate meat occasionally. But always out. (This gastronomic gender-disconnect cut across many Punjabi upper-caste families in the olden days. Dadima had once said, 'Your great grandmother made the best meat but she never once tasted it herself.' How did the system work? 'Well,' she said, 'after she'd prepared the masala, she'd place the vessel on a wood-fired stove outside the house into which the men would add the meat.')

I'd never been to Kolkata, but me being me, I had a list of places and items I wanted to try out: the Daab Chingri at 6 Ballygunge Place, the mutton kathi rolls at Kusum's, the Chello Kebab at Peter Cat… But how was I going to balance my meaty cravings on a trip full with vegetarians? I obviously couldn't count on Mayank and Rachna.

As is too often the case on family holidays, I wasn't the only one thinking of striking delicate balances. My aunts were too, and so Minna Masi decided to take one pre-emptive measure. She turned to mummy. 'I'll book rooms for us all in a nice hotel,' she said. 'I can't take your third-class journeys any more. If you want to go with Swamiji by train you're welcome.' She cast a glance around the table. 'But we'll fly.'

By this time my mother and aunts had crossed into their sixties, and although their faith in God never diminished, their energies surely had. Minna Masi was not one to compromise on her comforts and Rashmi Masi, in addition to comfort, had to have *proper food*. Which was Punjabi north Indian or South Indian, only *pure* vegetarian.

'Yes, you really like to glamorize self-deprivation, Shash,' Rashmi Masi said, savouring her daal *halwa*.

Mummy was beaming now and gladly took the barb. 'Agreed! Agreed! We can stay at whichever hotel. But I won't let you spend. This is my treat.'

'Not at all. I won't allow that.'

'No, no….'

And as the sisters began arguing I met mummy's eyes. Cutting through the din, I said, 'Look. I'll come with you by train. But if I want to break off and do my own thing, don't stop me. Okay?'

'Done!' Mummy got up and held out her hand for a high-five. She sat back down, met my eyes again then looked away, and I felt I could read her mind. 'Yes, taking everyone along is difficult,' she thought. 'But it's worth it. Totally worth it.'

And so, Dear Reader, this was how for the first time on a yaatra my family checked into a 5-star hotel: Kolkata's Taj Bengal.

April 2015

At the Taj, mummy and I shared a twin bedroom, Rashmi Masi and Minna Masi shared another, and Mayank and Rachna took a third. No doubt mummy had asked Swamiji to stay with us but he'd chosen instead to stay with his other devotees in an ashram attached to Adyapeath Ma Kali Temple in Daskshineshwar. And why wouldn't he? Even if his lodgings were frugal, surrounded by his own, Swamiji was always king.

Mummy and I had spent two nights in Puri together with 107 of Swamiji's devotees before we joined our family in Kolkata. The 107 yaatris were mostly over sixty and came from Delhi and towns in Haryana and UP, and everyone referred to everyone else by the proper honorific. So, the men were all *bhaisaabs, pitajis* and *unclejis* and the women were *behenjis, bhabhijis* and *matajis*. Among these brother-sirs, father-jis, uncle-jis, sisters, sisters-in-law and the many mothers, I was the solitary bhaiyya, brother.

There were three other men of around my age in our group but they'd come with their wives, so as the only youngish man accompanying his mother, I was the odd one out. My occasional discomfiture, however, was more than offset by mummy's open delight at taking on the role as the mistress of pooja ceremonies.

Sehdev Uncle had been unable to come. He had to take care of things at the ashram. I learnt that, although the others spoke of him with respect, his position as the ashram's manager was now more in name than substance. His role as Swamiji's caretaker, too, was a thing of the past.

A younger crop of devotees were now vying for Swamiji's attention and the frontrunner was Prahlad, a dark-skinned fifty-two-year-old man of average height and with a small belly, but much vigour. Prahladji was Swamiji's go-to man. He belonged to Faizabad in UP (which he proudly called Ram-janmabhoomi), but presently lived in Ghaziabad. He worked for the Delhi Jal Board while his wife, Saroj, a light-skinned plump woman, was a homemaker. The couple had an eleven-year-old son, Bharat, and a seven-year-old daughter, Srishti.

I'd visited the couple's home for a havan ceremony and was impressed by just how far out of their way they went for their guru. Before the pooja, Saroj washed Swamiji's feet, and afterwards, she set out for him an array of delicacies on a silver thaali. When Swamiji finished eating she swiftly stepped forward and poured water from a jug in a thin stream directly above his plate so he could rinse his hands without having to get up.

Not that Prahlad was one to simply stand around and watch. Prahladji was the man who did *everything that needed doing*. He sourced wood for the havan, purchased the samagri for the rituals, arranged the money to be handed to the pandits after the bhandaara, and ensured that the bhandaara feast itself passed without a glitch. And so in Puri, it was Prahladji who managed our boarding and lodging. It was Prahladji who arranged for two *maharajas* to cook our meals and it was he who organized the buses to the Alarnath and Konark temples for side trips.

Then there were scores of devotees who occupied junior roles: there was Sarla Aunty, a slim eighty-two-year-old lady from Saharanpur who always wore a crisp white saree and walked with a walking stick, even though she had a ramrod straight posture. Sarla Aunty was a former school teacher, which was why everybody called her *masterni*. She had lost her husband at a young age. Mummy said that despite the early loss 'she was a widow of high character'. I can't speak to her character, but I can attest that Sarla Aunty's eyes glimmered every time Swamiji began a sermon and she spoke only of two things: her son Anil who owned a garments shop, and her devotion to God.

There was the overweight Punjabi widow, Veeranwali Mataji, who at seventy-eight had far less energy and no walking stick. But even so, she was too happy to lean on one of the men to walk only a few steps. A Partition refugee, Veeranwali Mataji grew up in Sialkot but now lived with her son in East Delhi. She had bucked teeth, wore only salwar-kameezes and had heavy big-hooped earrings thanks to which her earlobes had grown long and saggy. And if Veeranwali Mataji looked like she belonged to another epoch she talked old, too. 'Cover your legs,' she said to little Srishti who'd worn a skirt one day. 'Stray dogs can smell virgin girls' legs!'

There was the sixty-year-old sweet shop owner from Haridwar, Tilak Raj. The man had a forbidding handlebar moustache and a severe demeanour to match it. Tilak Raj spoke very little and walked fast, and his wife, Savitri, who had her head covered with her saree at all times, walked a few feet behind him and didn't speak at all. Tilak Raj sent the first batch of mithai from his shop to Vairagya Teerath Gyanpeeth every month.

And finally there was the plump Subhadra Mataji who was seventy-five. Her family had long ago been wealthy residents of Burma. But when General Ne Win seized power in 1962 and many Indians were forced to leave the country, the family lost everything they'd built. Back in India, her husband fell into depression and soon died. Later, her daughter married a doctor and moved to Texas. Subhadra Mataji now lived with her brother in Meerut and according to mummy, 'had in her old age reverted to her life before marriage, occupied among the bhakts of Rishikesh'.

At Puri, the 109 of us sat down in a large hall whose floor was covered from wall to wall in ragged mattresses, and Swamiji asked aloud, 'I hope this is fine?' And everybody, like a classroom in unison, said, '*Bilkul* perfect, Swamiji.'

The arrangements were certainly adequate if adequacy was what you wanted. But gratefully, mummy and I got a little room to ourselves. Which, too, by the way, had no bed. A mattress was thrown on the floor, and a just-washed bed sheet was spread over it. The floor was recently swept clean but I could see dust collected in a corner. In the same corner where I spotted two strands of hair. Which then began to move and, I realized—*Oh shit!*—'it's a cockroach!'

I wrapped myself in my blanket. 'I'm checking myself into a hotel tomorrow.'

'You are just too spoilt,' mummy said. And five minutes later, she was snoring.

As I lay there that night staring at dried paint flaking on the ceiling, it occurred to me that I *was* rather spoilt. Certainly compared to these devout folk who didn't care for any comforts. Who seemed broadly content with their lot. Sarla Aunty was a widow, but she didn't appear lonely. Prahlad and Saroj weren't wealthy, but their lives seemed full, if not fulfilled.

It's amazing, I thought, how, despite the commotion, everything here *works*. How *everybody* works. The men take to disciplining their kids and organizing things, and the women dote on their kids and organize other things. The men in our group sourced kerosene-powered stoves, and the women took to making rotis. Once, Saroj even set up a stove using four bricks. And another time, during a bus ride, old Sarla Aunty distributed *matthis* she'd prepared herself, and the other women distributed homemade pickles. There was never a shortfall. Neither of food, nor of conversation, laughter and singing.

I was not in Goa, but I was not having a bad time, was I? This yaatra was a holiday for everybody so why couldn't it be one for me? *Why couldn't I relax?*

I laughed a sad laugh. Maybe I'll enjoy myself if I too hop on this elephant of faith, stopping at watering holes and drink it in: the folklore, the sermons, the mythology, the truths, the untruths.

But having just disembarked the faith-elephant, or rather the Jagannath Express from Puri that afternoon, while I still had left some reserves of faith, on the matter of food, I declared I was 'daal-ed out!' Now that we were at the Taj in Kolkata, what I was most looking forward to was some mustard fish curry. 'One yaatra has finished and the next one will start tomorrow, so it's cool,' I said. 'And we're in Bengal. Fish is practically vegetarian here.' My tone was deliberately provocative, but provocative in the sense that the listener knows you're being *you* and will only go so far. So, mummy didn't resist.

Rashmi Masi, strictly vegetarian though she'd been her entire life, at sixty-five seemed to have developed a curiosity for what she might have missed out on. She stepped forward and had a spoonful of the curry with a sly sliver of fish. She chewed it over and hobbled back to her seat.

'It's like paneer,' she said with a big smile. 'So, I'm not missing on anything.' She served herself another spoon of chaner daal. It was one of the Bengali delicacies I'd ordered.

Mummy and Minna Masi were sampling the banana blossom sabzi, and while my mother didn't mind this change from her usual food, Minna Masi was forcing it down.

Mayank forked through a piece of fish. 'It's nice,' he said tentatively. 'But bony.' So, Rachna asked the waiter for another portion of chaner daal. And as he turned around, I said, 'Also, one prawn cutlet.' And Rashmi Masi said, 'And one daal makhani.'

Swamiji had organized a two-day itinerary for Kolkata. On day one, we would visit the Dakshineshwar Temple at 6 am and at 2 pm we'd join the other yaatris at Adyapeath Ma Kali Temple.

Mummy had tried to wake me at 5 am, but when I didn't budge, she let me be. When I woke up at eight and went down to sample the breakfast buffet, however, I found that the others in my family were just as lazy. Only Mayank had accompanied my mother, and now, over fresh idlis, my aunts and Rachna were discussing the day's plan.

Minna Masi cast a dubious glance at my portion of bacon and eggs. 'Don't fill yourself up. We're going to Flury's at twelve.'

At Flury's, my first course was the ham croissant, while the others had the regular kind. The second was a round of coffee. And the third, an assortment of sweets. I was on the rum ball when mummy walked in through the cafe's glass doors. She was red-faced and her forehead was beaded in a film of sweat. 'You don't know what you all missed,' she said, gasping. 'You have no idea at all!'

A young couple beside us, lethargically scrolling through their phones, looked up, and she lowered her voice. 'You people are so silly not to have come.'

'Could you please bring another menu?' Minna Masi said to the waiter, and the young man handed a menu to my mother.

Mummy stared at the food before her, then at the menu, then at us. She shifted in her chair, shook her head. 'I've come from such a big pooja. And here you people are eating this. Everything has egg.'

'We have eggless options also, ma'am,' the waiter said in his polite waiter voice, and mummy shook her head again.

'What here is pure vegetarian? I want completely pure vegetarian. No egg. No egg at all.'

'Yes, ma'am, we have eggless cakes and pastries also.'

Mummy squinted hard at her choices. She nodded. She jiggled her chin. Then, as if she were deciding which food would earn her the least bad karma, she began enunciating the offerings: 'Masala bread, cinnamon roll, molten chocolate… Hmm. I dislike chocolate.'

She glanced up. The poor waiter was waiting with his hands locked behind his back: 'Would it be possible to do a simple pure vegetarian samosa?'

I rolled my eyes. 'Oh, just eat the damn pastry,' I said. 'I had a mutton roll from Kusum's down the corner. Big deal.'

Honestly, I wasn't planning on telling anyone about my little breakout but seeing mummy's pedantry on full display during what was initially meant to be a *holiday*, the words rushed out. It turned out to be a bad move. 'You're too much, Sid,' Minna Masi said, wincing, and Rashmi Masi, through a mouthful of chocolate truffle, seconded her.

As we got into the taxi to Kalighat temple, Rachna said: 'If you had it, fine. But why do you have to tell her?'

Our darshan of Mata at Kalighat was as fervid and joyous as anywhere, but it is what happened afterwards that has stayed with me.

It was a muggy, windless afternoon, the kind where sweat glistens on your face and you can literally see dust motes suspended in the air. We were walking back to our car, Rashmi Masi, Rachna, mummy and I. On either side of the lane were shops exhibiting pooja offerings for the goddess. Red dupattas with golden borders hung in long ribbons from the ceiling, and on countertops sat mounds of red vermilion, bangles and coconuts.

Doubly invigorated by two darshans of Kaali, mummy was trooping resolutely ahead. But she then suddenly stopped, turned around, and started jogging back in our direction. She crouched down. I caught up with her. On the floor lay scattered the *raksha dhaaga*, *mata ki chunri*, cardamom and *pedas*. The temple prasad had all fallen out of my mother's bag and she was scooping it up in feverish motions ('*So that nobody step on it! So that nobody step on it! So that nobody step on it!*') as pedestrians sidestepped and bicycles swerved around us. I helped her out.

It is wrong not to accept prasad if offered to you. But it's a sin to waste it. *Was she going to eat it?* I could feel my blood pressure rising in my veins.

'What are you trying to prove, Shash?' Rashmi Masi cried. 'Even inside the temple, she kept ringing the bell again and again for I don't know what.'

Mummy gave her sister an expression of amused dismay. She then put her hands on her knees and stood up and dusted herself. She looked to one side of the gully where, in her line of vision, a cow was tied up against a wall. She walked to it and fed her the pedas from her hands. Then she tied the red dhaaga around her neck, patted her face and whispered something in her ear.

As she joined us, she said, 'You people must think I'm really foolish.'

By the time we joined Swamiji and the 107 yaatris at Adyapeath Temple it was 2:30 pm. But I learnt that we weren't late as the idea was to have lunch. Or rather, to attend the bhandaara feast Swamiji and mummy had organized for local sadhus on behalf of Vairagya Gyanpeeth Ashram.

And so along with my family I fed 101 sadhus, ladling out precise portions of Bengali khichdi onto banana leaves that had been spread out in a long line on the floor, after which we ourselves sat down to eat our third meal of the day.

The food was ghee-laden and delicious. But seeing as my mother and aunts were overweight and diabetic, they ought to have paid some regard to portion size! Minna Masi tended to be careful. But when I told the other two that the food had a high glycaemic index, Rashmi Masi laughed melodramatically, and said, 'Ghee clarifies the air and warms my soul!' And mummy perkily added, 'I'll have your portion if you won't, Rachna. How can you waste this prasad?'

After our darshan, I was moving with the others towards a large banyan tree under which Swamiji was about to begin his sermon of the day: the story of Ganga Sagar. The sun was strong but the tree's branches provided the ideal cover so everybody was bunching up in the shade. Prahlad, Saroj and their children sat down in the front row beside Sarla Aunty, who was patting the sweat on her forehead dry. And Veeranwali Mataji, adjusting her hearing aid, sat behind them, as did Subhadra Aunty.

The front rows were thus occupied. Which was just as well, because Rashmi Masi said she couldn't sit on the floor anyway and Mayank had only just found a plastic chair for her. We found a place at the back.

Gracefully crossing his legs, Swamiji sat down on the tree's circular cement base. It made for the ideal podium. He then licked his lips. 'Everybody comfortable?'

'*Ji*, Swamiji!' Srishti said.

Swamiji smiled at her, clapped his hands. '*Sab* ready?' And the hubbub of voices went down a decibel.

'There was a King Sagar,' he began, and the chattering now altogether ceased. '… And one day, he summoned his kingdom's learned saints and astrologers to his court. He asked, "What *punya karm* [good deed] have I done to be king?" The astrologers analysed his birth chart and said, "In your previous life, you were a jackal. In that life, somebody had abandoned a baby girl in the jungle, and you picked her up and reared her as your own child. And this girl, she grew to become very beautiful. So, one day, a king passing through the area decided to grab her. But you and your pack blocked his path."

'You said: "O King, it does not behove you to take our girl like this! We are her parents and will not give her to you unless you first ask for her hand in marriage. And you must assure us you will treat her with respect and love, only then we will agree to this alliance."'

Rashmi Masi was straining to catch Swamiji's words. Mummy held out her hand: *I'll explain later.* Mayank met my searching gaze and gave a wry smile. He motioned ahead: *Listen!*

Swamiji said, 'The King, surrounded by all these animals, had to agree. He saw that the girl had the entire jungle's backing. So he begged the jackal for her hand in marriage and the jackal agreed to give his daughter to him.

'The astrologers then told the King that of all the charities in the world, *kanya daan*'—giving your daughter away to her husband and his family—'was the biggest, and it was because of this deed that the jackal became a king in his next life.'

For some reason, mummy decided to give us an English interpretation at the back: 'In our Hindu tradition, marriage is a sacrament,' she said. 'Kanya daan is regarded as the greatest charity because a child who you've nurtured with your whole heart is given to the groom to raise his family.'

Veeranwali Mataji spoke up: 'In our days, when a girl went to her husband's family, other kinds of daan were also given: household items and utensils to set up the new house. People used to do *chakki* [flour mill] daan, or give a *chulah* [stove].' She sat back and gathered her knees together.

'Yes, mataji.' Swamiji smiled and the old lady smiled back.

'King Sagar then had a sudden thought. He said to the pandits, "Tell me, what daan can I do to become a king of the devtas?" And the pandits said that if he did kanya daan of 60,000 girls, then his position as the King of Devtas was assured. And so King Sagar decided to undertake a great yagnya. But now'—Swamiji raised his eyebrows, produced his teasing face—'Indra got worried,' Indra, the King of Gods, whose weapon is the thunderbolt. 'His seat was under threat.

'As the King Sagar's yagnya progressed, the gods became pleased. But when he opened his mouth to state the object of his prayers, that he should beget 60,000 *putris*...daughters, just then, just at that instant'—Swamiji clapped his hands and looked to Srishti with playful eyes—'Indra struck his thunderbolt into the King's mouth so that he could not utter the "*I*" maatra,' the 'I' vowel that turns the word *putr*—son—into *putri*—daughter. 'And so the word which came out of King Sagar's mouth was "*putr*". And as a result, 60,000 sons were born to him!'

Srishti giggled and Sarla Aunty clapped her hands and there was the soft wind of murmurings that comes when a story has reached a pleasing denouement.

A small laughter escaped my lips, too. For this story showcased marvellous wordplay, didn't it? It was mythology, but like all good stories, it sparked the imagination. *Just like all those years ago while watching the Ramayana on TV the arrows of good and evil lit up the sky...*

Mummy continued: 'These 60,000 sons crossed all norms of decorum and even saints were not spared! ... Then, one day, these *Sagar Putras*, sons of Sagar, learnt that there was a wish-fulfilling cow, the *Kama Dhenu*, with the sage Kapila Muni who lived in an ashram by the Great Sea. And so they reached Ganga Sagar.'

'Kapila Muni is one of the earliest rishis of the Satyug,' Swamiji added.

(As per lore, I should add that there exists an alternate version of this story according to which the prayer that King Sagar wanted to perform was the Ashwamedha Yagnya, the Vedic horse sacrifice, for he believed doing this would give him dominion over the entire planet. But Lord Indra hid the sacrificial horse near Kapila Muni's ashram by the sea and when the 60,000 Sagar Putras discovered it there they mistook took him as the thief!)

As per both versions of the tale, however, the Sagar Putras prepared to attack the meditating Kapila Muni. But before they could, the rishi opened his eyes emitting a terrific fire bolt and reduced the 60,000 of them to ashes.

Kapila Muni cursed the Sagar Putras that they would never be forgiven for attacking him. He said that for this sin even their progeny would suffer. Then, many generations later, one of King Sagar's descendants, Bhagiratha decided to perform a *Bhagirathaprayatnam*, a penance of Himalayan proportions, to free his lineage from his forefathers' sins. Standing on one leg at Gangotri, he beseeched God to release the Ganga from the Heavens, and Lord Vishnu was so impressed that he sent the Ganga down to the Earth as a river. When the Ganga first descended, she came with such torrential force that the Earth was at risk of being obliterated. And so Lord Shiva stepped in to contain Her in his matted locks.

Watching the yaatris lap up Swamiji's every word, a maze of thoughts passed through my mind:

Faith began with story-telling, but you had to know when to return to reality, no? At what point did this traditional love for the daughter become an excuse for women's exploitation? How simple-minded these people were! Did you have to be so simple-minded to have faith?

Perhaps I should give a fuller setting to my jumble of thoughts at this juncture. Back in Puri, one young pandit had addressed us with much gusto about the great mysteries of the Jagannath Temple—'mysteries even science could not explain'. He said that the tallest temple dome never casts a shadow, and nobody knows why. He said birds don't fly over the temple spires, and nobody knows why. He said that while, usually, the wind blows from the sea to land in the day and from the land to sea in the evening, in Puri, the opposite happens, and nobody knows why. He said that when the prasadam is cooked, with one earthen pot placed on top of the other, seven of them in total, miraculously the topmost one cooks first, and nobody knows why. He said that even though thousands upon thousands of devotees are fed from the temple's kitchens daily, the amount is always right, with there never being a shortfall, or surplus. And finally, he said that the flag atop the temple always blows in the opposite direction to the wind, and people are still trying to figure out why.

As to why these things happen, he said, was a *rahasya*, a secret. And while I didn't bother to look up if any of his claims were true—seeing as prima facie they lacked scientific basis—the confidence with which the young man spoke and the gullibility with which everybody around believed was surreal. Surreal enough to make me doubt myself!

Veeranwali Mataji raised her dupatta in the air to show that the wind was indeed blowing in the opposite direction than what the flag atop the temple suggested. And Srishti dashed to the shrine's outer wall from where she said to her mother, 'Really, no shadow here,' and a tickled Prahlad brought her back to where we were gathered.

I was confident I could see the dome's shadow and I pointed it out to the pandit, and he said that I was not the first one to have made this mistake and won't be the last.

At the end of the day, though, this was good-natured banter I could live with. Even partake in. What was disheartening was the open abuse of power I also saw: the way in which some priests brazenly played with impressionable minds.

When Savitri from Hapur did a special pooja so her daughter find a good match, a passing pandit made his voice deep and low and said, '*Yeh pooja gupt rakho*...keep this pooja a secret.' When Swamiji overheard this, even he said, 'Don't put these fears in my devotees' minds, panditji.' And the pandit gave a big laugh, picked up his dhoti, and strolled on.

Another time, during an early morning pooja, one pandit asked a man in our group to place Rs 10 in front of him every time he poured a spoonful of ghee into the sacred fire, and when after the third time the man refused to comply, the pandit struck him lightly on his forehead with the spoon in his hand.

'Is this what you do in the name of God?' Prahlad said, his nostrils flaring. 'You will teach us how to pray, *haan*?'

And finally, on a visit to the Alarnath Temple dedicated to Lord Krishna, which lies at a distance of around twenty-five kilometres from Puri, mummy and I got a personal taste of pandit exploitation.

The legend behind this temple was that Lord Vishnu had once accepted *kheer bhog* offered to him by a child here. But the vessel was so hot his right hand got burnt. The burn marks are visible on the deity's hand even now and mummy wanted to see them. But by the time we arrived, it was 4:30 pm, and the local pandit said that the deity was resting. His hand was wrapped up in a cloth, and if we wanted a peek, we'd have to pay an additional Rs 500.

'But what will you gain from hiding the Lord from me?' mummy cried. 'It's not like the temple is closed. I've come here for darshan and you want to charge me extra for it?' But the pandit didn't budge, and for once, mummy wasn't easily swayed either.

She stood her ground. She prayed aloud: 'Dear Krishanji, I've come to pray to you in your full form. If somebody has created an obstacle, it is their fault. Not mine.' And the pandit stood by, silently smouldering.

Later that evening, I asked Swamiji how this could be acceptable.

'Yes,' he said, 'some men abuse their position... This kind of behaviour is why,' he let slip, 'so many people took to Buddhism in the olden days.'

And I thought, Swamiji's volte-face is just like my mother's from three months before.

In January 2015, rather than me going with her, for once, I made mummy accompany me on a trip. 'Where to?' she asked.

'Burma.' Burma fit into my itinerant ways at the time: of breaking away from the familiar but also finding new angles to dig deeper into it. The country seemed exotic, but was culturally proximate. I guessed there were no Hindu temples to be seen but plenty of Buddhist ones.

When at the Shwedagon Pagoda, before a line of oil lamps, she saw bald prepubescent Buddhist pupils offer their prayers, she said gaily, 'Just like Brahmin boys!' And when the boatman didn't haggle with us during a boat ride on Inle Lake, she laughed and said, 'Such a nice change from Banaras!'

'I'm so happy you brought me here,' she said. 'The simplicity of the people reminds me of Bangalore in the '50s.' And she was happy. Even though she found it challenging to find vegetarian food, she ate what she could without complaint: a bland noodle soup, a tea leaf salad, and once even steamed rice with ketchup.

During one meal, she was looking out the restaurant's window when a bunch of beggar boys dressed up as Buddhist monks came knocking on it. Mummy stepped out and dropped a few coins into one boy's begging bowl. In the same manner she'd employ for child beggars dressed as Hindu gods, I thought.

When she sat down she looked at me straight on. 'I used to think that non-vegetarians are morally bad people,' she said. 'But now I'm realizing what I learnt was...'

'Misguided?' I offered.

She shook her head. 'Was wrong.' She stared out again. The biggest boy of the posse of four swung his hand at the smallest kid, but the latter ducked away.

I smirked. *So, even the devout have reason hidden inside.*

Of course, mummy's self-doubt vanished the next morning when she saw me inhale a bowl of pork noodles for breakfast. 'You're really a true Kapila,' she said with disdaining eyes.

And this was also how Swamiji behaved the evening following our visit to the Alarnath Temple. Back in Puri, he said, 'Lord Vishnu works in four different ways. In Jagannath dham, God does *bhojan*. He eats. In Badrinath, He does tapasya. In Rameswaram, He bathes, and in Dwarka, He rests.

'The Buddhists had become morally depraved,' he said. 'They had left the way of the Dharma. They had converted so many Hindu temples to Buddhist ones... In those days, in the north, south, east, west—everybody was separate. Everybody was practising their own kind of religion. But when Shankaracharya went on his travels, he saw that there is one sanskriti everywhere and there's one Sanskrit language. So, to unify us, he established four mathas. It was he who took the pujaris of Kerala to Badrinath and Pashupati Nath in the Himalayas.'

He took a momentary pause and Saroj got up. Covering her head with the end of her saree, she fetched him a glass of water. Like an ideal daughter, I thought.

And if Saroj was an ideal daughter, the Puri temple priest's son, at whose house we'd had lunch the previous afternoon, was the perfect son. He, the young Puri pandit, who said to me, 'I had the option of studying engineering. But how can I leave this and go? Who will carry our tradition forward?'

Sitting under the banyan tree that afternoon, I thought, yes, religion was story-telling before it was faith. And if our stories laid down moral codes that millions still lived by then it was worth examining them, wasn't it? Maybe what mummy said *was* worth looking into: 'It's foolish to dismiss the truth of millions!'

After Swamiji finished his discourse I even said aloud: 'Maybe I should write a book about our temple yaatras one day.'

From the city to the sea. April 4, 2015

I awoke at 7 am and by 8 am had joined my family in an eight-seater van. By nine, we picked Swamiji up from Adyapeath Temple and the seven of us were on our way to Kakdwip, a coastal town about one hundred kilometres south of Kolkata. By ten, having passed greying apartment blocks on the city's fringes, we were zipping through the lush greenery of Bengal. We were flying past rice fields speckled with palms quivering in the wind. Past thick-trunked trees standing over ponds and pools, their branches casting reflections alongside clouds scattered across a vast blue sky.

And as I imbibed these images along with nuggets of Swamiji's sermon ('Bathing here doubly re-enforces the karmic cleansing a river offers'), I couldn't help but think that the man had figured me out over the years. It was as if Swamiji had learnt only to please those who pleased him. To only talk when he knew he'd be taken seriously.

I turned outside: Women in sarees of bright primary colours—green, blue, pink—working the land. Men in checked *lungis* sitting around a courtyard, playing cards. A boy squatting in the fields taking a shit looking up at the sky. Up, where white birds flew across in a chevron so neat that I imagined, *The sky was a lake! And the 'V' formation, a ship!*

Now a pair of schoolboys walking hand in hand. Now a group of school girls. Now an egret on a buffalo soaking in a pond. Now a scarecrow, its wicked smile askew.

Another pond. And another traffic jam!

Like an insect just freed from a spider-web flying into another entanglement, we were stuck in a net of cycle rickshaws and bullock carts, and the breeze that had been lapping my face was replaced by sweat and grime.

'This is what I don't like,' Mayank said. 'This mess. Why can't they build a highway?'

Rashmi Masi opened a packet of potato chips, popped one in her mouth, then offered it to us. 'Because, beta,' she said, making a faux-serious face, 'you have to have some difficulty on a yaatra, na? As Maji used to say: *Baaki tirath baar baar. Ganga Sagar ek baar.*'

Maji was my great-great-grandmother, my maternal grandfather's paternal grandmother, who died at the age of 106 in 1966.

'Did Maji come here?' I asked, incredulous.

'I think she did,' mummy said, brightly munching on chips. 'In those days, people would cook food and carry it with them. There were no facilities or anything. And coming from Machhiwara'—my maternal grandfather's ancestral village in Punjab—'to Ganga Sagar was a once in a lifetime experience. Trains were infrequent and I think she covered a part of her journey by bullock cart.' More munching of chips. 'Most people didn't travel overseas.'

Years later, I'd come across an article entitled 'The English in India' by James Mascarene Hubbard published in *The Atlantic Monthly* in June 1908, in which one paragraph would catch my eye:

'In the ante-British times there were no roads, only bridle-paths. Today there are more than one hundred and eighty thousand miles of road, and twenty-eight thousand miles of railway on which two hundred and forty-eight million passengers were carried in 1906. This fact means more than lies upon the surface. In times not very long ago the pilgrimages, which every Hindu endeavours at some time to make, were done mostly on foot. The rivers in their way were rarely bridged, and if they were swollen by the rains so that the customary fords were impassable, the multitudes going and returning from the shrine became congested on either bank. Their supplies were soon exhausted, and famine and its attendant diseases were the inevitable result. Even when there were no extraordinary difficulties to be overcome, the old and feeble, whose strength was exhausted by the journey merely, died in countless numbers by the way. For fifty miles from Juggernaut [Jagannath] in every direction the paths were lined with the bodies of those who had perished in the attempt to prostrate themselves before the car of their god. The pilgrimages have not ceased, but the excessive mortality consequent upon them has.'

'Did this reluctance to travel abroad have anything to do with the old Hindu prohibition on seafaring?' I voiced my thought aloud. And because Swamiji was there, he answered.

'*Dekho*, India is a *punyabhoomi*,' he said, a pure spiritual land. 'While the rest of the world has always been concerned more with worldly pursuits... And if you leave these holy lands, you'd have to mingle with people who'd pollute your foods, your rituals. You would have to compromise on your habits and this would affect your spiritual progress.'

I'd heard that as recently as the nineteenth century, caste Hindus were discouraged from travelling abroad. *But was this true?* My recent travels in Southeast Asia had shown me much proof to the contrary and I was now more inclined to believe that this travel ban was probably more prevalent in northern India, in places distant from the sea.

Thailand, which once fell under the Hindu-Buddhist Khmer Empire, still revered Hindu deities like Brahma and Ganesha. The Ramayana played such an important role in the country's culture that its episodes were even painted on the Grand Palace's walls. The country's old capital was even called *Ayutthya*! The churning of the oceans between the devtas and asuras was one of the many Hindu fables engraved on the walls of the Angkor Wat in Cambodia and there were crumbling Shivalingams as far even as Mo Son in Vietnam!

So how could Hindus have been against travel if what you saw east of India was an overabundant evidence of it? The detractor in me wanted to dismiss Swamiji, but what he said rang true somewhere. To this day, it rankled to see a Western chef tasting a dish only to put the jootha spoon back into it. Even today, I find it absolutely disgusting to clean my bottom with anything other than water.

Like many that came before, the village we were now passing through had one or more Hindu temples, but there also rose above it a minaret with a green dome. Perhaps Swamiji had also noticed this because what he said next was this:

'The punyabhoomi in ancient times extended not only to today's India, but to Pakistan and even Afghanistan. They say that Gandhari'—wife of the blind king Dhritarashtra in the Mahabharata—'came from what is now Afghanistan and,' he stalled, licked his lips, 'I don't know if it's true, but I have heard that there is even a powerful Shivalingam in Mecca…' He turned around, assessed our faces, 'A Makareshwar Mahadev. I don't know, but I've heard it.'

He went on: 'See, I've heard there was once a raja from Nepal who came to know about Makareshwar Mahadev. So, he reached Mecca in disguise. Shiva had come to him in a dream and asked him to put Gangajal on the Shivalingam there. So, after some investigation, he found out where Mahadev resided. But before he could get to it, he was stopped. I believe guards are protecting this place even today.'

'I wonder if Swamiji himself believes all this,' I muttered under my breath and mummy shot me a glare.

Those of a more balanced persuasion, though, certainly have a way of discarding things that don't fit their worldview and taking the things that do. Here's how Mayank responded: 'You know, Swamiji, I have an astrologer. His name is Raees. He's Muslim. A decent chap from Tamil Nadu and his prophecies are often true. He says many religious places have the same vibrations and these energies are born from lakhs gathering to pray at the same spot. Actually, he says he's felt the same vibrations in Mecca and Tirupati. Only a few places in the world have such powers.'

Swamiji nodded. 'Yes, this is true. It takes a lot of tapasya to take a rock out of the Ganga and pray so hard that Shiva Himself enters it. Only few can do this.' He gave mummy a knowing smile.

Our speed picked up, wind came streaming back into the van, and I fell back to staring outside.

Mayank tapped me on my shoulder. 'Sid.' He looked like he wanted to get something off his chest and his wife held out her hand. 'See, nobody is stopping you from eating what you want,' Rachna said. 'But you're very rude to your mother. You don't realize it.'

'And,' Mayank said, his words now taking on a virtuous quality, 'it's about discipline also. If you've come here, then do things properly. Why pray at all if you'll do it in this half-baked way?'

I turned from Mayank to Rachna, and back to Mayank. I raised my eyebrows: *Are we really going to have this conversation?*

'Look, I also eat chicken sometimes, but would I do it today? You should have some sense.' He turned to the green fields rushing outside. A young girl was pushing down on a steel hand pump and her friend, laughing, was collecting water in a bucket. 'It's like you want to do these things to be fashionable.'

I thought mummy was busy talking to Swamiji, but she also piped up. In a jesting voice, she said, 'Mayank, he'll listen to you. Not me.'

During the few seconds I struggled to hide my irritation and Mayank struggled to be tactful, Swamiji spoke up. '*You* eat chicken?' His eyes were fixed on my cousin.

'*Ji*, very little. Maybe once a month,' Mayank said. 'And only outside the house,' Rachna added. Swamiji stayed quiet for a whole thirty seconds.

'Nowadays, I know people have meat out of temptation,' he said. 'But I wish you'd give this one thing up. *Maans khaane se pooja ki pavitrata kam hoti hai*...eating meat really weakens your prayers.'

Their jaws still energetically working on those chips, Rashmi Masi and mummy nodded.

'Okay, Swamiji,' Mayank now said. 'This is easy for me.' In a brushing-off motion, he shook his hand away from his body. '*Samajh lo ho gaya*...consider it done,' he said. 'I've left it.'

How extraordinary, I thought. My cousin made it sound like he was giving up something big, but also rather small: a thing he could easily live without. And as I knew he was a man who stuck to his word, I considered: *Faith* can instantly change your mind. To which I now add another thought: Faith can shape the future, too. For seven years later, just before Mayank's daughter left for her studies abroad, he asked her only to promise one thing. 'I don't care about anything. But just don't eat beef,' he said. And his daughter pursed her lips and said, 'Papa, please! I don't even touch eggs.'

The hot, sticky air in Kakdwip, a non-descript coastal town, was thick with the smell of fish and the chatter of incoming Bengali pilgrims. A juxtaposition which created in my north Indian mind a clash of two mutually exclusive things: fish and faith.

We parked our van near a large bus stop and Swamiji led us to the place we were meant to 'stretch our legs' that afternoon. The resthouse, a Yaatri Vishram Sthal, couldn't have been a bigger contrast to Taj Bengal. The waiting room had a corrugated green plastic roof and similarly bright green walls. Five or six plastic chairs were loosely thrown about on a smudged floor and a broiling sweaty sink was attached to a wall. A ceiling fan lethargically churned the humid air. Luckily, this room opened into three bedrooms with working high-speed fans.

A slim helper, Biju, a boy of about sixteen, welcomed us with a broad smile. Overeager to please Swamiji, he picked up his bags and then brought us tea.

'What's there for lunch?' I asked, and Biju said there was lots of *moori* (puffed rice) and chana daal.

'Arre wah!' mummy said. 'Swamiji makes such good arrangements for us.'

But Rashmi Masi scoffed and asked if he could get her a masala dosa from somewhere. Biju shook his head and Minna Masi laughed. Not that she was any better. Sure, she ate her food without complaining. But when she went to the sink to wash her hands and found the tap emitted only air, she asked a clueless Biju to get her a finger bowl. 'Just warm some water and add a slice of lemon,' she said, and now we giggled at her.

Licking her fingers clean, mummy said, 'This is what happens when you 5-star people come on a yaatra.'

We napped, had tea, had more puffed rice and more tea, and before we knew it, it was 2:45 pm. Rashmi Masi came up to our room. Mummy and I were lying down.

'Why are we waiting here so long, Shash?' she said in a sweet voice.

'Yeah, why?' I turned to mummy. I knew we were meant to visit Ganga Sagar during the lunar eclipse. But what was going on?

Look, Dear Reader, I'd done my research. Although the lunar eclipse today would last for five hours and fifty-eight minutes, beginning in India at 14:31 and ending at 20:29, it was only partially visible here. It was fully visible only in faraway Australia. But what I didn't appreciate, and what mummy and Swamiji had been discussing all along, was that the *full eclipse* would begin at 17:27 and end at 17:32; the moon would reach its maximum eclipse at 17:30, and that this was the proper time for a dip in the Ganga Sagar.

But where was the logic in this? Why must you bathe during the *peak* eclipse when there was only a *partial* eclipse anyway? Plus, Biju had said not to delay our departure as the waters could get choppy and 'uncomfortable for the old ladies'.

'Who are you calling old, Biju?' mummy said, and the boy blushed.

'Look, the movement of the moon dictates the exact time of all our festivals. Ekaadashi'—the eleventh lunar day, which honours Lord Vishnu—'and Pradosh'—the transition from the twelfth to the thirteenth day of the waxing and waning of the moon cycle, which honours Lord Shiva—'and Ashtami'—the eighth day, which honours the Divine Mother. Sitting upright in bed, mummy was in her moralizing mode. 'The moon represents the mind and the respiratory system and because his power is obstructed we have to follow dos and don'ts.'

Bathing and reciting mantras was especially propitious at this time. But Swamiji had further explained that although bathing during an eclipse was good, improvements could be made. Bathing with normal water was better than with hot water. Bathing with fresh water was better than stored water, and flowing water was better than still water. Bathing in the Ganga was better than bathing in any other river. But bathing in the sea was even more favourable. And as Ganga Sagar was where the Ganga met the sea, it was the best place of all.

Usually, my aunts were keen on my mother's sermons, but today Rashmi Masi's fear of the irrational sea trumped her zest for prayer. 'You don't have to be a superwoman every day, Shash!' she said. She rotated herself to face Biju. 'When is the last boat back?'

The poor chap looked around desperately. 'I think 7:30 or eight.'

'That is too late!' She spun back. 'Look, it took us four hours to come here and Rachna's father said that the ferry to Ganga Sagar takes an hour.' She began counting the hours on her fingers. 'Shash, do you want to be in a situation where we spend the night on the beach?'

She marched to Swamiji's room. His door was open but he was sitting up in bed with his eyes fixated on a prayer book. So, deflated, she returned to mummy, her stomach heaving, now looking too distraught even to speak.

As if releasing an ectoplasm from some medium only known to her, mummy had her eyes closed and was moving her fingers away from her chest in a stringing motion. She directed a lazy eye at her sister. 'Relax, bhai. Let the others first get here.'

'Look, let's forget your eclipse,' I said, keeping my voice on an even keel. 'Let's go now.'

'She's been like this since childhood,' Rashmi Masi said. She then turned to me, her eyes broadening. 'Sid, let's us go. These people can come later.'

And now stifled giggles from Minna Masi, Mayank and Rachna

broke into open laughter. Mummy got off the bed. The light-heartedness on her face was transfiguring into open displeasure.

'But the whole purpose of this trip is to bathe in the Ganga *during* the eclipse!'

'But the eclipse is on!'

And now Swamiji appeared. He placed his hand on my shoulder. '*Shant ho jao*...quieten down, please,' he said. 'Again, you're troubling your mother?' He gave a paternal smile. 'Don't worry. I'm with you, aren't I? Don't you have faith in me?'

I turned to Rashmi Masi who was still muttering, 'Since childhood, since childhood...'

'I think you better pack some more moori for the beach, masi,' I said, then nodded to Swamiji. As we were getting on choppy waters to chase an eclipse I had better invest some faith in him, too.

The usual way yaatris get to Ganga Sagar is to hop on a bus from Esplanade, Kolkata, to Harwood Point in Kakdwip: a total distance of about ninety kilometres, which takes around three hours to cover by road. From Kakdwip, you cross the Muriganga (or the Hooghly) by ferry to get to Kachuberia jetty on Sagar Island, from where it takes another hour by road to get to Ganga Sagar beach.

It was 3:10 pm when the three bus loads bearing the 107 yaatris rolled into a bus stop near our resthouse. Standing at one 'Tourist Bus' door like a conductor, Prahladji was offloading everybody one by one, taking a headcount. Some of the women, Sarla Behenji, Veeranwali Mataji and Saroj among them, walked over to a shaded spot and took a seat. But when they saw mummy approaching, they stood up. The two older women took her into an embrace, and now the foursome were conferencing on the vital pooja ahead and the samagri required.

Ganga Sagar was the last earthly place to celebrate the Goddess's femininity, specifically her marital bliss, so one would need to offer to the sea red vermilion, a red dhaaga, a coconut, and of course a saree. Mummy and Saroj had each bought a red one with them. But we nevertheless accompanied the others to the bazaar, where Savitri and Tilak Raj bought a bridal red cloth, presumably a good omen for their daughter's marriage, and Rashmi Masi and Minna Masi bought shell necklaces, bangles, incense sticks and what have you.

When Prahladji bought a large *shankh*, a conch shell, mummy told him with dancing eyes that she'd brought one with her. But then he clarified that there were actually two kinds of shankhs. The *dakshin mukhi* (south-facing) shankh, which had an opening on the right side, was associated with the Samudra Manthan, the churning of the cosmic ocean, as well as Lakshmiji, and it was the more appropriate sort for the prayers today. And so mummy bought one, too.

As she was paying for her things, she spontaneously also paid for Saroj's items, who was standing beside her. But Saroj naturally resisted. 'No, behenji,' she said, shaking her head. 'I won't let you do this.'

'Oh, it's nothing. Let me do at least this much,' mummy said.

And Saroj placed her hand on my mother's arm. 'You know how much I love dressing up Mata, na?' Her brown eyes welled up with tears. 'You know, na? Don't stop me from putting ornaments on Devi myself.'

Mummy observed Saroj momentarily, then placed her hand on her shoulder. 'You're right,' she said. 'I won't take this joy away from you, but please allow me the honour of looking after you at my house. You and Prahladji do so much.' Saroj wiped away her tears and nodded.

I learnt that at one pooja Saroj had been possessed by Mata, the feminine divine. Her face went pale, her eyes widened, and she fainted. Prahladji splashed water on her and when she awoke she couldn't quite explain what had happened. All she knew was that a wave rose from within her, an *inexplicable shakti*. And while I hadn't witnessed this incident myself, enough yaatris had. Enough said, 'Yes, it was true,' Saroj *had* come under Mata's spell.

As I was to make a connection between the Bhootha Kola spirit dancers and Aghoris years later, I drew a similar link here too. After the Bhootha Kola dancers concluded their holy dance, a priest in the audience went mad before my eyes. In front of some thousand spectators he grabbed a fire torch lying to the side (the same one the dancers used in their performance) and sprinted across the temple courtyard yelling at the top of his lungs. His eyes were aflame and his shriek murderous. But then, in the nick of time three men pinned him to the ground and he passed out. He lay limp and lifeless for more than a minute before somebody stepped forward and splashed water on his face after which he awoke seeming totally normal.

'The shakti that had entered the Bhootha Kola dancers before had seized him,' a young man in the audience said. 'But he was unable to handle it.'

Was this priest acting? No. He couldn't be. For if he were acting, it was an Oscar-worthy performance. And not just him, everybody around—the men who restrained him, the man who splashed water on him, indeed the entire village watching—had to be acting to some degree for the performance to work. So, no, this wasn't acting. This was something different. *Something inscrutable, something fundamental...*

Perhaps this was belief altering reality? Maybe faith coloured not only *how* you saw things but *what* you saw?

At the jetty, a line of beggars.

A blind man pounded his dholak as his friend played the harmonium. A woman held out a hand for coins as she cradled her baby with the other one. And her companion clanked his metal bowl to the ground like a grief-stricken percussionist. Among this lot I saw two young boys with dark luminescent skin diving into the water below. Only to climb up to the jetty and repeat their exercise.

Was this a river or sea? I couldn't decide. The Muriganga had the burbling currents of the deep, but lacked sea waves. If it was a sea, it was hemmed in by land. If it was a river, it was waiting to burst free. It was an iridescent, unrestrainable thing.

I was admiring the sun and the sea and the boys' spirit when I noticed that the duo wasn't playing a game but retrieving coins from the water. The same coins which Sarla Aunty tossed in along with marigolds, before she pottered onto the ferry, her face beaming, her walking stick drumming the floor. After which, Veeranwali Mataji, taking support from Prahlad, did the same.

A woman ahead said to her friend how she and her husband had taken out the time to visit the Victoria Memorial the previous morning but that Swamiji had no interest in these touristy things. 'No interest beyond God, so he'd stayed back to pray.' Then she brushed off the outstretched hand of one of the diving boys who'd come up alongside her. And I found I did the same.

A strange assemblage of emotions shot through me. I felt a twinge of self-loathing, at the incongruity of my surroundings, at how badly

I treat the poor, at how they are beholden to me. And I felt the old urge to extricate myself from this, *all of this*. An urge that produced in me a sense of superiority as well as powers of observation. Which is to say, I understood that my privilege gave me a clearer view of things, as one gets when sitting on a plane looking down at the earth from up high. But at the same time, I asked, *Why, then, are you moving with the faithful along the Ganga?*

I let out a sad laugh to which Rashmi Masi added her sardonic chortle from the front. She shook her head. 'I don't know how I let your mother drag me into these situations!' she said, and stepped onto the boat.

I laughed again. 'Me neither.'

And now I felt another thing. A thing I can admit only with hindsight. *Envy*. Yes, I was envious of these believers. I was envious of how everybody so unquestioningly and wholeheartedly believed, and how I was unable to do the same.

Prahladji was at the boat's edge pulling the old ladies on board. 'Come,' he said to me with a grin. A few women behind him had begun singing a kirtan. (*Maiyya, Hey Gange, Maiyya, Maiyya! Hey Gange, Maiyya!* ...) I smiled at them and they smiled back.

But back in Puri, I'd believed for the most part, hadn't I? I'd put my rational mind to rest, so many times. I'd merged with the others. I'd connected with God. Yes, despite myself I had prayed sincerely and wholeheartedly. I *really* had.

I hopped on: And so I would again.

Sri Jagannath Express

On the Sri Jagannath Express from Puri to Kolkata, still high from my darshan at the Jagannath Temple the previous day, I found myself in the inner coterie of Swamiji's devotees. We had adjoining berths in the AC two-tier carriage, Swamiji, Prahlad and his family and mummy and I.

Swamiji was always served dinner first and he seldom spoke as he ate. But now that he'd finished, he was looking back fondly at the heyday of Shivsagar Ashram in the '80s.

'Initially, I used to doubt what Maharajji said,' he said. 'But with age, I'm seeing that everything was true.'

Mummy, Prahladji and Saroj were sitting at Swamiji's feet. Saroj had just put his tiffin boxes back together and was now laying out our dinner: more khichdi prasad, pickles, papad.

'Every single thing,' mummy said.

Prahladji sighed deeply. 'I feel the love you have for Maharajji, I have for Swamiji,' he said.

It is truly a curiously humbling experience, Dear Reader, to see grown men and women investing so profoundly in the arcane secrets of God. It was something I'd seen so many times before and will no doubt see again and again.

'Can I ask you something, Swamiji?' I said. He was in a receptive mood, and I knew he'd entertain me. 'Why did you take up sanyaas?'

Swamiji laughed lightly. 'I can tell you how Maharajji became a saint. Do you know how?'

I did. I'd heard that far back in the early twentieth century, Maharajji was born to a wealthy Rajput family in Kota, Rajasthan. His family was so rich that he wore shirts with diamonds for buttons as a child. He had a sister and brother and loving parents. A happy childhood. But when he was eight, his uncle killed his father and his mother died from shock. Maharajji was mistreated by his uncle, so he ran away from home. He was only eleven when he somehow reached Banaras and there at an ashram he decided he wanted to renounce the world. He wanted to take up sanyaas. But the sadhus said that he was just a child; he would have to wait. So, Maharajji stayed in Kashi studying the scriptures, and when he was eighteen, he received *deeksha* (initiation) from one mahatma. This mahatma saw that Maharajji was no ordinary boy and he said he knew just the guru for him: a deeply learned sadhu named Krishnadevanand who had unparalleled knowledge of Vedanta, but lived in Rishikesh.

So, Maharajji began walking from Varanasi towards Rishikesh. He walked and walked and faced many hardships along the way. Because his uncle had killed his father for money, he had vowed never to touch it. He only ate if somebody gave him saatvic food. So many times he went hungry.

When Maharajji reached Rishikesh, he learnt that Swami Krishnadevanand paid his respects at the Someshwar Mahadev Temple every morning, so he camped outside it. Every day he implored Swami

Krishnadevanand to take him as his pupil, but the elder sadhu paid him no heed. Then one day, Swami Krishnadevanand gave a young Maharajji a pencil and paper. He said, 'I have a test for you,' and asked him to write down what he could and began reciting a lengthy shloka.

'When Krishnadevanandji saw that Maharajji had not only kept up with his speed, but that there wasn't an error in what he wrote, he knew he had to take him in.' Swamiji gave a plaintive smile.

I smiled back. 'And what about you, Swamiji?' I said, and again Swamiji prevaricated.

'Why do we take up sanyaas?' he said. 'Sanyaas means that you've burnt your body. So, your life is now dedicated to God. You must kill your ego. One of the steps in our path is to seek alms from our family, to affirm we have no attachments left.'

As Swamiji elaborated on the implications of *satya* (Truth), *ahimsa* (Non-violence), *brahmacharya* (to stay in conduct within yourself), *asteya* (a non-stealing, non-possessing nature) and *aparigraha* (non-attachment to material things), I was thinking rather about how it was the twin ill-fates of poverty and tragedy that had spurred so many to adopt this way. (Hell, isn't my own much less grave depression the reason I began this journey down the Ganga?)

I'd started to eat when Swamiji said, 'So, are you interested?'

I nodded.

'Do you have the patience to listen?'

And I didn't say anything. Swamiji spoke and I listened. The guru expounded and the student imbibed. And just like that, a little gap opened up in the cosmos between ardent believer and sceptic in which an honest conversation could happen. A conversation, Dear Reader, you could say was about the allures of faith, but which was equally about those nagging questions we seldom voice: *Why did we do what we did? Who makes us, us? Ourselves or Fate?*

'It was 1981 and I was nineteen,' he said. 'I was studying engineering in Madras, and one day, I don't know what happened, but I woke up on the beach. Either I'd fainted, or drowned and someone pulled me out of the water, I don't know. I have no memory at all. But the next thing I remember is that I was in a cottage in a jungle and there was a swamiji in white clothes looking after me.'

Swamiji would later tell me this cottage lay somewhere in Karnataka even though he couldn't recognize it today.

'I was so scared, and I asked that swamiji, "How am I here? Who are you?" And he just said, "Rest. Big changes will come in your life."'

He chuckled lightly. 'At that time, I didn't know whether this man was a Vaishnava or Shaiva or what. He said I was a Brahmin because there was a janeu around me, but other than the *Gayatri Mantra*, I didn't even remember any prayers. He said that my journey would begin in the Himalayas, that I would begin my penance there. *Aur main bhavuk ho gaya…*I got emotional. I asked again, "Who am I? Who are my parents?" And he said, "Be patient. Little by little, things will return to you."

'That swamiji gave me a diary. He asked me to put down whatever came to my mind. And so I'd write in it every day… At the start, I would get some flashes. Like I remembered I had a sister. And I got more and more flashes of my mother, so I wrote this down. But when I finished a page, the swamiji told me to rip it out and stick it upside down on the previous one and begin the exercise afresh. He said that in time everything will become clear… But what was so strange was that my memories started weakening after a few days. I started writing more about my present than my past.

'I stayed in this cottage for a year and in this time the swamiji taught me many things. Things I can't tell you. Like mantras for specific situations. He said you won't feel hungry if you recite this mantra.' He hesitated. '… I can't tell you everything, but I can say that *jo craze tha, padhai ka, family ka, sab wash out ho gaya…*the desire to study, to find out about my family, it all washed away.

'Then, one day when swamiji and I were alone, a man came to see him. I had never seen him before. He said he was from Mangalore, and swamiji told me to go with him. I was reluctant, but I went. This man turned out to be an MD of a big company. He was wealthy and gave me a place to stay and a job in his factory. I didn't like the work, but he looked after me well, so I didn't say anything. Then, one day, we both went to meet swamiji together, and I heard him say he had a son. He said his son was studying in America and had died. He said he was very sad and directionless and his missus was in a deep depression. And swamiji said to him, "Who says your son is dead? Your son is alive. Even after seeing him, you can't see him?" The MD said, "Who's my son? Who's my son?" And swamiji pointed to me. "God has sent this boy to you in your son's place."

'So, I now went to live in this man's house, and I tell you, his wife had such love for me that after some weeks, she told me, "I have forgotten my own son. You are my son now. All the pain from my heart has got totally dissolved." And whatever I wanted she'd give me. Clothes, food, anything… Then after maybe a month, the MD told me, "This company that I'm building will be yours one day. Everything will be yours." And that night, I just could not sleep.'

Swamiji swallowed. 'I was very disturbed. I felt something was wrong about all this. So, I returned to swamiji's cottage and this time, he said, "So, you have your answer. Now you must leave. You must begin your journey."'

Swami Shraddhanandji then packed up his meagre belongings—some clothes, a little cash and his diary of memories—in a small *potli* and walked out of the cottage. But before he was out of the door the white-robed swamiji's said, 'Don't open your diary until you're fifty. Just carry on and you will find your way.'

'I was so naive. I just knew the Himalayas were these big mountains in the north, nothing more. And I knew that Delhi was in the north, so I got on a train to Delhi.

'When the TTE asked me for my ticket, I didn't know what to say, but he let me travel in the general class… Then the next morning the train stopped in Mathura. The stop was only for two minutes. And I thought, why not get off? I thought, Mathura is the birthplace of Shri Krishna. What will I do in Delhi? And I jumped off. I was in such a hurry that one shoe got left behind on the train. I thought, I'll look so stupid walking with just one shoe on so I threw the other one away too.'

Swamiji gave a self-deprecating laugh and a nod of acknowledgement, and I turned around. A middle-aged Bengali couple in our carriage was listening in. The man said, 'Swamiji, please carry on.'

And so he licked his lips. 'I asked one man, where is Shri Krishna's temple, and he said, "Keep going straight." So walking, walking, I reached the Jamuna. I bathed in it and put on a fresh dhoti from my bag. Then I went and sat down at Krishanji's temple.'

Swamiji slept in the temple courtyard for a month subsisting only on the food the temple-goers gave him, a lone brahmachari sitting at the temple's entrance. On some days, he ate two meals, and on others, he went two days on only two cups of tea.

'So one day I asked Krishanji, "Oh Lord, what is happening? I am constantly hungry. I am lost. I am not even in the Himalayas. God, what games are you playing with me?" And that same afternoon, a man came up. He said, "Oh Brahmachari, have you eaten today? Will you have *bhog* [temple prasad]?" It was *Janmashtami* that day and there was a *Chhappan Bhog* feast on. So, that man took me to a big bhandaara and sat me down. He said, "Here, eat. Eat what you want. Eat to your heart's content. Nobody will stop you." There was an unlimited supply of the choicest dishes, I tell you. Poori, aloo, sabzi, kheer. Everything. And I was so hungry'—he smiled sadly—'I felt like nobody can stop me today. I had hardly eaten anything for three weeks, and I thought, I'll now eat for the whole year!'

Swamiji gently raised his hand. Prahlad had tears in his eyes.

'Then that night, I woke up at 1 am. I had to rush to the toilet. I got such severe dysentery that I spent the whole night going to the bathroom and washing myself in the Jamuna. One minute I'd go to rest, and the next my runs would start up again. So, I thought, this is it. This is my karma. *Aaj mera shareer samapt ho jayega...* today, my body will die... But I thought, if I die near the temple, they will just dispose of my body as a beggar, and I wanted some final control over my fate, you know? So, I decided to go to the Jamuna, and I kept walking along its banks. I had no strength in me but I kept going. I remembered that there was an area where little crocodiles would come and play and I thought I'd leave my body there, and the *magarmach* can eat me up, and that will be the end of me and my story.'

This time when Swamiji laughed, it came out as a melancholy cry.

'I found a rock to sit on and I was near passing out. And I now thought: What if my diary is discovered? Then my identity will become public. My family will find out about me. And this I could not accept. So, I tied some stones around my potli and threw it into the Jamuna.'

'Your diary also?' the Bengali woman said.

'Yes, everything. And I fell into a deep sleep... When I awoke, I had the sun blinding my eyes, and I felt myself.' He felt his arms. 'And

I realized I was fine. Oh, I was more than fine. So, I went straight to Krishanji and thanked him for giving me a new chance.'

A few days later, sitting in the temple courtyard, Swamiji overheard two wandering sadhus talking among themselves. One said to the other, '*Waise*, Rishikesh is a lovely place. There are mountains and the Ganga and there is plenty of food in the ashrams.'

'I was still thinking about how to keep hunger away so this place sounded very attractive. And it was near the Himalayas also.'

Swamiji got on a train for Haridwar that evening. When he got off, he asked a rickshawaala, 'Where is the temple, bhai?'

'Which temple?' the man said.

'I thought Haridwar too would have one big temple like Puri and Mathura. But the man said, "The town is full of temples. Which one?"'

But at long last, here in Haridwar, Swamiji found a break from his cycle of hardships. Every morning he'd bathe in the Ganga after which he'd pay his respects at a local temple where there was always enough prasad to fill his stomach. Sated, he'd attend the Ganga aarti by the ghats in the evenings.

Swamiji stayed in Haridwar for five months. 'But, *mere man mein dhun lagi thi*...a tune was playing in my mind, that I want to go to the Himalayas.'

During a bhandaara at a Haridwar ashram one day he came into contact with visiting sadhus from Shivsagar Ashram. Hearing his story, one man invited him to meet Maharajji in Rishikesh. When Swamiji told Maharajji about himself, about his time in Mathura, the MD from Mangalore, and the swamiji in the jungle, Maharajji simply said, 'So, what will you do now?'

'I will go to the Himalayas and do tapasya there,' Swamiji said.

Maharajji laughed uproariously. 'But you're already here! Where do you think you are, oh Brahmachari? These are the Himalayas.' Then with a stern face he said, '*Swadhyaaya hi tap hai.*' Swadhyaaya, or recitation of the Vedas, by itself is penance.

I didn't think it then, but I wonder if it was on this train that the seeds for my journey began germinating. Was it here that the wheel of questions began turning in my mind. Questions like: Is there a clean dividing line between rationality and faith? Can the two things ever go hand in hand?

Despite my supposedly logical outlook, even I instinctively touched money fallen to the floor to my forehead. Even I did a pranaam to the gods if I happened to drive past a temple, with my hands unconsciously coming off the steering wheel. When a black cat crossed my path, my mind surged with shlokas to ward off the animal's evil spirit. This was my upbringing! These were my beliefs. And even if they were irrational, acting on them never failed to bring comfort.

But there were degrees of faith, weren't there? Mummy will kill me for telling you this. But I kid you not, she once even sprinkled our house with *gaumutra*, cow urine, to purify it. So, if there was a clear dividing line between believers and atheists, there lay deep boundaries *between* believers, too. Between those who had unquestioning faith in the elders and those who searched out their own paths. Between those who believed God was who the Books said He was and those who defined Him, or Her, as they wanted.

I didn't think about these things as copiously seven years ago as I do today. But I did think of them in some rough form. And so I asked Swamiji, 'Don't you think having too much faith is also dangerous? Even doubting has a place, no?'

It was Prahlad who answered. 'Do you know the story about the couple who prayed for a child at Tirupati?' he said.

I shook my head, looked to Swamiji for support. 'But what I'm saying is entirely something else,' I said. 'I'm saying…'

'Listen,' Prahlad said. 'There was a couple from South India, and they could not have a child. So, at Tirupati, they prayed to God. The wife, she prayed very, very hard. She told God she'd give Him anything to become a mother. And within a year Lord Balaji blessed her with a healthy boy… So, on the boy's first birthday the couple returned to thank the Lord. After their darshan they went to make an offering at the *hundi*.' He stopped. 'You've been to Tirupati, no?'

The hundi is a temple collection vessel, and the first time I saw the one at Tirupati as a child, I couldn't get over how big it was. One woman dropped a gold bangle into it and a man chanted a mantra and fed it a fat envelope of notes. When I told mummy of this she placed Rs 100 into my hands to do the same.

'So, the couple came here. The father put money into his boy's hand, and the mother raised him to the hundi's lip so he could drop it in. But just then'—he enlarged his eyes—'she lost her grip, and the baby fell inside!'

'*Arre baba!*' the Bengali woman said and I turned to Swamiji with raised eyebrows.

'There was a lot of noise and everything,' Prahlad said, 'but the priests told the parents that as they had offered their boy to God he was temple property now. Of course, they fought, but you can't take back from the Lord what you've given him, na?'

Prahlad saw me covering my incipient smirk. 'And wait,' he said, irritated, his tone betraying that easy confidence that comes to men who are used to being fully heard. 'The story isn't over, bhai. That same boy…tell me, who's he today? He's one of the main priests at Tirupati!'

Of course, my mother had caught me stifling my snigger. And, of course, she later chastised me. 'You keep doubting people,' she said. 'It's good to doubt. But do you know what Swamiji has done for Prahlad?'

I didn't. And so mummy now told me how Prahlad had first met Swamiji, many years ago.

At the time, Swamiji was having troubles at Shivsagar Ashram and had gone on a long yaatra along the Narmada River. Prahlad heard that he might settle in Ujjain, and he searched him out. He begged him to live close to him.

In those days, Prahlad had his son, Bharat, but he badly wanted a daughter. He wanted to complete his family. Swamiji warned him against going forward with his plan. He said that trying for another child was a bad idea as he could envision a danger to Saroj's life. But Prahlad didn't listen and went ahead. At the time of delivery, Saroj had a seizure. She slipped into a coma, and the doctors said only one person would survive: the child or the mother. That was when Prahlad fell again at Swamiji's feet. He said he'd do anything, but Swamiji had to save his Saroj.

Swamiji didn't say a word. He only said, 'Go home.' Then he went into samadhi—the highest state of meditative consciousness during which your soul unites with the Ultimate Reality. Swamiji stayed in samadhi for three days and in the end both Saroj and the newborn daughter emerged whole and healthy.

As per Swamiji's advice, Prahlad and Saroj then named their daughter Srishti, meaning the Earth, or of the Universe, and conducted an elaborate yagnya in Lord Shiva's honour. They did an abhishek pooja of a Shivalingam, which Swamiji had himself found on the banks of the Narmada. Through a *shringi*—a conical brass jar with a tiny hole at the bottom—the couple bathed Shiva with Gangajal, ghee, milk, honey and sugar continuously for hours.

Prahlad started doing this pooja in November 2008, when Srishti was born, and they've done it every November since. Since which time the couple has gone on an annual yaatra as well. Every year they pay their respects at a new temple and take Swamiji with them. At the time I was writing this chapter, Prahlad was gearing up for a yaatra to Sri Sailam in Andhra Pradesh. It was the only one of the twelve sacred jyotirlingams left for him to visit.

'What about you?' I asked mummy. 'Have you seen any miracles like this?'

And she told me once again about how Maharajji had given her a birthday present like nobody had before or has since.

It was mummy's twenty-fifth birthday and Maharajji was staying at my grandparents' house at the time. At a small party, she received several presents from family and friends, and when everybody left, Maharajji said he wanted to speak to her.

'I feel bad that I've nothing to give you,' he said. 'And I've been wondering what I can give you. I have no money or understanding of what you like. So, I've been thinking, what will be of value.'

'Swamiji, it's enough you are here,' mummy said. But Maharajji then raised his right hand, and she bowed her head in obeisance.

'*Main aap ko abhay ka daan deta hun*...I give you the boon of fearlessness,' he said.

As a kid I found this story so very magical. Mummy really was intrepid. Unlike my friends' mothers, ours had taken us all by herself on so many trips. Not just to temples but to the Gir Forest (*where I saw lions!*) and Kanyakumari (*where I saw the merging of two seas!*) and Goa (*where I saw the miraculous body of Saint Francis Xavier that had not decomposed for over four hundred years!*). Once, she even chased a thief at Bombay Central Station after the man grabbed her purse and ran.

But now I said maybe this was just confirmation bias. 'Maharajji could see you for who you are!'

'Okay, Mr Doubting Thomas,' mummy said. 'I *know* what I saw.'

In 2023, however, as I was concluding this book, I asked again if she'd seen any proof of God. Any evidence of a paranormal force. I put to her pointed questions designed to preempt her old cycle of stories. Not that this was helping much. Mummy's frustratingly opaque replies were already driving us to an argument.

Too much about my mother still didn't quite add up. As religious as mummy was in her personal life, in the professional sphere, as I've said before, she was correspondingly pragmatic. Unlike footloose-me, who'd simply decided to travel and write, my mother remains focused. Even at seventy-four, she's a practising lawyer and efficacious ashram trustee. Even today, she can operate both Microsoft Excel and her smartphone with practiced ease.

'So, in all these years, you haven't seen any miracles?' I said. 'How do you resolve your contradictions?'

'What contradictions? I have none.' She giggled.

And I thought, maybe she's right. Maybe everything does add up, in a way. Mummy was a creature of norm and routine, whether pooja or court appearances. She wasn't the one looking for side trips from the set river of life, I was.

Mummy was observing me, her eyes distant, then near. Perhaps after all this time, we finally *saw* each other, as sometimes you see in a photograph a new aspect of a house you've lived in your whole life. Mummy and I were the same, but different. Two vessels floating down life's waters, each adhering to our ineffable internal flow. It really was unfair to expect her to swim against her currents, wasn't it?

I was about to say, 'Let's leave it,' when she said: 'I haven't told anybody this. But I can tell you now. Enough time has passed.'

She began, 'Yes, I did see something once, many years back… I told you. But you've probably forgotten.'

I looked her in the eyes. She wasn't being frivolous.

'I was having tea in Swamiji's room [in Rishikesh] one day, and I said, "I miss our Maharajji. I miss his guidance. I miss his insights." And he said, "Do you want to meet him?" I stared at him. I was trying to make out what he meant. But I said, "Yes."

'I thought he would walk me through a prayer. But he took me to meet another man. He was not a saint but an ordinary man, also a devotee of Maharajji. His name was Prasad. When Prasad saw me, he raised his eyebrows to Swamiji, but Swamiji said, "Let's go."

'So we got in a car and started driving uphill and after maybe ten minutes, Swamiji and Prasad kept looking at the hills to the left hand side. They asked each other a few times, "Is it here?" The place looked very ordinary. Just rolling hillside, trees, monkeys—nothing new. And then, Prasad said, "Here! The *pagdandi* is here." So, we got off and started climbing up the trail. Swamiji and Prasad were going fast like they eagerly wanted to get somewhere and I was running out of breath. But I was getting excited too, so I kept up.'

'Where is this place? When was this?'

'You must have been in your twenties and I've never been able to trace it again… So, we climbed uphill for maybe twenty minutes, and I remember they were also trying to figure out where to go. They weren't sure. Then, at one place, we went past a cluster of trees and found ourselves in a clearing where the sun was bright and sharp and there was a small stream. And Prasad gave us a nod and Swamiji told me to sit down.

'Swamiji said that this is where Maharajji used to meditate for hours. He said, "If you want to invoke him, you must do the same." I remember I had a terrible headache from the trek. But Swamiji said, "Sit here and clean your mind. Clean your thoughts." So, I sat down.

'At first, nothing happened, but then I saw little clouds leaving me.'

'What do you mean?'

'Like blobs of doubt and negativity were leaving me. First, there were very black clouds, then I saw pink clouds and then light, whitish clouds. And Swamiji kept saying "Clean, Clean, Clean", and I kept cleaning my aura.'

Mummy straightened her back and brought her hands above her chest then pulled them away, her fingers pinched and quivering. 'Swamiji said, "You must clean the mind and when you feel it is totally pure only then ask Maharajji to come." And I noticed that within ten minutes my headache disappeared and my mind started becoming alert.

'Swamiji said, "Can you see anything?" I said, "No." Then he asked after a few minutes, and again I said no. Then, that other man, Prasad, said, "Maharajji has come." And now Swamiji stopped talking to me and went directly to Maharajji.'

'What?'

'Swamiji started speaking to Maharajji through Prasad.'

'What do you mean? How do you know this Prasad wasn't acting?'

'Okay. Fair enough. But you hear his words.'

'Did Prasad's expressions change? His voice?'

Impatiently now, like she wanted to retell the story more to herself than to me: 'His expression was peaceful. But the voice was Prasad's voice.'

'How can…?' But let me not stop water in flow.

'Swamiji told Maharajji that he wanted to leave Shivsagar Ashram. He said things were getting difficult. He said he wanted to set up his own place. And Maharajji said to him, "Whatever you start in life, complete it. Be certain of it." Maharajji then gave him some solutions, certain mantras. He told him to set up a Sankat Mochan temple on the northwest side of the new ashram and some other things, and after a few minutes, Swamiji said, "Maharajji, please speak with Shashiji." And now I stepped forward.

'I said, "I felt very, very bad after you left us, Maharajji," and I could feel myself trembling with sorrow.

'And he said, "Why do you have doubts? I'm always with you."

'I said, "Are you happy with me?"

'And he said, "Please set the food and drink right in your house. If you do, everybody will stay on the correct path."

'I then said, "Will my children be okay?"

'And he said, "If you act like a true mother then how can your children get spoiled?"'

Mummy could sense I was getting jaded, but she carried on: 'Maharajji told me many things. But I remember at one point, Prasad's face had gone, and I saw my Maharajji sitting right before me. And he asked me with his full intensity, "Tell me, Shashi, do you want wealth or peace?" I thought, how can there be peace without wealth? So, I stayed quiet. Swamiji said in my ear, "*Bolo shanti, bolo shanti!* Say peace, say peace!" And then, Swamiji said, "Maharajji, Shashi wants peace. Give her peace." And Maharajji said, "*Tathastu.*" So be it.

'Maharajji then scolded Swamiji. He said, "How could you disobey Nature's laws and summon me like this? Don't you dare do this again." Maharajji never liked any saint displaying his siddhis in public. He was always against it. So, Maharajji told us to ask Mother Earth for forgiveness and to drink water from the stream nearby, sprinkle it on ourselves.'

Mummy was beaming now and her ebullience made me loosen a smile. I think I was smiling at simpler times when I unreservedly believed in her. When I was always on the same page with her. As a part of me still wanted to be.

'I was so illuminated after my experience that when I came home, I told you about it. But you forgot so I kept it to myself.' She beamed again. 'Swamiji told me later that day, "Never ask for money over peace. Look at rich people in their big palaces who are all miserable. Always ask for peace!"'

She laughed, daubed her moistening eyes. 'So, till today, I am grateful to Maharajji, to Swamiji, to Rishikesh… And I think you too sensed something extraordinary about Shivsagar Ashram when you were little. When I used to touch Maharajji's feet, you'd push me aside to get his blessings first. That was your direct relationship with something divine.

'Once I took you to Ganeshpuri and you said, "Mummy, this place is like a club." When I took you back to Rishikesh in the summer, you said, "Now here there is God's energy." You felt something.'

I remembered making this remark. In the early '90s, at one ashram in Ganeshpuri, Maharashtra, I saw white people praying to Hindu gods for the first time. I saw white people singing kirtans in exotic accents and eating egg sandwiches. *Egg sandwiches! In an ashram!* The place was preposterous. The place was wonderful. I laughed. 'That was your influence! I was a kid!'

'Maybe. But those were your impressions. You were very enthusiastic as a child. You learned pranayama from me. The *Shiva Mahiman Stotra*. So many good things. You were so good.' She gave a laugh. Neither bitterly nor sarcastically, but openly, flowingly. 'Then you hit teenage-hood, and boy…'

Parting glances

Seagulls drifted down, then rocketed back up. As the ferry pulled away from the jetty, some birds lingered above us, fascinating some and repelling some others. But then the boat sounded its horn, and vendors came streaming down the aisles and a rush of wind swept through my hair and the mutterings of the still humid world was supplanted by movement, by water, by communal singing.

Rashmi Masi craned her neck in the direction of one man selling packets at the end of our aisle. 'What's there?' she shouted. Somebody said there was more puffed rice, so she fell back in her chair with a huff.

We were sitting on a long wooden seat, Rashmi Masi, mummy, Sarla Aunty and I, and Sarla Aunty pulled a packet of matthis out from her bag and handed it to Rashmi Masi. She hugged mummy. 'Do you remember how we once went with Maharajji at three in the morning in winter to bathe in the Ganga? But we just couldn't do it… It was so cold!'

Mummy laughed. 'How can I forget, behenji?'

With a straight face, Veeranwali Mataji said she'd once gone down to the Ganga at 4 am, and everybody giggled. As did she. And I wondered if she was laughing at her joke or hiding her embarrassment at having convinced nobody.

Subhadra Aunty meanwhile admitted she never could wake up early, but she once had the pleasure of accompanying Maharajji on a long walk along the Ganga. 'He was skipping across the rocks like a boy,' she said, her eyes gleaming. 'He was running on the water's surface.'

The women got up and went to the ferry's handrail where each one brought a few coins out of her bag, held it in her fist, chanted a prayer and tossed the lot in.

Waves broke at the hull releasing sprays of water and laughter and for a few moments I was taken by it all. By the vivid atmosphere, the fervour. That act of sacred communion. Sure, I could say it was all illogical. But why must I be cynical?

The boat wobbled and I dashed to mummy. 'Let's sit down.' But mummy was fishing out more things from her purse, preparing for a more private communion.

Sarla Aunty opened her bag and asked mummy if she needed anything. Other than the saree, she had a coconut, a packet of red vermilion, turmeric, cloves and cardamom. Mummy said she didn't have the cloves and cardamom but had flowers and camphor and so the women made a trade.

I returned to my seat and tried to relax, but in vain. The ripples on the water's surface were morphing into waves and our gentle bob was turning to an active bounce. But mummy was still at the ferry's edge. Still tossing in *rewari* sweets, cardamom, cloves, red vermilion, coins. With one hand on the railing, she was again poking through her purse, from which she pulled out a coconut.

She was holding it steadily above the water when a boat quake forced it out of her hands: *Splash!*

'Can you please sit down!'

The women nearby, half-drenched and leaning on one another, were laughing, hysterically.

I clenched my teeth. 'Mom, sit down. You can't swim! Do what you want from the seat.'

And now Rachna stepped forward. She held my wrist tight. 'Come with me.' She took me aside. 'You know some things are funny. But she's your mother. Remember, you're in public.'

She re-joined my family from whom I could hear snatches of a conversation they made no attempt to conceal: 'Badly behaved…' '… No sense of propriety.' '… Not funny at all.'

Prahlad, Saroj, Bharat and Srishti were sitting with Swamiji on the aisle opposite them and Swamiji was saying something, and the children were silently listening. The bunch of women in front of me were still laughing. Still half-praying, half-singing.

There really was laughter and bonhomie on this boat, I thought. There was warmth and conviviality. And there was me: all fuming, all alone. *Really, why am I here?*

With her hands quivering above the water, mummy was mouthing a prayer. I stood up, then sat down. I exhaled and inhaled. The air, salty. I went over and stood beside mummy. I looked out at the changing skies and waters. The Ganga was the sea now or something very sea-like, and I couldn't tell where one world ended and the other began. Whether that white bulge was a ruffle or a wave. A swell of water or a water-hill?

We returned to our seats. 'I prayed for everybody,' mummy said. She turned to me, giggled. 'Especially for you. So you lose this anger you have for me.'

At Kachuberia jetty on Sagar Island: more beggars. And on the road beyond: scores of buses and taxis. We got into two cabs and sped off towards the Ganga Sagar beach to the island's south, and within minutes, I was again passing through broad open fields fringed with tall palms and sal trees and banana trees. I was going past lakes and ponds reflecting the setting sun.

At first came concrete houses. Then flimsy ones. Then a village of hutments. And five minutes later, another like it. As I observed the wrinkled faces of farmers on Sagar island, I had the distinct feeling of traversing a once-hidden subculture.

A culture that long ago had its own separate identity (Tribal? Animistic?) but whose uniqueness was now lost. All subsumed in the Hindu cosmos…

And then we'd reached.

Reached where? I could see no sea.

The sea was a short distance away, about eight hundred metres, the driver said, so we'd have to walk. But we couldn't walk, could we? Too many of us were old, and all of us were tired, plus there was little time. And so it was decided post-haste we'd take cycle rickshaws.

A long line of rickshawaalas were waiting for us at the road's edge, from where I saw that the beach was so big that a concrete path had been paved over it. Many rickshawaalas were Muslim men, like the porters at the Vaishno Devi shrine in Jammu.

I was about to verbalize my observation when a man with a skull cap caught me staring. He beckoned, and as I looked closer, I saw that his right foot below the ankle was missing. He had his leg's stump end, hideously scarred, resting on the pedal. He smiled.

Did faith bring him relief? I hoped it did.

'Did you see that guy?' I said. But nobody heard me.

Negotiations between the yaatris and the rickshawaalas were under full swing and they seemed to go on and on. This was getting too much, this picture of a cliche: we, the wealthy pilgrims and the poor waiting to serve us. We, the able-bodied, using the disabled poor as our servants.

'I'll walk,' I said.

'*Arre*, come back,' Mayank called out. 'Do you know the way? You don't.'

'I'll figure it out.' I continued, but then Minna Masi said in a wearied voice: 'Sid, why must you be difficult?' So, I quietly returned and sat down with my family on the edge of a rickshaw. Which I saw now was not quite a rickshaw but a rectangular wooden platform. It was a cart. A vegetable cart.

I felt my eyes smart. 'I'm making it difficult? You guys are fighting over how much? How much did we spend on dinner last night?'

'It's not about the money,' Swamiji said calmly. 'It is about the principle.' And Prahlad, who'd ended up on our rickshaw with his back pressed against mine, said in my ear, 'You know how they are, na? They just want to cheat us.'

It was a touch of bigotry I'd seen shades of before and of which I'd see louder and louder colours in the years ahead.

Further on came three red temple domes, each with a triangular red flag perched on top. The Kapila Muni temple was grand but due to the eclipse it was closed and presiding over an empty beach.

'Many temples close during eclipses,' Swamiji said. 'But it is key to remember just who Kapila Muni was. He was an avatar of Vishnu. He had given us Samkhya Yoga, a path of yoga whose final aim is to realize the difference between the *purusha* [consciousness] and *prakriti* [matter].'

As we made a turn, across the last three hundred yards of swelling sand—*On which a couple of dogs were playing chase! On which the wind coaxed a two-second mini-hurricane!*—I saw it: the sea—ceaseless and grey.

Mummy was saying to Mayank, '… Now, why is this bath important? I've told you the short answer. But the real reason is because…because…you must ask, what is the strongest human need?'

She turned to Rachna. 'Love. And all of us fail in understanding each other. So, what should we do? We must look within… And all faiths evolved ways of entering the world within. Hinduism came up with the method of worshipping idols who represent divine qualities, and because the most basic act of relationships is energizing each other and ourselves, we must do this first with God.

'And this act of energizing is what we're doing today. These rituals energize you, and through repetition, they can take you to a deeper place.' She glanced at me. '… But yes, there is no one set path. Wherever somebody seeks with a true heart, their prayers get answered.'

I wanted to say, 'Then why have we come here?' But I stopped myself. I was still meant to be sulking, wasn't I? And although I was now only a little vexed, seeing me quiet, Swamiji said to me in his fond way: 'See, Siddharth, people spend their whole lives finding a guru, and here you were born to one.'

Mummy squinted her eyes in Swamiji's direction, then mine, and produced a prankish smile. Her eyes twinkled in the evening light, and for an instant I felt we saw in each other something subtly new, as when you wake from a long sleep and your dream world just tints the real one.

She grinned. 'Swamiji,' she said, 'we fight, but in the end we make up.'

At the far distance, the sea united with the sky in a perfect grey. And at my feet, the sands joined the waters in imperfect wonderful shades of puddly grey, red and brown, as only beaches at evening time seem able to produce. It was 5:22 pm, and I thought, *How amazing!* How amazing that we'd made it in time.

A hawker came ambling down selling empty plastic bottles for the collection of sacred seawater, and a woman from a bunch squatting on the beach bought one. Then she returned to her business: making rotis on a wood-fired stove.

The women's red, yellow and blue sarees had been spread out on the sands like magical carpets leading the Ganga to her final abode. Or simply—*Why must I always imagine things?*—laundry put out to dry without a washing line.

Veeranwali Mataji saw me daydreaming and beckoned. I went over.

'What are you doing, aunty?' I said and she put a finger to her lips and began placing little things—thirty-two seashells and camphor, to be exact—into an earthen pot.

'It's a small thing.' A pooja to remove a dosh, a fault, in her horoscope, she'd later say. 'Can you put this in the sea for me?'

Like many men, I'd shed my shirt and trousers and was only in my shorts, but the women all kept their clothes on. The 109 of us were standing on the verge where Swamiji was reciting the *Shiva Ganga Stuti* imploring the Ganga to remove our sins, and we repeated after him.

Then, we stepped into the sea.

'O Ganga Maiyya, I beseech you,' mummy said. 'I beseech you, Ganga Sagar, to confer on my family good health, good fortune, security. *Shanti, Lakshmi, Saraswati*.'

I held out my hand and mummy and I waded into the shallows. We reached a point where the water was just waist high and it felt warming rather than chilling, and Swamiji now stopped. '*Bas*.'

He then sat down. Or, although he was half-floating, he appeared to have sat down, for he looked comfortable. He looked comforting even, with everybody settling around him in bubbling circles, the women's clothes vibrating with the waves, their chants quavering with the water's rhythms.

Mummy brought out a red saree from a cloth bag and closed her eyes. 'O Ganga Maiyya, I offer this to you.' She was about to place it in the water when Sarla Aunty stopped her.

In her school-teacher voice, the old lady said that the proper way to make the offering was to fold the cloth into a triangular shape as this represented the Holy Trinity of Lords Brahma, Vishnu and Mahesh. And so the women now all properly folded their sarees.

Then they brought out their flowers and bangles and coconuts. They opened their plastic sachets of red vermilion and turmeric and cloves and cardamom. And chanting '*Ganga Maiyya ki Jai!*' everybody immersed their offerings into the sea.

I heard my name and turned around. It was Rachna. About a hundred metres away, Mayank and she were paddling in the waves, soaking in the goodness.

Wah! 'After preaching to me, *haan*? Just look at you!'

'We've done our pooja.' Rachna giggled. 'Now, fun time!'

'Come.' Mayank splashed water in my direction. 'You've done enough.'

Flowers, coconuts and plastic sachets were bobbing at my waist and I couldn't help but think I was standing in the middle of an exotic shipwreck. *Who could I share this thought with though?* Mummy, of course. But not now. Later.

Right now, she had her head turned towards Swamiji, who was about to commence his next preachment. Right now, Bharat, then Srishti, went underwater to touch his feet. They surfaced up, their eyes stinging, laughing. And a young mother, much younger than me, brought her toddler forward to do the same.

Swamiji stopped her, but she had already dunked the kid's head and the boy was crying. Oh, dear. He was bawling.

Swamiji cleared his throat. '*Shant ho jao*...everyone, quiet.'

I tapped mummy on her shoulder. She was looking ahead, squinting hard.

'I'm going to the other side,' I said.

She nodded.

Rachna splashed water at me and laughed. 'See, it's just like Goa.'

Many things would happen in the years ahead. Things I've told you and things I can't tell you. Things that led me deep into myself and things that took me far away from everything.

What did I know now that a month later, on a trip to Japan I'd try beef for the first time and enjoy it? Only to feel very guilty afterwards. Only to promise myself I'd never commit this sin again.

What did I know that a year later I'd meet Armaan? Armaan, who one day trapped a spider in the bathroom under a mug and released it into the open so nobody would kill it. Armaan, who calls himself a 'Buddhist Spinozan'. Armaan, a vegetarian flirting with veganism who's persuading me, yet again, to give up eating meat.

What did I know now that six years later, when I'd fall ill with Covid, I'd ring mummy and ask her to do Pranic Healing for me.

'Oh, I thought you didn't believe all this,' she'd say. 'What's happened now?'

'Nothing. Will you do it or not?' I'd say.

And she'd say, 'Okay, Tell me your symptoms.'

And what did I know now, Dear Reader, that seven years later, my father would fall terminally ill? My dear atheist papa, who stayed true to his materialist spirit till the end, would die, and mummy, Mala and I would take his earthly remains to Haridwar where, as his only son, I'd carry out his funeral rites.

That sitting on the Ganga's banks, I'd solemnly make twelve balls of rice, wheat flour, dried milk, honey and sesame, each representing my non-believing father's soul, and of my forefathers who passed before him. That I'd pour ten buckets of Gangajal at the roots of a sacred Banyan tree, then shake the tail of a cow. *Why?* 'To make your pitaji's passage to heaven easy,' the pandit would say. 'Because after one dies, their soul has to pass through the Baitarni river which is full of blood and gore. But one can make the crossing easily by holding on to this.'

But all this would happen later. *Much later.*

Today, a wave came in and pulled mummy's bag into the deep and she went after it. Right now, her head went under then surfaced again. I panicked: *Mummy can't swim!* From the beach, Rashmi Masi and Minna Masi got up from their plastic chairs and began yelling, crazily waving their hands.

Mummy saw my face and laughed. She steadied her feet to show that she was okay. To show that she was fearless. But another wave knocked her down.

Swamiji held up his hands: *Don't worry!*

But I could see mummy had swallowed water. And this was water not of the Ganga, but the open sea. A sea I was already wading in, already swimming in, cutting into in ungainly strokes, determined, totally determined, to bring my mother back to shore.

A Brief Note on Sources

It would be difficult to produce a complete bibliography of the books, essays and articles that have informed my views on the Hindu faith, especially since so much of what I've imbibed was passed down to me orally. But I must acknowledge my debt to the authors of the following. I've provided, to the extent possible, publication details as well as specific page numbers for the quotes and observations that I've borrowed from elsewhere. This list is not exhaustive, but it will offer opportunities to further travel down the streams of thought explored in my journey.

The quote that gives the link between Ganga and Vishnu in the section 'A Synthesis of Rituals in Badrinath' is taken from page 3 of *The Many Pasts of a River* by Sudipta Sen (Penguin Viking, 2019). The bits about Buddhist institutions being seized by Brahmins and about Shankara expelling the Buddhists with the help of the Parmar king, respectively, are taken from *A Social History of India* by S.N. Sadasivan (APH publishing Corporation, 2000), page 211, and *The Unquiet Woods: Ecological Change and Peasant Resistance in the Himalaya* by Ramchandra Guha (University of California Press, 1990), page 64.

On the rate of the glacier's retreat in Gangotri, which I talk about in Part III, there's a lot of literature online. Readers may start their inquiry with 'Is the Gangotri Glacier Receding at an Alarming Rate?' by V.K. Raina, which appeared in the *Journal of the Geological Society of India*, vol. 64 (December 2004) (https://www.geosocindia.org/index.php/jgsi/article/view/82699/63828, last accessed on July 1, 2024).

In the section 'A Brief Immersion in the World of the Naga Babas in Prayagraj', for Hiuen-Tsang's account of the Kumbh, see *Encyclopedia of Global Religion*, edited by Mark Juergensmeyer and Wade Clark Roof (SAGE, 2011), page 677. About the Allahabad mela before 1760, see *Pilgrimage and Power: The Kumbh Mela in Allahabad, 1765–1954* by Kama Maclean (Oxford University Press, 2008). For the contemporary importance of the Kumbh Mela, see 'The Kumbh Mela festival processions' by James G. Lochtefeld, in *South Asian Religions on Display: Religious Processions in South Asia and in the Diaspora*, edited by Knut A. Jacobsen (Routledge, 2008), pp. 31-33. I also refer to an article by David N. Lorenzen, entitled 'Warrior Ascetics in Indian History', which appeared in the *Journal of the American Oriental Society*, vol. 98, no. 1 (January-March 1978), pp. 61-75.

In the section 'A City in Flux: Varanasi', the 1890 description of the Varanasi ghats by W.S. Caine is quoted from page 15 of Diana L. Eck's *Banaras: City of Light* (Penguin, 1988), but is originally from W.S. Caine's *Picturesque India*, page 302. James Kennedy's quote on the *Great-Indian-Free-For-All* is similarly from Eck's book, page 17, but originally from Kennedy's *Life and Work in Benares and Kumaon* (1884), page 68. And so is Count Hermann Keyserling's quote about Benaras. The original source for the latter is *India Travel Diary of a Philosopher* (1925), pages 118–22.

The comparison of Varanasi to a palimpsest is also from Eck's *Banaras* (page 9). And the quotes at the start of the section 'A Trip Down Varanasi's Lanes of History and Politics' that relate to the history of the temple are from the following pages in the same book: 83, 84, 132, 133, 134. The quote about the anandavan is also taken from the Eck's book; see pages 55–56. Eck's comment on Kabir's death in Magahar can be found on page 87.

All quotes by Madhuri Desai are from her book *Banaras Reconstructed: Architecture and Sacred Space in a Hindu Holy City* (University of Washington Press, 2017). M.A. Sherring's quote about Hindus not allowing '*the Mohammedans to pluck a single leaf*' from the peepal tree at Gyanvapi is from page 164 of Desai's book. Her observations on Kashi's Purana literature and the discovery on Sarnath in 1794 are taken from pages 168 and 156, respectively. And her observations on H.R Neville, Gazetteer of Benares, are taken from page 159 of her book, and the colonial view of all confrontations as Hindu–Muslim ones from page 163. Her prescient observation on the city's built environment can be found on page 29. The point made by her about Aurangzeb having turned Vishweshwar into the 'undisputed centre and fulcrum of the city's ritual landscape' appears on page 69.

Catherine B. Asher's quote on Aurangzeb's mosque is from *The New Cambridge History of India: Architecture of Mughal India*, pages 278–79.

The quote from Michael Dumper about the destruction of the original temple housing the linga is from pages 108–9 of his book *Power, Piety and People: The Politics of* Holy Cities in the Twenty-First Century (Columbia University Press, 2020; Kindle edition). I further allude to observations he makes in this book (on page 106) when I talk about the pluralistic nature of Lord Hanuman's Sankat Mochan Mandir.

The interview of the historian Romila Thapar, in which she says that as recently as the 1800s many people who identified as Hindu or Muslim freely partook in the festivals of the other, can be seen here: https://www.youtube.com/watch?v=J8HhLJzpx3Y&t=1185s, last accessed on July 1, 2024. And here's the link to Thapar's paper, 'The Tyranny of Labels', *Social Scientist*, vol. 24, no. 9/10 (September–October 1996), pp. 3–23, which I also quote: https://www.jstor.org/stable/3520140.

Sherring's derisive quote about the 'sons of the Ganga' can be found on pages 45–46 of his *The Sacred City of the Hindus: An Account of Benares in Ancient and Modern Times* (London, Trubner and Co, 1868).

For the classification of the Upanishads into Early, Middle and Late, I refer to Hajime Nakamura's *A History of Early Vedanta Philosophy* (Motialal Banarsidass, 1983), pages 42–43.

The quote from the *Shvetashvatara Upanishad* can be found on page 32, *The Upanishads, Volume 1: Katha, Isa, Kena and Mundaka* by Swami Nikhilananda.

In the philosophy subsection, 'Loops of Clarity', at the end of Part V, I mention Nagarjuna's philosophy of emptiness, which is taken from *An Introduction to Buddhism by Peter Harvey* (Cambridge University Press, 1990).

The mention of Shankaracharya appropriating Buddhist ideas to attract Buddhists to the Sanatana fold is from S.G. Mudgal in his book *Advaita of Shankara: A Reappraisal* (Motilal Banarsidass, 1975).

You may also find interesting this academic thesis entitled 'Shankara: A Hindu Revivalist or a Crypto Buddhist?' by Kencho Tenzin, Department of Religious Studies, Georgia State University (see https://scholarworks.gsu.edu/cgi/viewcontent.cgi?article=1003&context=rs_theses, last accessed on July 1, 2024).

Although I haven't quoted from it here, there's a YouTube channel I often listened to on Buddhism which you may find interesting called Doug's Dharma (https://www.youtube.com/@DougsDharma).

Likewise, on Vedanta, I found stimulating the writings of Christopher Isherwood. *Vedanta for Modern Man* (Harper & Brothers, 1951; published in England by George Allen & Unwin, 1952), which he edited and introduced, in particular was a good read.

On meditation and mindfulness I found thought-provoking the books *Why Buddhism Is True: The Science and Philosophy of Meditation and Enlightenment* (Simon & Schuster, 2017) by Robert Wright and *The Awakened Brain: The New Science of Spirituality and our Quest for an Inspired Life* by clinical psychologist Lisa Miller (Penguin, 2022).

The long David N. Lorenzen quote from his *Two Lost Śaivite Sects: The Kāpālikas and Kālāmukhas* (1972) in the section 'A Whirlpool of Encounters in Varanasi' is taken from page 4 of the book.

Some of the philosophical themes Armaan alludes to in our conversations can be traced back to the writings of Spinoza, particularly his *Ethics*. Equally, for cogent arguments on atheism the writings of Richard Dawkins and Sam Harris, both hat-tipped in these pages, are invaluable.

Regarding the discussion on Soma in the subsection 'A Last Swim Back to the City of Death', I referred to R. Gordon Wasson's 'The Soma of the Rig Veda: What was it?', *Journal of the American Oriental Society*, vol. 91, no. 2 (April–June 1971), pp. 169–87, and *The Story of India* by Michael Wood, which is available online (see https://d2onlinesite.wordpress.com/wp-content/uploads/2018/06/michael-wood-the-story-of-india.pdf, last accessed on July 1, 2024).

And finally, James Mascarene Hubbard's article 'The English in India' from June 1908 in *The Atlantic Monthly*, which I mention in the final section, can be found here: https://www.theatlantic.com/magazine/archive/1908/06/the-english-in-india/639131/, last accessed on July 1, 2024.

Acknowledgements

This book written over seven exploratory years would not have been possible without the love, support and guidance of many good people.

My wholehearted thanks:

To my family for allowing me to write about our stories; to my sister Malvika Kalra for her tacit support and encouragement; to my brother-in-law Bikram Kalra and my nephew Jai Singh and niece Seher for theirs; to my father Sharat Dev Kapila for his reassurance and criticism over the years; to my masis and cousins for letting me do this with complete freedom; to Amir Sarwari for our endless debates and cogitations, for shaping the latter part of this book, for continuing this journey together.

To all the dear friends I hectored to read each chapter as soon as I finished it: Sonali Bagai, James Jenkins, Rinchen Kalon, Swati Singh, Neera Choudhary and Samir Singh Solanki; to those who made time for excerpts: Brahma Prakash Gaur, Manav Kapur, Rohit De, Soumya Kapoor, and Julia Foden; to those who read early drafts: Ajoy Acharya, Manish Mishra, Aju John and Arjun Kapoor.

To my dear friends Madhavi Misra, Amrita Datta, Himani Gupta, Miha Schnabl, Sumeet Popli, Shivan Gupta, Aditi Banerjee, Radhika Arora, Nandita Bhan, Emma Bentham and Vipul for nudging me along with good meals and good humour.

To Mahant Rajendra Tiwari from Banaras who helped vivify the city for me; to Diana Eck and Madhuri Desai for injecting academic rigour into these pages.

To the many swamijis and pandits of Rishikesh for your interviews and clarifications.

To the innumerable other sadhus, pandits, kanwariyas, Nagas, Aghoris, Buddhist monks, backpackers, non-Hindus, sceptics, agnostics and atheists I met on my journey.

To my co-yaatris over the years whose stories I've shared even if in a lightly disguised way.

To my publisher Ravi Singh for reading the incomplete manuscript and accepting it; for his patience and encouragement along the way.

To my editor Nazeef Mollah for believing in this book from the beginning, for his insightful comments and suggestions, for seeing it through to publication.

To Maithili Doshi Aphale for designing the cover; to Devashish Verma for drawing the maps and preparing the photo insert; and to Rajinder Ganju for the page layouts.

But most of all, thank you to my mother Shashi Malhotra Kapila. No trip to the Ganga would have been thinkable without you.

ALSO FROM SPEAKING TIGER

Tales of Hazaribagh

An Intimate Exploration of Chhotanagpur Plateau

Mihir Vatsa

'Vatsa's prose has three components that are vital for writing about a place and its people: love, earnestness and humility. This is a book that will be remembered.'—Hansda Sowvendra Shekhar

In January 2017, Mihir Vatsa, a young poet, gives up his life in the big city and moves back home to Hazaribagh, a small town on Jharkhand's Chhotanagpur Plateau. Battling depression and uncertainty, he is seeking a 'sanatorium' amidst the sal trees and the temperate climes of home—just like the British soldiers and Bengali settlers and visitors before him.

Rejuvenated by the fresh air and lush landscape of his childhood, he spends the next three years exploring local landmarks and their fascinating history, and the deep, wondrous escarpments, the secret waterfalls and serpentine rivers of the plateau. Travelling partly on foot and partly in his trusted Alto, he encounters trees destined for death and waterfalls ravaged by mining; passes through Surajkund—the country's hottest geological wonder—and Karanpura Valley—home to prehistoric humans ten millennia ago; and takes selfies with emus.

In between, he wonders what makes a landscape beautiful and how language shapes such notions; muses on the arbitrary boundaries of administration and government which, try as they might, cannot tame rivers and hills; and plumbs the archives of previous residents of the plateau and his own memory to understand his love of home. With empathy and in unhurried prose, *Tales of Hazaribagh* combines the best of nature, life, history and travel writing into an unforgettable portrait of a place and a journey back to one's self.